PLAY FOOTBALL THE NFL WAY

PLAY FOOTBALL
THE NFL WAY

Position-by-Position
Techniques and Drills for
Offense, Defense, and
Special Teams

By Tom Bass

St. Martin's Press/New York

Editor-in-Chief: John Wiebusch
Senior Editor/Project Editor: Jim Natal
Associate Editor: Jim Gigliotti
Design: David Johnston
Photographic Coordinator: Paul Spinelli
Photographic Services: Mark Sherengo,
   Kevin Terrell
Production Coordinator: Tania Baban
Production: Morrissey Gage,
   Beverly Kohake
Diagrams: Violet Lee, James Whitaker
Typesetting: Sandra Gordon,
   Rick Jermain, Rick Wadholm

Library of Congress Cataloging-in-Publication Data

Bass, Tom.
   Play football the NFL way / Tom Bass.
      p.   cm.
   Includes index.
   ISBN 0-312-05947-7 (pbk.)
   1. Football—Training.   2. Football—Coaching.   3. National Football League.   4. n-us.   I. Title.
   [GV953.5.B37   1991]
   796.332′07—dc20   90-27861
                                             CIP

First U.S. Paperback Edition: July 1991
10 9 8 7 6 5 4 3 2

The authors contend that football is a physically demanding sport, not suitable for everyone, and that the practice techniques and drills described in this book may result in injury. Any user of the techniques and drills described herein assumes the risk of injury resulting from performing the exercises and using the equipment suggested. The exercises and techniques described herein are not to be attempted without consultation with and clearance from a physician. Adequate protective gear and proper coaching and supervision in conjunction with sound physical conditioning are essential.

The football helmet never should be used as a weapon in blocking or tackling or in any facet of the game.

The instructions and advice presented in this book are in no way intended as a substitute for professional coaching.

The authors, publishers, participants, and distributors of the manual disclaim any liabilities or loss in connection with the exercises and advice herein.

Another Official National Football League book from St. Martin's Press you will enjoy:

THE NFL ALL-PRO WORKOUT
   by Michael Creedman
   A complete conditioning program for people of all ages, shapes, and fitness levels from NFL trainers, coaches, and players.

Contents

Notes for Coaches 7

Key to Diagrams 9

1. Quarterback 15

2. Running Back 53

3. Receivers 101

4. Offensive Line 151

5. Defensive Line 201

6. Linebackers 249

7. Defensive Backs 295

8. The Kicking Game 339

Glossary 395

Index 407

ACKNOWLEDGEMENTS

The author and editors gratefully acknowledge the contributions and assistance of the following people and teams in the writing and production of this book:

The late Lew Erber, one of the outstanding teachers of the game of football
    David Bass
    Los Angeles Rams
    San Diego Chargers
    Ed White

Special thanks to head coach John Featherstone and the Warriors of El Camino College, Torrance, California:
    Brett Austin
    Dave Blakes
    Larry Bonner
    Aaron Craver
    Steven Danzy
    Darrin Dolce
    Frank Dolce

Greg Franklin
Donovan Gallatin
Paul Hunt
Mike Jones
William Lackey
Alfred Lowe
Ismael Peralta
Scott Peters
Robert Reid
Raul Rodriguez
Niu Sale
David Samperio
Darryl Smith
Rod Smith
Tui Suiaunoa
Shannon Thompson
Ed Togia
James Wicks
Dan Wilbanks

PHOTOGRAPHY

Training Camp/Practice: Paul Spinelli/NFLP with additional photography by Paul Jasienski

NFL Action: Bill Amatuci 152, 324; David Boss 20, 271; John Biever 107, 303, 360; Vernon Biever 184, 331; Peter Brouillet 378; Rob Brown 104; Thomas J. Croke 72; Jonathan Daniel 222, 272; David Drapkin 267; Malcolm Emmons 43; Michael Fabus 83; Richard Gentile 40; Pete J. Groh 202, 291; John McDonough 161; Al Messerschmidt 105, 162; Michael Minardi 39; Jerry Pinkus 390; George Robarge 102; Bob Rosato 262, 286, 340; Manny Rubio 186; Jerry Soifert 138; Paul Spinelli/NFLP 213; Tom Strattman 128; Tony Tomsic 221, 357; Greg Trott 297; Jim Turner 240; Ron Vesely 16; Herb Weitman 146, 316, 386; Michael Zagaris 65.

Notes for Coaches

This book is about football, both the way it is played in the NFL and in any sound athletic program, no matter the level. This book also is about teaching, and creating an evironment in which players not only succeed, but want to learn and have fun doing it. Even though football is mentally and physically demanding it is, after all, a game. It should be challenging, but it should be fun, too.

The objective of *Play Football the NFL Way* is to present the necessary techniques for beginning offensive, defensive, and special teams players, along with drills designed to teach the requisite skills each player must master. The text in this book generally refers to practice, but it does apply to most game situations. Actual game conditions that may be different than practice have been noted.

The drills described here will teach offensive players how to best contribute to achieving their unit's main goal—to score. For defensive players, the drills teach what to look for from the offense, the individual keys on which defensive players should focus, and the reactions necessary to overcome the inherent offensive advantages of knowing the play and when it will begin.

Each drill is designed to teach one skill or technique that will help a player improve, regardless of the particular offense or defense used by his team. These drills teach and develop the basics every player needs to be successful at his position, helping to build a solid foundation of fundamentals.

It is important for a coach to vary the drills daily, constantly challenging his players without subjecting them to endless repetitions. Boredom is one of the greatest enemies of learning, especially in football. Practice time must be interesting and focused, not disorganized. For example, while defensive players should practice tackling every day, the actual tackling drill should vary with each practice. Short, crisp, well-defined drills that concentrate on only one skill

keep the players' attention and help eliminate long, tedious practice sessions.

Certain elements are key to all of the drills (and hold true for teaching any position or aspect of the game). For example, it always is the responsibility of the coach to make certain that he positions himself properly to oversee his players' form and technique. Suggested position is indicated in the drill diagrams.

If there are certain skills that you want your players to have, don't just talk about them, *practice* them. If a drill for a specific skill is not in this book, make one up. Let your players know what you want, then teach them how to do what you want. Communicate with your players. Praise accomplishment in the skills you want to emphasize (e.g. blocking ability in running backs). Tell your players what it takes to make the team or to be a starter. If you are working with young players or beginners, allow them to try different positions; just don't categorize them from the start.

It is better to run most drills with only offensive (or only defensive) players. Having offensive players take the roles of defensive players in practice (or vice versa) serves two purposes: First, the coach can work as long as necessary with one unit or group without wasting the practice time of another unit or group. Second, a player's ability to perform his job is greatly enhanced when he understands the job and techniques of the players he will be facing. For example, a defensive lineman will be a better pass rusher if he has had the experience of being a pass blocker in practice. A coach who thinks he is helping his starters by giving them a rest and not subjecting them to playing the roles of their opponents, actually is denying them a valuable learning opportunity.

Eventually, the real players from the opposite unit will be added to most drills. This can have both positive and negative consequences—positive because the players will get a chance to work against people who are skilled at their positions, which better simulates game conditions; negative because a high degree of competition may enter the drills, making them more combative than instructional.

Most drills should begin at a relatively slow pace. This is especially true where contact is involved. The coach must make sure that all players are using correct technique and have overcome their natural fear of contact before increasing the speed of a drill. If players are afraid of being injured, they will learn very little. Also, safety and form must be stressed in any contact drill or scrimmage. And *under no circumstances should a player be allowed ever to use his head as the initial point of contact*.

Remember to run most drills to the right *and* to the left. You want your players to be "ambidextrous," so to speak. No matter the drill, though, do not allow your players to practice bad habits or incorrect techniques. That only reinforces the unwanted behavior. Point out bad technique immediately. Then change it and practice it correctly. In some instances, it may be beneficial to break technique down into individual segments to analyze what is being done wrong. Correct mistakes and provide encouragement rather than berating or losing patience with a player who is having a difficult time with a specific phase of the game. Yelling at a player will cause him to lose concentration and confidence. Negative coaching will have negative results. Tell a player what *to do* instead of what *not* to do. Often a player will do exactly what he last heard from his coach, no matter if it is positive or negative instruction.

The best way to stop or end most drills is by blowing a whistle. This conditions players to respond to the sound that stops play in a game. Nevertheless, a whistle can be distracting to other players who are involved in other drills being run nearby.

One final note: do not neglect physical conditioning. Drills that have conditioning side benefits are noted in the text that follows. Football is a demanding sport that requires strength and endurance. Players need to be in top physical shape. Each position has its own physical requirements, but you must be sure that all players work on flexibility and aerobic capacity, not just strength- or bulk-building exercises. And, no matter the level of the football program, body-building or performance enhancing drugs have no place in athletics.

The emphasis of coaching football should be on teaching and on fun. Winning is the icing on the cake.

Tom Bass
Rancho Santa Fe, California

Key To Diagrams

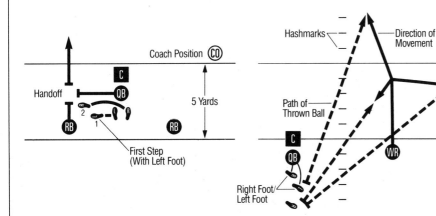

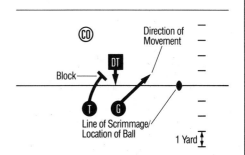

Coach Position (CO)

Handoff

5 Yards

First Step
(With Left Foot)

Hashmarks

Direction of
Movement

Path of
Thrown Ball

Right Foot/
Left Foot

Direction of
Movement

Block

Line of Scrimmage/
Location of Ball

1 Yard

(CO) COACH

(QB) QUARTERBACK

(WR) WIDE RECEIVER

(TE) TIGHT END

(RB) RUNNING BACK

(OL) OFFENSIVE LINEMAN (UNSPECIFIED)

(G) OFFENSIVE GUARD

(T) OFFENSIVE TACKLE

C CENTER

DL DEFENSIVE LINEMAN (UNSPECIFIED)

DE DEFENSIVE END

DT DEFENSIVE TACKLE

NT NOSE TACKLE

LB LINEBACKER

DB DEFENSIVE BACK

CB CORNERBACK

S SAFETY (UNSPECIFIED)

SS STRONG SAFETY

FS FREE SAFETY

BC BALL CARRIER

K PLACEKICKER

P PUNTER

KR KICK RETURNER

OFFENSE

QUARTERBACK

1

Quarterback

- Quarterback Stance   **16**
- Quarterback-Center Exchange   **18**
- Handoffs   **20**
- Making the Handoff   **24**
- Faking the Handoff   **25**
- The Forward Pass   **26**
- Gripping the Ball   **27**
- Dropback Passing   **28**
- Developing a Throwing Motion   **31**
- Pattern Passing   **34**
- Play-Action Passing   **44**
- Passing on the Move   **46**

There is no question that quarterback is the most glamorous position on a football team.

An offense must have a proficient player at the quarterback position. Lack of ability at the other offensive positions may be covered up, or compensated for, but if a team attempts to play with a quarterback who lacks the physical skills and mental abilities for the position, the weakness quickly will become evident to everyone.

Because of the importance of the quarterback to a team's success, the player at this position also will come under closer scrutiny and be forced to play under greater pressure than many of his teammates. The ability to play under pressure is a vital part of a great quarterback's makeup.

When the offense is successful, most of the praise will be directed toward the quarterback. Should the offense falter, the quarterback often will find much of the criticism directed at him. Young quarterbacks need to understand early in their careers that neither the praise nor the criticism really is justified, that both are magnified out of proportion, and that, though a quarterback, he is just one player on a team. Many young quarterbacks' careers often are ruined before they develop by undue pressure applied by parents, coaches, teammates, and the players' own perception of the importance of the position.

In order to survive, the young quarterback, even though he is the offensive leader, must realize that the pressure of winning or losing is not resting solely upon his shoulders, but that his teammates also must share the responsibility for the team's success or failure.

Many coaches, at all levels of football, believe that the quarterback position requires a player with exceptional athletic skill. This is especially true if the quarterback is asked to direct a team in which one of his primary responsibilities is to run with the ball.

For a passing team, pure athletic skill —speed and running ability—is not nearly as important as the player's ability to set up correctly and throw the ball accurately with good velocity to the proper receiver.

Height and weight may vary considerably from one quarterback to another, but all successful quarterbacks have an inner strength and belief in themselves. Each time they lead their offense out onto the field, the great quarterbacks truly believe they will move the ball and guide their team to victory.

Great quarterbacks bring an air of confidence to the field and the huddle that is quickly transmitted to every player on the offensive, and sometimes defensive, unit. Their mere presence conveys the message that whatever it takes will be done to get the ball down the field and score the winning points.

Along with determination, mental toughness, and physical skill, a quarterback must be a leader. When he steps into the huddle, he must command the respect and attention of each offensive player. He must be able to take control and cause the other 10 men to execute whatever play he calls to the very best of their ability.

If a quarterback calls a play with any indecision, the other offensive players quickly will recognize his lack of conviction and often will not perform with

The quarterback is in complete control when the offense is on the field.

the same intensity. It is especially important for young, beginning quarterbacks to understand this fact and never enter the huddle until they are absolutely certain of the play to be called.

A successful quarterback must enjoy taking charge of the offense, he must speak with conviction and dedication, and he must leave no doubt in anyone's

mind that he is running the offense on the field.

Quarterback Stance

Each position on a football team requires certain physical skills that the player can and should practice by himself in the offseason, without the need to have other players present.

The quarterback position has a number of these individual physical skills that can be developed by the player himself. Each of these skills can be practiced over and over again. They should be executed so many times that they become automatic, requiring no thought by the quarterback in a game situation.

The stance a quarterback uses is one of those things. Poor performance by a quarterback often can be traced to his very first movement. A quarterback must originate every play from a proper stance. If there is one key word to describe the essence of the quarterback stance, that word would be "comfortable."

When getting into a comfortable and balanced stance, the quarterback should start with the placement of his feet, which should be parallel and shoulder width apart. The player's weight should be distributed evenly on the balls of both feet, allowing him to step with either foot and to move with equal ease forward or backward, to the right or to the left. If his feet are less than shoulder width apart, the quarterback will not have the balance that he needs and often will lean to the right or the left. It also is important to make certain that he does not have his weight back on his heels, which will cause him to lean backwards, away from the line of scrimmage.

At the start, it is best to give the quarterback a line of reference to use for checking to see if his feet are even. Foot placement should be observed from both the front and the side. It is important for a coach to check the width of the space between the feet, to be sure that they are even, that the toes are pointing straight ahead, and that the weight of the player is on the balls of his feet.

The next area to consider in the quarterback's stance is the position of his legs. It is important for the knees to be flexed, but it must be understood, both by the coach and the quarterback, that the actual degree of flex in the knees is determined by two factors. The first is the actual height of the quarterback; the second is the height of the center. A tall quarterback who has a short-legged center requires a greater flex in the knees than a shorter quarterback with a tall center.

The quarterback must understand that he will have the responsibility of getting enough bend in his knees so he can be in position to receive the ball from the center. *It is the quarterback who always must adjust to the height of the center, and not the other way around.*

In the beginning, however, the quarterback should work without a center, setting up with a comfortable 45-degree-angle flex in his knees for his practice stance. This is a good starting position. The amount of knee flex can be adjusted easily once the center becomes part of the drill. Again, observe the quarterback's stance from both the front and the side to check on the knee flex of the player.

Because the quarterback will be asked to practice getting into his stance hundreds and hundreds of times prior to

The best way to check the quarterback's stance is to view it both from the front and the side. In the correct stance, the quarterback's feet are set parallel along a straight line, his knees are flexed, his back straight, head up, and eyes focused ahead.

the start of actual full-team workouts, it should be emphasized that the total stance, and especially the flex of the knees, must be comfortable and not fatiguing.

Now, let's move the focus to the quarterback's upper body. The quarterback should have a slight forward lean at the hips. His back should be straight and his shoulders should be in front of his hips.

With his body in this position, the quarterback should have his head up, eyes focused straight ahead. As he settles into his stance, the quarterback should be able to move his head from one side to the other easily, viewing the entire defense prior to the beginning of each play. The quarterback's arms should be extended forward and toward the center of his body. His hands should be placed on top of each other with the palms facing. *The passing hand of the quarterback always should be the top hand of the two.*

Because a ball or a center won't be used in the initial drill, the quarterback may place the heels of his hands together, fingers spread, with hands held at a 90-degree angle to one another. The hands should be midway between the quarterback's knees and hips in a position that will be near where he will re-

ceive the ball from the center.

Learning the proper stance is vitally important to every quarterback. The tendency of many players and coaches is to brush over this critical phase quickly and move into areas in which there is movement and action. Young quarterbacks must be forced to practice stepping up to the line and assuming a proper, relaxed, and comfortable stance in every practice session.

WINNING POINTS
- Feet parallel, shoulder-width apart, toes pointed straight ahead.
- Weight distributed evenly on balls of feet.
- Knees flexed.
- Slight forward lean at hips.
- Back straight, shoulders in front of hips.
- Head up, eyes focused straight ahead.
- Arms extended forward toward center of body.
- Hands placed on top of each other, palms facing in.
- Passing hand always is top hand.

Quarterback-Center Exchange

Once the quarterback has developed a stable, comfortable stance, he can move

on to learning the method of receiving the ball from the center. The obvious importance of this exchange must be impressed upon the beginning quarterback. An offensive play has little chance to succeed if it begins with a fumbled exchange.

The quarterback must feel that he is connected to the center. He must understand that as the center delivers the ball to him, the center will not remain stationary. Depending on the play, the center may be moving straight ahead, to the right or left, or, in the case of a pass, dropping straight back.

The quarterback should take the time early in his career to know all the blocking assignments of the center so he can anticipate the center's movement without even thinking about it. The quarterback always must take the responsibility for not pulling out or away from the center too quickly. Controlling the football from the center has to be the number-one priority of the quarterback.

When working on these basic physical skills without the benefit of an actual center, a coach can take the place of the center and hand the ball to the quarterback. In that situation, the coach lines up in front of and facing the quarterback. Down on one knee, the coach can grasp the ball and lift it up to the waiting

Practice taking snaps without a center.

hands of the quarterback. It is important for the coach to deliver the ball in the very same manner as the center. Ideally the ball should be brought up to the quarterback's hands in such a manner that it is turned sideways and the laces make contact with the top hand. The fingertips of the quarterback's top hand should be over the laces of the ball. As the ball makes contact with the top hand, the bottom hand, which is the most important hand in securing the snap, should wrap around the ball to assure that the ball is completely under control.

As soon as the player becomes proficient at receiving the ball, the coach can increase the velocity with which he delivers the ball to the quarterback's hands. The harder the snap, the more

chance there is for the hands to separate and the snap to be fumbled. The quarterback must understand this and be prepared to grasp the ball quickly with his bottom hand.

Once the ball has been secured, the quarterback should allow the middle finger of his passing hand to become the dominant grip point on the ball. Because the ball seldom will reach the quarterback's hands in perfect position from the center, the quarterback must be aware that he often will have to adjust the ball once he has it in his control.

When the center is available to take the place of the coach, the quarterback

The quarterback must adjust his knee flex to fit the height of the center.

should take his stance directly behind the center. Remember, the quarterback need only have enough flex in his knees so that he can comfortably reach his hands under the center to receive the ball.

In order to achieve good hand placement, the quarterback should place the index finger of his top hand (passing hand) directly on the center seam of the center's pants. It is important for the quarterback to let the center know that his hands are in position by exerting pressure upwards with the knuckles of the top hand.

WINNING POINTS
- Stand directly behind center.
- Flex knees to accommodate height of center.
- Index finger of top hand on center seam of center's pants; alert center hands are in position with upward pressure of knuckles of top hand.
- Controlling football is number-one priority.
- At snap, fingertips of top hand cover laces of ball; bottom hand wraps and secures ball; middle finger of passing hand is main grip point.

DRILL:

Quarterback-Center Exchange

When first working on the snap between the center and quarterback, the center should move forward only one step after releasing the ball. As the exchange becomes more and more secure, the center can go through the entire range of movement that he will execute when he is blocking on all running plays.

The coach should call a play, making certain the quarterback knows the direction the center will move once the ball is snapped. The quarterback must gain a feel for the center moving away from him —either straight ahead, to the right, or to the left.

The coach should position himself so he can be certain the quarterback is not pulling away from the center while the center's body is moving forward.

The next step in the exchange is to have the center set back in pass protection rather than firing across the line of scrimmage. Now the quarterback will get a feel for the center's body coming back toward him rather than moving away. The quarterback also may feel the center's buttocks come down upon his hands as the center brings his shoulders, arms, and hands up to pass protection position.

Because of the tremendous impor-tance of a good exchange between center and quarterback, the more practice time and the greater number of snaps the two men can have prior to actual team practice, the better off they will be. Remember, rather than merely going through the motions of taking the snap, the mental part of the game should be included by always calling a play and simulating the actual center's movement on the play. By doing this, the quarterback quickly will learn to anticipate and associate the center's movement on the snap with every type of play.

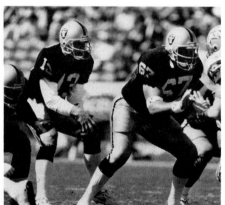

The movement of the center after the snap complicates the ball exchange.

Handoffs

Proper footwork is vital on every hand-off. Improper steps can result in the quarterback not quite reaching a ball carrier on a handoff. The result can be an insecure handoff, or the quarterback may miss the handoff completely and find that he has the ball and nowhere to go. *It is the responsibility of the quarter-back to get the ball to the ball carrier properly. Once the handoff has been ex-ecuted, the ball carrier assumes the re-sponsibility for making certain the ball is secure.*

Because a variety of offenses are used these days, the numbers and types of running plays have increased greatly. The basic steps needed for the running plays found in most offenses will be de-tailed here. If some other style of foot-work is desired by a coach, the quarter-back should learn the desired footwork and incorporate it into his practice rou-tine. But no matter the offense, foot-work, carefully choreographed and me-ticulously practiced, ensures that the quarterback is in the best possible posi-tion to hand the ball to the ball carrier on each running play.

Learning footwork does not require a running back or a center in the drill. In the beginning, it is best if the quarter-back works alone, or with just his coach. The quarterback's steps and the body movement he needs for each run-ning play should become relaxed and automatic before the running back enters the drill.

Initially, the quarterback can grasp the ball as if he already has received it from the center. Because physical techniques and skills are learned much better when the drill focuses on only one technique, the quarterback should not concern himself with taking the snap or actually handing the ball to the running back when he is concentrating on his footwork.

DRILL:

Shallow Handoff Footwork

If working with a coach, the coach will tell the quarterback which way he wants him to move—either to the right or to the left. By lining up on the side of the quarterback's movement, the coach can observe the footwork. He also can make certain that the quarterback has turned his head around and is focusing on the spot where the running back will originate his movement.

On the command "Hut!," the quarterback should take a short cheat or lead step with his foot in the direction in which he is moving. This step need not be more than six inches.

The quarterback should hold the ball in both hands, belt high and close to his stomach. It must be emphasized to the

Footwork is critical; the quarterback must be in position to hand off.

quarterback that he must protect the ball at all times, that it always should be securely grasped in both hands, and that it should never be away from his body until he is ready to give it to a teammate.

The next, more elongated, step with the far foot should be down the line of scrimmage, bringing the quarterback to a point at which he can extend his arms and his hands, plus the ball, away from his body in preparation for the handoff.

While he takes the second step, the quarterback should be certain he has

turned his head and located the position of the coach. Later in his development, the quarterback will be focusing on the running back who is to receive the ball.

After simulating the handoff, the quarterback can take three steps away from the line of scrimmage, then continue to the outside.

DRILL:

Deep Angle Handoff Footwork

A two-step movement by the quarterback also is required prior to a deep angle handoff. The difference is that the handoff now takes place away from the line of scrimmage, in the offensive backfield.

For this handoff, the coach is aligned seven yards deep and closer to the quarterback than he was in the previous drill. This positioning allows the quarterback ample area to move, in addition to giving him an area to focus on and a good idea where the running back will be coming from to receive the ball.

Once again, the quarterback's first step is a short cheat step with his foot in the direction in which he is going. Because the quarterback is moving away from the center, the length of the first step should be cut down to ensure that the snap is executed correctly. More than anything else, the first step estab-

Deep angle handoffs primarily are used when running out of the I-formation.

lishes the direction the quarterback must go to execute the handoff. This step takes the quarterback away from the line of scrimmage. It also opens his hips so that the second step allows him to move farther from the line, at an angle to his right or left.

On the second step, the quarterback turns his head and shoulders around and focuses on the coach. As he completes the second step, his arms and hands and the ball can be extended to simulate a handoff.

Once the quarterback has finished the motion of the handoff, he should return the ball to his stomach and continue to move to the outside.

This type of deep handoff is most common on I-Formation tailback plays in which the objective is to give the running back an opportunity to cut in either direction after receiving the ball.

DRILL:
Far Back Handoff Footwork
In this exchange, the quarterback comes almost straight back from the line of scrimmage to hand off the ball. The cheat step will be taken by the foot oppo-

The quarterback does not extend the ball until he is ready to hand off.

site the direction in which the quarterback is going. The slight step guarantees that the quarterback will be able to take the snap from the center.

The quarterback should turn his body away from the line of scrimmage to take a longer second step, putting him in position to make the handoff as the back comes across the backfield.

The quarterback's head and shoulders should be turned so that he sees the coach instantly. On the second step, the quarterback should extend the ball as if handing off. After extending his arms, the quarterback may take two more steps away from the line of scrimmage, then continue to his right or left.

DRILL:
Reverse Pivot Handoff Footwork
The quarterback actually pivots away from the center for this type of handoff. The cheat step is a short step up with the foot in the direction that he desires to go. This ensures that the quarterback will not separate too quickly from the center (when the center is incorporated into the drill).

The quarterback then pivots on the cheat step foot, bringing his hips and body around as he takes a second step with the far foot. The quarterback actually will be turning his back to the line of scrimmage briefly as he pivots and takes the second step.

Because the quarterback is pivoting and not opening up directly to the side of the ball carrier, it becomes more important than ever that the quarterback turns his head around as quickly as possible. The quarterback must focus on the coach as soon as he can.

As soon as he completes his second step, the quarterback extends the ball in the motion of the handoff. After the quarterback has made the movement, he pulls the ball back in and continues moving to the outside.

This type of footwork is used when the quarterback gives the ball to a fullback who is lined up directly behind him.

DRILL:

Reverse Pivot Pitch Footwork

To pitch the ball instead of handing it off, the quarterback uses the same footwork he used on the previous drill. The difference is that instead of extending the ball away from his stomach to make a handoff, the quarterback now moves the ball more to his hip on the side of the pitch and forcibly extends his arms to simulate the movement he will use when he flips the ball underhanded to the running back. After simulating the pitch, the quarterback should quickly drop straight

On pitch plays, the quarterback must focus instantly on the running back.

back, away from the line of scrimmage.

This technique is used when the ball is pitched in single-back formations or to I-formation tailbacks on wide running plays.

As in all the drills, the quarterback's speed in locating and focusing on the coach or running back is critical. The coach must be certain that the quarterback turns his head around quickly and that he is not looking out into space.

Because the footwork used by option quarterbacks varies greatly with the actual style of option offense being run, it is not included in this book. Should

your team be an option team, it is essential that you understand and practice the footwork desired by your coach. The manner of pitching the ball on the option pass also will vary, but it is similar to a chest-high basketball pass, with the ball pitched back by the hand that is farthest from the line of scrimmage.

Once the quarterback feels comfortable with the basic footwork, the center should be introduced to the drills. The quarterback and the center then should practice all of the handoff plays together.

Once the quarterback-center exchange is taking place correctly, a coach can stand in the position of the ball carrier. From this position, the coach can observe the movement of the quarterback, making certain that he is focusing quickly and is using the proper footwork on each play.

At first, the quarterback may feel that he is slow in his movements. But, as he and the center work together more and more, his speed of movement should increase.

In this center and quarterback practice, it is imperative that the center go through his normal blocking motion. By moving as he would in a game, the center gives the quarterback a feel for actual game conditions. This movement also forces the quarterback to stay under the center and not pull away too soon. The emphasis, even in practice, is on the quarterback always securing the ball before moving away from the center.

Making the Handoff

Once the quarterback and center begin working together smoothly, the running back is introduced to the drills.

Both the quarterback and the running back must execute precise footwork for any handoff to be successful, but it is the quarterback's job and responsibility to make certain that the ball is placed firmly against the runner's midsection.

When the quarterback approaches the handoff spot, he should be holding the ball securely in both hands. As he extends his arms and hands away from his stomach toward the ball carrier, the hand closest to the runner should come off the ball and the ball should be placed into the runner's midsection with the hand farthest away. Many coaches tell the quarterback to place the ball on the far hip of the runner. These coaches obviously do not expect that to happen, but they are trying to make certain that the quarterback understands the importance of getting the ball into the runner's stomach area rather than merely placing the ball on the near hip of the running back, where it likely will be fumbled.

DRILL:
Dive Handoff

A coach should be positioned where he can observe both players and the execution of the handoff. The drills should be repeated for each type of run that will be used by the offense.

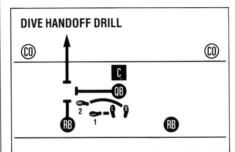

DIVE HANDOFF DRILL

It often is advisable to give the quarterback and the running back some time to work together before reintroducing the center to the drills. The ball carrier can align himself in the proper position and the quarterback starts the drill with the ball already in his grasp. On the snap count, both players then should execute their respective footwork for the play that was called, and the handoff is made.

DRILL:
Deep Handoff

If there is a problem with any one segment of the play when all three players

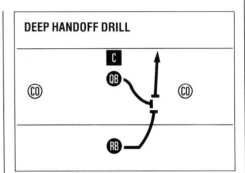

DEEP HANDOFF DRILL

The quarterback puts the ball in the runner's stomach with his far hand.

are working together, the coach should stop the drill, separate the players once again, isolate the problem skill, and work on it individually until it is corrected. Allowing players to practice bad habits or to execute incorrect physical techniques only enforces that action by the player. The sooner a bad technique is pointed out to a player—and especially to the quarterback—the quicker it can be changed and practiced correctly.

All quarterbacks spend hours practicing passing the ball, but only the great ones realize the importance of a well-executed running game and how much it ultimately contributes to the success of a team's offense. They understand and use the running game to make the passing attack even more dynamic. Rather than hastily going over ball handling, quarterbacks should spend the time needed to make the running game an integral part of the offensive attack he directs.

Faking the Handoff

When a quarterback forces the defense to try to stop a strong running game, he has set up one of the best plays in football—the play-action pass. This play looks like a run as it starts, but in reality is a passing play.

Both the quarterback and the runner must "sell" the fake to the defense.

In order to insure the success of this type of play, the quarterback and the running back must convince the defense that the handoff has taken place. The quarterback must look like he is placing the ball into the running back's stomach and the running back must run as if he has the ball.

Two techniques are used by a quarterback when executing this type of fake. The first is putting the ball on his hip

away from the line of scrimmage and then faking giving the ball to the running back with the other (empty) hand. If it is done quickly enough, this may momentarily fool the defense. But with this type of fake, the ball is not really secured in both hands by the quarterback; should he be hit from the rear there is an excellent chance for a fumble.

The second method of faking play-action is for the quarterback to extend the ball into the running back's stomach

Two-handed fakes look more real and afford better control of the ball.

with both hands, withdrawing it before the running back covers it with his hands and arms. As on every play-action pass, the running back must make the

---

WINNING POINTS
- Secure ball immediately on center exchange.
- Take short cheat step.
- Hold ball in both hands, belt high, and close to stomach.
- Never hold ball away from body until ready to hand it to teammate.
- Turn head and shoulders to focus on running back to receive ball.
- Quarterback has responsibility to place ball firmly in runner's midesection; runner has responsibility to secure ball.
- On handoffs, as ball is extended away from body, hand closest to runner comes off ball; ball is placed in runner's midsection with hand farthest away.
- On pitches, move ball to hip on side of pitch and flip ball underhanded to running back.
- On play-action fakes, extend ball into running back's stomach with both hands, withdrawing it before back covers it with hands and arms.

---

defense think that he has the ball by running as hard as he would on an actual running play.

The two-handed fake is preferred because the defensive players really see the ball being extended to the running back. By having both hands on the ball at all times, the quarterback has greater control over the ball, hence there is less chance of losing it. Also, after extending the ball and then taking it away from the ball carrier, the quarterback has the ball in both hands and is in an ideal position to set up and pass to a receiver downfield.

The important thing for the quarterback to remember is that all his hard work in learning the proper footwork for the running game, and the hours of practicing with the running back on the handoff, will pay off doubly—in a strong running attack, and subsequently, in a devastating play-action pass attack. As New York Giants general manager George Young once said, "You win with the pass—but if you can't run, you can't pass."

The Forward Pass

Every young quarterback dreams of throwing a long touchdown pass on the last play of a championship game. It's never difficult to get a quarterback to practice throwing the ball. But what may be hard is to make the quarterback practice the proper body mechanics needed to set up, step, and start his body moving correctly prior to releasing the ball.

Because passing the ball requires great concentration, correct grip, proper body movement and arm action, control of the football until the moment of release, and good follow-though, it is extremely important that the quarterback practices the basics of passing over and over again until they become second nature to him.

Passing a football with accuracy has been compared to hitting a great golf shot. The motion of the two athletes is smooth, almost without effort, and the action of both is the same time after time. This consistency of movement is what each quarterback should strive to attain as he learns to pass the ball. His goal must be to grip the ball the same, to use identical footwork in setting up for each pass, to execute the same body movement as he moves forward to throw the ball, and to release the ball with as close to the same action as possible on every forward pass.

In addition to learning the mechanics of passing the ball from classic drop-back style, the quarterback also must master the proper footwork and action for the various other types of passes that he will be asked to throw.

Depending on the type of offense being run, the quarterback often will be asked to execute a play-action pass as well as some type of movement pass where the quarterback does not drop directly back from the center, but instead moves to the outside of the center, either to the right or the left, to throw the ball. Often this type of moving pass will require the quarterback to learn the added skill of throwing the ball on the run.

The quarterback also needs to develop a grasp of the mental aspects of the passing game. On a running play, the quarterback's primary responsibility ends when he places the ball securely into the hands of the running back. With the exception of option plays, he is not required to make any decisions when executing a running play. This is not the case on passing plays.

Offensive coaches who like to run the ball have an old saying that there are three things that can happen every time a quarterback passes the ball and two of them are bad. A pass can be complete, or it can be incomplete or intercepted. The job of the quarterback is to make certain that the one good result, a completion, occurs more often than the two bad ones.

Once the quarterback is proficient in the mechanics of passing, he must learn how receivers run particular patterns, when the different patterns will open up, and the keys to the various types of defenses that he will face. The ability to read the defense is a skill that a quarterback will learn to master only after he has had years of playing experience.

In the beginning, the quarterback should limit himself to determining the difference between zone and man-to-man coverages, and to focusing on the pre-selected area of the field to which he will pass.

Many young quarterbacks get so wrapped up in trying to look for the first, the second, and finally the third receiver on a pass pattern that they forget to throw the ball. That is one of the reasons why it is so important for a coach to define and pinpoint the intended receiver for a novice quarterback. It is vital for both the coach and the quarterback never to forget that indecision is one of the greatest hindrances to good performance. For the beginning quarterback, a primary receiver and, if he is covered, one backup receiver, are all that should be considered.

Should the quarterback find that neither receiver is open, he must be prepared to run with the ball, gaining as much yardage as possible, rather than throwing an interception or incompletion, or taking a sack for a loss.

Gripping the Ball

The passing grip that is used by each quarterback will vary slightly from player to player, usually relating to the size of the quarterback's hands. The larger the hand of the player, the farther back from midpoint that he can grip the ball. Most beginning quarterbacks should start with a grip that is near the center of the ball.

The top hand always is the passing hand; the bottom hand secures the ball.

When learning to grip the ball correctly, the quarterback should start with the index finger near the tip of the ball, across the seam, and slightly off the laces. If the quarterback has extremely big hands, the index finger can be closer to the tip of the ball than it is to the laces.

The middle and third fingers should extend across the laces so that the fingertips rest on the surface of the ball and not on the laces; the tip of the little finger will usually rest on the laces, with the hand pressure exerted just behind the center point of the ball. It is very important that the quarterback feels that he has the ball completely under control in his hand. The non-passing hand should rest lightly on the underside of the ball, insuring that the player has the ball firmly in his grasp.

When learning the proper grip, it is best for a young quarterback to start with a coach, kneeling, handing the ball up to him. As the quarterback feels the ball make contact with his hands, he should automatically learn to adjust so that his passing hand is in the proper position on the ball. A center can be added to the practice, taking the place of the coach, whenever the coach feels that the quarterback is ready.

From his kneeling position the coach should concentrate on the hands of the quarterback, making certain that the grip is correct and that the quarterback has complete control of the ball, cra-

dling it securely in both hands as he moves.

So the quarterback learns to adjust the ball as he moves into position to pass, the quarterback should accept the ball from the coach and then sprint back five steps from the line of scrimmage. Remember, we are teaching the proper grip to the quarterback, so do not simultaneously work on setting up or passing the ball.

Dropback Passing

A successful passing game requires exact timing between the passer and the receiver. The receiver aids this cause by running precise and disciplined pass patterns. The quarterback can fulfill his part by learning to become very consistent in the manner and depth of his drop away from the line of scrimmage.

There are four distinct depths in the dropback passing game. The depth of each drop should be coordinated with the depth of the particular pattern that is being run by the primary receiver.

When teaching the footwork for the various drops, it is best to concentrate solely on the quarterback's footwork and not allow him to actually pass the ball. And because the ball is not going to be thrown, it is not necessary to have a receiver involved in the drill. If a center

is available, have him snap the ball to the quarterback, though a coach easily can hand the ball to the quarterback during this preliminary work. The primary point is that the player should correctly accept the ball prior to starting his sprint away from the line of scrimmage.

In setting up a dropback drill, a coach should be positioned on the side of the quarterback's passing hand. From this vantage point he can easily observe the footwork of the quarterback during his drop and quickly make the appropriate corrections. When practicing the drops for the quarterback, it is good to have the drill run near the hashmarks so that the depth of his drop can easily be determined.

In all dropback passing, the quarterback will take an extremely short step forward with the foot opposite his passing hand. As the quarterback becomes more and more proficient in taking the snap from the center and dropping away from the line of scrimmage, he will find that he moves the cheat foot less and less. The purpose of the cheat step is to guarantee that the quarterback does not pull away from the center before he has received the ball.

In practicing the footwork for the various drops, have the quarterback use crossover steps, not a backpedal away

On dropbacks, the ball is carried in both hands at jersey-number height.

from the line of scrimmage. The quarterback should carry the ball securely in both hands, at a height even with the numbers on his jersey. It should be emphasized that he keep the height of the

ball constant and that he does not fall into the extremely bad habit of carrying the ball in a lower position, more even with his belt buckle.

Drop drills, with the player retreating to each of the determined depths without passing the ball, should be run at the start of every practice so that the importance of consistent drop mechanics are never lost, but are constantly enforced by daily repetition.

Beginning quarterbacks will be impatient to get through this phase of training and to start throwing the ball down the field. Stick it out; without the proper mechanics of setting up you never will be a good passer.

DRILL:
Three-Step Drop

SHORT PASS DRILL	—
—	—
— ⓒⓞ	—
—	—
—	—
Ⓒ	
— ⓆⒷ	—
—	3-Step Drop
—	—
—	—

The first drop that should be learned is the short, three-step drop that is needed for the quick passing game. For a right-handed passer, the first step away from the line of scrimmage is with the right foot, the second with the left, and the final set step with the right. The third and final step should be slightly longer, ending with a firm foot plant to stop the quarterback's backward movement and put him in position to immediately step forward and pass the ball.

DRILL:
Five-Step Drop

The next drop the quarterback needs to learn and perfect is the five-step drop. This depth of set should put the quarterback approximately seven yards from the line of scrimmage on his final step. For the right-handed passer, the proper steps should be with the right, left, right, left, and finally the right foot.

As you work on the five-step drop, remember the ball should remain at a constant height even with the quarterback's numbers. This drop is used when the quarterback throws medium-depth passes and certain deep passes which require a quicker release.

The quarterback will find that because of the added steps of the five-step drop, he will generate more momentum as he

The quarterback uses crossover steps to retreat from the line of scrimmage. He then stops the backward momentum of his drop with a plant step.

moves away from the center. This makes his final step, the longer set step, where he stops his backward motion and brings his body under control, more critical.

After planting with the set step, the quarterback should then bring his left foot closer to the right so that both feet are planted directly under his hips and body. From this position, with his feet under his hips, the quarterback will be balanced and able to step and throw the ball to any area of the playing field.

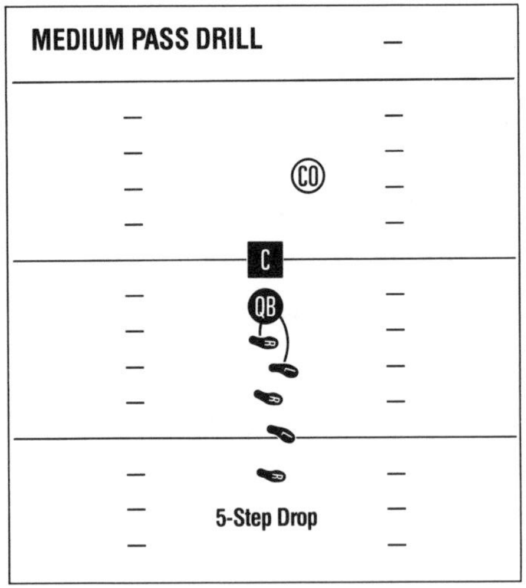

MEDIUM PASS DRILL —

5-Step Drop

Seven-Step Drop

The third type of drop that the quarter-

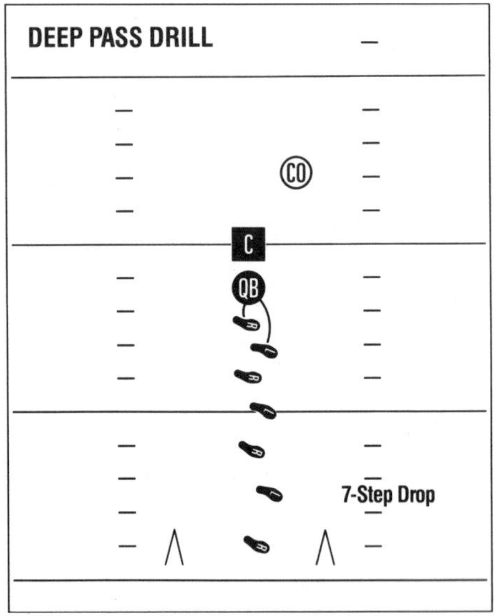

DEEP PASS DRILL —

7-Step Drop

back needs to master is the seven-step drop. This should take the quarterback about nine yards from the line of scrimmage. The seven-step drop is used when throwing deep pass routes that take a longer time to develop.

By placing a cone or a towel on the ground, the coach can give the quarterback a quick, additional point of reference for the depth of his drop.

DRILL:

Screen Drop

The fourth and final quarterback drop is a variation of the seven-step drop that is used when throwing a slow screen pass. For this drop, the quarterback takes his normal seven-step drop, sets up as if he were preparing to pass, and then retreats an additional five or six steps away from the line of scrimmage.

Developing a Throwing Motion

Once a quarterback has learned to take the snap from center, grip the ball correctly, and drop properly, he is ready to develop an accurate, automatic, grooved throwing motion. In order to insure accuracy, the player should attempt to have his throwing motion as identical as possible on every pass thrown, and his body should move to throw the ball with little, if any, conscious thought.

The passing motion can be broken down into four distinct elements. The first is the set (the last step in the quarterback's drop), where he stops his momentum backward from the line of scrimmage, brings his body under control, and plants his feet closer together directly under his hips. At this point, the ball should be held firmly in both hands and it should be carried at a height even with the top of the player's jersey numbers.

Next is the step with the foot opposite the passing hand. As the leg moves forward, the toe of the foot should be placed so that it aims directly at the quarterback's target area. Simultaneous with this forward step, the non-passing hand will release from the ball, and the passing arm and hand will be brought back, elbow cocked, ball held high, behind the helmet.

The third stage in the passing motion is the delivery of the ball. This is a criti-

A good passing motion has four elements: the set step (left); *a forward step* (middle); *the delivery, release, and follow-through* (right). *The passing motion should remain consistent on every pass, no matter the depth.*

cal stage because the player must initiate the throwing motion with the trunk of his body and not merely his arm. A player who throws only with his arm, and not his body, usually is inaccurate and loses velocity on the ball.

The hips of the player should open up and be square with the target area. The belt buckle of the quarterback should precede the passing arm's forward motion, with the center of the buckle being pointed directly at the target area. As the trunk of the passer starts forward, the upper body also will begin to move forward with the shoulder leading the forward movement of the passing arm. The elbow of the passing arm should remain bent at a good angle, as the ball, which is held above the shoulder pads, is brought forward.

It is important for a coach to check the quarterback's arm movement, making certain that his passing hand is not extending straight out from the elbow as the throw begins, causing him to have a sidearm throwing motion. Quarterbacks who use a sidearm passing motion lack accuracy, their ball usually does not have a good spiral, and, because of the lack of height at which the ball is released, they stand a greater chance of having their passes batted down at the line of scrimmage by defensive players.

This flaw in a player's throwing motion is much easier to correct if caught at the beginning of the quarterback's career. Once a quarterback becomes accustomed to delivering the ball with a sidearm action, it is almost impossible to change his throwing motion to a correct overhand delivery.

The fourth, and final, stage is the actual release of the ball from the quarterback's passing hand and the follow-through of his arm and passing hand. As the passing arm continues its forward movement, the forearm should come over the top of the elbow and extend toward the target area. At the moment of release, the passing hand should be extended directly at the target and the ball should be allowed to naturally leave the passer's hand, rotating in a nice tight spiral. The middle finger of the passing hand is the dominant grip point on the ball and should be the last released from the ball.

After the quarterback has released the ball, his passing arm should reach full extension. At this point, the passing hand should be allowed to rotate inward toward the center of the quarterback's body so that the palm of the passing hand ends up facing down toward the ground. The fingers of the passing hand should end up pointing directly toward the intended receiver or the target area.

DRILL:

Passing Delivery

Sometimes it is easier to teach the me-

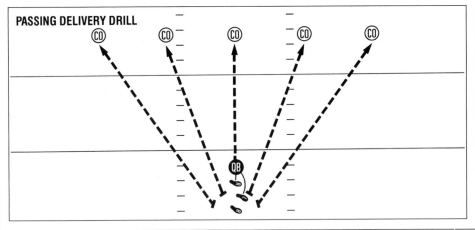

PASSING DELIVERY DRILL

chanics of proper passing motion without using a ball. The coach can position himself downfield as the target and have the quarterback set, step, and go through the throwing motion over and over again. In this type of practice, we are only concerned about teaching the throwing motion; the quarterback should take just a three-step drop before executing his passing delivery.

Once the quarterback and the coach both are satisfied that the quarterback has learned the fundamental passing motion, a ball can be introduced. Holding the ball in both hands, the quarterback can take his short drop, set, step with the front foot, and actually go through his entire passing movement while throwing the ball to the coach.

Beginning quarterbacks often will have a great amount of difficulty passing to the side of the field opposite their passing hand. If the quarterback has this problem, the first thing to check is the step foot. In a majority of cases, a quarterback who is having trouble throwing to the opposite side of the field is not stepping in that direction. Rather, his foot ends up pointing more down the center of the field. With this improper step, the quarterback does not have an open throwing motion, his hips and belt buckle don't end up pointing toward the target

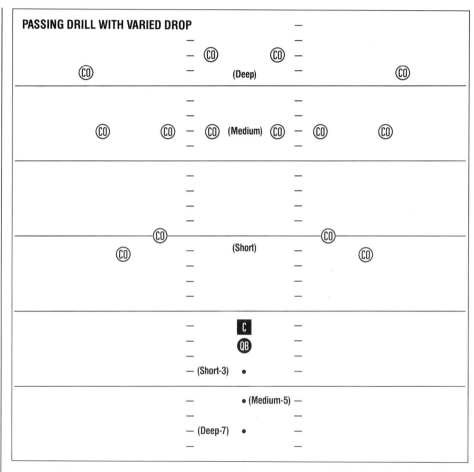

PASSING DRILL WITH VARIED DROP

area, and he has to bring his passing arm across his body as he releases the ball.

Next, the center can be introduced to

the practice with the quarterback taking the full appropriate drop for each of the passes called by the coach. This way the quarterback begins to get a feel for the

WINNING POINTS

- Strive for relaxed, smooth, and consistent passing motion.
- Grip ball with index finger near tip of ball across seam, and middle, third, and little fingers across laces with fingertips on ball.
- Non-passing hand rests lightly on underside of ball.
- On dropback, carry ball securely in both hands at height even with jersey numbers; use crossover steps to retreat to the proper backfield depth.
- Use final (set) step of dropback to stop backward motion and bring body under control.
- Plant with set step, then bring left foot closer to right foot directly under hips and body.
- Step with foot opposite passing hand, toe pointing toward target area; release ball with non-passing hand; cock passing arm.
- Initiate throwing motion with trunk, not only with arm.
- Shoulder leads forward movement of passing arm.
- Follow-through on passing motion leaves fingers pointing at intended receiver or target area.

depth of drop corresponding to the depth of each pattern run. Remember, the emphasis of the practice should still be on developing an automatic passing motion.

Above all, the quarterback should be relaxed and throw with a smooth motion, with each pass released in a nearly identical way. What we are trying to develop is a consistent, comfortable throwing motion, which leads to accuracy, velocity, and the ability to pass to all field depths from a variety of drops.

Pattern Passing

For a quarterback to be a successful passer, he must know the different pass routes that each of the receivers will be running. In football terminology, these patterns are often referred to as limbs of the *passing tree*. Each pattern or route not only will be given a name but also will be assigned a number so that the pattern may be called at the line of scrimmage during a game.

A quarterback must know the names and numbers of the patterns in order to call a play during a game, plus he must understand where the receiver will be throughout each pattern. Close work between the passer and the receiver, called the *timing of the pass* , is essential if the pass is to be completed.

Passing to Wide Receivers

One of the hardest things to learn about passing is how to lead a receiver. Most beginning quarterbacks find it difficult to anticipate the speed of a wide receiv-

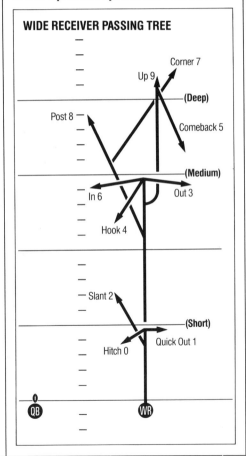

WIDE RECEIVER PASSING TREE

er as he runs a pass pattern and to gauge how far ahead of the receiver to place the ball. In order to help the novice passer develop pass timing and the techniques of throwing to a moving target, it is good to start with the "hook" pass. When run correctly, the "hook" pass should bring the receiver directly back toward the quarterback and not across, up, or to the outside of the field.

In setting up a wide receiver "passing tree" drill, the quarterback does not need to take a complete drop nor does the receiver need to run a full pattern. Our concern is with the final break on the pattern by the receiver and the final set, step, and throw by the quarterback.

DRILL:

Hook Pass

For the first pass pattern, the "hook," the receiver can line up, facing upfield, 12 yards from the line of scrimmage. He can begin to run in place and then on the command "Hut!," he moves up the field two more steps, turns to the inside, and comes back in a straight line directly to the quarterback.

The quarterback lines up in a position four yards from the line of scrimmage, takes a two-step drop, and plants his set step at seven yards as he would on any of the five-step drop patterns. Next, he

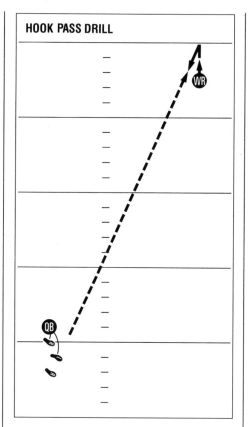

HOOK PASS DRILL

should initiate his passing motion by stepping directly toward the receiver with his lead foot.

The quarterback should try to deliver the ball so that it reaches the receiver chest high. With the ball at this height, the receiver can protect the ball as he

makes the catch. The worst thing a passer can do is to throw the ball high over the receiver's head. More often than not, this pass will go directly to a defensive player and lead to an interception. Also, a high catch puts the receiver in an exposed position. Ideally we want the pass to reach the receiver chest high, but if the pass is lower, the receiver can go down to make the catch where it is extremely difficult for a defensive man to make a play.

The quarterback must throw the "hook" so that the receiver not only makes the reception at his numbers, but also so that he has to come back toward the passer in order to easily catch it. In a game, this habit of throwing the ball so that it brings the receiver back toward the line of scrimmage will accomplish two important things. First, it will cause separation between the defensive player and the receiver, and second, it will decrease the opportunity for interceptions by the defense.

DRILL:

In, Out, and Up Passes

Once the quarterback is delivering the "hook" pass on time and with accuracy, we can begin teaching the other two medium pass patterns, the "in" and the "out."

The drill to learn these passes is set up

in the same manner as above for the quarterback and the receiver. If a young quarterback has not developed good arm strength, it is wise to shorten the length of the receiver's pattern by moving him closer to the line of scrimmage in his initial position. This adjustment is especially important when introducing the "out" pass. Instead of having the receiver line up 12 yards out, you might start him 10 yards from the line of scrimmage so that he will be only 12 yards downfield when he makes his final break to the sideline.

When passing to a moving receiver, the quarterback adjusts his throwing motion, beginning with the placement of his step foot. For the "in" pattern, this step foot should be aimed at a point six yards inside of where the receiver breaks his pattern and not directly at the receiver as on the "hook" pattern. The quarterback must release the ball so that he leads the receiver back to the inside of the field and at the same time, brings the receiver slightly back toward the line of scrimmage as he makes the catch.

The step foot for the "out" pattern needs to be directed at a point eight to ten yards in front of the receiver's breaking point. The difference in the amount of lead yardage between the "in" and the "out" pass pattern is based on the

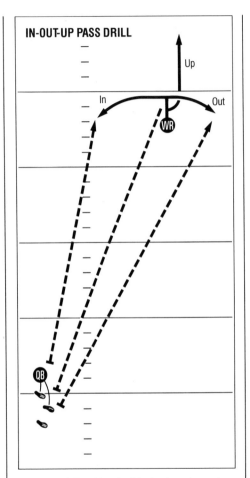

IN-OUT-UP PASS DRILL

amount of time the ball is in the air and the distance it must travel for each pass.

Because the ball is in the air for a longer time on the "out" pattern, the receiver

has a greater opportunity to run under the pass. This also gives the defender more time to react, so it is important for the quarterback to bring the receiver back toward the line of scrimmage. Again the pass should be chest high, but it is far better to throw the ball low and to the outside than it is to pass it high or behind the receiver.

The "up" pattern is a deep pattern that is best thrown off of the five-step drop that we have been using for the "hook," "in," and "out" patterns. While the drop is the same, there is one big difference in the manner this pass is thrown—it is the first pass requiring a throw with greater trajectory. When throwing the "up" pattern, the quarterback must pass the ball in an arc, giving the receiver an opportunity to run under the pass and make the catch.

The vital stepping foot of the quarterback should be directed to a point five yards inside the receiver's path up the field. The quarterback should place the ball five yards in front of the receiver and five yards to the inside. By throwing to this inside position, the normal flight of the ball takes it directly to the receiver. If the receiver does not run to this inside position, the passer usually will end up throwing the ball over the receiver's head, well out of bounds.

Throwing the pass too far to the inside of the receiver will also have undesired results, often ending up in an interception. Ideally, the ball should sail over the inside shoulder of the receiver and drop into his outstretched hands as he runs up the field.

For the quarterback to throw the "up" with proper loft, the point of the ball must be pointed upward at the moment of release. To accommodate this release, an adjustment must be made in the passing motion.

As the passing arm comes forward, the quarterback should get a little more bend in his elbow, bringing his passing hand slightly closer to his helmet. At the same time, he should cock his wrist a few degrees backward so that he can easily release the ball with the nose

On an "up" pass, the ball is tipped up and is released at a higher point.

pointed in the air. The quarterback will be releasing the ball at a higher point in his delivery, and his follow-through will be pointed higher, down the field and not directly at the receiver.

DRILL:

Post, Corner, and Comeback Passes

As the quarterback becomes comfortable and develops accuracy in throwing the five-step drop patterns, work can begin on the other deep patterns.

Don't worry initially about passing velocity. In fact, it is important for a coach to guard against allowing the player to throw too hard. Accuracy, a groove passing motion, and an understanding of the various deep patterns should be the primary concerns.

In this drill, we start the receivers and quarterbacks in the same postion as the previous drill. The difference in the execution of the two drills is that the quarterback takes a deeper drop before he sets and the receiver runs farther downfield before he breaks on his pattern.

When throwing any passes using the seven-step drop, the quarterback must keep in mind the added distance the ball has to travel and the added time the ball must be in the air.

Starting with the "post" pattern, the passer must anticipate the receiver's

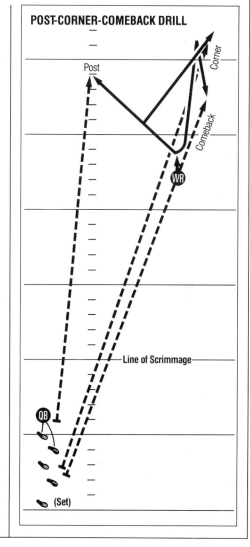

break toward the center of the field. As with the "up" pass, the quarterback should throw the ball with arc, allowing the receiver the opportunity to run under the pass to make the catch.

The stepping foot must be pointed at the center of the field, giving the passer's hips room to initiate the throwing motion. If the step foot is directed at the receiver and not the center of the field, the ball will usually end up behind the receiver as he runs his pattern. The step foot placement and the direction of the hips are keys to deep, accurate passing.

The quarterback should throw eight to ten yards in front of the receiver as he makes his break. This target area is often referred to as the "reception point," the first place where the receiver can make the catch while running at full speed.

The "post" pass does not require as great an arc as an "up" or a "corner" pattern. There is loft, but because of the fear of a defensive man in the center of the field, the quarterback should get the ball to the receiver as quickly as possible.

Of all the passes in the passing tree, the corner pass is usually the most difficult for quarterbacks to master. First of all, it is the pass requiring the ball to be in the air the longest. Second, it requires pinpoint ball placement by the quarterback. Third, it is the route that takes the longest for the receiver to run. Consequently, the quarterback is forced to hold the ball for a greater length of time before starting his throwing motion.

The passer will find that he has to wait, with his feet under his hips, body erect, eyes focused down the field, and the ball held in both hands chest high after he has taken his set step. The quarterback must keep his body and the ball in this position until he sees the receiver begin his final break. At that moment, he can start the passing motion with the step foot directed toward the corner of the field. The reception point should be 12-15 yards in front of the receiver. It is important for the passer to bring the receiver to the sideline as well as the corner with the pass.

The point of the ball should be up at the moment of release, allowing the ball to travel downfield in a high arc. For the quarterback, the "corner" and the "up" patterns should be thrown with a similar arm and wrist position and action.

The "comeback" pattern begins by looking like an "up" route. As the receiver starts upfield he will plant, turn his body to the sideline, and come back toward the line of scrimmage.

For the quarterback, this pass should be thrown with as little loft or arc as possible. The ball should be delivered like an "out" route, except the passer will not lead the receiver to the outside of the field but instead will bring him back to the line of scrimmage.

The step foot should be directed at a point five to six yards back toward the line of scrimmage and in a direct path toward the receiver's anticipated movement. When the timing is perfect, the pass will actually leave the quarterback's hand prior to the receiver turning back to the ball. Because this pass can be timed so well and because it is thrown to the outside of the field away from the defensive players, the "comeback" pass is one of the safest passes for the quarterback to attempt.

DRILL:

Hitch, Slant, and Quick Out Passes

Finally, we will introduce the quarterback to the three-step drop for short pass patterns. Because these short patterns require great timing, they are learned most successfully by using a center in the drill and starting the receiver in his normal position.

By using a center, the quarterback will become accustomed to receiving the snap, taking his drop, stepping, and delivering the ball on time to the receiver.

The passing motion for the "hitch" pattern is very similar to the motion used

A "slant" pass must not be delivered too high or behind the receiver, or the defender will have a better play on the ball.

when throwing the "hook" route. The step foot should be directed at the receiver and the ball should bring him slightly back toward the line of scrimmage.

The "slant" pass is thrown with the step foot directed five to six yards in front of the receiver. The ball should be delivered to this point with velocity and at a height just above the receiver's waist.

Throwing the slant pass either too high or behind the receiver will create problems in that the receiver cannot protect the ball with his body as he makes the

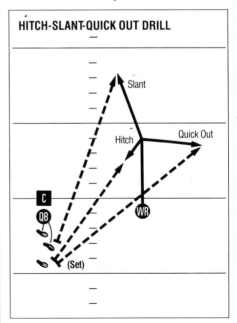

HITCH-SLANT-QUICK OUT DRILL

Slant

Quick Out

Hitch

C

QB

WR

(Set)

catch and the defenders will have a greater opportunity to make a play on the ball.

The throwing motion for the "quick out" pass and the "out" pass are very similar. The passer must anticipate the break and step and pass the ball seven or eight yards in front of the receiver and slightly back toward the line of scrimmage. As with the "out" pass, the one area we do not want the ball to go to is behind the receiver. A "quick out" thrown late and behind the receiver will almost always be intercepted and often the interception will result in a touchdown for the defensive team.

As a quarterback becomes more and more proficient throwing each pass, the drills can be adjusted so the receivers run full routes and the quarterback takes his full drop on each pass. By starting with both quarterback and receiver off the line of scrimmage, many patterns can be practiced without running the receivers to exhaustion.

Obviously, the same drill will have to be run with the quarterback throwing each pattern to his right and to his left. It is important for coaches and the quarterbacks alike to remember that we are looking for the quality in the pass; repetitions that are done incorrectly only enforce bad habits and do nothing to make

the player more successful. When warming up his shoulder and arm, the quarterback should throw each pattern, starting with short passes and working down the field to the deep routes.

Passing to the Tight End

For the quarterback to learn passing to the tight end, he first must learn and understand the different pass routes that the tight end uses. The tight end has a passing tree that includes short, medium, and deep patterns. The quarterback must learn which drop to use with each corresponding pattern run by the tight end.

The tight end often is a clutch, third-down, possession-type receiver.

DRILL:

Tight End Passes

We can start the drill by first learning to throw the medium route patterns using a five-step drop. The same techniques we emphasized in teaching passing to the wide receivers should be employed at this time. The major difference is that the intended receiver is now much closer to the quarterback and that the ball will be in the air a shorter time before it is caught.

When the quarterback understands this difference, he will know that he need not lead the receiver as much as he did when throwing to the wide receivers.

On both the "center" and the "hook" patterns the tight end will stop his movement, turn and face the quarterback, and begin moving back toward the line of scrimmage. This pass requires a step directly at the tight end, with the ball thrown at the numbers.

The "in" and the "cross" patterns require the tight end to keep running toward the center of the playing field. The quarterback should step toward an area in front of the tight end's path and deliver the ball to a point five to six yards in front of him.

Passes that are completed close to the line of scrimmage like the "cross" route, should not be thrown with the same ve-

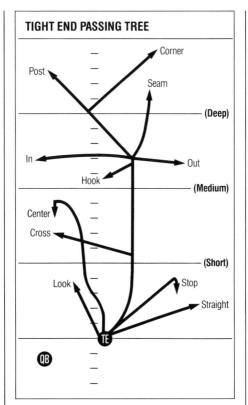

TIGHT END PASSING TREE

locity as passes that are thrown farther downfield, but they still must be delivered with authority.

For a beginning quarterback, learning to pass with "touch" may become one of the hardest techniques to master. Often the young passer thinks he must change his entire passing motion and throw only

with his arm. He forgets to step, disregards his normal passing motion, and ends up throwing at the receiver rather than leading him as he runs his route. All "touch" requires is that the passer not throw the ball as hard as he normally does—everything else should remain the same.

The "out" pass should be thrown to a spot six to eight yards in front of the tight end as he breaks to the sideline. The quarterback should deliver the ball with good velocity, making certain that he gets the ball to the tight end at chest height. A pass high, behind, or too far out in front of the tight end can be disastrous.

The quarterback should use a seven-step drop for the deep patterns that are run by the tight end—the "post," "corner," and "seam" routes. The passer must remember to adjust the release of the ball and use good loft and arch on the "corner" and "seam" pass routes, allowing the tight end to run under the ball. The "post" can be delivered with less loft and less lead yardage.

When throwing short passes, the quarterback uses a three-step drop. Again the quarterback must understand that a pass like a "look" must be thrown with touch, while others can be thrown with greater velocity on the ball.

Passing to Running Backs

Passing the ball to a running back is similar to throwing to a tight end in that a running back often is close to the quarterback on many of his patterns. This means that the ball should be thrown with a soft "touch," particularly in those instances when the receiver is running his pass pattern on the offensive side of the line of scrimmage.

The running back may delay his release on his pattern, often checking first to see if he is needed to block before running his route. This results in a pass pattern in the short area, near the line of scrimmage. But for timing purposes, the passer will use a five-step drop as he sets up and throws.

In the passing game, running backs are not always primary receivers but often serve as outlet receivers should everyone else be covered. This is the important role of "dump-off man," a receiver to whom the quarterback can throw at the last minute to avoid being sacked.

Running backs also use a passing tree to define their pass patterns, just like the other receivers. Many patterns, such as the "wide," "stop," and "hook" routes, are designed for the running back to go

to a designated area, turn and face the quarterback, and be prepared to receive the ball at the last moment should the passer get into trouble.

A smart quarterback, one who wants to avoid getting hit, will always know exactly where these outlet receivers are; he must be ready to throw to them the instant it becomes necessary.

Practice throwing to the running

backs with the same kind of drills used for passes to the wide receivers and the tight end. The quarterback usually uses a three-step drop when throwing the "wide" pattern, the "split" route, and the "flat" pass. The three-step drop becomes a necessity when the running back is a primary receiver on one of these routes. If the running back is checking to block before releasing, the

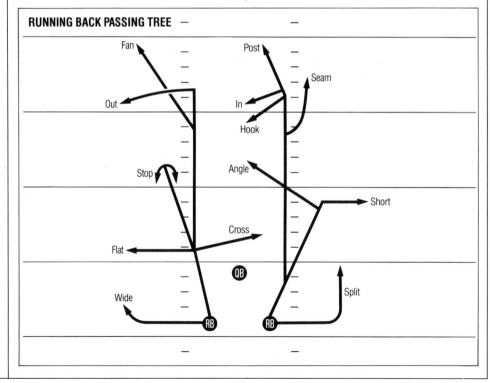

RUNNING BACK PASSING TREE

A quarterback must know where his receivers are on every play, whether wide receivers, tight ends, or running backs.

quarterback utilizes a normal five-step drop prior to passing the ball.

The quarterback also uses the five-step drop when throwing a majority of the other pass patterns executed by the running backs. These routes range from the "short" and "cross" routes—patterns run four or five yards past the line of scrimmage—to passes caught farther downfield like the "in" and "out" patterns.

The three-deep patterns run by a running back ("post," "fan," "seam") require a seven-step drop by the quarterback. The pass must be thrown with enough loft to allow the running back to run under the ball.

One thing to remember is that due to the initial alignment four yards or more back in the offensive backfield, running backs must cover added ground before they begin to work on the defensive side of the line of scrimmage. Because of this, the running backs' patterns will often come open slightly later than the patterns run by the wide receivers or the tight end, who are lined up on the line of scrimmage at the start of every offensive play.

All of the techniques that we covered for proper passing to the wide receivers and tight ends must be utilized when the quarterback is passing to a running back. In fact, the quarterback's motion when passing the ball should be identical regardless of who is receiving the pass. Except for minor adjustments, every young passer should strive to keep his set, step, forward motion of the hips and body, and arm and hand action constant on each and every pass play.

Play-Action Passing

One area which requires a great deal of practice time for passers is play-action passing. A play-action pass initially looks to the defense like a running play,

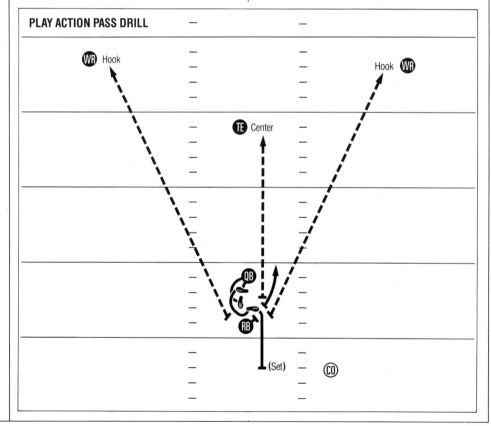

PLAY ACTION PASS DRILL

and then ends up with the quarterback passing the ball.

Obviously, the success of this type of play relies a great deal on convincing the defense that the play is a running play. In order to achieve this deception, the quarterback must indicate that he is handing the ball off and the running back must run as if he has the ball. It is also important for some members of the offensive line to block aggressively as if it were a running play. Coaches talk about the offense "selling" the run to the defense in order to open up the pass.

Excellent fakes by the quarterback, running back, and offensive line will cause linebackers to move into the line and the defensive backs to leave their zones to tackle the ball carrier. Skilled fakes also result in a slower pass rush by the defensive linemen and any other assigned pass rushers.

DRILL:

Play-Action Passes

When working on play-action passing, the quarterback, one running back, and at least one receiver downfield are needed. The receiver can remain stationary until the quarterback's faking and passing skills develop; he then can run his pass route from the line of scrimmage. The running back's alignment should be

A play-action fake requires convincing performances by the entire offense.

varied to represent his proper position to run each play.

For the quarterback a play-action pass can be broken down into three segments. The first is the proper footwork he normally would use for the running play that is being faked.

The second segment is faking the handoff. This can be done by putting an empty hand into the ball carrier's stomach or, if we are after maximum effect, holding the ball in two hands, placing it into the runner's stomach, and then pulling it out at the last instant as the ball car-

With a two-handed fake, the defense actually sees the ball handed off.

rier fakes receiving the ball.

Obviously, the two-hand fake, where the defense actually sees the ball being given to the running back, is the one that has the greater opportunity of deceiving the defensive players.

After the fake, the quarterback should move to the final segment of the pass by going into a normal drop-back type of motion, retreating to the depth of a five- or seven-step drop (depending on the type of pass pattern run by the receivers). A play-action pass usually is thrown from the pocket, not with the quarterback on the move. Ultimately, the quarterback will use the very same techniques that he has practiced and perfected on any five- or seven-step dropback pass.

Passing on the Move

Many quarterbacks become comfortable executing a dropback pass or a play-action pass where they have the opportunity to drop, set, step, and throw. They find that with hard work they can achieve a proper delivery and a consistent throwing motion for all pass routes.

This comfort level can change dramatically when the quarterback is asked to throw the ball as he is running to either his right or his left. Then, the quarterback loses the luxury of dropping back and setting to initiate his passing motion; he must get his body in proper throwing position as he runs with the ball.

There are a number of different plays that require the quarterback to throw the ball while he is moving to one side of the field or the other. The type of movement pass a quarterback is taught depends to a great extent on the offense his team is featuring.

DRILL:

Passing on the Move

For this drill, we need only the passer

and one receiver or a coach acting as a receiver. As in all of the previous passing drills, the quarterback needs to throw to both sides and all areas of the field because the mechanics of passing change radically when a passer is moving toward the side of his passing hand as opposed to away from it.

At first, it is best for the quarterback to open up, stepping first with the foot in the direction he desires to go. The quarterback executes a "sprint out" pass in this

fashion.

This allows the quarterback to easily pick up the receiver in his field of vision on his first step away from the line of scrimmage. The receiver or coach should be in a stationary position 10 yards downfield, creating an easy target for the passer. As the drill is practiced more and more, the receiver can line up just outside the hashmarks and move toward the sideline in the same direction as the quarterback's movement.

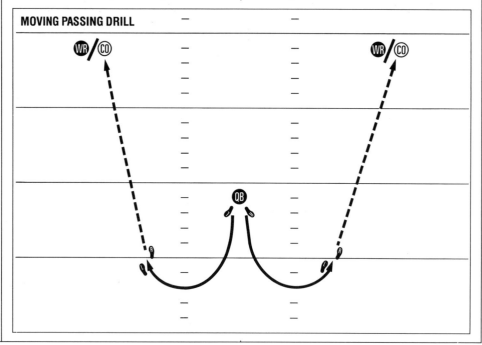

MOVING PASSING DRILL

When throwing on the run, the quarterback must be sure to get his hips turned upfield and to step directly at his target. The velocity and accuracy of the pass will be increased if the quarterback is moving upfield as he throws and does not stop after the release.

Regardless of the offense a team uses, there are some techniques that remain critical whenever a quarterback throws on the move.

The primary technique a passer must learn is to make certain that he has turned his body so that his hips are facing down the field toward the opponent's goal line and his intended receiv-er as he prepares to throw the ball. If the quarterback does not get his hips turned and leaves them directed to the sideline, he will end up throwing across his body with poor accuracy and minimal velocity.

The next important technique is for the quarterback to step directly at the intended receiver or the reception point with the foot opposite his passing hand. This step establishes the path the ball follows on each pass. Consequently, it is necessary to take this step in the proper direction.

As in dropback passing, the hips and belt buckle must initiate the throw and precede the passing arm and hand. The quarterback will usually be in good position if he aims his belt buckle toward the target area. When moving to the side away from his passing hand, the quarterback will find that he may have to move a little farther away from the line of scrimmage so that he can have ample room to turn his hips and face up the field.

Throwing on the run to the opposite side of the field can be dangerous.

It is beneficial if the quarterback is moving upfield at the time of the pass. This way, the passer's body adds momentum to the throw. And because the body and passing arm of the quarterback are going in the same direction, the velocity and accuracy of the pass will be increased.

As the quarterback delivers the ball on the run in his normal throwing motion, he will find that he rolls over the step foot as he throws and steps with the foot on the side of his passing hand. As the ball is released with good follow-through and hand position, the quarterback should allow his body to continue down the field and not come to an abrupt stop.

Most beginning quarterbacks get into trouble when they think their arm is stronger than it really is. They attempt to throw a pass while on the run to a receiver who is located in the center or on the opposite side of the field, and the result is almost always an incompletion or an interception.

In addition to the "sprint out" pass, there are other plays designed to get the quarterback to the outside and enable him to pass on the run. Each one is a little different, but the throwing motion of the passer always should remain the same.

On a "roll-out" pass, the running backs provide moving pass protection.

DRILL:

Roll-Out, Dash, and Waggle Passes

The "roll out" pass requires the quarterback to roll to the outside usually behind both running backs. In this instance, the quarterback will momentarily have his back to the line of scrimmage and he will need to turn his head around to see the receiver and the defense. The "roll out" pass gives the quarterback the added benefit of additional blockers to protect him as he throws.

For the "dash" pass, the quarterback executes his normal five-step drop action. When he reaches the position where he would normally set up to throw, the quarterback hesitates and then escapes, running to either his right or left. This has the advantage of drawing the pass rushers in toward the quarterback and then allowing him to quickly move to the outside away from their grasp.

One of the best movement passes for the quarterback is the "waggle" pass. The "waggle" is a pass where the quarterback fakes giving the ball to the running backs who are going in the opposite direction and then, with one offensive lineman in front of him, runs to the other side of the field to throw the ball.

"Waggle" and "Bootleg" passes are misdirection plays with the quarterback and running backs going in opposite directions after a play-action fake.

Often the defense is caught off guard, moves in the direction of the running backs, and is out of position to react to the quarterback's throw.

There are some coaches who run a very similar type of action, only without the pulling lineman. This is usually called a "bootleg" pass. Because of the lack of protection, the quarterback usually has the option of passing or running with the ball on a bootleg. Whatever his decision, it must be made quickly or he will find himself buried by defensive players.

Throwing on the run, attacking and moving directly at defensive players as he throws, challenging the defense to stop him as he moves up the field—all

these abilities are found in all successful quarterbacks.

It is not enough to develop only physi-

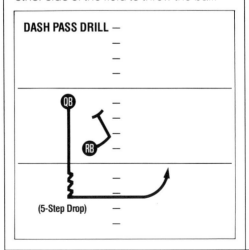

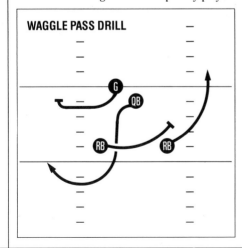

cal skills in a young quarterback. While he is learning footwork, body mechanics, and the proper throwing motion, a quarterback also must develop the necessary mental tools to lead the team.

The quarterback must lead not only with his complete knowledge of the game and his attitude in the huddle, but also by his actions when things are not going well. He must be an enthusiastic cheerleader, offering encouragement at the moment of adversity; a commanding general, telling the offensive players in no uncertain terms what they are going to do; and a taskmaster coach on the field, demanding from the offensive players that they give their best in the final moments of the game when they are dead tired.

In addition to all these things, great quarterbacks lead by example. They never give up and they are the first to jump up off the turf even after suffering a devastating hit by a defensive lineman. They have a toughness, courage, and confidence that is eagerly shared with each offensive player on the field.

WINNING POINTS
- When passing on the move, turn body so that hips are facing downfield toward intended receiver.
- Step directly at intended receiver or reception point with foot opposite passing hand.
- Continue moving upfield as pass is thrown; roll over step foot and step with foot on side of passing hand; maintain normal throwing motion and good follow-through; do not stop abruptly upon releasing ball.
- When moving to side away from passing hand, stay slightly farther from line of scrimmage to allow more room to turn hips upfield.

RUNNING BACK

2

- Stance   **54**
- Start   **58**
- Ball Handling   **60**
- Running With the Ball   **64**
- Run Blocking   **69**
- Pass Blocking   **76**
- Pass Receiving   **81**
- Screens, Delays, and Draws   **91**
- Running Back Passes   **97**

Running Back

The running back, like the quarterback, often will be given credit for a victory. But unlike the quarterback, a poor performance by a running back often is blamed on lack of blocking and not the back's running skills—unless he consistently fumbles the ball away to the defensive team.

Teams that want a balanced offensive attack, teams that run the ball as much as they pass it, or teams that want to emphasize the run more than the pass, need and depend upon a good, solid ground game. In some offenses, two or more players may have to share the load. But because there are few truly great ball carriers, most National Football League teams feature only one player at running back.

The role of the running back has changed dramatically in recent years. Being able to carry the ball, make people miss tackles, and run over smaller defensive players no longer is enough. Today's running back must be a multifaceted athlete. He must be able to carry the ball 20-30 times a game, pick up blitzing linebackers and defensive backs, plus, on occasion, block the bigger defensive linemen. At the same time, he must have the ability to catch passes like a tight end or wide receiver.

To be a successful running back, young players especially need to understand the importance of working hard in all areas of the game, instead of strictly concentrating only on carrying the ball. Very few teams have the luxury of keeping a running back on the roster who can not or will not take responsibility for blocking and pass receiving.

Because of the constant pounding that all running backs endure during the course of a game, one of the most important traits for a player at this position is mental and physical toughness.

Great running backs seldom give defensive players the satisfaction of knowing that they have been hurt by an aggressive tackle. Instead, the running back jumps up off the ground the minute the whistle blows. Often the running back will be nearing the offensive huddle before the defender has managed to get up off the ground. The ball carrier may be aching all over, but he never will give the tackler the satisfaction of seeing his pain.

Some NFL running backs have carried this toughness one step further by actually challenging the defensive man to tackle them, heading directly at a potential tackler rather than trying to make him miss.

The opposite type of running back is the ball carrier who, because of limited size, relies on making potential tacklers miss, rather than running over them. These players lack the size to repeatedly challenge defensive players head-on, so the effectiveness of their running comes from their ability to change direction quickly and never to give the defender a straight shot at their body.

Then there is the third group, the runners who combine both traits. These are the ball carriers who have the quickness and agility to make a tackler miss and at the same time have the size and leg strength to attack a defensive man whenever a collision cannot be avoided.

Another important skill, which has become a premium for all running backs, is the ability to catch the ball. This has put added pressure on the play-ers who line up in the offensive backfield.

Defenses are at an extreme disadvantage on passing downs when the running back can come out of the backfield quickly, catch a pass while running at full speed, and instantly be in the defensive secondary. More and more, running backs with pass receiving ability are set in motion prior to the snap, causing the defenders to cover even more of the field with pass coverage personnel.

Almost every running back is tough when he is carrying the ball. Many show this same toughness when they go into a crowd to make a difficult reception, knowing that they are going to be hit by one or more defensive players. But only the complete back will demonstrate the same toughness and desire when it comes to blocking. Top backs play with a competitive and unselfish attitude, blocking to protect the quarterback or when someone else is running with the ball.

The final characteristic common to all great running backs is the desire to compete for the duration of the game. Such backs seem to get stronger as a game goes on. While other players on the team tire and lose intensity as the game progresses, great running backs get more powerful and run harder with each successive offensive play. They are so well conditioned that it seems as if they could run forever. Defensive players who made tackles in the first half of the game often find that in the third and fourth quarters they are bouncing off a great running back. It is only at the conclusion of a game, when you view the running back sitting at his locker, that you can tell how exhausted he really is.

Stance

There is a great deal of variation in the stances used by running backs. The differences are based on alignment, the style of the offense, and the type of start the back is called upon to use.

The first stance is the two-point stance, which is commonly used by a tailback running from the I-formation. When aligning in this stance, the running back should first spread his feet evenly, so that they are about the width of his hips. Next, the back bends his knees slightly, assuming a shallow squat position. The amount of bend in the running back's legs should only be enough so that he can stand comfortably while reaching down with each arm and placing the palms of his hands on the top of each knee.

In this position the running back should be lightly balanced on the balls

The two-point stance, commonly used by I-formation runners, affords a wide view of holes on the line of scrimmage and aids in setting up for pass protection.

scrimmage. In this upright stance, the running back has the benefit of full vision of both the offensive and defensive lines and the quarterback, and can quickly focus on the area in which he is to run the ball once the play begins.

The two-point stance also may be used by running backs in passing situations when they need to have a good view of the defense prior to the start of the play. The increased field view this stance affords helps the running back set up for pass protection.

When a back is not running out of the I-formation or is not involved in pass protection, he normally will use a three-point stance. A three-point stance must be balanced, affording the running back the ability to move quickly in any direction with equal ease.

In the three-point stance, the running back should start with his feet spread the width of his shoulders. Because the running back will have to go to both his right and left, he must have his feet even, with his weight equally distributed on the balls of both feet. From this position, the running back should flex his knees, bending them enough so that he can rest his forearms on the insides of his thighs.

The next step is for him to reach straight out, with one hand or the other,

of both feet. It is very important that a coach check to make certain that the back is not leaning in one direction or the other. Often a coach will find that a young running back, in his eagerness to get the ball and run in a certain direction, will start leaning even before the play begins. Early correction will stop the beginner from developing this bad

habit, one that can greatly aid linebackers who will be keying on him and reading his lean during a game.

In the two-point stance, the player's shoulders should be even with his hands and knees, and his back should be slightly forward and straight. The running back's head should be up, his eyes looking directly ahead toward the line of

lightly placing the fingertips of the extended hand on the ground. The arm with the hand on the ground should extend straight down from the running back's shoulder, and should not be placed too far to the inside or outside of the back's shoulder pads. When the hand on the ground is placed correctly, the running back's shoulders will be even.

In this three-point position, the player should have his back straight and level with the ground, with his other forearm remaining on the inner thigh. As noted above, his shoulders should be even. He should be in a comfortable position with his head up and his eyes focused straight ahead.

Both player and coach must understand that the ability to see the total defense is greatly decreased when a player is using a three-point stance. While the running back will not have the expanded field of vision he does in a two-point stance, it also is true that he is not as easily seen by the defensive players.

The third stance that may be used by a running back is the four-point stance. In this stance, the player will have both hands on the ground and usually will be balanced with more weight forward.

The main reason for using this stance is to allow the running back to have a quick, fast charge straight ahead or on a slight angle to either his right or left. You generally will see the fullback in a Wishbone attack utilizing this stance. Some running backs also will go to this stance on short-yardage or goal-line plays where they are going to be driving directly into the line.

When taking a four-point stance, the running back should start with his feet even and spread slightly less than the width of his shoulders. Once again he should flex his knees until it is possible for him to comfortably rest both forearms on the inside of his thighs.

From this position he should reach out with both hands, placing them on the ground two to three inches in front of his shoulders. As he reaches out with his hands, his heels will come off the ground; his weight will end up on the balls of both feet and on both hands.

In this stance, the running back often will raise his hips up into the air, by

In a three-point stance, the runner's back should be straight and his shoulders level. There should be no leaning in the direction the ball is to be run.

The four-point stance is best for a quick charge straight ahead, or at a slight angle, into the line of scrimmage because most of the runner's weight is forward.

straightening his legs, so that they are slightly higher than his shoulders. As in each of the other stances, a coach must check to make certain that the runner's back is straight, his shoulders even, and his head up with his eyes focused straight ahead.

Remember, a four-point stance is best for charging directly ahead as quickly and as powerfully as possible. A four-point, weight-forward stance is not good if the player is going to be required to move laterally along the line of scrim-

mage in either direction or to set up and pass protect for the quarterback.

When teaching a player any of the stances, the coach should begin by having the players line up facing him four yards away. The coach should then have the running backs, first individually and then as a group, go through the steps in getting into a proper stance. It is a good idea for the coach to view each player from the front, side, and back as he makes his corrections.

The main question to consider when

choosing a proper stance is, does the stance allow the player to move and do the things that he will need to do during the course of the game? The stance must be comfortable and, above all else, functional if the running back is to have any opportunity for success.

Start

For any running back, the ability to have a quick start in any direction is vital. Many beginning running backs will take a stance where they are forced to take a false step or to shift their weight before they can attack the defense. This is a bad habit that should be cured immediately by stressing stance fundamentals.

When a back is called upon to move laterally to the line of scrimmage as he runs with the ball, it is best for him to use a crossover step when leaving his stance. In a crossover start, the back merely leans his body into the direction he wants to go. As he is leaning, the opposite foot should automatically come off the ground and become the first step.

For a back who is moving to his right out of a two-point stance, this first step will be with his left foot. By leaning with his shoulders and upper torso to the right, the running back is able to swing his left leg across his right leg, which has remained stationary. Once the left foot makes contact with the ground, the right leg and foot will follow naturally, allowing the player to move to his right

easily in a smooth running motion.

DRILL:

Crossover Starts

The running backs form a line, single file. One at a time, each back steps forward. After the back has gotten into his two-point stance, the coach gives the player the snap count and points either to the player's right or left. Prior to calling the cadence, the coach checks each back to make certain that he is not leaning in the direction of his start. This is the most difficult tendency to overcome.

The coach then calls the cadence, and on the snap count, the running back executes a crossover start in the direction indicated by the coach. Because this drill is designed only to develop a proper start for the young player, no ball is used and each back need only run 4 or 5 yards before returning to the end of the line.

Using a crossover start when coming out of a three-point stance is sometimes more difficult for beginning running backs because when coming out of a three-point stance, the back cannot easily use his shoulders and upper torso to initiate the movement. Instead, the back must think in terms of leaning with his hips and midsection in the direction he wants to go. As he leans, the player also

can swing the hand and arm on the side of his movement back and around. By doing this motion with his hand and arm, the running back quickly turns his shoulders and head in the direction of his run.

When running the three-point start drill, it is important for the coach not only to have the players start to their left and right, but also to have them vary their initial alignments. They should start to the coach's left and right as well as directly in front of him. As with the two-point stance, the player must be reminded not to lean in the direction of his movement prior to the snap count.

On some running plays, the back will be asked to move directly toward the line of scrimmage. When executing this start, it is best for the player to take a lead step with the foot on the same side of his movement, rather than rolling over with the opposite foot as he has done in the previous drills.

The big difference for the running back in this start is that instead of leaning to initiate the start, he can now step with the near foot while pushing off with the opposite foot. The first step, with the foot on the side of his desired movement, should be a short, quick, directional step. The purpose of this step is to get the back's body headed immediately for the proper area on the line.

When coming out of a two-point stance and lead-stepping to his right, the running back also can use his left hand to push into his left thigh and thus generate additional thrust to the first movement with his right foot. The following drill can be set up the same way as the roll-over start drill with the players first working out of a two-point stance and then executing from a three-point stance.

DRILL:
Lead-Step Starts
The first player in line leaves a two-point stance with a lead step in the direction indicated by the coach. After the player has started in the proper direction, he should continue running to the line of scrimmage past the coach for only a yard or two. This drill is designed to teach the back a proper start, not to tire him.

When starting from a three-point stance, the player usually can use the hand on the ground for a little added push if he is moving in the opposite direction. Most of the initial thrust for the start will have to come from the push of the foot opposite the direction in which the back is moving.

As with the crossover drill, the coach must check for any lean by the running back prior to the snap count. In lead-step starts, it also is important for the coach to make certain that the running back is not taking too long of a first step. The first lead step starts movement and continues the runner's body in a desired direction. It is not taken to cover a great deal of ground. If he is taking a long first step, it will be very difficult for the back to have good body control as his hips will be centered between his feet and not over them. Good balance, body control, and the ability to change direction quickly are only possible when the running back has his hips directly over his feet.

The drill can be expanded to include clearly defined running lanes once the coach determines that the players can execute proper crossover and lead-step starts going to the right and left. Strips of cloth or towels can be placed on the ground to define the running lanes for the backs. The coach then can call out by number the running lane or hole that he wants the back to cut into after the player has started properly.

The running backs should line up in all three running back positions (shown in the hole numbering diagram) and be asked to run to both their right and left. The tailback would use a crossover step on all plays to the 9, 7, 6, and 8 holes, and a lead-step start when running in the 5 and 4 holes.

Running backs using a three-point stance and starting in the split back positions would use a crossover step start for all plays which are to be run on the opposite side of the coach and for a wide play to the same side as the coach. The running back should use a lead-step start when attacking the two inside holes on the side of his initial alignment.

Hole Numbering
Each hole, or space, between or beside

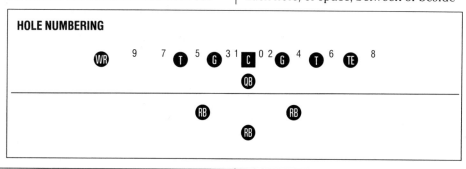

HOLE NUMBERING

the interior linemen is designated by a number; odd numbers to the left of the center, even numbers to the right. These numbers are included in play calls.

> **WINNING POINTS**
> - Do not give away direction of play by leaning prior to any start.
> - On starts, do not take too long a first step; keep hips over feet.

Ball Handling

A smooth exchange of the ball between the quarterback and the ball carrier is vital. It is the primary job of the running back to run the exact path necessary to bring him in position for the quarterback to hand him the ball. The back must understand that the quarterback will be executing predetermined footwork on every running play that will bring him to a specific spot for the exchange.

The back also must make certain that he forms a pocket, with his hands and arms, to receive the ball from the quarterback. Though it is the quarterback's responsibility to place the ball properly in the runner's stomach, once the ball is there it becomes the back's priority to make certain that he has the ball securely in his grasp and well protected until

the play is blown dead.

To have a successful rushing attack, there must be a bond of faith between the quarterback and his running back. Each expects and counts on the other to do his job properly. The ball carrier cannot afford the luxury of looking at the ball as he receives it from the quarterback. His vision must be directed to the area of the line where he is supposed to run. It is imperative that he see the blocking as it develops while using his peripheral vision to see the reaction of the defensive players.

NOTE: *In all running back drills that follow, refer to the quarterback chapter for quarterback movements, footwork, and drops.*

DRILL:

Dive Handoff

The easiest play to start with when working on ball handling is the straight-ahead dive play. For this drill, the running backs can line up, in two lines, four yards off the line of scrimmage on either side of the quarterback.

When first teaching the drill, the quarterback should have the ball in his hands as he begins his cadence. Prior to the start of the cadence the coach should designate which back is to run the drill and receive the ball.

At the snap count, the running back should charge straight ahead from a three-point stance. At the same time, the quarterback should be moving down the line, preparing to place the ball into the runner's stomach area.

At the point of the exchange, the running back should form a pocket to receive the ball by raising up his inside elbow so that it is almost even with his shoulders. A large percentage of the fumbles which occur on the exchange are caused by the running back not raising his inside elbow high enough and his elbow actually hitting the point of the ball. The forearm of this upraised arm

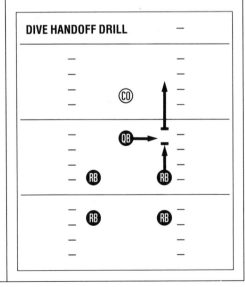

DIVE HANDOFF DRILL

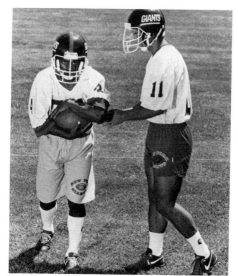

On a handoff, the running back forms a pocket to receive the ball. Once the ball is delivered, it is his responsibility to secure and protect it.

should be horizontal to the ground, extending straight across the runner's chest and forming the top of the pocket. The hand of this arm should bend down so that the palm can grasp the point of the ball.

The bottom of the pocket is formed by the other arm and hand. The forearm of the outside arm should be extended straight across the ball carrier's stomach. The palm should be up and fingers extended toward the quarterback.

The quarterback needs to place the ball firmly between the running back's two arms and into his stomach. The running back must clamp down on the ball as soon as he feels it placed against his body. In the beginning, it is good to have the ball carrier continue to grasp the ball with both hands as he crosses the line of scrimmage.

This same ball-handling technique should be practiced with the back lining up in various positions and running all of the plays in the offense. Each time a play is run, the coach must check the path of the ball carrier and the footwork of the quarterback, while paying special attention to the actual exchange of the ball between the quarterback and the running back.

Executing a front handoff will be easy for the running back and quarterback to master. The next step is to learn the correct exchange of the ball on the plays where the quarterback is turning back toward the running back, instead of stepping directly at him, as he places the ball in the runner's stomach.

DRILL:
Reverse Pivot Handoff

DRILL:
Fake Toss/Inside Trap

In both drills, the running back should take a path that initially heads directly at the coach. In the reverse pivot drill, the running back will establish this path with his first step of the far foot. In the fake toss-inside trap drill, the back's first step will be a lateral one with his inside foot and then his second step, with the far foot, will establish his path toward the coach.

As the back receives the ball from the quarterback, he should cut inside the coach and head up the field. If a coach

REVERSE PIVOT DRILL

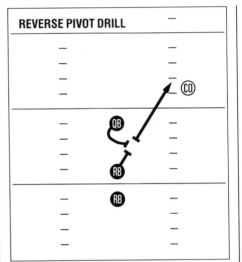

FAKE TOSS-INSIDE TRAP DRILL

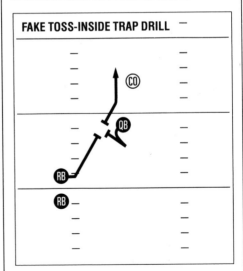

The path of the running back to the point of the handoff must be exact.

same and the manner of the handoff from the quarterback to the ball carrier should remain constant.

Once the running back feels he is taking the handoff correctly, it is time to learn the proper method of receiving the ball on plays where the quarterback laterals, rather than hands off the ball. This will happen on two basic running plays—a pitch play and on any option running play.

DRILL:

Taking a Pitch

The running back starts his lateral move-

is not available, a shirt or towel may be placed on the ground to give the back a target to run toward.

Because the quarterback is starting one direction and then turning back to the running back to give him the ball, the path of the running back is vitally important. If the running back goes too wide, the quarterback never will be in position to reach him with the ball. Should the back run too close to the quarterback, then a collision can occur and the handoff has a good chance of being fumbled.

The pocket formed by the running back to receive the handoff will be the

PITCH PLAY DRILL

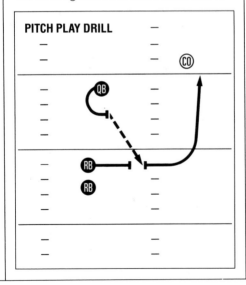

ment in the direction of the play with a crossover step. As he runs to the sideline, his hips should be facing the sideline and he should turn his upper body and head back toward the quarterback.

The running back needs to keep in mind that the quarterback will release the ball with an underhanded motion. The ball should reach the running back at his belt level or just above it. Because of the height of the ball, the running back must catch it by reaching back with his hands, making sure to keep his little fingers together. The palm of the near hand should be up to form a cradle for the ball,

When taking an underhand pitch, the runner must reach back for the ball.

while the palm of the far hand should serve as the mitt for the catch, making contact with the point of the ball. Once the running back makes the catch, he should bring the ball across his body and secure it with his hand and arm farthest from the line of scrimmage.

DRILL:

Option Pitch

For a running back, receiving an option pitch from a quarterback differs from receiving a pitch in two major ways. First, the ball will not be coming in a spiral, but instead will be floating with much less velocity. Second, the ball usually will

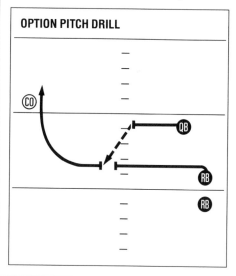

OPTION PITCH DRILL

On an option pitch, or any lateral, the first priority is catching the ball.

reach him at a much higher level. Rather than throwing the ball in an underhand motion, the quarterback running an option play will be flicking the ball from chest level to the running back.

Because of this, the ball carrier usually will catch the ball at his shoulders or above rather than at belt level. This makes it necessary for the running back to place his thumbs together to form the catching pocket when receiving the ball, and not his little fingers as on a pitch play.

When making this type of catch, the running back must try to remember to cock his wrists back toward his helmet so that the palms of both hands are facing slightly up and not pointing down toward the ground. With the palms down, there is a good possibility the ball will deflect off the player's hands down toward the ground.

On both option and pitch plays, the running back must turn his upper body to be in position to receive the ball. He also must try to have his hands in position so that he can simultaneously see the ball and his fingers as he makes the catch.

When receiving any type of lateral, the running back's first thought should be to catch the ball. Obviously, without first making the catch, the back has no chance to make the play a success. Next, he must think about securing the ball in his hand away from the line of scrimmage, and be prepared for any contact from the defense. Once the ball is caught and secured, the running back can think about turning up the field and making yards.

Running With the Ball

Much of a running back's ability is natural talent. But that does not mean it cannot be improved upon or developed. While certain elements of a player's physical attributes, such as speed and quickness, most often are genetic, they can be augmented with a proper start and good running techniques.

Most great runners have tremendous leg strength and explosion, and many of them develop this not by lifting weights but by actually running. Their offseason conditioning programs usually include running up and down hills rather than merely running sprints on level ground. Running up steep hills gives running backs the leg strength and high knee action they need to explode through potential tacklers.

Another trait of great running backs is the manner in which they practice. Every play is run down the field a full 20 yards and is not stopped after the back has gone two or three yards past the line of scrimmage.

When working with young running backs it is important to emphasize that it is neither necessary nor smart to always try to run over the defensive players. While there will be times in a game when the running back is given no choice but to explode into the defense, the running back must always be looking for opportunities to make the defenders miss.

For the young running back, it often is best to start with a drill that gives him the skill to avoid a tackler who is coming straight at him. The running back should understand that when this occurs in a game, he has the advantage over the tackler, because he knows in which direction he is going to cut.

WINNING POINTS

- Run the correct path to be in position for handoff.
- Form pocket with hands and arms to receive ball from quarterback by raising inside elbow shoulder-high, forearm horizontal, hand bent down; forearm of outside arm is horizontal across stomach, palms up, fingers toward quarterback.
- Secure ball immediately on handoffs, laterals, and pitches, and protect it until end of play.
- Catch pitches with hips facing sideline; upper body and head turn back toward quarterback; reach back for ball with little fingers together, palm of near hand up, palm of far hand as contact point.
- Catch high option pitches with thumbs together and wrists cocked back toward helmet.
- When catching laterals and pitches, position hands so that fingers and ball can be seen at same time

Top running backs exhibit quickness, power, grace, and balance, along with exceptional field vision and endurance.

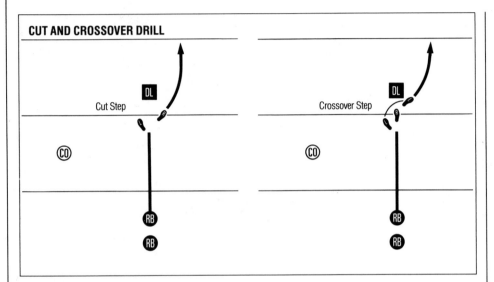

CUT AND CROSSOVER DRILL

Cut Step

Crossover Step

DRILL:

Cut and Crossover

This drill teaches the running back two different change-of-direction moves. The man on defense will be stationary; there will not be any contact. Either the coach or another running back can take the place of the defensive player. The defensive player should line up six yards away and facing the ball carrier. The defensive player will step to the side of the fake, and serve as a point of reference for the running back.

The first technique which we will work on is a simple fake in one direction and a cut to the other side. The running back starts toward the defensive player. As he approaches a distance of about two yards from the defensive man, he should shorten his stride and prepare to make his cut.

If the running back has determined that he will cut to his right, at five yards he should step slightly to the left of the defensive man with his left foot. At the same time, his head and shoulders should give a quick, short jerk to the left.

When the left foot makes contact with the ground, the ball carrier should push off it, directing his body at a 45-degree angle to the right. It is important that the

next step with the right foot be a very short change-of-direction step to the side of the defensive man. By using a short change-of-direction step, the ball carrier is able to keep his feet under his body as he cuts past the defender.

In the beginning, the running back may have to run at half speed in order to execute the technique properly. As he gets better and better at coming under control, faking, pushing, and stepping, he can run the drill faster.

This drill should be repeated with the ball carrier cutting to both his left and right. The back should have the ball held securely in the hand on the side of his final cut. If he is cutting right, the ball should be in his right hand; it should be held in the left hand when cutting left.

It is not a good idea for a running back continually to change the hand that is holding the ball, but whenever possible, the ball carrier should try to carry the ball in the hand that is farthest away from any potential tackler. By carrying the ball on the proper side, the running back is cutting down on the possibility of the ball being bobbled or fumbled.

The second technique for a running back to use in avoiding a potential tackler is a crossover step. This is similar to the first technique except that the ball carrier will not push off the foot opposite the direction of his final cut.

In this technique, the running back again will approach the defensive man in a straight path. At a distance of three yards the running back should shorten his stride and step slightly to the left of the defender with his left foot. His head and shoulders will also lean, but not jerk, slightly to the left.

His next step, with his right foot, should be at the center of the defender's body. At this point the defensive man should be convinced that the ball carrier has gone into his final cut to avoid a tackle. As the right foot makes contact with the ground, the running back should lean toward his right with his upper body. This will allow the player to quickly bring his left leg across his right, changing the direction of final cut to his right.

As the players become more proficient at using these two techniques they can be incorporated into a normal tackling drill, where the running back on defense comes up and actually tries to grab the man with the ball.

When adding this action to the drill, the two players line up 10 yards apart and then move toward one another on the coach's command. The drill should first be taught at half speed and the coach should emphasize that neither player is to leave his feet. The defensive

man's movement makes the drill more realistic for the ball carrier.

The next type of cut, or change of direction, to be introduced is the inside cut up the field from a lateral run with the ball.

This is the kind of maneuver a running back would use on any play which looks like it is going wide but is really designed to be run in an inside hole. In this type of play, the running back generally starts on the opposite side of the ball, but it can also be used by a back who is lined up in an I-formation.

DRILL:

Inside Cut

The running back starts with the ball in

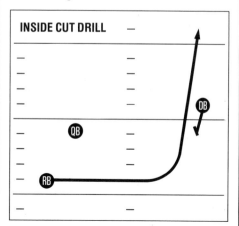

INSIDE CUT DRILL

his possession so he does not have to be concerned about taking the handoff. It is more important for him to concentrate on setting up the defensive player and making his cut. After the back has run the drill a few times, the coach or another player can hand him the ball as he comes across the formation.

The defensive player should hesitate a few seconds after the drill begins and then come straight up the field two or three steps. He will not be involved in any tackling or contact with the ball carrier. The running back should roll over and start his controlled, half-speed, lateral run to the opposite side of the quarterback. It is important for him to run laterally and not start directly into the hole at the beginning of the play. His movement should convince the defensive man that he is going to attempt to run outside. When he sees the defender moving up the field, the ball carrier must continue his path for another two or three steps and then, rolling over the leg nearest to the line of scrimmage, cut to the inside and continue his run up the field.

The initial position of the defensive player can be moved wider or closer to the quarterback, allowing the running back to get a feel for all of the different running holes he will attack. With a tight position the defender can give the look

INSIDE CUT DRILL WITH BLOCKER

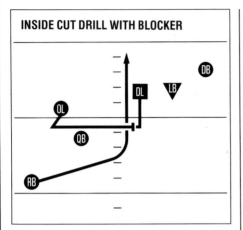

of a defensive lineman who is to be trapped. Given little wider alignment, he can simulate an outside linebacker. And, in the widest position, he can play a defensive back coming up to stop a wide sweep. Regardless of the width of the defensive man, or the defensive player that he is simulating, the running back should remember to start laterally and then to cut up the field at the last possible moment after the defender has made his commitment across the line of scrimmage.

As the running back gets proficient at executing this cut, a lead blocker can be added to the drill. The blocker would have the responsibility for blocking the defensive player to the outside, giving the ball carrier an inside running lane.

The ball carrier now will get a much better feel for how the play actually will develop in a game. The running back also will see that if, by his path, he can get the defensive player to come across the line of scrimmage, the offensive blocker will have a much easier job and be in better position to make his block.

The running back should be given the opportunity to run into all of the play holes, going both to his right and left. In this drill, the running back also should get a feel for following his blockers. With a blocker in the drill, the ball carrier gains an understanding for varying and controlling the speed of his run, using his body movement and position for setting up the defensive man who is to be blocked.

Even though there is no tackling in this drill, and the defensive player allows himself to be blocked, it is important the running back understand that there is a potential for defensive tacklers to be hitting him from all sides as he makes his cut during an actual game. Consequently, an added emphasis should be made on protecting the ball. Many running backs, as they explode across the line of scrimmage, will grasp the ball in both hands, holding it tightly against their stomachs to guarantee that they will not fumble when they are hit.

DRILL:

Spin Technique

The final technique a running back can use to avoid being tackled is a spin move. Because most young backs incorrectly try to execute this maneuver from a straight-up body position, it is vital that good forward body lean be stressed.

SPIN TECHNIQUE DRILL

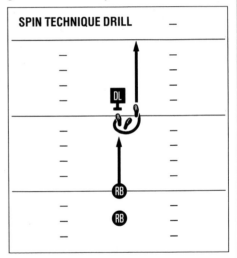

In this drill the defensive player stands with his feet parallel to the line, his knees flexed, and his shoulders slightly forward of his hips. His arms should be flexed, elbows tight to his sides, and the palms of both hands open, number high and facing the running back. The job of the defensive man is to provide resistance to the running back as he executes his spin technique. If a small, hand-held blocking shield is available, the defender can use that instead of his hands to make contact with the ball carrier.

Initially the ball carrier should approach the defensive man at half speed, aiming his helmet between the defender's hands. If a blocking bag is being used by the defensive man, the ball carrier's head should slide to the side of the bag opposite the direction of his spin.

As the running back makes contact with the defender, he must lean into the defensive man and step to the center of the defensive man's body with the foot on the side of the spin. As this foot makes contact with the ground, the ball carrier must throw his opposite shoulder, leg, and foot back, spinning completely around, separating and momentarily turning his back to the defensive player.

The defensive player can help the running back learn this technique by absorbing his first hit and then extending his arms and pushing the ball carrier into his spin.

All running backs must understand that they need good forward lean for this technique to work. If they do not challenge the defensive man aggressively, and merely run with their bodies positioned straight up and down as they try

to spin, they will have little success.

During the actual spin, the running back must understand that he is especially vulnerable and must protect the ball and himself by staying compact and ready to explode down the field the instant the spin is completed.

> **WINNING POINTS**
> - Do not always try to run over defenders; avoid them or make them miss tackle.
> - Do not constantly change hand holding ball while running.
> - Consider grasping ball tightly against stomach with both hands when exploding across line.

Run Blocking

In order for a player to become a complete running back, he must be able to do more than simply run with the ball. One of the other important skills he must master is blocking. Often, a running back will be asked to block on running plays where he is not carrying the ball or on pass plays when he is needed to help protect the quarterback. The ability and willingness to block is what helps an average running back become more valuable.

Every coach needs to praise good

blocking by the running backs as much as he does good running with the ball. If blocking is truly important to the coach, he must tell the players at the start of practice that being a good blocker is one of the prerequisites for being a starting running back on the team.

It often is easiest to teach the beginning player run blocking by having him block first on a hand-held blocking dummy, if one is available. The main point for a beginning back to realize is that proper technique in blocking is very important, especially when the back is asked to block a defensive player who is much larger.

There are a few important points and techniques which the running back needs to learn regardless of who he is asked to block. First, the player needs to understand that the quicker he gets to the defensive man, the less time the defender will have to position himself to defeat the block.

Next, the blocker must know that he only will be blocking one side of the defensive man and should think in terms of getting to the defensive man's hip, on the side of the block, as soon as possible. In college and in some high school leagues the rules allow a running back to block below the hip, at the knee. If this is the case, the back can come in lower in his approach.

These two techniques can be taught in a drill where the coach holds the blocking dummy and the running back attacks it, getting the feel for the speed needed in his attack.

DRILL:
Dummy Blocking

In this drill the emphasis is placed on the running back attacking the dummy as quickly as possible in a straight line, then at the last instant sliding his head to the right or left and making contact with his shoulder on the side of the block. The coach should indicate to the player which side of the dummy he is to block and then start the drill with the command, "Hit."

Coming out of his three-point stance, the running back shortens his stride as he nears the dummy, making certain that his feet always are under his hips. If the running back is going to make contact with the dummy with his left shoulder, he should use his left foot as the explosion foot for his block. A block by any offensive player must start with the explosion from the power foot and continue up through his body with the thrust generated by the big muscle groups of the upper legs and hips.

At the point of contact, the running

back must strike the dummy with his shoulder pads and forearm in a forceful manner. This first explosive hit, with the shoulder pads and forearm, often will be the only advantage a smaller running back has when blocking on a larger defensive player, so it must not be wasted by a half-hearted attempt. *The head should never be used as the first contact point.*

During the actual block, the player's back should be straight, with his shoulders square, head up, and eyes open. Once contact is made, the running back must take a few straight, short, choppy steps before trying to turn the defensive player.

More often than not, a block by a running back is not expected to drive a defender off the line of scrimmage. Instead, the block is considered successful if the blocker merely occupies the defensive man and positions himself in between the ball carrier and the tackler.

DRILL:
Blocking the End Man

One of the first run blocks a back should learn is blocking the end man on the line of scrimmage. This usually will be an outside linebacker or a larger defensive lineman. The running back will be asked

to block this defensive player both out, toward the sideline, and in, toward the center of the field.

One important point for the running back to understand and remember is that his path toward the defender should be the same regardless of whether he is going to block the defensive man out or in. The running back has the advantage of knowing which way he is going to block the defender and he should not give this advantage away by starting on an inside or outside path, thus alerting the defensive man to the final block.

On the coach's command, the defensive player should take one step directly across the line of scrimmage and turn to face the running back. The running back should start directly at the defensive player and adjust his path as he sees the defender crossing the line of scrimmage.

If the running back is going to block the defender in, toward the ball, he should aim at the defensive man's outside hip. Using his inside shoulder and forearm, the running back delivers a blow to the outside hip of the defensive man using the same techniques he learned when he was hitting the dummy.

Should the objective of the running back be to block the end man on the line out, away from the center of the field, he will drive his outside shoulder at the inside hip of the defensive player. At contact, the back slides his head to the inside and uses his outside foot as his explosion foot, making contact and driving the defensive man with his outside shoulder and forearm.

When blocking, the running back must guard against getting his shoulders too far in front of his hips, in an overextended position. If the blocker makes contact with the defensive man when his body is in this overextended position, the defender easily will absorb his block and push him to the ground. Instead, the blocker must keep his shoulders slightly in front of his hips, his hips over his feet with knees flexed, and he must think of gathering, rather than extending, himself prior to the explosion of first contact.

Blocking a Defensive End

Most running backs will have a natural desire and tendency to line up even with or outside of the man they are going to block. This is the worst thing the back can do because he will come into the sight path of the defensive player prior to the start of the play and draw attention to himself.

In particular, by staying to the inside of a defensive end in his initial alignment, the running back will find that he is partially hidden from the defensive end's view by the offensive tackle. Using his speed and quickness, the blocker often can reach the defensive player before the defender has the opportunity to react. Quickness in reaching the defensive man and getting into the block is one of the most important advantages a smaller running back has when blocking a larger defensive player.

Remember, the running back's blocking technique is the same as when he is blocking in or out on the end man on the line of scrimmage. If the play calls for the defensive end to be blocked toward the ball, the running back will aim at the outside hip of the defensive player. Contact on the defender by the running back should be made with the inside shoulder and forearm. If the play is designed with the running back blocking the defensive man toward the sideline, contact would then be made on the inside hip with the outside shoulder and forearm of the running back.

With either block, the running back must remember to explode at the point of contact, using short, choppy, powerful steps to make contact and turn the defender in the desired direction.

DRILL:

Blocking Defensive Tackles

The running back may be aligned either

When the guard pulls, the running back may be assigned the uncovered tackle.

directly behind the quarterback or in a split-back location to be in position to block a defensive tackle. This is a unique type of block in that it usually will be used when the offensive guard, who will be lined up in front of the defensive tackle, is pulling out and trapping or lead blocking on another defensive player.

From the position behind the quarterback, the running back will aim for the outside hip of the defensive tackle. On this type of play the guard usually will be pulling to the outside, away from the ball. The running back must understand that the guard's movement often will cause

Being a lead blocker demands as much timing as closely following a lead blocker and cutting off the block that is thrown.

the defensive player to start to the outside, moving to a position that is wider than where he initially lined up.

For this drill, the player on defense should start in a three-point stance. On the command "Hit," he takes a step to the inside and then takes a reaction step to the outside. As he makes this second step he should get his hands up so that he can absorb some of the block by the running back. As in all drills, this drill should start at half speed and then increase in speed as the coach and the running back feel that the techniques of the block are being executed correctly.

The running back can take a little wider approach path if he anticipates this outside reaction by the defensive man. First and foremost, the running back must remember that he must get to the defensive man as quickly as possible. Speed and quickness are his greatest allies in getting his job accomplished.

The actual technique will be the same as the other blocks where the running back is approaching the defensive man from the inside and blocking the defender's outside hip with his inside shoulder.

If the running back is executing this block from a split back alignment, a position outside the defensive tackle, the path to the block can be direct. On this type of play, the man in front of the de-

A running back must hit a nose tackle fast and low when the center blocks away.

fensive tackle will be moving toward or behind the ball. Consequently, the defender usually will also be moving toward the inside, and his outside hip often will be open and exposed for the block, if the running back makes contact quickly.

A running back will perform a similar type of block when he is asked to block a nose tackle who is lined up directly in front of the center.

The running back must understand that the center will be moving and block-

ing away from the running back's block. Because of this, the nose tackle, unless he is on a predetermined stunt, usually will be moving, or at least leaning, in the direction in which the running back wants to block him. Again, the running back must think in terms of coming in low and quickly to the defensive man, making contact with his inside shoulder and forearm, and exploding off his inside foot and leg into the near hip of the nose tackle. As contact is made the blocker can use the palm of his off hand to strike the buttocks of the defensive man. This will help the blocker maintain contact and can help stop the defender's reaction into the block.

During a game, because of the difference in size, a running back often will not be able to drive the nose tackle off or down the line of scrimmage. Instead, the running back will be able to create only a stalemate and stop the defender from moving down the line toward the ball carrier. If he accomplishes this, the block is considered successful.

Next, the running back needs to learn the technique he will use when he is asked to block a linebacker who is lined up three to four yards off the line of scrimmage. This block is somewhat different in that the defensive player will have more time to react before the running back can execute his block.

The running back must not think of blocking the linebacker where he initially lined up; he must anticipate and be prepared for the linebacker to be moving to the ball and charging the line of scrimmage.

DRILL:

Lead Block on a Linebacker
On the command "Hit," the man serving

as the linebacker should be instructed by the coach to do one of three maneuvers. First, he can stay where he is and move slightly to his left or right as he takes on the running back's block. Or, he can hesitate a second and then charge straight ahead, moving either inside or outside of the running back's block. Finally, he can take two steps up and then move laterally to either his left or right.

No matter what the linebacker does, it is of vital importance that the running back completely concentrate and focus

A running back must be prepared for the movement of a linebacker he is to block.

on him. If he does not have this focus, he will not see the movement of the linebacker and he will not be prepared to adjust his path and make the proper block.

The second thing the running back must understand is where the play is designed to be run. Is it a play where the ball carrier is following him directly up the field, or is it designed to go outside the linebacker's initial position?

If the ball carrier will be following the blocker directly into the line, the running back must take a path straight at the linebacker. He must not predetermine the shoulder with which he is going to block the linebacker. Instead, he must think in terms of seeing which side the linebacker is playing his block and then use the shoulder and forearm on that side to execute the block. The blocker must block the linebacker the way he is going, and he must have confidence that the ball carrier will be prepared to cut in the opposite direction of his block.

Should the running back see that the linebacker is stunting completely out of the hole, he must be prepared to continue to lead up the field and look for any other defensive player who may come into his area. The one thing he must not do is stop and look for someone to block, thus causing the ball carrier to have to

LEAD BLOCK VS. LINEBACKER

Double-Team Block

On almost all of the blocks that a running back is asked to execute during the course of a game, he will be blocking by himself. The one variation that is being used more and more is the double-team block by a center and running back on a nose tackle.

When working on this type of block, the defensive man should play into the center with both hands and only react into the running back's block at the last instant.

For the block to be a success, the center must drive into the nose tackle as he would on a straight one-on-one drive block. The objective of the center is to get the defensive man to be focused and intent on defeating his block and not to be prepared or in position to react to the delayed block by the running back.

The coach will tell the two offensive players prior to the beginning of the play on which side the running back will attack.

On the command "Hit," the center will drive into the nose tackle, sliding his head to the opposite side of the block by the running back. At this initial stage of the block, the center should concentrate on maintaining contact with the nose

hesitate and not hit the hole at full speed.

For a play where the ball carrier definitely is running outside and not following the blocker into the hole, the running back must continue to adjust his path so that he is in position to block the outside hip of the linebacker with his inside shoulder and forearm.

On all three blocks the running back's first two steps should be the same, first his right foot and then his left foot directly at the linebacker. If he sees that the defensive man is sitting and waiting, he should charge straight at him and veer off to the outside of the linebacker only at the last second.

When the linebacker is charging the line of scrimmage, it is important for the blocker to adjust his path much sooner and be prepared for an early collision, with the block occurring much nearer the line of scrimmage.

If the blocker determines, after he has taken his two steps, that the linebacker is stunting to the outside, then he must adjust his path so that he can be in position to block with his inside shoulder and forearm to the outside hip of the linebacker. There may be occasions in this type of block where the running back will find, as he prepares to make his block, that the linebacker is not squared up, facing the line of scrimmage. When this occurs, and the linebacker has turned and is facing more toward the sideline, the running back must drive his inside shoulder into the nearest hip of the linebacker.

When double-teaming a nose tackle with a center, the running back must drive his inside shoulder and forearm into the nose tackle's near hip. Then the running back and center, driving hip-to-hip, turn the nose tackle out of the hole.

tackle and driving him back.

The running back should drive as close to the center's hip as possible, keeping out of the view of the defensive man for as long as possible. If the running back sees that the defender is occupied with the center's block, he should quickly drive his inside shoulder and forearm into the near hip of the nose tackle.

Once contact has been made by both blockers, they should immediately try to get hip-to-hip, slowly turning in unison and driving the defensive man not only back off the line of scrimmage, but also away from the side of the running back's block. This drill must be set up and practiced with the back going to both the left and right side of the ball.

Pass Blocking

Pass blocking differs from blocking on a running play in that the running back will not attack the man he is responsible to block. Good pass protection requires the running back to wait for the defensive man to charge and then to block him away from where the quarterback is setting up to pass. Often the running back will not stop the charge of the defensive player, but will merely redirect the path of the rushing defender away from the quarterback.

In pass protection, the running back first must think in terms of placing his body in a relative position between the defender and the quarterback. Knowing where to set up to take away the defender's path to the quarterback is a necessity for the running back. By physically taking away this path with his body, the running back forces the defensive man to adjust his path and to think in terms of defeating the block before ever proceeding to the passer.

Even though the running back is not firing out, as he would when blocking on a running play, at the moment of contact he must be aggressive, striking out at the defensive man.

DRILL:

Setting Up to Pass Block

The first technique the running back needs to learn is how to move from a pre-snap stance quickly and set up in a position that affords the greatest opportunity to block the defensive pass rusher effectively.

In this drill no players are used on defense. The inside and outside rush lanes and the target area can be marked with towels or blocking dummies. The running back is concerned only with coming out of his two- or three-point stance, moving into a position between the imag-

inary defensive man and the target area, and aligning his body in proper position to pass protect.

In the beginning the coach should only have one running back set up at a time. The running back must be told, prior to the start of the drill, whether he is blocking on a defensive man who is rushing from the outside or up the middle. If the rush is from the middle, the running back must step up and in with his inside foot. He must then bring his outside foot up so that it is even with his inside foot, allowing his body to face straight down the field. The running back should feel that he has placed his body directly in the path of the inside rush man to the target area.

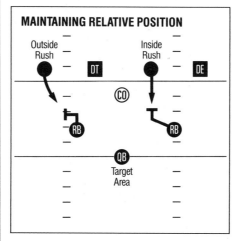

MAINTAINING RELATIVE POSITION

Should the coach designate that the rush is coming from the outside, the running back will need to adjust his initial setup. He will once again step in and up with his inside foot. But now, with his second step, he must swing his outside foot, leg, and hip back, so that he ends up with his feet parallel and his body facing toward the sideline, instead of straight up the field.

The coach should have the player move into what he perceives to be a proper position. Then the player should be allowed to turn around and see if he has actually achieved a position in the rush lane to the target area.

Once the running back understands the proper location of his setup versus either an inside or outside rush, he then can assume the proper stance for pass blocking.

In the pass protection stance, the running back should have his feet parallel and spread slightly less than the width of his shoulders. He should lower his body by flexing his knees and not by bending over at the waist. It is important for him to keep his back straight and his head up, with his eyes focused straight ahead. The elbows of both arms should be just above belt high and close in to the sides of his body. The elbows should be flexed, allowing the forearms to come up

'he running back does not go out to meet the charge of a pass rusher. He sets up and waits for the defensive man, maintains relative position, and either stops the rusher's momentum or redirects it away from the quarterback.

into a position directly in front of the running back's chest. The hands should be four to five inches in front of the blocker's jersey. Both hands need to be close together, thumbs almost touching, fingers up and spread, facing directly toward the path of the defensive man's rush.

DRILL:

Blocking an Inside Pass Rush

The drill will start when the coach gives the command "Hit." In the beginning, the drill should be run at half speed, thus allowing the running back to concentrate on proper body position and good pass-blocking technique.

An offensive player, acting as a line-backer, rushes directly toward the target area, allowing himself to be blocked to the outside, away from the target area, by the running back. Remember, in all drills of this nature, we are teaching pass protection blocking, we are not teaching the technique needed by a linebacker to rush the quarterback.

The running back should step to the inside at the start of the drill, and staying square to the line of scrimmage, position his body so that he is slightly inside the path of the linebacker as the linebacker rushes toward the target area. By staying inside of the rush, the running back is physically taking away one side of the linebacker's rush lane, the inside path, and is inviting and forcing the linebacker to rush to the outside.

The force for stopping and redirecting the rush of the defensive player must start at the ground, come up through the big muscle groups of the running back's legs, and be transferred out the arms and through the palms of the blocker's hands. The running back must learn to focus on the numbers of the linebacker's jersey. As the linebacker gets near, the running back must gather himself and prepare to strike.

The running back must make certain, at the moment of contact, that he does not lunge forward, overextending himself and losing his balance. The running back should try to deliver as hard a blow as possible with the palms of both hands. As the palms make contact, the blocker must press out with both arms and gain some separation from the defensive man. When striking out at the linebacker, the running back must think in terms of momentarily stopping the pass rush of the defender and pushing the defensive man's body to the outside, away from the target area.

When the running back has stopped the linebacker's momentum, he must quickly reset his hands and arms and shuffle his feet so that he keeps his body in an inside position between the rush lane of the linebacker and the target area. In this shuffling motion, the running back should be coached to take short, quick steps. Elongated steps or steps in which the running back crosses one foot over the other should be eliminated as

they will only result in the blocker losing his balance and being unable to complete his block.

In the drill, the linebacker should continue to try to reach the target area until the coach calls out "Stop" or blows a whistle. After his initial hit, the running back must expect the defensive man to continue rushing toward the target area. As he sees the defender once again starting his charge, the running back must gather himself and prepare to strike out to stop the defensive man's charge. The running back must continue this action until the drill is stopped.

When the running back can execute a pass protection block with the linebacker redirected to the outside, the coach can then instruct the linebacker to attempt to rush to the inside of the running back.

Anytime the running back finds that the linebacker is attempting to rush to the inside, he must adjust his thinking and technique in pass protection blocking. First of all he must be certain that the linebacker is truly going to attempt to rush to the inside.

When the linebacker begins to cross the running back's nose, moving on his inside pass rush, the running back must step slightly back with the foot to the side of the rush. As this foot makes contact with the ground, the running back should

When taking on an inside pass rush, the running back stays square to the line of scrimmage and positions himself slightly inside the rusher's path.

explode off of it and strike out into the defensive man.

The running back should make forcible contact with the palm of the inside hand into the sternum area of the linebacker's chest. As this hand makes contact, the running back should continue to push off his inside foot.

As the inside foot and hand are being used partially to stop the rush of the linebacker to the inside, the running back must step quickly with his outside foot, keep his balance, strike the shoulder area of the defender with the palm of the outside hand, and drive the defensive man into the middle of the field and well past the target area.

When blocking versus an inside pass rush, the running back must understand that he will not have the opportunity to hit and reset and hit again. Instead, the running back must think in terms of stopping the linebacker's initial momentum to the inside, and then drive blocking him as he would on a running play, until the drill is over.

DRILL:

Blocking an Outside Pass Rush

The major difference in this drill will be the path of the defensive man's rush, and the initial setup by the running back in preparation for the block. The linebacker's

When blocking an outside pass rush, the running back faces the sideline.

rush lane will now be coming from the far outside, and the running back must make certain that he ends up facing squarely out to the sideline as he moves into his setup position. If the blocker faces squarely at the linebacker, rather than at the sideline, he will afford the linebacker the luxury of rushing to either the running back's right or left side with equal ease. By facing the sideline the running back is inviting the rusher to rush up the field, and the blocker now

has a much easier time of stopping the linebacker's rush and redirecting it past the target area.

WINNING POINTS

- On runs, the quicker blocker gets to defensive man, the less time defender has to react to block.
- When run blocking, attack aggressively; aim for defender's hip on side of block; keep head up, back straight; use short, choppy steps to turn defender.
- The head never should be used as first contact point.
- On double-team blocks, get hip-to-hip with lineman as soon as initial contact with defender is made.
- In pass blocking stance: feet parallel, slightly less than shoulder width apart; knees flexed; back straight; head up; eyes focused straight ahead; elbows held belt-high and close to body; forearms in front of chest; hands four to five inches in front of jersey, palms out, fingers up and spread, thumbs almost touching.
- In pass blocking, stop and redirect defender's charge; stay in relative position between defender and quarterback.

The action of the running back in making the block will be the same for the legs and lower body. The difference will come with the manner in which the arm and hands are used. The blocker's hand farthest away from the line of scrimmage will become the hand that delivers the major blow into the sternum of the rushing defensive man, thus slowing his momentum. The palm of the other hand usually will strike the defender in the shoulder area, not the chest, and will be used more to redirect the defensive man's path up the field away from the target area.

As in the previous drill, after the initial hit, the running back must gather himself, shuffle his feet to stay in proper position, and be prepared to strike again and again until the drill is ended by the coach.

When the running back has mastered the fundamentals of proper pass protection, the linebacker can increase the speed of his rush. The linebacker, as he comes from the inside or outside, should also be allowed to rush to either side of the running back.

Pass Receiving

Becoming a proficient pass receiver is the final skill a player needs to master in order to be a complete running back.

Catching a ball is a learned skill, one which requires proper body position, correct location and alignment of the hands, good hand-eye coordination, and complete concentration on the ball.

Many young players will spend great

amounts of practice time running pass pattern after pass pattern, and will not have spent the necessary time learning and practicing the proper method of catching a ball. Often they will find themselves getting open and then drop-

Pass receiving techniques for running backs are the same as for receivers: Thumbs touch on passes above the numbers, little fingers touch on passes below.

ping the pass as it comes to them, never really understanding why.

The very first thing that a beginning player must learn is the proper positioning of his hands to make a reception. For the reception of any pass which is even with or above the top of the numbers on his jersey, the thumbs and first fingers of the running back's hands should be together. The rest of the hands and fingers should be slightly forward, forming a cone in which the ball will be caught. With his hands in this position the running back should be able to think in terms of cradling the ball as he makes the catch.

If the pass is to be caught even with the numbers or below, the running back must change the position of his hands. For this height of reception, the player must place his little fingers, rather than his thumbs, together, allowing his hands to come forward thus forming the mitt in which to make the catch. In making a reception, one hand will almost always serve as the mitt; this will be the hand which makes contact with the point of the ball.

DRILL:

Hand Position

To teach proper hand position for making a reception, the coach can have the running backs line up facing him. Without actually throwing a ball, the coach can call out the position of the pass and the running backs should put their hands in the proper position to make the catch.

The running backs should stand in a comfortable stance with their feet spread shoulder width apart and with a slight bend in their knees. Their arms and hands should hang in a relaxed fashion at their sides and the players' complete focus and concentration should be on the coach. The coach will call out the location of the imaginary pass and each of the running backs should react to that location. The coach should then check each player, making certain that each of their hands is in the proper relationship to make a reception in that location.

For this drill, there should be 15 possible locations for the players to place their hands. There should be five distinct height locations: high (well above the player's head); pad (even with the shoulder pads); numbers (even with the jersey numbers); belt (even with the hips); and low (even with the thighs). These five distinct height locations should be followed with a directional call of left, center, or right, thus telling the running back exactly where the ball is to be caught. Because this drill requires no movement, it is a drill that the running backs can go

through on their own prior to start of actual practice.

The next important pass-receiving technique for the running back is, whenever possible, to extend his hands and arms so that he can see his hands and the ball as he makes the reception. To learn this, modify the previous drill. The coach, once again, calls out the location of the pass. This time, though, the players should not only place their hands in the proper position, but they also should reach forward as they would to bring their hands and the ball in view at the same time as the catch is made.

With the running backs in the same drill setup, the coach should have them turn so they are facing toward the sideline on their side of the field. The coach will call out one of the 15 positions and the players should reach out simulating a catch at that position. Next, the players should all face into the center of the field and the drill should be repeated.

Finally, the running backs should be instructed to turn around and face down the field, away from the coach. In this position, the players will be simulating making a reception on a pass which is thrown over their head from behind. The coach will now call out only the direction of the pass—either left, center, or right—and not the height. When making a re-

On short passes it is important for a running back to quickly look back at the passer while keeping his body turned upfield.

The little fingers are held together, arms extended, on over-the-head passes.

ception on a ball which is thrown over one shoulder or directly over his head, the running back must position his hands as if he were making a reception on a pass thrown below his waist. It is im-portant that the tips of the little fingers of both hands be touching, the fingers and thumbs forming the catching cone. The player must also attempt to reach his hands high and back toward the imaginary ball, allowing him the opportunity to see the ball and his hands as he makes the catch.

DRILL:
Ball Reception I

The ball now should be introduced into the receiving drills for the running backs. In setting up this receiving drill, the coach should have the running backs line up first to his right and then to his left. The purpose of the drill is to give each player the opportunity to catch as many passes as possible, so the players should have to run only a few steps before turning to make the catch. The coach, by the location of his pass, should force the running back to catch passes at each of the five height positions. The drill is run with one player at a time.

DRILL:
Ball Reception II

A running back lines up facing away from the coach. The coach then tells the player whether he is to turn to his left or his right to make the reception. On the command "Hut" from the coach, the running back should drive up the field four yards and then turn to the proper side and come back toward the coach. As he starts back toward the coach, the player must locate the ball, reach out with his hands and arms, place his fingers in the proper position to make the catch, and finally use the proper hand to serve as the mitt for receiving the tip of the ball. The mitt hand should always be the hand on the side of the pass and the other hand should be used to surround and control the ball.

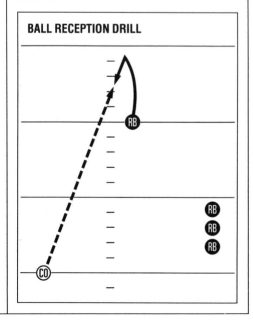

BALL RECEPTION DRILL

If the ball arrives on the right side of the running back, he should use the palm of his right hand as the mitt or contact point with the front tip of the ball. The left hand would then help the player control the ball and aid in securing the ball for carrying.

Starting with this simple drill, each time the running back makes a reception

The hand to the side of the pass is the first contact point with the ball.

he must be instructed immediately to "put the ball away," grasping it firmly by the point with his mitt and squeezing it tightly to his body with his forearm. As the catch is made the player should use his mitt hand to start turning the ball in toward his body. His other hand should continue to turn the ball so that the running back is able to place the uncovered part or back of the ball securely up into his armpit area.

Players may find that they are not catching passes that are in the high area. Usually the inability to make this reception is due to the fact that the player has not cocked his wrists back toward his helmet. Without cocking his wrists, the running back will find that the palms of both hands are pointed down, directly toward the ground in front of him. Consequently, when the point of the ball makes contact with the mitt hand it is immediately deflected down into the turf and the pass falls incomplete.

Once each running back has worked to the right side sufficiently, the coach should flop the drill over and repeat the same maneuvers with the players on the left side.

Finally, the players should be lined up, one at a time, facing downfield directly in front of the coach. The coach now will tell the players left, center, or right, and he

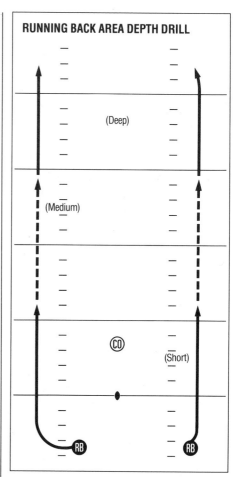

RUNNING BACK AREA DEPTH DRILL

(Deep)

(Medium)

(Short)

CO

RB   RB

will throw the ball over their heads or shoulders as they run straight down the field. When a running back is making a reception over his head in this manner, he will find that he does not need to turn the ball to put it away; he can pull it directly into his side with the mitt hand.

When the mechanics of pass receiving have been mastered, the running backs should be introduced to the pass routes which they will be asked to run during the course of a game.

The first step in learning pass routes is to see the three different depths (short, medium, deep) at which different pass patterns will be run. In order to get a feel for the actual distance down the field at which the area occurs, the first practice should only deal with each running back striding down the field in a straight line and calling out the area he is in as he runs.

As the player is running up the field, he will call out "short, short, short" for the first six yards past the line of scrimmage. From 7 to 13 yards he will call out "medium," and after 14 he will call out "deep." By calling out the depths as he moves up the field, the player quickly becomes familiar with the depths at which different pass patterns are run and he also demonstrates to the coach that he understands where the three areas are located.

Pass offense is based on timing. The coordination of the quarterback's drop and delivery of the ball will be based on the precise running of a pass pattern at a certain depth and time by the receiver. Consequently, each running back must know exactly where he must run the various pass routes, the "passing tree" concept, and the actual pass patterns (routes) that he will use.

In order to help the young running back not become overwhelmed when first learning all the routes on the running back's passing tree, it is best for the coach to introduce the patterns by the depth areas where they are run. In other words, the coach first teaches the running back all the patterns that are run in the short area, then medium, then deep. In the beginning it is best to run the patterns without using a ball in the drill. After the player has mastered running the patterns for each of the areas correctly, a ball can be added.

DRILL:
Short Patterns

Because passes in the short area often are thrown quickly by the quarterback, the running back must be instructed to immediately turn his head around, focus his eyes on the quarterback, and get his

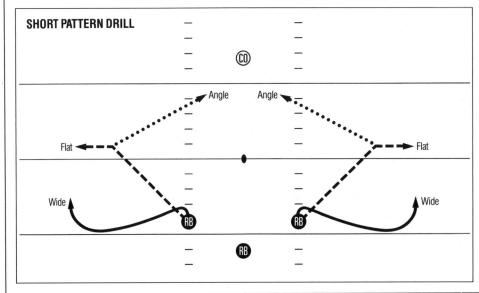

SHORT PATTERN DRILL

hands in proper position to make the reception.

In running the "wide" pass pattern, the running back should use a crossover start to the sideline, arcing back slightly away from the line of scrimmage as he runs, so that he will be able to turn his body up the field as he makes the catch. The pass usually will be caught on the offensive side of the line of scrimmage. The running back should think in terms of using his hand nearest the sideline for his mitt hand.

When running a "flat" route, the running back should attack the line of scrimmage. Once he is one yard past it, he should break directly toward the sideline. Again, it is very important for the running back to turn his head quickly and look for the ball. The hand that is farthest up the field will serve as the mitt hand when catching a "flat" pass.

On the "angle" pass pattern, the running back should be instructed to attack the line of scrimmage in the same manner that he did when running the "flat" route. But as he crosses the line of scrimmage, instead of breaking toward the sideline, the running back should break at an angle, back toward the center of the field. As with the flat pass, the upfield hand should be the mitt hand when making the reception.

On a "wide" route, the running back arcs away from the line of scrimmage and turns upfield as he makes the catch with the hand nearest the sideline.

On a "flat" route, the running back breaks toward the sideline one yard past the line of scrimmage. His upfield hand will be the mitt hand.

On all pass patterns, but especially on passes caught in the short area, the running back must expect to be hit and tackled immediately after making the reception. Because of this, it is of vital importance that the running back secure the ball the instant it reaches his hands. Any player who is going to be a pass receiver has to understand that there is a good chance he will be hit whether he catches the ball or not, so he might as well make the reception and gain the yards.

DRILL:

Medium Patterns

The object of the "stop" pattern is to get downfield as quickly as possible, stop, and turn back to the quarterback to receive the ball. In the drill, the coach should tell the running back to turn either to the inside or the outside, but later the back must learn to turn away from the nearest defensive man in coverage.

Prior to the play ever beginning, the running back should pick out a spot seven yards across the line of scrimmage and seven to eight yards outside of where he originally lines up. As he sprints to the point, the running back must gather himself, lowering his backside, and be prepared to stop and turn. As he turns back to the quarterback, it is very important that the running back

bring his head around, focus quickly on the quarterback, and bring both hands up in a position to make a reception. The hand on the side of the pass should serve as the mitt hand for the catch.

The initial release by the running back on all of the remaining pass patterns should be the same. At the snap the running back should release wide enough so that he can easily avoid the block of

his own offensive tackle and the rush of any defensive players. Once he has gotten enough width to clear these obstructions, the back must turn and sprint straight up the field. The success of the remainder of the running back's pass routes in the medium and deep areas will depend on the defensive players never being certain if he is going to run up the field or not.

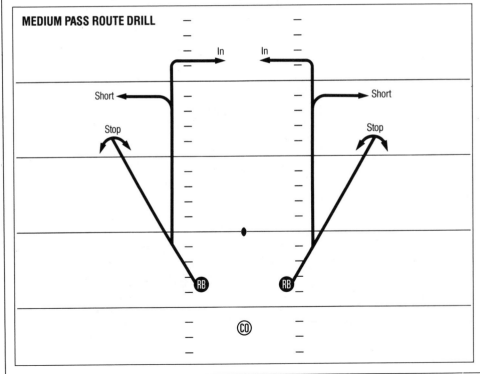

MEDIUM PASS ROUTE DRILL

For the "short" route, the back should sprint up the field for eight yards past the line of scrimmage. At nine yards the running back should roll over his outside foot and break toward the sideline. It is important for the running back to understand that he will come back slightly toward the line of scrimmage as he proceeds to the sideline. The player must be reminded to reach back with his hands so that he has his fingers and the ball in his vision at the same time prior to making the catch.

The "in" route starts with the same release, only now the running back will continue his sprint up the field for 10 yards. As he crosses the 10-yard area, he should roll over his inside foot, breaking on a path directly to the center of the field. In this pattern, the running back must be prepared to make the reception at any point as he proceeds across the field. The important thing is that the player not slow down or, worse yet, stop his movement across the field.

DRILL:

Deep Patterns

For all deep-area pass routes, the quarterback will take a deeper drop from the line of scrimmage and usually will hold the ball slightly longer before he throws the pass. When executing a deep pass

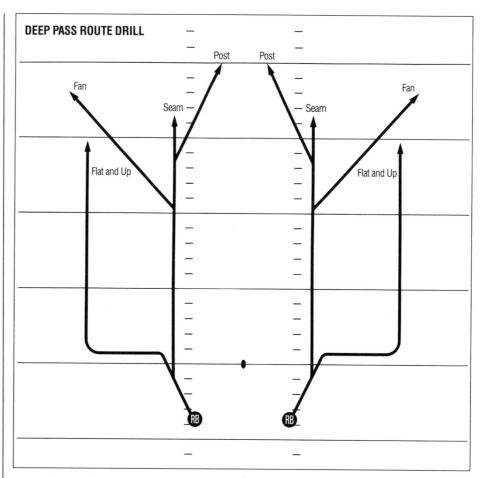

DEEP PASS ROUTE DRILL

route, the running back also must realize that the pass will be thrown with more loft and hang in the air longer, thus allowing him the opportunity to run under the ball as he makes the catch.

The "flat and up" pass pattern begins with the running back running a "flat" route exactly as he did in the short area patterns. As he nears the sideline, he should look back for the ball and the quarterback should pump his arm in his direction. As soon as the running back sees the pump, he must turn up the field and sprint toward the goal line. Usually on a pass of this type the ball will come over the player's inside shoulder, and the palm of the outside hand will serve as the mitt on the reception.

If the running back is called on to run a "seam" pattern, he should release from his position in the same manner as he did when he was running the "short" or "in" route. On the seam, the running back will continue to run straight up the field. Ideally the pass should come over his inside shoulder as he runs up the field. But because of the way the defense may be playing, the running back must be prepared for the ball to arrive on either his inside or outside shoulder.

The "fan" pass route is different in that the running back will be breaking at an angle deep toward the sideline after running up the field for 10 yards. The ball usually will reach the running back by coming in over his shoulder nearest the sideline. This is one pass pattern where, because of the difficulty in throwing it, the running back often will have to adjust his path so that he can be in position to make the catch. It is very important for

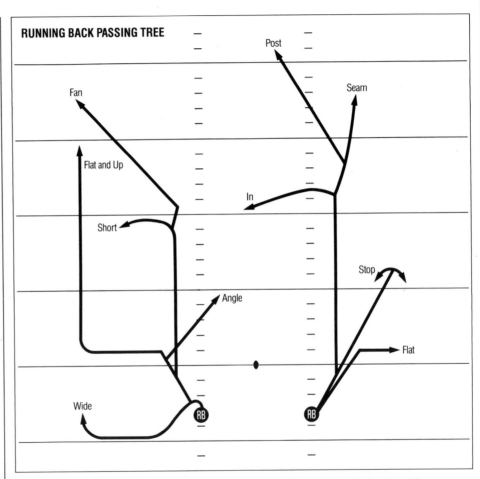

RUNNING BACK PASSING TREE

Post

Seam

Fan

Flat and Up

In

Short

Stop

Angle

Flat

Wide

RB

RB

the running back to get his head around as soon as he makes his break so that he has the maximum time to locate and adjust to the flight of the ball.

The final pattern is the "post" pattern. Again the running back will release outside and head straight up the field. At 14 yards, instead of continuing to run

A "fan" route may have to be adjusted to get into position for the catch.

straight up the field as on a "seam," the running back should adjust his path so that he bends in and heads in the direction of the goal post. For this pass to be complete, the ball needs to be thrown over his inside shoulder, allowing the player to use his outside hand as the mitt for receiving the point of the ball.

Once all the pass patterns have been introduced and taught to the running backs by using the three depth areas, the coach can then present the entire running back passing tree for the play-

WINNING POINTS
- To catch pass even with, or higher than, jersey numbers, hands are held with thumbs touching, wrists cocked back.
- To catch pass even with, or below, jersey numbers, hands are held with little fingers touching.
- To catch pass coming over shoulder or head, reach for ball with hands held with little fingers touching; try to see ball and hands as catch is made.
- The hand on side of pass is mitt, or contact, hand; other hand surrounds and controls ball, and helps secure it.

ers to see.

The players need to learn all the patterns running both to their left and right. Remember, players only become great pass receivers by learning to run routes correctly, by understanding the proper method of catching each pass, and by catching a number of passes at practice every day.

Screens, Delays, and Draws

Screens, delays, and draws are run in conjunction with the normal passing attack that an offensive team might use during a game. Each of these three types of plays begins with the entire offensive team executing as they would on a normal pass play. The real success of these plays results from the defensive team thinking and reacting as they would for a regular drop-back pass.

There are basically two types of screen passes which the running back will be asked to learn. The first type is called a "slow screen" and as the name indicates, it is a pass that takes a few seconds to develop.

DRILL:

Slow Screen

The first thing that the running back needs to understand about running a "slow screen" is that he must sell the de-

The success of a screen pass depends on the running back making the defense think he is staying in the backfield to block. The running back delays, then releases toward the sideline, and positions himself for the catch behind his blockers.

fensive players that he is staying in the backfield to help pass protect for the quarterback.

Only one back should execute the screen during the drill. The coach should indicate on which side the screen will be thrown. On the command "Hut" from the coach, the running back should step in and up as he would if he were preparing to pass block.

As the running back sets up to the inside, he should mentally count "a thousand one, a thousand two, a thousand three," and then move up to the line of scrimmage before releasing out toward the sideline. If, in a game, the running back sees that there is a linebacker blitzing on his side that is not accounted for or is unblocked by one of the offensive blockers, then he must make certain to hit the linebacker and momentarily slow his rush to the quarterback before releasing to the outside.

This delay by the running back, prior to releasing out to the sideline, is necessary so that the offensive linemen have time initially to block the defensive men, and then to release to the outside to form a wall for the running back who is to catch the screen. One of the worst things that the running back can do is to release to the outside too quickly and end up waiting for the pass without the offensive linemen there to block for him.

When executing a "slow screen," the running back should expect to receive the ball over his shoulder farthest from the line of scrimmage. As he makes the reception, it is a good idea for him to shout "Go" to the offensive linemen who are preparing to block for him. This call will alert the offensive linemen that he has the ball and is running up the field.

The second type of screen that a running back will be asked to run is called a "speed screen" and it differs from the slow screen in the action of the running back. Instead of stepping in and up and delaying before releasing to the outside, the running back turns and immediately runs to the sideline.

DRILL:

Speed Screen

On the command of "Hut," the running back runs to the outside to a point halfway between where he lined up before the play began and the sideline. When the running back reaches this point he must stop, turn back toward the quarterback, and be prepared to receive the ball.

The "speed screen" not only differs from the "slow screen" in the instant release of the running back, but also in the fact that the offensive linemen are not leading the play, but are coming out to block after the running back has set up to make the reception.

When teaching this type of screen pass it is good to alert the running back

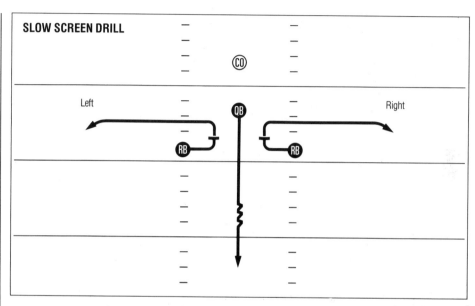

SLOW SCREEN DRILL

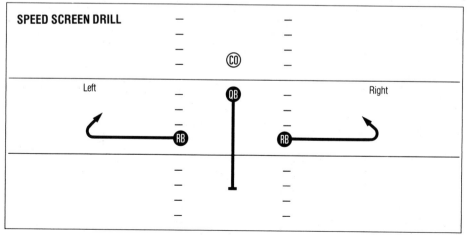

SPEED SCREEN DRILL

The running back does not delay on a speed screen as he does on a slow screen. At the snap the running back turns and immediately runs toward the sideline.

When the running back is halfway to the sideline, he turns to make the catch. The offensive linemen come outside to block after the running back is in position.

that he may find, after he has made the catch, that he has to start toward his blockers before turning to run up the field. This slight initial movement to the inside usually will allow the blockers to be in much better position to execute their blocks on the defensive players.

DRILL:

Delay Pass

Another type of running back pass is a "delay" pass. The drill should be run the same way and the running back should be instructed to set up as he would if he were going to run a "slow screen" to his side. Again the running back should mentally count to himself, "a thousand one, a thousand two, a thousand three," before releasing on his pattern. Success

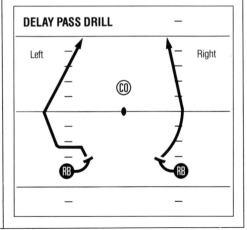

On a delay pass, the running back sets up the same as on a slow screen and waits to release inside between the blocks of his guard and tackle. Once across the line of scrimmage, the running back adjusts his path to the center of the field.

on this type of pass will occur only if the defensive players drop back into pass coverage, thinking that the running back is staying in to help with the pass protection.

Once the running back has delayed, he then must try to release between the blocks of his offensive guard and tackle.

During a game, the inside area may be completely congested and the running back may be forced to release outside of the blocks of the offensive linemen.

With either release, once he crosses the line of scrimmage, the running back must adjust his path to the center of the field and immediately turn his head, look

for the ball, and be prepared to make the reception. Usually on this type of pass, the reception will be made three to four yards past the line of scrimmage, giving the running back time to make the catch, secure the ball, and turn to run up the field before the defensive men arrive to make the tackle.

A draw play actually is a running play that looks to the defense like a pass. As the quarterback begins his drop, the running back steps inside, checks the line blocking, and waits for the quarterback to give him the ball.

The last play of the special running back pass plays is the "draw" play. This really is a running play and not a pass play, but because of the fact that the offensive team begins as they would on a drop back pass play, most coaches teach the "draw" as part of the pass offense.

DRILL:

Draw Play

When running the draw play, the running back, on the coach's command of "Hut," should take a long, quick, lateral step to the inside with his inside foot. It is important that he not step up and in, but in-

stead he must make certain that his step is directly lateral. When his inside foot makes contact, the running back should quickly slide his outside foot to the inside so that he ends up in a comfortable, balanced stance with his feet only slightly wider than his hips and his knees flexed.

As the quarterback begins his pass

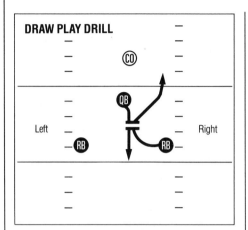

DRAW PLAY DRILL

Left

Right

drop, the running back should keep his head up, focusing his eyes on the offensive line and observing how the blocking is developing. At the same time he should get his hands and arms into position as he would if he were taking a handoff on a dive play to his side.

It is not necessary for the running back to look for the handoff; the quarterback has the complete responsibility of placing the ball into the running back's stomach as he moves past him on his pass drop. The main responsibility of the running back is to be set up in the proper location and to get himself in the correct position to take the handoff. Once he has secured the ball, the running back must immediately start up the field, running to any hole that he has seen open up.

Running Back Passes

One final skill that can be a very positive addition for any running back is the ability to pass the ball. This skill is one that will differ greatly from one running back to another, but it is a skill that can be taught and developed with practice.

Prior to throwing a "run" pass, a running back may receive the ball from the quarterback by a handoff, a quick toss, or a pitch deep to an I-formation tailback. Regardless of how the running back gets the ball, there are critical techniques which will remain constant anytime he is trying to throw the ball while he is on the move.

The number-one technique for the running back to learn is that he must make certain that he has turned his body so that his hips are facing down the field toward the opponent's goal line and his intended receiver as he prepares to throw the ball. Failing to turn his hips properly will cause the running back to end up throwing across his body, resulting in poor accuracy and very little velocity on the ball.

Once the running back has good body position to throw the ball, the next important technique for him to learn is to step directly at the intended receiver with the foot opposite his passing hand. This step is essential to set the direction

and establish the path the ball will follow on each pass.

The running back should continue the throwing motion by allowing his hips and belt buckle to initiate and precede his passing arm and hand. The young player should be reminded always to think of aiming his belt buckle directly at the target area anytime he throws a pass.

When the running back has started running to the sideline away from his passing hand, he often will need to get slightly more depth away from the line of scrimmage. This added depth should give the running back ample room to get his hips turned up the field as he prepares to pass the ball.

The actual delivery of the pass is greatly aided if the running back is moving up the field at the time he releases the ball. With this movement up the field, the running back's body will give added momentum and greater accuracy to the pass.

At the moment of release, the running back should be rolling over the foot opposite his passing hand and stepping directly at the receiver with his foot on the side of his passing hand. The ball should be released with good follow-through, the palm of the passing hand turning naturally down toward the ground. The body of the running back should continue down the field and not come to an abrupt stop after throwing the pass.

Most offensive plays that are designed for the running back to throw the ball are usually option types of plays. If the running back sees that the receiver is in the open, he can throw the pass. If the receiver is covered, the running back should be prepared to secure the ball, turn up the field, and run for as many yards as possible. It is a good idea for a running back to think of this type of play as a run first and a pass second; in that way he will not be inclined to force throwing a pass to a receiver who obviously is covered.

DRILL:
Run Pass

The running back begins the drill with the ball, so he does not have to be worried about taking the handoff or catching the pitch from the quarterback. Initially, the receiver should be stationary, turned, and facing the running back.

To give the running back an idea of the decision he has to make, the drill can be developed further to where the receiver will sometimes turn his back to the running back, indicating that he is covered and that the running back should run

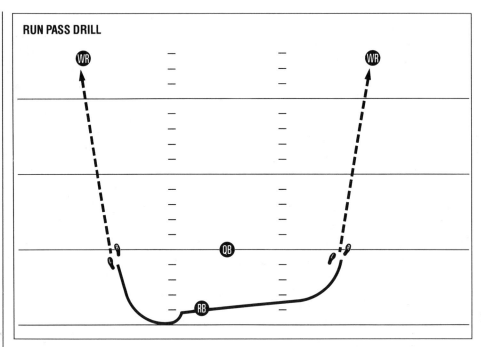

RUN PASS DRILL

with the ball.

Once the running back has demonstrated that he has the techniques for throwing a "run" pass, the quarterback exchange can be added and the receiver can run his normal pass route.

Later in practice, another offensive player can simulate a defensive player by either coming up and forcing the run or dropping back in coverage, thus causing the running back to decide quickly whether he is going to run or

pass the ball.

Any running back who is being asked to throw a "run" pass should also be cautioned about trying to throw the ball to a receiver who is in the center of the field or on the opposite side of the field. In order to make this type of throw, the running back usually will have to throw across his body, not stepping directly at the receiver. The result of this type of throw will almost always be either an incompletion or, worse yet, an interception.

RECEIVERS

3

Receivers

- Characteristics of a Wide Receiver **101**
- Characteristics of a Tight End **103**
- Wide Receiver Stance **105**
- Tight End Stance **106**
- The Release **107**
- Running Pass Routes **111**
- Catching the Ball **115**
- Wide Receiver Pass Patterns **121**
- Tight End Pass Patterns **129**
- Blocking **135**
- Reading Coverage **145**

The wide receiver is considered the thoroughbred of the receiving corps. His primary job is to get far enough away from any defender so that the quarterback may deliver the ball where he can make the catch.

If the wide receiver is the thoroughbred, his partner in the passing game, the tight end, can be viewed as the quarterhorse of the offense. Like the wide receiver, the tight end must be able to get free from a defender at the line of scrimmage, run his pass route so that he comes open quickly , and then make the reception. In addition to his receiving role, the tight end also has the vital job of blocking in conjunction with the offensive linemen on a majority of the offensive running plays.

Any player who desires to become either a wide receiver or tight end must understand the basic principles of running good pass routes, how to maneuver to get open, and the need to have a conviction that he will catch every ball.

Receivers learn that getting hit, by one or more defensive players, is inevitable. Further, they realize they will be hit with the same force whether they catch the ball or not. So the great ones maximize the situation by making every effort to make the reception on each pass thrown their way.

Characteristics of a Wide Receiver

There are many athletes who have the ability to run fast in a straight line, but to be a top wide receiver, the athlete must have the one quality that cannot be coached—quickness. He also must be able to change direction without losing any speed, run at full speed the minute he comes off the line of scrimmage, and continue to run flat-out throughout his entire pass pattern. You can almost always pick out a receiver who has great speed by his average yards-per-catch figure for the season.

However, if a player has a desire to be a wide receiver and he does not have tremendous speed, he should not auto-

Speed and quickness are the trademarks of most wide receivers, but the ability to run precise pass routes also is a key.

matically give up on his dream. With a great deal of hard work and dedication, there can be an opportunity for him to make the team at the receiver position. Even though all coaches would like to have receivers with great speed and quickness, there is a place for the receiver who, lacking speed, makes up for it with precise pattern execution, complete focus on the ball when it is thrown his way, and the ability to get away from defensive players or to find the hole between zone coverages.

Along with a thorough grasp of offenses and defenses, another important trait found in any successful wide receiver is concentration. First, he must concentrate on getting off the ball on the snap count. As he releases off the line of scrimmage, the receiver must concentrate to recognize the defense that is being used. While still running at full speed, he must concentrate on running the pattern called in the offensive huddle, running it in the exact manner that will allow him to be in the best position to defeat the coverage being executed by the defense. Finally, as he moves into the final phase of his pass pattern, the wide receiver must be able to shut everything out of his mind, focusing his eyes and all of his attention on the ball as it moves toward him. He must be

consumed with total and complete concentration on making the catch.

This ability to focus on the catch and the understanding of the importance of the catch are demonstrated by great wide receivers every time they walk on the field to practice or play football. They know that if they practice with intensity and dedication, attempting to catch any pass that they can touch, their performance in a game will become automatic.

Conditioning, the ability to run on play after play without slowing down, is also a vital characteristic of any great receiver. All football players should be ready to run when practice begins, but the very nature of the job of a wide receiver requires that they come to the practice field in the very best physical condition. Fatigue and a lack of conditioning will turn a good receiver into an average pass catcher faster than anything else that might happen to him during practice or a game.

Playing as a wide receiver on a football team can be exciting for any young player, but he must understand that it is not an easy position to play. He will be required to run continuously during the entire practice session or game when he is on the field. Prospective wide receivers also must realize that while they may

not be required to block like an offensive lineman or even a tight end, they will be involved in contact. They should be prepared for this, and especially to "take a hit" after a catch, accepting this inevitable collision as a part of playing the game as a wide receiver.

Characteristics of a Tight End

Size is not really an issue when it comes to playing wide receiver. There are too many 5-foot, 9- or 10-inch, 175- to 180-pound wide receivers in the NFL, who are having success year after year, for physical proportions to become an important consideration.

This is not the case for the tight end position. Because of his responsibilities in blocking defensive linemen and linebackers, the tight end must have the size to get the job accomplished. He also must have the same ability as a wide receiver to run accurate pass patterns, to get open, and to make the catch. Some tight ends even possess the speed to be deep threats.

But blocking ability is the one vital characteristic found in all good tight ends. Often they will be smaller in stature than the man they are asked to block. Consequently, it is very important for the tight end to have good quickness off the ball, plus the understanding

Sure-handed receptions in crucial possession situations, plus solid, consistent blocking, distinguish the tight end.

and mastery of good blocking techniques.

A tight end also must be as tough mentally as he is physically to play in the middle, fighting against strong, active linebackers, finding just enough room to make a reception for a first down. Top-notch tight ends demonstrate time and again this tremendous determination, particularly on third-down situations when they release off the line of scrimmage, taking hits from opposing defensive players as they run, and still execute their pass routes. They make clutch receptions despite the defense keying on them and everyone in the stadium knowing they will get the ball.

A successful tight end must possess sure hands. It is important for everyone on the offense to feel that if the ball is thrown in the tight end's direction he will make the catch. When a team has a tight end with demonstrated clutch receiving ability, defenses are not able to blanket the two wide receivers with double coverage, thus greatly increasing the chances of one of them getting open.

Wide Receiver Stance

The stance, the manner in which a wide receiver lines up prior to the beginning of the play, varies from wide receiver to wide receiver and team to team. There still are coaches who favor the wide receiver in a three-point stance usually with his outside hand down on the ground, thus allowing a clear view of the ball. Being able to sight on the ball often is necessary due to the noise of the crowd and an inability to hear the quarterback's signal count. There will be times when the wide receiver will know when a play has begun only by observing the ball's movement as the center snaps it.

In the three-point stance the receiver should start with this feet spread a little less than the width of his shoulders. Because there is no need for a receiver to move laterally on the scrimmage line, he can place his feet in a narrower stance than the one used by his offensive teammates. The receiver should then move his outside foot back so that the toe of the foot is even with the heel of the inside foot. From this position the receiver should flex his knees, bending them far enough to allow him to rest his forearms on the inside of both thighs. Next, the player should reach out with his outside hand, placing it on the ground slightly in front of the outside of his shoulder pad. In this stance the receiver should now be on the balls of both feet, heels off the ground, with a majority of his weight being transferred to the ball of the forward

The upright two-point stance is better against bump-and-run defenses.

foot, so he can take off quickly.

In this basic three-point stance, the wide receiver must concentrate on having his shoulders level, his back straight, and his head up with his eyes focused on the defensive player who is lined up in front of him. It is very impor-

The three point stance, with outside hand down, less stagger, and wider foot placement, affords tight ends more balance for blocking.

tant for a young player to practice seeing the ball with his peripheral vision, and not by turning his head toward the ball. Always try to keep the head pointed as straight downfield as possible.

More and more coaches and players are using a two-point, or upright, stance for wide receivers. In this upright stance, the player gets a quicker read on the defense and is usually in a better position to avoid any type of bump or collision instigated by a defender.

For the two-point stance, the wide receiver should have his feet in the same relationship as in the three-point stance.

The weight should be centered more on the front foot, though, allowing the receiver to start by rolling over his foot on his release. He should have his knees slightly flexed and he should be bending forward at the waist. His shoulders and head will be in front of his forward foot. Many wide receivers, rather than allowing their hands and arms to hang down, will bend their elbows in their stance, bringing their hands more to the middle of their bodies.

Tight End Stance

With the tight end's added blocking re-

sponsibility, his stance will, by necessity, be more like that of an offensive lineman than a wide receiver. Most tight ends use a three-point stance, with their feet spread about the width of their

WINNING POINTS

- For wide receiver three-point stance: feet spread slightly less than shoulder width; toe of outside foot even with heel of inside foot; knees flexed enough to allow forearms to rest on insides of thighs; outside hand on ground slightly in front of outside of shoulder pad; heels off ground; majority of weight on ball of forward foot; back straight; head up; eyes focused downfield.
- For wide receiver two-point stance: same as three-point stance, except no hand on ground; weight on forward foot; forward bend at waist; head and shoulders in front of forward foot; elbows may be bent to bring hands to middle of body.
- For tight end three-point stance: same as wide receiver, except feet are shoulder-width apart and toe of back foot is even with instep of forward foot.

shoulders. The toe of the back foot will usually be even with the instep of the "up" or forward foot.

In learning to get into a proper stance, the tight end can follow the same procedure as the wide receiver. After adjusting his feet to their proper location, he can flex his knees, allowing him to comfortably rest his forearms on the inside of his thighs. From this position, with his back straight and head up, the tight end can reach out with his hand on the side of his back foot. The hand should be extended straight out from the player's shoulder and should make contact with the ground slightly in front of his shoulder pad.

In this stance, it is very important that the tight end's back is straight, his head up, and his eyes focused directly ahead. The heels of both feet should be slightly off the ground. The player now should feel his weight on the balls of his feet with most of his weight being centered on the front foot.

The Release

The intent of the release from the line of scrimmage of either a wide receiver or tight end, is to get up the field as quickly as possible. The sooner a receiver can attack the defense, the greater the opportunity he will have to make a reception.

Whether the player is a tight end or wide receiver, he should roll over his forward foot, making certain that he is physically taking a step up the field with his back foot.

For a wide receiver who has aligned himself in a comfortable two-point stance, making this initial step up the field should be easy. As this first step is taken, the receiver should maintain his forward body lean with his head and shoulders. The receiver's arms should

begin pumping in a normal running motion.

DRILL:

Wide Receiver Release

During this drill, the coach must make certain that the wide receiver starts in a good stance and that the player understands that the drill is being run only to develop the fastest release down the field from the line of scrimmage.

The receiver need only run five yards

A quick release from the line of scrimmage is critical to any pass route.

down the field in order for a coach to determine if he is releasing correctly. On the command of "Hut!" by the coach, the player should burst forward, stepping with his back foot while rolling over and pushing off of his front foot.

It is very important that the coach make certain that the player is not stepping back with the front foot as he first begins to move. This unnecessary or "false step" will stop the player from attacking down the field and will make it more difficult for him to quickly threaten the defense.

Releasing from the line of scrimmage is more difficult when the receiver has a defensive player lining up directly in front of him. This either can be a defensive back who is on the line in a press coverage in front of a wide receiver, or a linebacker who is aligned over a tight end. In either instance, the release used by the player must not only allow the receiver to get up the field, but it also must be executed in a manner that will allow the receiver to free himself from the defensive player.

In the next phase of the drill, another wide receiver can assume the position of a defensive back. As the receiver releases off the line of scrimmage, the player on defense should attempt to bump the wide receiver and to momentarily grab

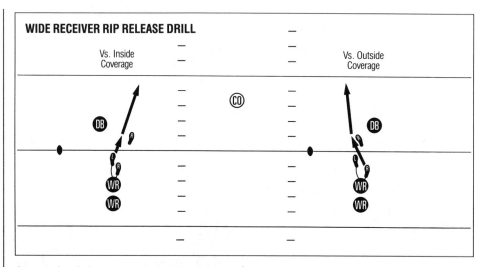

WIDE RECEIVER RIP RELEASE DRILL

Vs. Inside Coverage

Vs. Outside Coverage

the receiver's jersey, stopping his release. Remember, this is not a drill to teach defensive back technique, but the player on defense should give the receiver a good feel for what may occur during a game.

The first step of the release, with the back foot, usually will not be straight ahead but will be angled slightly away from the defensive player. The important thing for the receiver to remember is that he must attack off the line and not waste valuable time trying to fake the defensive player without really moving from his original location.

The arm on the side of the receiver which is closest to the defensive player

is used to "rip" away from the defender. As the wide receiver feels the defensive man's hands attempting to make contact, he must "rip" up with his near arm making contact with the defender's wrist and knocking the defender's hands up into the air.

DRILL:

Tight End Release

The release used by a tight end will be somewhat different from the wide receiver's in that the defensive player often will be aligned directly in front of the tight end. When faced with this type of defensive alignment, the tight end is forced to make his initial release step with his back foot more to the side than straight ahead.

A fellow tight end should play the part of the linebacker and the players can rotate going from offense, where they can execute their release, to defense, acting as the coverage man. As the tight end releases off the line of scrimmage, the linebacker should attempt to make contact by striking the tight end in the chest with both of his hands.

In the beginning, the tight end should be taught to rip up with the arm on the opposite side of his release. As with the wide receivers, the arm should strike the defender's wrist with force, directing the defender's hands and arms up into the air away from the tight end's jersey.

The tight end rips up with the arm on the opposite side of his release.

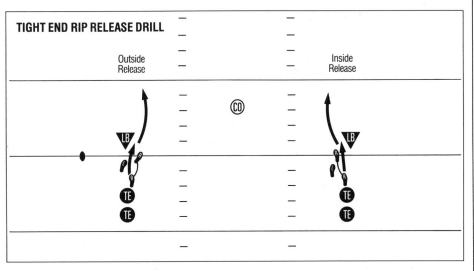

TIGHT END RIP RELEASE DRILL

Outside Release   Inside Release

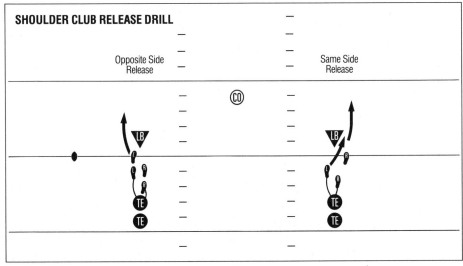

SHOULDER CLUB RELEASE DRILL

Opposite Side Release   Same Side Release

In the "shoulder club and arm-over" release, the tight end steps to the side of the release and hits the defender's arm with his forearm (left), then reaches over and drives past the defender (right) with his elbow.

The tight end must advance up the field with this first step and not merely stand up and fight off the defender while barely moving his feet. The longer the offensive man takes to move from his original stance position, the greater the possibility will be for the linebacker to make good contact with both hands and stop the tight end from releasing down the field. A quick, explosive, and decisive release move by the tight end is essential.

Once the tight end has mastered the rip release, he can move on to another type of release. This release can be learned with the same setup as the previous drill.

When executing this new release, called the "shoulder club" release, the tight end should step, with the foot in the direction of the release, to the outside of the linebacker's shoulder pad. If the release is to the side of the back foot, the tight end can attempt to get this position with his first step. If the release is opposite the back foot, the tight end will be forced to take two quick steps before gaining his desired position.

As the tight end steps to the side of his release, he should swing his forearm on the side of the release so that it makes contact with the defensive man's arm just below the tip of his shoulder. As the inside of his forearm makes contact, the tight end must reach over the defender with his opposite arm, driving the point of his elbow into the back of the defensive man. At the same instant he is reaching over the linebacker's shoulder, the tight end must step past the defender, and accelerate his hips past the defensive man's body. This action should propel the tight end past the defender, allowing him to attack up the field into the defensive secondary.

WINNING POINTS

- Roll over forward foot, while taking step up field with rear foot.
- Do not take step back with front foot as movement begins.
- Maintain forward body lean with head and shoulders.
- For wide receiver "rip" release: first step is angled slightly away from defender; rip up with arm nearest defender, hitting defender's wrists as defender reaches to make contact; do not waste time faking defender at line; attack directly.
- For tight end "rip" release: initial step with rear foot to the side; rip with arm on opposite side of release; do not fight defensive man —get upfield.
- For tight end "shoulder club" release: step with foot in direction of release to outside of defender's shoulder pad; swing forearm on side of release into defender's arm; reach over defender with opposite arm, bringing elbow into defender's back; step past defender and accelerate.

Obviously a tight end using the shoulder club and arm-over release is not going to have much chance for success if he is shorter in stature than the linebacker who is playing in front of him. If this is the case, the tight end is better off concentrating on using the rip release to free himself from the linebacker's grasp.

Running Pass Routes

Every receiver must have in his mind the four essential segments of any pass route: the release, glide, sprint, and burst. The first of these elements was covered in the preceding drills.

The next segment of the pass route is referred to as the "glide" phase. This is where the receiver may alter his path up the field in order to be in the best possible position to break free from the defensive man. In the glide segment of any route, the receiver must understand that speed is an essential factor and he must not slow down as he is in his glide.

Initially, the receiver should think about two things in the glide phase: First, where he wants to go, and, second, where the defensive man is located in relationship to the receiver's final path.

All wide receivers and tight ends must apply this basic principle: *If the defensive player is away from where you desire to go, run at him and keep him where he is. But if he is located where you want to go, you must run away from him and force him to come with you.*

DRILL:

Wide Receiver Glide

In this drill, the wide receiver should not be concerned with learning how to run the complete "out" pass pattern. The focus, instead, is on teaching the receiver how to use the glide phase of the pass pattern to maneuver the defender away from the final area of the intended route. The receiver will not actually break to the outside, but should continue running up the field until he has passed the coach. The same drill setup will be used for teaching the tight end how to adjust his glide based on the coverage location of the defensive player.

The defensive player in the drill (usually another wide receiver) attempts to keep the same relative relationship to the receiver during the entire drill. If he starts on the inside he should attempt to stay on the inside, and if his initial position is on the outside he should stay there for the duration of the drill.

When a receiver running the "out" pattern releases off the line of scrimmage and sees that the defender is playing on his inside, then the path of his glide should be directly at the defender. The defensive man has placed himself away from the area of the final cut, consequently the receiver must think only of keeping him there and possibly moving him farther to the inside. In his glide, the receiver should set a path at the inside hip of the defender. Obviously the receiver is not really trying to get to the inside of the defender, but this path will force the defender to move farther and farther to the inside. As he drives at the defensive player, the receiver should threaten to run by the defender, forcing the defensive man not only to the inside but also back with each step.

On the other hand, when the receiver observes that the defensive man has lined up where the receiver ultimately wants to go, he must change his tactics. Now instead of merely keeping the defender where he originally lined up, the receiver must alter his glide so that the defender is forced to move out of the area. After the receiver has run a few yards straight up the field, forcing the defender to start moving back, the receiver must alter his glide, slanting in toward the middle of the field. This action will pull the defender more to the inside. When the receiver observes the defender coming to the inside with him, he should then redirect his path straight up the field, giving the defender the feeling that he is going to run a deep pass pattern. By moving the defender more toward the ball, the wide receiver should

GLIDE DRILL FOR WIDE RECEIVER RUNNING "OUT" PATTERN

Keep Defender in Position

Move Defender from Position

CO

DB

WR

During the glide phase of a pass route, a receiver must stay aware of where he wants to go and where the defender is located in relation to his pattern.

gardless of the movement of the receiver as he releases off the line of scrimmage. If he starts on the inside of the tight end at the beginning of the drill, he should remain on the inside, as both players run up the field past the coach. An initial outside position also should be maintained during the course of the drill.

The tight end running the "in" pattern knows that he ultimately wants to run to the inside. As he releases off the line, the tight end's job is to determine if the defensive man is positioned where he desires to go, or if the defender is on the opposite side of the receiver's final destination.

When the defender is lined up on the side of the receiver's final path, the tight end must release away from the defensive back, pulling the defender with him. If the defender is away from the tight end's final path, he must drive directly at his far hip, forcing the defensive back to move farther and farther away from his final break.

The third segment of a pass pattern is the "sprint." This includes the last four steps of the glide, just prior to the receiver making the final break on his pattern. In these four steps the receiver is trying to convince the defender that he is attempting to run by him. If possible, this

give himself ample area to run his out pattern.

DRILL:

Tight End Glide

In this drill, the tight ends will be learning the same principles that were taught to the wide receivers in the previous drill.

One tight end should serve as the defensive back for the drill. Remember, it is the defender's job to try to maintain the same relationship to the tight end re-

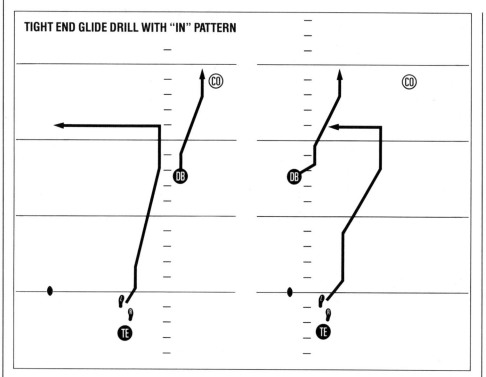

TIGHT END GLIDE DRILL WITH "IN" PATTERN

"burst." This is the last stage prior to catching the ball and occurs as the receiver makes his final cut on each particular pass route. In the burst phase the receiver must not allow himself to slow down or to stop his momentum. Running at full speed the receiver must turn his head around so that he can look back to where the quarterback will ultimately be throwing the ball. He also must be prepared to get his hands up in position to receive the pass.

When first practicing the burst phase of a pass route, it is best for wide receivers and tight ends to work only with the "in" and "out" pass patterns. Later, after players have been introduced to all of the pass patterns they will use, they can work on the burst for every route.

DRILL:
Wide Receiver/Tight End Burst

When practicing the burst, the same drill setup as in the previous drills can be used, with an offensive player posing as the defender and no quarterback in the drill. The final break of the pass pattern and the burst away from the defensive man are the points to be emphasized.

For the burst phase of either the "in" or "out" route, the receiver must remember to keep his momentum going at all cost. In order to maintain his speed as he

threat of being beat deep will cause the defender to physically turn and start running directly toward his own goal line, thus giving the receiver a better opportunity to break free.

The sprint phase of the pattern can be added to the glide drill once the coach is satisfied that the receivers have the idea of moving the defensive player into the desired location.

In practicing the sprint phase, the receiver should allow his head and shoulders to come slightly forward and accentuate the pumping of his arms when he has run a minimum of 10 yards downfield. This slight change in the receiver's body position and motion hopefully will cause the defensive player to feel that the receiver actually is going long.

The final stage of a pass pattern is the

makes his break, the receiver should think about making two 45-degree cuts rather than one 90-degree break, which often forces the receiver to slow down as he cuts.

Another point to be stressed is that the path of the receiver's burst should bring him back toward the line of scrimmage. This adjustment in his final path will cause greater separation from the defender and will minimize the likelihood of the pass being intercepted.

During practice, the defensive man should try to maintain his original position on the receiver, but it is not necessary for the defender to react to the final burst phase of the tight end or wide receiver's pass pattern. The defensive man may continue backing up toward his own goal line when the cut is executed.

WINNING POINTS
- In glide phase, run at defender if he is away from reception point.; run away from defender if he is near reception point.
- In sprint phase, convince defender of intention to go deep.
- In burst phase: do not slow down or lose momentum; look back at quarterback; get hands in position; come back toward line of scrimmage to minimize interception risk.

Catching the Ball

Catching a pass is a learned skill that requires proper body position and alignment of the hands, good eye/hand coordination, and an intense concentration on the ball.

The first thing a receiver needs to learn is the correct way to hold his hands to make a reception. For all passes that are even with the receiver's numbers or above, the thumbs and the first

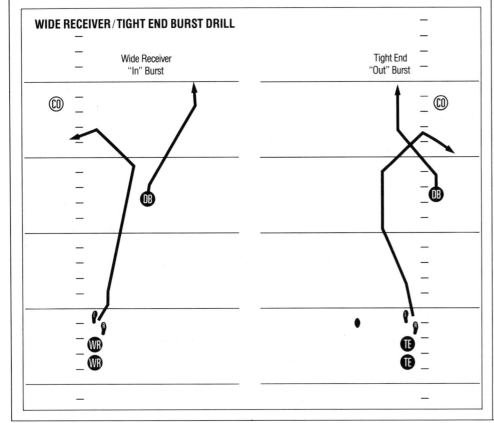

WIDE RECEIVER/TIGHT END BURST DRILL

Wide Receiver "In" Burst

Tight End "Out" Burst

The receiver keeps his thumbs together to catch passes above his numbers.

fingers of the receiver's hands should be together. They should form a basket or cone in which the ball will be caught.

With his hands in this position the receiver should be able to cradle the ball and make the catch. If the receiver is · having trouble making receptions and dropping passes, the problem usually will be that he has not cocked his wrists

and the palms of both hands are facing down. With the palms of his hands in this position, the ball on contact will have a natural tendency to be deflected down into the ground.

If the pass is delivered below the numbers, the receiver will have to change the position of his hands as he makes the catch. Instead of having the thumbs together, the receiver must put his little fingers together, causing his hands to form a basket or mitt in which to make the reception.

DRILL:

Hand Position I

The receivers line up facing a coach 10 yards away. There will be neither a ball nor movement in this drill. The receivers line up with their feet spread shoulder width apart, with a slight bend in their knees. They should be concentrating on the coach, with their arms and hands hanging relaxed at their sides. The coach calls out one of 15 possible locations for an imaginary pass and the receivers should reach to that position, making certain that their hands are being held the proper way.

The drill includes five distinct height positions, with each different height location further divided into right, center, and left. The height positions are high

(well above the receiver's helmet), pad (even with his shoulders), numbers (in the area of the center of his chest), belt (even with his hips), and low (an area even with the receiver's thighs).

As the location in called out, the players should instantly react by moving their hands to that area. The coach should

On low passes, the receiver forms a mitt with his little fingers touching.

Along with holding the hands in proper position, three important things receivers must do are reach out for passes so that the hands and ball are in sight, keep the wrists cocked back on high passes, and form a receiving mitt, or cone.

check each player, making certain that his hand relationship is correct, before allowing the group to move on to another pass position. This is a drill that receivers also can do on their own or with a teammate prior to practice.

One of the most important rules a young receiver can learn is, whenever it is physically possible, he should always extend his arms toward the pass so that he has his hands and the ball in his vision as he makes the reception. Most

young receivers do not reach out for the ball, and consequently end up desperately trying to locate their hands at the last second as the ball arrives. Work this rule into the above drill so that in addition to properly aligning their hands, the re-

No matter the location of the pass, the receiver should attempt to extend his arms in the direction of the ball (left). *On over-the-head passes* (right), *the hands are held in the same way as for passes below the waist.*

ceivers now make a point of extending their arms and hands toward the coach.

DRILL:
Hand Position II

Using the same drill setup as above, the coach now should have the players turn their backs toward him, facing down the field. When making a reception on a pass that is coming over a shoulder or directly over his head, a receiver must place his hands and fingers in the same position as he would when catching a pass thrown below his waist. For this type of reception the tips of the little fingers of both hands should be touching, fingers spread, with the thumbs forming the outside of the catching area.

The coach will call out one of three areas (right, center, left) for the receivers to react to: for each call they will reach up with their arms and hands with their fingers in the proper position. Once the coach is certain that each player understands the proper finger alignment, he should repeat the drill, this time concentrating on having the receivers reach back so that they are able to see their hands and the ball at the same time.

Now introduce the ball to the drill. We are concerned only with the receiver making the reception with his hands in the correct position. The player should have the opportunity to catch as many passes as possible in the various locations that were covered in the previous drills.

It is best for the coach to have the wide receivers and tight ends line up and make receptions first on the right side of the ball. After the receivers have caught balls in a number of locations on the right, the coach can then switch the drill and have them work on the left side of the ball. This also is a drill that is excellent for two players to conduct by themselves, alternating as the passer and the receiver.

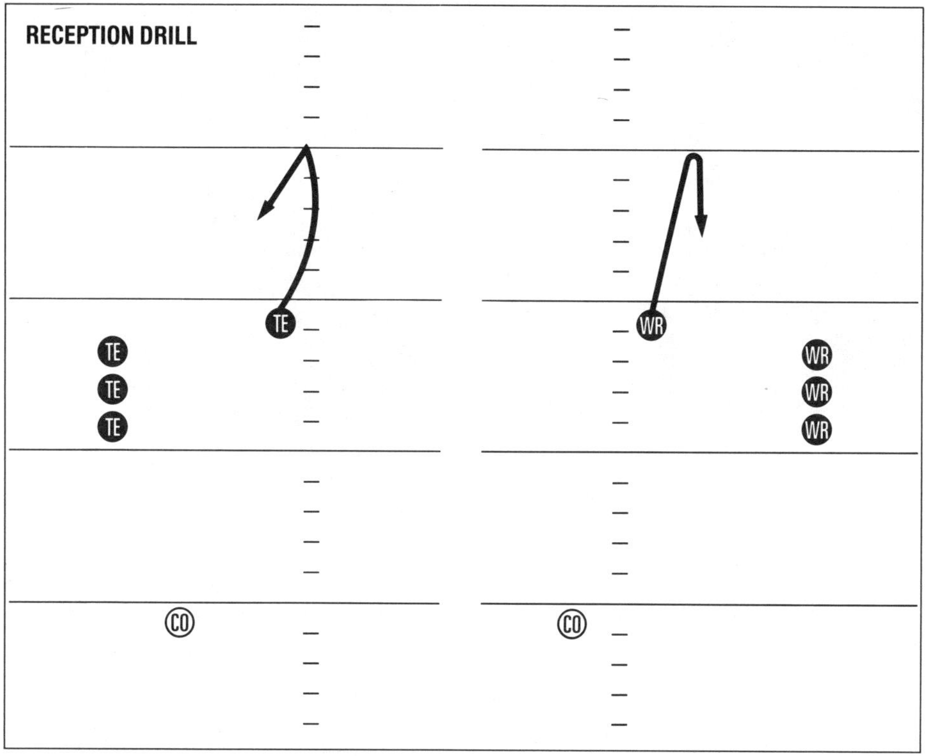

DRILL:

Hand Position III

The drill is run with one player participating at a time. The tight end and wide receiver, who are in the drill, should line up with their backs to the coach. The players alternate making the reception. As they line up, the coach will tell the designated receiver in the drill either left or right. On the command of "Hut!" by the coach, the player who is to receive the pass will drive up the field and turn to the side designated. As he turns, he must come back toward the coach, locate the ball, reach out with his arms and hands, place his fingers in the correct alignment, and make the catch.

One teaching point that will help young receivers is that they should think of using the inside of the palm of one hand as the area for making contact with the point of the ball. The hand used

RECEPTION DRILL

TE TE TE

CO

WR WR WR

CO

It is important for the receiver to "put the ball away" as soon as a reception is made. The mitt hand is the hand that is used to turn the ball into the body. With the other hand the receiver turns the ball securely into his armpit.

as the mitt of the catch always should be the hand on the side of the pass; the other hand should be used in surrounding and controlling the ball. If the ball arrives on the right side of the receiver, the player should think of using the palm of his right hand as the mitt or contact point. The left hand then helps secure the ball during the catch and, later, in securing the ball between his arm and body.

Each time that a tight end or wide receiver makes a reception it is vital that they immediately "put the ball away," grasping it firmly by the point and squeezing it tight to their body with their forearm. The hand of the receiver that serves as the mitt, making contact with the point of the ball, should remain on the point, and he should use this hand to begin turning the ball in toward the center of his body. Using his other hand, the player should continue turning the ball, allowing him to place the uncovered end or back of the ball securely up into his armpit.

On a pass that comes over the receiver's head, it will not be necessary to physically turn the ball. Contact with the mitt hand will take place with the point of the ball that is farthest from the receiver's body. In this case, the receiver need only guide the ball with his oppo-

The hand to the side of the pass is the hand the ball will contact first.

site hand into the armpit position and grasp it firmly to his body with the mitt hand and arm.

Whenever a receiver makes a catch in a game, he is going to be hit by a defensive player. Because of this fact, the receiver must know how to secure—and

---

WINNING POINTS
- Hold thumbs and first fingers together to catch the passes even with jersey numbers or above; be sure wrists are cocked so palms are not facing down.
- Hold little fingers together for passes below jersey numbers.
- Extend arms toward pass so that hands and ball are in field of vision.
- For passes coming over a shoulder or directly overhead, hold hands with little fingertips touching, fingers spread.
- Use hand on side of pass as contact point; other hand secures ball.
- Put the ball away immediately, turning it with contact hand and using other hand to place ball in armpit.
- Expect to be hit, whether reception is made or not.

---

must concentrate on securing—the ball immediately after each catch. One of the cardinal sins that can be committed by any wide receiver or tight end is to make a great reception, run for a big gain, and then turn the ball over to the defense by fumbling when he is hit.

Before a receiver can think of running with the ball, he must accomplish two things. First, he must make the reception, and second, he must secure the ball. Every yard he gains after making the catch is frosting on the cake. But it only can be done if he has the ball in his possession.

Wide Receiver Pass Patterns

Four things must happen for any passing attack to be successful. First, the quarterback must have sufficient time to set up and throw the pass. Next, the pass must be accurately thrown. Third, the receiver must run the proper pass route so that he is in the correct location to make the reception, and finally, the receiver must make the catch.

Obviously the wide receiver does not have any control over the first two factors in the passing attack, but he does have full responsibility for parts three and four.

In the preceding section, the physical techniques and skills needed to properly make a catch were covered in detail. Now come the various pass patterns or routes that a wide receiver runs.

NFL coaches usually refer to a "passing tree" when discussing all of the various patterns a receiver must learn. Each different pattern will not only be given a separate name, but often they will be given a number. Referring to a particular pattern by only a number shortens the time needed to call a play in the huddle and also gives the quarterback the flexibility of using the numbers when he is calling an audible at the line of scrimmage.

Pass patterns, along with being individually named and numbered, are placed into groups based upon the depth (distance from the line of scrimmage) that they are run. There usually are three groupings of patterns based on the distance that a receiver will run down the field from the line of scrimmage before he makes his break and goes into the burst phase of his pattern. These three area designations are short (six yards from the line), medium (10 to 14 yards from the line), and deep, which refers to any pattern run deeper than medium depth. The receiver needs to get a good feel for these different depths, so that he automatically knows where he is as he runs up the field.

DRILL:

Pass Depths

Prior to ever having a receiver run an actual route, it is good for the coach to set up a drill where the receiver runs straight up the field and verbally calls out the depth grouping that he is in at that moment.

As the wide receiver runs up the field, he should begin by calling out, "short, short, short." Once he has passed six yards from the line of scrimmage, he should begin shouting, "medium, medium, medium." After 14 yards, he would call out, "deep, deep, deep." For some passing attacks, the medium area may end and the deep area begin at 12 yards. It is up to the coach to decide upon and teach his players the beginning and ending depths of each passing zone.

A receiver must understand the importance of running every pattern at the exact distance specified by his coach. Only when the wide receivers execute exact pass patterns can the timing of the pass offense ever be achieved. If the receiver does not go far enough up the field before he breaks on his pattern, the quarterback will not be ready to throw, giving the defenders a greater opportu-

nity to react to the pass. When a receiver goes too far upfield or if he is slow in running his pattern, the quarterback usually will lose his throwing rhythm. Worse, because he must hold the ball for too long a time, the passer will be forced to run out of the pocket and often will be sacked by the defense.

Wide receivers and quarterbacks must develop a complete trust that the other will do his job correctly. Each of them understands and accepts that his success, and that of the offense, is dependent upon the actions and abilities of the other. Through hours of practicing together and talking about what they are trying to accomplish, they soon learn to think and act almost as one.

Once the coach and receivers are comfortable that the receivers understand the different depths at which groups of patterns are to be run, the wide receivers can learn the various individual pass patterns from the passing tree.

Due to the way plays and audibles are called at the line of scrimmage, some of the patterns in the passing tree (such as "delay," "cross," and "seam") will not be given corresponding numbers. Often an offensive coordinator will refer to a seam pass as a "Q 8," indicating to the receiver that it is a quick "post."

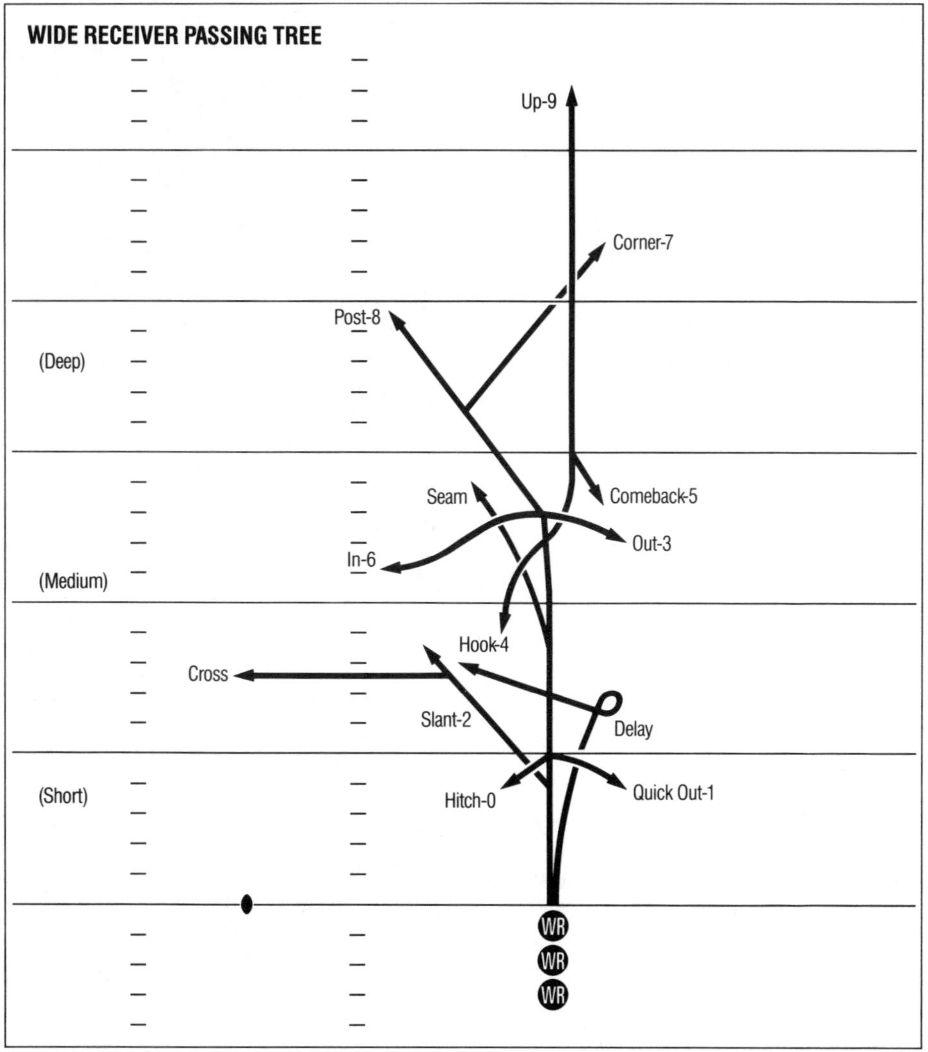

WIDE RECEIVER PASSING TREE

Up-9

Corner-7

Post-8

(Deep)

Seam   Comeback-5

Out-3

In-6

(Medium)

Hook-4

Cross

Slant-2   Delay

(Short)

Hitch-0   Quick Out-1

WR
WR
WR

In order that receivers not become overwhelmed when first learning all the routes on the passing tree, it is best for them to be introduced to the patterns by their depth designations.

DRILL:

Short Patterns

It is best to learn to run all patterns without using a ball in the drill. After the players can run the routes correctly, a quarterback and ball can be added. Because these are patterns which are thrown quickly, the receiver should drive straight up the field, breaking the pattern at the designated depth, immediately turn his head and eyes around to the quarterback, and get his hands in position to make the catch.

When running the "hitch" pattern, the receiver should drive hard for five yards, making the defender think he is going to run deep. He then should plant his outside foot to stop his momentum up the field, instantly turning his body back toward the ball, with his hands chest high ready to receive the pass.

For the "quick out" route, the receiver again drives off the line. At four yards he starts his two 45-degree turns to the outside. Once he has redirected his momentum toward the sideline, he should further adjust his path so that, as he

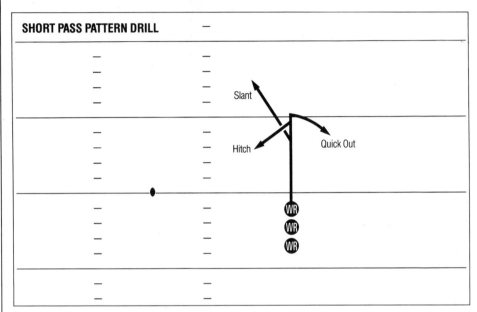

SHORT PASS PATTERN DRILL

Slant

Hitch

Quick Out

WR
WR
WR

goes out, he is also coming slightly back to the line of scrimmage. It is very important for all wide receivers to expect the "quick out" pass to be delivered low, often arriving well below the receiver's waist, necessitating a catch with the little fingers together, forming the receiving cone.

The "slant" pass is different from the other two short-pass routes in that the receiver will continue running up the field after making his break. As he reaches a depth of four yards, the receiver should redirect his path in toward the center of

the field at a 45-degree angle. Because he has not had to stop his sprint off the line of scrimmage, he must expect to run at least six yards before receiving the pass. All receivers must be prepared for a collision when running any pass pattern of this type into the center of the field where the majority of defensive players are. This makes it all the more important that the receiver instantly put the ball away, protecting it against a possible fumble upon impact.

As the wide receiver begins to learn to

When running a "hitch" route, come back to the ball with hands chest high.

Wide receivers should expect a "quick out" pass to be delivered low.

run the six medium pass patterns, it is a good idea to have another wide receiver line up as a defensive player using either inside or outside coverage. It is not necessary for the defender to react to the final cut, but by having a defensive player on the field, the receiver will be forced to run his pattern in the manner that we

introduced in the beginning of the section. The player must think to himself as he releases, "If the defender is where I want to go, I must move him from the area. If the defender is opposite of where I want to go, then I must keep him there with my pattern."

When learning to run the pass routes in the medium area, the receiver must concentrate on the position of the defender and he must remember to focus on the four parts of his pattern—the start, glide, sprint, and burst. As he releases from the line of scrimmage, he

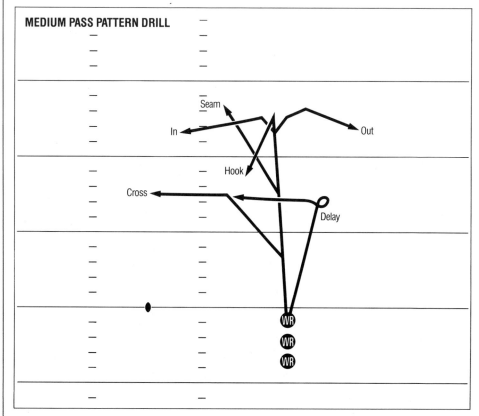

MEDIUM PASS PATTERN DRILL

Seam

In

Out

Hook

Cross

Delay

WR

WR

WR

must have decided on the exact method he will use and path he will take when running the pass pattern called by the coach.

DRILL:

Medium Patterns

The "delay" pass route is run by the wide receiver releasing off the line of scrimmage at a slight angle away from the ball. On this type of pass, another eligible receiver from the inside runs deep through the wide receiver's area first. When the wide receiver reaches six yards, he should pivot in, running back at a slight angle toward the center of the field. This is a type of pass which is not caught far down the field. However, because of the time it takes the pattern to develop, the quarterback will use a medium pass drop. The receiver should be prepared to receive the ball anytime after breaking to the inside.

The "cross" pattern comes off the slant pass route, which is run in the short area. After angling in at four yards, the receiver breaks off his slant path at eight yards and continues running directly across the field. He can continue to allow his path to take him slightly away from the line of scrimmage, but he must be certain that he does not go so deep that he runs into defenders who are dropping into zone coverage. The ball usually will not get to the receiver until he is nearing, or has just passed, the center of the field.

When the receiver is learning the "hook" pattern, he must be reminded to use his glide to best position the defensive player. When he has reached a depth of 12 yards from the line of scrimmage, the receiver should lower his hips, plant his outside foot to stop his momentum, turn to the inside with his body, and begin coming back in a direct line to the quarterback. The ball should be delivered chest high, at the numbers, for the receiver to make the catch.

Both the "out" and the "in" pass patterns must be run in relationship to the play of the defensive man. The wide receiver should run up the field 12 yards and then begin to make his two 45-degree cuts to either the inside or the outside. With both patterns, the receiver must have a slight angle back to the line of scrimmage. Because the ball is in the air for a longer time on the out pass, thus giving the defender a greater opportunity to react while the ball is in the air, it becomes even more important for the receiver running the "out" route to come back toward the line of scrimmage to make the catch.

The final pass pattern in the medium area, the "seam," is really a quick post pattern. Because this is a pass route that relies on speed, the receiver usually will sprint straight up the field. At eight yards, the receiver should adjust his path, angling slightly in toward the center of the field. Based upon the coverage run by the defense, the receiver can expect to get the ball any time within the next six or seven yards. When running a seam route the receiver must make certain that he angles in only enough to get away from the defender and not enough to carry him into the center of the field. Any wide receiver running a seam route should expect the ball to be drilled into his chest and not lofted over his head so that he can run under it.

DRILL:

Deep Patterns

There are four pass patterns for the wide receivers to master in the deep area. As with the other drills, we should have a wide receiver on defense; the quarterback and ball should not be brought into the drill until after the coach is certain that the receivers have learned and can execute each pattern correctly.

These deep pass patterns, with the exception of the "comeback," usually require the receiver to catch the ball as it reaches his hands in front of him as he runs toward the opponent's goal line. The

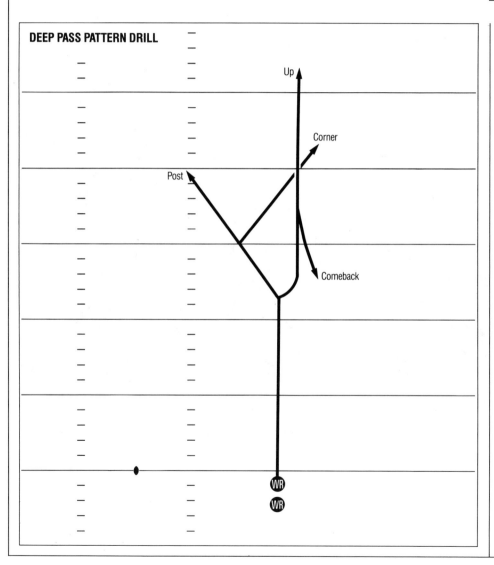

DEEP PASS PATTERN DRILL

coach and the player should review the method of catching a pass that reaches a receiver in this manner, and the player must remember to keep his little fingers together. The receiver needs to make every effort to reach for the ball with his hands, always trying to keep the ball and his fingers in his line of vision.

The first deep pass route, the "post" pattern, is a route that is run toward the center of the field at a deep angle toward the goal post. The receiver will attack up the field for 12 yards and then break in at a 45-degree angle toward the center of the field. The quarterback usually will loft the pass to the receiver, giving him an opportunity to run under the ball at full speed to make the reception.

The "corner" route is a pattern that comes off the post pattern. When a receiver is running a "corner," he again will attack up the field and break into the center of the field just as he did on the "post" route. But after he has driven in five or six steps, instead of continuing into the middle of the field, he will break on another 45-degree angle back to the corner of the field. To complete a "corner" pattern, the ball must be in the air for a great deal of time and the wide receiver must continue running and never give up on making the catch. The ball should be delivered just over the receiver's out-

On deep patterns, such as a "corner," receivers must be ready to stretch or make a diving catch, while running flat out.

side shoulder. But because it is such a difficult pass to throw with accuracy, the receiver must be prepared to make a diving catch on the ball.

Many young receivers do not understand that the "up" pass pattern only becomes effective when the receiver has been running the medium pass routes correctly and with success. The defensive back must become so concerned with stopping the completions on the medium routes that he forgets to stay deep and allows the receiver to get even with him. Wide receivers like to refer to the "up" pass pattern as the "even and leav'n" route. Whenever a wide receiver can cause a defender to stop retreating, thus giving the receiver an opportunity to get even with him while running full speed, he should be able to speed past him toward the goal line.

On the "up" route, the receiver should run up the field using his glide to get the defender into the proper position. At 12 yards, the receiver should angle his path to the outside of the defensive player. This adjustment in his pass pattern should bring the wide receiver about three yards closer to the sideline. He then should continue his route straight up the field, looking over his inside shoulder to determine the path of the ball. Ideally, the ball on an "up" pass

should be thrown so that the receiver can make the reception on his outside, after it has sailed over his head.

The final deep pass pattern is the "comeback" route and it is run off of the up pattern. When running a comeback route, the wide receiver should do exactly the same maneuvers as he did when running the "up." The difference is that instead of continuing up the field, the receiver breaks the pattern and comes back toward the line of scrimmage to make the reception. As the wide receiver reaches 15 yards, he should begin lowering his hips, thus allowing him to plant his foot at 17 yards, stop his momentum, turn his body toward the sideline, and come back. Once the receiver makes the reception at about 14 yards, he should be prepared to put the ball away, turn to the outside of the field, and gain as many yards as possible.

Tight End Pass Patterns

Tight ends have their own passing tree to learn and to use as a map of the different pass routes they will be called upon to run.

As with wide receivers, tight ends first must learn the different depths at which their patterns will be executed, before actually learning the pass routes. Based upon the drop of the quarterback, the

style of pass blocking, and the timing of the passing game, the tight end's passing tree has three depths: short (line of scrimmage to six yards), medium (7 to 14 yards), and deep (more than 15 yards).

The tight ends should run the same depth drill as the wide receivers, where they release up the field, one at a time, and call out the different depths they are in as they run 20 yards upfield. Like the wide receivers, tight ends must understand the importance of running the routes at very specific distances so the quarterback can develop complete confidence that they always will be where they are supposed to be as the pass is thrown. It must be reiterated that a successful passing game is based on everyone doing his job just as it is drawn up and designed on every play. The last thing a quarterback needs, in a game or practice, is a receiver who constantly is running patterns incorrectly.

Tight ends then should be introduced to the entire passing tree so that they gain a general idea of the different patterns used at each depth.

Once a feel for the depths of the patterns and a general knowledge of the pass routes has been demonstrated by the tight ends, they can begin learning how to correctly run the various pass routes on their tree.

TIGHT END PASSING TREE

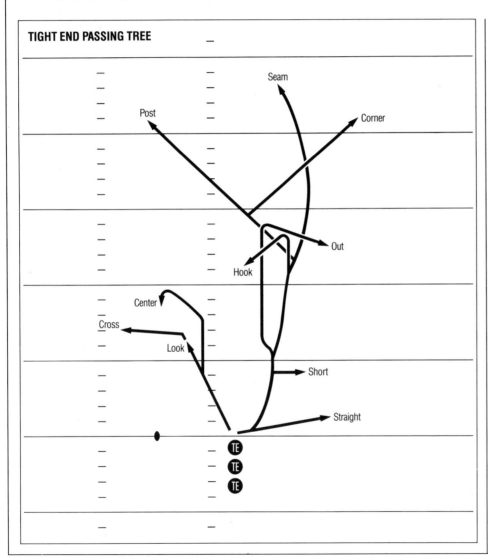

Seam

Post

Corner

Out

Hook

Center

Cross

Look

Short

Straight

TE
TE
TE

Tight ends must quickly look back for the ball when running short routes.

The players should start working in the short area, learning how to execute the "straight," "short," and "look" pass patterns. The tight ends must remember that passes thrown in the short area are delivered very quickly and they require the receiver to quickly turn his head and get his hands immediately into position to make the reception. Another tight end can line up as a linebacker in the drill; he does not need to react.

DRILL:

Short Tight End Patterns

The "straight" pass pattern requires that the tight end run at an angle directly away from the ball to the sideline. The tight end must keep in mind that he probably will receive the ball by his fifth or sixth step, so he must look quickly over his outside shoulder and get his hands up and back, little fingers together, ready to make the catch.

When running the "short" pass route, the player should release to his outside past the linebacker, go up the field four yards, and break directly toward the sideline. As he makes his break, it is important for the tight end to look immediately for the ball and be prepared to make the reception.

The "look" pass is different in that the tight end will release inside of any de-

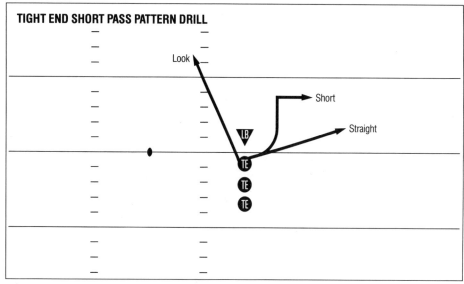

TIGHT END SHORT PASS PATTERN DRILL

fender who might be playing in front of him. Now, instead of looking for the ball over his outside shoulder, as he did in the straight and short pass routes, the tight end must look immediately to the inside. Again, this is the type of pass that is delivered very quickly by the quarterback and often is used if the quarterback sees the defense in very loose coverage. The look pattern demands that the tight end be conscious of putting the ball away as soon as he gets it, because when it is run during the course of a regular game, there usually will be a very quick collision with a defensive player.

DRILL:

Medium Tight End Patterns

When moving on to drills for the patterns in the medium area, it is a good idea not only to have a player lined up as a linebacker, but also to have a player lined up as a defensive back either inside or outside of the tight end. This player should only try to keep his initial position relative to the tight end, and need not react to the pattern being run; he merely backpedals up the field as the tight end runs.

The tight end must think in terms of running his route, either moving the de-

TIGHT END MEDIUM PASS PATTERN DRILL

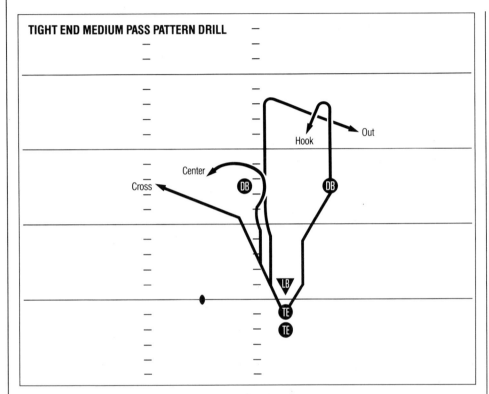

Out

Hook

Center

Cross

DB   DB

LB

TE

TE

crease his distance from the defender.

If he is running a "center" route, the tight end can bend slightly to the outside after his release, driving a few steps directly at the defensive player, thus keeping the defender away from the tight end's final destination, which is directly

A tight end's "center" route is most effective against outside coverage.

fensive back from his initial location or keeping him in his relative position.

When the tight end runs either the "cross" or the "center" pass pattern, he must release on the inside of the linebacker. If the defensive back is playing him to the inside, he must attempt to drive the defender straight back a few steps prior to making his break and go-

ing into the burst phase of the pass route. The tight end's job on a "cross" or "center" pattern is much easier if the defensive back is using an outside technique to cover him.

On the "cross" route, versus outside coverage, the tight end should think, as he releases to the inside, of running as hard as possible across the field to in-

in front of the quarterback.

The release from the line of scrimmage that will be used by the tight end when executing either a "hook" or "out" pass pattern will depend on the position of the linebacker and the initial pre-snap location of the defensive back. Often in a game the linebacker physically will take away the inside or outside by his alignment. When this happens, the tight end must go to whichever side the linebacker has left vulnerable and understand that the most important thing is to get his release as quickly as possible.

If the linebacker lines up directly in front of the tight end, as he will in this drill, the release by the tight end may be either inside or outside depending on the location of the defensive back.

For the "hook" pattern, when the tight end sees the defensive back stationed to the inside, he should release outside the linebacker and drive up the field a few steps before beginning to angle to the outside bringing the defender with him, hopefully widening the area in which he may run his pattern. Should the defender be to the outside prior to the snap, the tight end would again take an outside release, but instead of driving straight up the field initially, the receiver should now immediately drive to the outside hip of the defensive back, causing him to move farther and farther away from the tight end's desired final destination.

The tight end needs to drive up the field at least 12 yards into the "hook" pattern before he begins to lower his hips, coming under control in preparation for stopping and turning his body back into the inside of the field, facing directly toward the quarterback. Remember, it is very important for the tight end to keep coming back toward the quarterback and not merely turn and stop.

The tight end should be prepared to receive the "hook" pass chest high at his numbers. Once he has secured the ball, the tight end should think about and practice immediately turning up the field, fighting to gain additional yardage.

Because the route for the "out" pass goes away from the ball, the release of the tight end must be exactly opposite than on the "hook" pass in terms of how he leaves the line in relationship to the positioning of the defensive back.

From the tight end's perspective, the ideal position of the defensive back on an "out" pattern would be to the inside. That would mean the tight end could release inside and drive immediately at the defender's inside hip, moving him away from the final destination. Once the tight end sees that he has the defender moving to the inside, he can begin driving straight up the field. At 12 yards, the receiver should execute two 45-degree cuts, allowing him to break to the outside of the field toward the sideline. (Remember always to work back toward the line of scrimmage as you run the burst phase of the "out" pattern.)

If, however, the defender is on the outside, the exact place where the tight end wants to go, the job of the tight end becomes more difficult. Again using an inside release, the tight end now will drive straight up the field for a few yards, causing the defensive back to work at keeping his separation. After four yards, the receiver should angle to the inside for a few yards before driving straight up the field in the glide segment of the pass route. Hopefully, the defensive back will be turned in toward the center of the field by this time and not be in position to react quickly as the tight end breaks to the outside. The final burst phase of the "out" pattern should be the same versus inside or outside coverage.

DRILL:

Deep Tight End Patterns

For all three of the patterns in the deep area, the tight end should make his break at about 12 yards. As with the patterns in the medium area, the receiver must be aware of the technique being used by the defensive back who is in coverage.

While it is good to be able to position the defender away from the final destination of the pass pattern, the tight end must not sacrifice speed in getting into the deep area. Usually the outside release off the line of scrimmage by the tight end will not only be the easiest but also the quickest. Tight ends should be reminded that most of these deep passes will be coming over their heads and the reception should be attempted with the little fingers touching to form the mitt for the ball. Often a tight end will find that he is running a pass route against a safety and not a cornerback. While most tight ends do not have the speed or athletic ability of a wide receiver, the safety generally will not be equal in strength and physical ability to a cornerback. Hence, the tight end's opportunities to get open should even out.

When running a "post" pattern, the tight end should attack up the field for 12 yards and then break at a 45-degree angle into the center of the field. The quarterback usually will lead the tight end on the post route. He should loft the ball, allowing the receiver to have an opportunity to run under the pass as it makes its downward descent, and catch it while still running at full speed.

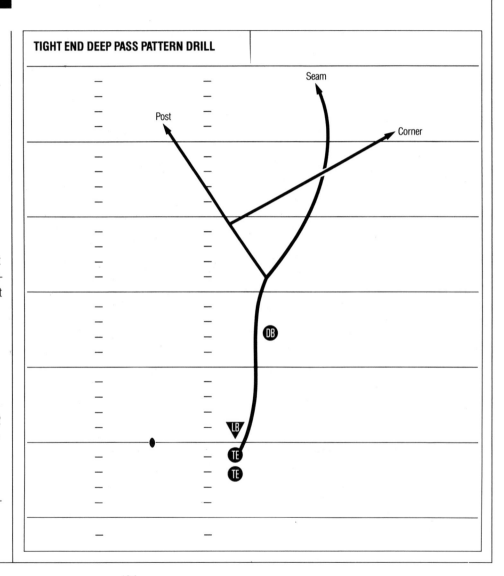

TIGHT END DEEP PASS PATTERN DRILL

The "corner" pattern will be run off the post route. Once the tight end has driven to the inside on the post route, he should break a second time. This second break should be to the outside at a 45-degree angle and should put the tight end on a path toward the corner of the field. Because the ball is in the air a long time on a corner route, the tight end must expect to run a considerable distance before the ball comes over his outside shoulder. A "corner" pass is a very precise pattern to throw and complete and it will require a great deal of timing by the quarterback and the tight end if it is to be successful.

For the tight ends, the "seam" pass will serve the same function as does the "up" pattern for the wide receivers. When running the seam, the tight end should release outside of the linebacker, attack up the field, and, at 12 yards, bend slightly to the outside of the field. After bending out for a few yards, the tight end must adjust his path so that he is again coming back toward the center of the field. Because of the outside position of most safeties, the tight end will seldom be in position to break to the outside of the defender as a wide receiver would do when running an "up" pattern.

Blocking

Being a good blocker may not be as im-portant for a wide receiver as it is for a tight end, but it is a tremendous asset for players in either position. Many long runs, or short receptions that turn into long gains, are the direct result of a wide receiver's willingness to block. The block by a wide receiver may not be as devastating as the block thrown by an of-fensive lineman, but it can be just as ef-fective in preventing a defensive player from tackling the man with the ball.

Wide Receiver Blocking

The major method of blocking on run-ning plays for most wide receivers will be the mirror type of block. In this block, the receiver should approach the defensive back at speed, as he would if it were a pass play. The receiver should always try to create in the mind of the defender as much doubt as possible about whether the play is a run or a pass.

It is important for the receiver to con-tinue running down the field if he sees that the defender is fooled and is contin-uing to backpedal, playing pass de-fense. When the defensive back realizes that it is a running play, stops his back-pedal, and prepares to attack the line of scrimmage, the receiver must stop his movement upfield and bring his own body under control.

The wide receiver then should begin to shorten his stride, widening his feet so that they are a little wider than his hips. As his steps become more choppy, the receiver should begin to slightly flex his knees and lower his hips. It is impor-tant for the receiver to keep his back straight, his neck bowed, head up, with his eyes focused on the numbers on the defender's jersey.

At this point, the number-one objec-tive of the blocker is to stay in front of the defender, positioning his body so that he is between the defender and the ball carrier. The wide receiver must an-ticipate the defensive man's movement to the ball and, consequently, must al-ways be aware of where the ball is being run.

DRILL:
Mirror Blocking

This drill requires two wide receivers, one posing as a defensive back. The man playing on defense begins to back up into coverage and then, at any time, breaks his coverage and tries to go to the ball carrier.

On a running play that is attacking the middle of the field, or is being run to the opposite side of the field, the wide re-ceiver should try to adjust the glide por-tion of his release so that he moves to the inside of the defender. With this inside re-

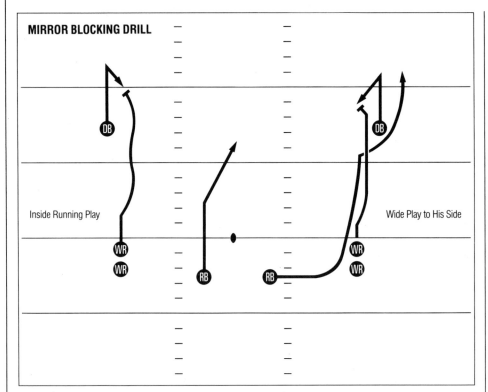

MIRROR BLOCKING DRILL

Inside Running Play

Wide Play to His Side

DB

WR
WR

RB

RB

WR
WR

DB

ing, and hitting should continue until the whistle blows and the play has ended.

When mirror blocking on a wide running play to his side of the field, the wide receiver and the ball carrier must work as a team. The wide receiver must

Always stay between the defender and ball carrier when mirror blocking.

lationship to the defensive man, it will be much easier for the wide receiver to position his body to stop the defensive back's pursuit of the ball carrier.

As he makes contact with the defensive back, the wide receiver should not lunge and overextend himself. Instead, it is very important for the blocker to strike the defender's chest in an upward mo-

tion with the palms of both hands. As contact is made, the wide receiver should recoil away from the defender, reset himself in a good position, and prepare to once again make contact.

In the drill, this action should continue only for two or three hits. But each wide receiver must understand that in a game, this continuous action of hitting, recoil-

On run blocks, the wide receiver forces the defender to take a side. Once the defender commits, the receiver blocks him in that direction.

be the same as he used when blocking from an inside position.

One important fact needs to be reemphasized to wide receivers: the importance of driving off the line of scrimmage in the same manner on every play, whether it is a run or pass. When a receiver releases the same way, the defender is constantly threatened with being beat deep with a long pass for a touchdown. This continuous threat causes indecision in the defender's mind and allows the receiver to run all of his patterns with greater ease. It also creates much better opportunities for the wide receiver to successfully block on running plays.

Tight End Blocking

The requirements for blocking by a tight end are much more complex and varied than those of a wide receiver. Often the tight end will find that he is at the exact point where the ball is being run and his block will determine the success or failure of the play.

In many instances the tight end will serve the offense as an additional offensive lineman, one required to be able to execute a number of different blocks on a variety of defensive people. Because of the complexity of his blocking, adequate time must be allotted in practice

know that the running back will key off of his block and will cut to the opposite side. At the same time, the running back must be confident that the receiver will continuously try to block the defender.

Knowing that the ball carrier is going to cut away from the defensive man, the blocker must approach the defensive back straight on, forcing the defensive back to take a side. Once the defender has committed to either the right or left, the wide receiver must continue to block him in that direction. The wide receiver's actual blocking technique will

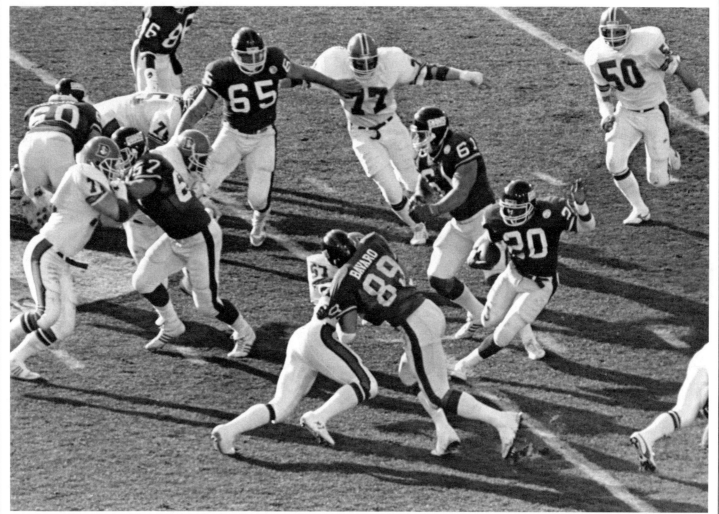

Tight ends (such as number 89, above) serve as additional offensive linemen, often blocking at the point of attack.

for the tight ends to learn and develop the necessary techniques for each block.

The first tight end block is the drive block. In this block the tight end's major objective is to drive the defensive man, who is lined up in front of him, off the line of scrimmage. It is not necessary for him to turn the defender to either the right or the left.

DRILL:
Drive Block

The drill begins with one tight end playing a linebacker and lining up in a two-point stance, feet spread the width of his shoulders, knees slightly bent, back straight, head up, and the palms of both hands open facing the offensive man at a position just even with his jersey numbers.

A coach should give the tight end the snap count to start each drill and call out a cadence when he sets at the line of scrimmage. It is also very important for the coach to position himself correctly so he can observe the blocker, making certain that the tight end is using proper blocking technique.

The defensive man should merely react to the block and not attempt to charge across the line of scrimmage. That way, the tight end is not worried about penetration from the defensive

man, and he is free to concentrate on rolling off the front foot and taking a good short power step, straight at the defender, with his back foot as he starts the drive block. The blocker must also concentrate on making certain that he does not raise his upper body straight up into the air. Keeping his shoulders low, his back straight, and his head up is very important for the tight end as he moves into the block.

When the actual contact is made, the tight end must have both feet on the ground shoulder width apart and be prepared to take short, powerful steps as he drives the linebacker backward. The blocker must explode with his legs in a forward and upward motion. Using the palms of both hands, he should strike the linebacker in the numbers, extending his arms as he feels the contact of his hands on the defender's jersey.

Finally, the tight end must finish off the blocking by thrusting his hips forward, driving his feet, extending and pressing up and back with his body, arms, and hands while attempting to drive the defender off the line of scrimmage.

The next block that a tight end will have to use on a linebacker playing in front of him is the hook block. The hook block is necessary on running plays that

are going wide to the tight end's side of the alignment, and it is used to keep the defensive man from going to the outside (toward the sideline).

DRILL:
Hook Block

In practicing the hook block, the linebacker first lines up head-up on the tight end. Later, he shifts into the more difficult position to block, which is slightly to the outside of the offensive player. The defensive man should play without penetration as he did in the drive-block drill.

When a tight end is attempting to hook block a man who is directly in front of him, he should step with his back foot to a point slightly to the outside of the linebacker's outside hip. The tight end must once again make certain that he keeps his body low and square as he begins his block.

As the blocker takes his first step, he should begin driving the palm of his inside hand directly at the center of the defender's chest. The tight end should then drive the palm of his other hand into the outside armpit of the linebacker. He should then push up with the hand on the chest of the defender and back with his outside hand, thus causing the defender to be turned toward the middle of the field.

The tight end's first step on a hook block is to the outside with his rear foot. He then attacks the defender, hitting him in the chest and outside armpit, and moving him toward the center of the field with short, choppy steps.

From this position the blocker must take short, choppy steps, working his hips quickly to the outside of the defensive man. Once he has turned the defender back to the inside, the tight end should finish the block by thrusting forward and driving the defensive player back toward the center of the field.

When trying to hook a linebacker who aligns himself in a wide position, the tight end usually will find that he has to adjust his style of blocking and steps. In order to hook block a wide defensive player, the tight end must start the block as if he were drive blocking the linebacker. The tight end must attempt to get the line-

backer to come back into him, rather than widening out, as he would versus a drive block.

Rolling over his front foot, the blocker should take a short step with his back foot directly at the center of the defensive man's chest. He should make contact with the linebacker as he takes a quick power step with his inside foot. The third step, with his outside foot, should be to the outside of the linebacker's hip. As the blocker takes this third step, he must slide his outside arm into the armpit of the defender and prepare to turn him back to the inside. Once the tight end has achieved this outside position, he should finish off the block in the same manner described above.

In the previous two blocks the tight end has learned to block on a man who is lined up directly in front or slightly outside of him. The next two blocks, the angle block and the double-team block, are used when the tight end is asked to block a defensive player who is lined up to his inside.

This inside defender usually will present two distinctly new and different problems for the tight end. First, the inside defensive player normally will be a defensive lineman who is bigger than the blocker. In addition to the size difference, the defensive man usually will be attempting to charge across the line of scrimmage at the snap of the ball, trying to get penetration, rather than reacting to the tight end's block as the linebacker did in the previous drills.

Again use another tight end as the defensive man when first working on the angle block. As the tight end becomes proficient in these blocks, a defensive player may be used to give the blocker a realistic feel for game conditions.

DRILL:
Angle Block

Whenever a tight end is called upon to execute an angle block, the first thing he must do is square up his stance on the line of scrimmage so that he can step with his inside foot as he initiates the block. On the snap, the tight end takes a short, three-inch angle step down the line of scrimmage, with the foot that is closest to the man he is assigned to block. This short step not only allows the blocker to get his head in front of the defensive man's charge, stopping penetration, but it also opens the blocker's hips, making it possible for him to attack the defender with a low, square blocking surface.

The tight end then must bring his far foot quickly across his body, keeping his feet spread and maintaining a wide base. This second step serves as the power base for the angle block, and the tight end must make certain to plant it aggressively on the ground.

Once the power foot slams into the ground, the blocker should explode into the defender using the big muscles of his legs. With this explosion, the tight end should jam the palm of his far hand, with as much force as possible, into the side of the defensive player. As opposed to the drive and hook blocks, where the tight end had the luxury of using both hands as he made the block, the angle block really only allows him to effectively use one hand. This one hand should generate as much force and explosion as possible and not merely be used to balance the blocker as contact is made.

Finally, the tight end must finish off the block by staying low, maintaining a wide base, continuing to drive his legs in short, choppy steps, thrusting his hips forward, and lifting up through the defender. The goal of the tight end in an angle block is to drive the defensive man down the line of scrimmage as far as he can before the play is stopped.

The next block for the tight end to learn is the double-team block. This block is similar to the angle block in that the tight end will be blocking on a defensive man who is lined up to his inside. However, for the double-team block the tight end will be joined by the offensive tackle who is lined up next to him.

The double-team block is the most forceful block the offense can use against a defensive player. The size, strength, explosion, and momentum of two men are pitted against one defender. It is a block which is designed to drive the defensive player laterally out of the hole and back toward his own goal line.

When a tight end and offensive tackle execute the double-team block correctly in a game, they not only will bury the defensive man, they will cut off the pursuit paths of many of his defensive teammates who are trying to reach the ball carrier.

DRILL:

Double-Team Block

The essence of this drill is the offensive tackle executing a drive block on the defensive player and, simultaneously, the tight end angle-blocking the same man.

Because the offensive tackles will take part in the drill, it is better to use a big offensive lineman as the defensive player. The play and reaction of the player posing as a defender is very important when we are teaching the double-team block. In the beginning, the defender must attack into the offensive tackle and then lean into the angle block as he feels it coming from the tight end. As the two blockers become more and more proficient in using the double-team block, the defensive man can be instructed to drop

The tight end's first step on a double-team block is toward his blocking partner. Then, hip-to-hip, they drive the defender backward off the line.

to the ground, creating a pile, and making it more difficult for the blockers to drive him out of the hole.

The primary thing for the offensive men to realize is that they are working together and must get into position so they are driving in the same direction and not pushing against one another.

In order to insure good position, the tight end needs to direct his first step more toward his blocking companion. This first step will allow the tight end to come hip to hip with the offensive tackle and permit both of the blockers to drive the defensive man back toward his own goal line.

Both offensive blockers must explode into the defensive man with a low, hard charge, with each of them striking the defender's body with the palm of the near hand. As this contact is made, the blockers must make certain that they are staying hip to hip and that each of them is driving up and through the defensive player.

If the blockers lose this hip-to-hip position, the defensive man usually will be able to create a seam between the two offensive players and split the block apart.

Once the offensive men have succeeded in starting to move the defender backwards, they should try to turn slightly and drive the defender away from the direction of the angle block. It is important to emphasize to young or beginning blockers that it is much more crucial to drive the defensive player back off the line of scrimmage than it is to turn him out of the hole.

Both blockers must concentrate on finishing off the block together, coming up and through the defensive man, driving him onto his back if possible, and continuing to block the defender until the coach calls the drill to a halt (or, in a game, until the whistle blows).

Tight ends also will become very important blockers for all goal-line and short-yardage running plays. Often, when blocking on these types of plays, the tight end will want to completely adjust his stance prior to the snap of the ball. Because a majority of his blocks will be straight ahead on a defender lined up directly in front of him, the tight end must get into the best stance for exploding across the line of scrimmage.

Most blockers will revert to a four-point, balanced stance with both hands on the ground four to six inches ahead of the front of their shoulder pads. In this position the blocker will want to put as much weight on his hands as possible. The tight end should have his feet slightly wider than his hips and his hips should be up in a position higher than his shoulder pads. By having a slight bend in his arms, the tight end can move his shoulders into the desired position.

Once the tight end has gotten into his stance, the next most important thing for him to concentrate on is getting off on the snap count. Knowing the exact instant the play is to begin is a tremendous advantage for all offensive players, and utilizing this advantage to the fullest is even more crucial in short-yardage or goal-line situations.

DRILL:

Short-Yardage/Goal-Line Blocking

The first block the tight end needs to learn on the goal line is the drive block. In setting up the drill, the tight ends who are playing on defense assume a stance similar to the one being used by the offensive blocker. The defender's weight needs to be forward, shoulders low, hips up, with his feet slightly wider than his hips. When the defensive man sees the tight end move, he should explode forward, driving with his legs, trying to get penetration across the line of scrimmage.

The blocker must get off on the snap count, exploding forward from the ground, using the big muscle groups of his upper legs, hips, and lower back. As he moves across the line of scrimmage, the tight end must keep his shoulders low and with quick, short steps drive the defender off the line. It is very important for the blocker to anticipate the forward charge of the defensive man and to focus on the defender throughout the entire block.

This is a type of block where the tight end should use his shoulder pads to facilitate the block and utilize his hands and arms on the ground to aid him in his forward movement. Each tight end must exhibit the resolve and dedication nec-

For drive blocking on short-yardage/goal line situations, the tight end may assume a four-point stance with weight forward, shoulders low, and hips up.

essary to push the defensive man as far off the line of scrimmage as possible.

In addition to the drive block, the tight end also may be asked to execute a hook block against a defensive man on short-yardage and goal-line running plays. This block often is required on running plays designed to go outside of the tight end.

Using the same drill setup as before, the tight end should get into the same four-point stance. At the snap of the ball, the blocker comes off the ball in a low, hard charge directly at the defensive player. As he makes contact, instead of driving the defender straight back, the blocker, scrambling with his hands and feet, will now swing his hips around so that he is in an outside position on the defensive man. The goal of the blocker when using a hook block must be to guarantee that the defensive man does not get either penetration across the line of scrimmage or have the ability to pursue the ball carrier toward the sideline.

WINNING POINTS
- Wide receivers must release off line of scrimmage the same way on running or passing plays.
- On wide receiver mirror blocks, anticipate defender's movement to ball or force him to commit; stay between defender and ball carrier.
- Do not lunge on blocks; make contact, recoil, and make contact again; continue hitting until play has ended.
- On tight end blocks, stay low and square; take short, choppy steps; explode forward and upward into defender; finish block until whistle blows.
- On tight end double-team blocks, maintain hip-to-hip position with offensive tackle; drive in same direction.
- Get off on snap count on short yardage/goal line plays.

To gain an outside position on a hook block, the tight end fires out of his four-point stance and, instead of driving forward, swings his hips around.

Reading Coverage

The job of learning to play wide receiver or tight end is difficult enough without the added pressure of having to know and recognize the different types of pass coverages that the defense may present. But it is never too soon to begin impressing on young players that they will never enjoy real greatness as a pass receiver until they begin to understand what the defense is trying to do.

One of the easiest ways to start learning defenses is with a simple recognition drill using four offensive men on defense and two wide receivers and one tight end on offense. This drill should not require all-out running by any of the players.

DRILL:
Pass Coverage Recognition
The three receivers release straight up

In man-to-man coverage, each cornerback takes a wide receiver and the strong safety stays with the tight end.

In two-deep zone coverage, both safeties drop deep, each taking half the field (top). *In a three-deep zone* (bottom), *both corner-backs drop to the outside deep zones while the free safety drops to the deep middle.*

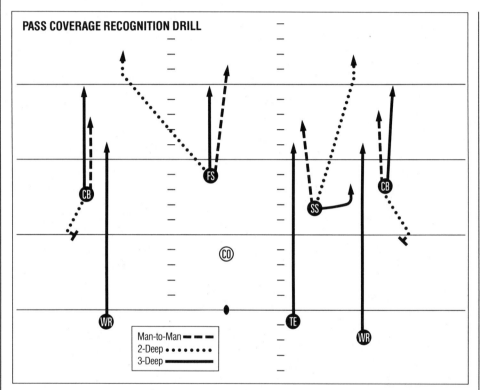

PASS COVERAGE RECOGNITION DRILL

Man-to-Man ▬ ▬ ▬
2-Deep • • • • • • •
3-Deep ▬▬▬▬▬

the field and yell out to the coach the instant they can recognize what type of pass coverage the defensive backs are using. Because this is a drill designed to help receivers learn to pick out defensive coverage, the players on defense should move quickly to their assigned positions and not try to fool the receivers as they release off the line of scrimmage.

Initially, what we want the receivers to be able to see is the movement to a three-deep zone, movement to a two-deep zone, and the reaction of the defensive men in man-to-man coverage. Each wide receiver should watch the movement of the corner and safety to his side; the tight end should watch the action of both the strong and free safeties.

When showing the receivers a three-deep zone picture, both cornerbacks should drop quickly back into the outside deep third of the field, the free safety should drop into the middle deep third, and the strong safety should leave his position, sprinting to the nearest sideline, rather than dropping deep.

For the two-deep simulation, the two corners should rotate up and try to get in front of the wide receiver to their side. Both safeties must drop very deep to a position where they can cover half of the field on their side.

To show man-to-man coverage, the free safety should drop into the deep center of the field, the strong safety should stay with the tight end as he goes up the field, and both corners should run with the two wide receivers as they release up the field.

This is a good drill to run in a pre-practice situation or after practice if the receivers need extra work. As the players learn to easily recognize the coverages, the coach can add any changes that he feels they will see in the game.

OFFENSIVE LINE

4

Offensive Line

- Stance   **153**
- Center Snap   **155**
- Run Blocking   **158**
- Drive Blocking   **160**
- Hook Blocking   **165**
- Angle Blocking   **166**
- The Running Drive Block   **168**
- Combination Blocks   **174**
- Short Yardage/Goal Line Blocking   **180**
- Pass Protection   **183**
- Picking Up Stunts   **193**

When they're executing correctly, offensive linemen go unnoticed by the average fan. In fact, about the only time you will hear an offensive lineman singled out in the NFL is after he has committed a penalty and the referee announces his number.

Recognition and fame on the offense usually starts with the quarterback, then goes on to the running backs, wide receivers, and tight ends. Then come offensive linemen. But the truth of the matter is that the others would have little success if the offensive linemen weren't doing their jobs.

This anonymity is one of the reasons that good offensive linemen must have an enormous amount of self-esteem and self-confidence. They must believe they are good performers, capable of blocking anyone they may face. Without this inner confidence, an offensive lineman always will be thinking about being defeated and not focusing on what he must do on every play.

When you look at great offensive line-men in the National Football League, you see a common trait—all of them possess a great amount of intelligence. While playing defense is more often than not reacting to a play, offensive linemen must be intelligent enough not only to know their assignment and those of the players lined up next to them, but also to understand and anticipate the movement by the defense before the play ever begins.

It is this complete knowledge of the offense that allows a good offensive lineman to know where the ball is being thrown from or where the ball will be run, thus making it possible for him to position himself between his assigned defensive player and his teammate with the ball. The execution of this assignment is referred to as maintaining a "relative position" for the duration of the play. Great offensive linemen constantly strive to maintain relative position on each offensive down.

Mental toughness is another important characteristic of an offensive line-

Offensive linemen not only must be physically big, strong, quick, and tough, they must be mentally quick and tough.

man. Often the success of the offense will not be determined by the first few series in a game. Instead, offensive successes will come later in the game as the offensive line begins to dominate and frustrate defensive players. Mental toughness allows an offensive lineman to take the field on series after series, knowing that each time he is winning little battles that ultimately will be rewarded with a team victory. With mental toughness comes a willingness and stubbornness to keep on trying, plus an enormous pride in individual performances on every down.

Because offensive linemen play in the area referred to as the "Pit," they must by necessity be the biggest and strongest players on the offensive team. Their primary job is to block, play after play, the big linebackers and huge linemen on the defensive team. In the NFL, it is not uncommon for offensive linemen to be 6 feet 5 inches or taller and weigh close to or more than 300 pounds. Height is most important for offensive tackles, but some of the most successful and most experienced NFL offensive guards and centers are in the 6-foot to 6-foot 2-inch range.

While good weight and height are desirable, one of the most important physical characteristics needed by an offensive lineman is quickness. An offensive lineman may not be the fastest player in a 40-yard dash, but all good offensive linemen are extremely quick in their movement for the first 5 or 10 yards. Great quickness allows an offensive lineman to get into proper position on a defensive player, physically placing himself between the defensive man and the ball carrier, or between the pass rusher and the quarterback.

Offensive linemen who do not totally understand the offense they are running or the defense they are facing, often will appear to lack good quickness, when in reality they often are slowed by indecision, not physical limitation. More often than not, intelligence and quickness go hand-in-hand, and both players and coaches must realize this. Top offensive linemen move immediately upon the snap of the ball. Quickness combines, along with size and strength, to give an offensive lineman the explosiveness to drive a defensive opponent off the line of scrimmage.

Quickness can be developed by drills and by gaining a total understanding of each assignment. Strength can be developed by a well-supervised weightlifting program that focuses on the development of the big muscle groups. For younger players, it is essential that any weight work be done under qualified instruction and that there never be any use of weight-enhancing drugs such as steroids. These drugs not only can seriously damage certain organs in the body, but, especially in the case of young men, can cause severe mood swings that often result in aggressive behavior off the field. It is far better for the young player to learn to stay away from the so-called "shortcuts" and realize he must work hard for his strength gains and muscle development.

As a lineman grows naturally, as his strength is increased by proper weight training, and as drills and study increase his quickness, then he will begin to become the explosive blocker that coaches love. Like the other positions on the football team, success in the offensive line will only come with desire, dedication, and a great deal of hard work.

Stance

The stance, the manner in which an offensive lineman positions himself prior to the beginning of a play, is very important.

Because an offensive lineman is required to drive straight ahead, block at angles to the right and left, pull laterally in either direction, and move backward from the line of scrimmage, it is impor-

The three stances used by offensive linemen are the three-point (above, left) the most common; the four-point (middle), for straight-ahead blocking; and the upright (right), for sure passing downs.

tant that he assume a stance that will allow him to execute each of these maneuvers with the greatest ease.

Offensive linemen generally find that it is most comfortable to use what is commonly termed a three-point stance, a stance with only one hand on the ground.

Often, teams that run the ball a lot use only straight-ahead blocking. Those teams have their offensive linemen in a four-point stance, with both hands on the ground. At the other end of stance

adjustment is the passing team, which often will have its linemen with both hands up in an upright body position on certain passing downs.

Each of these variations in the offensive lineman's stance is assumed for a specific reason and is designed to put the offensive lineman in the best possible blocking position. While each of these positions differs in appearance, there are some very constant rules that should apply to any stance used by an offensive lineman for any style of of-

fense. The basic stance is what should be learned first; other adjustments that can be used for specific types of plays come later.

To get into a proper stance, the lineman should stand in an upright position facing a coach. The lineman should have his feet no wider than his shoulders. Then the coach should have the player squat down, bending at the knees and resting both forearms on the inside of each of his inner thighs. With the player in this position, the player's back should be straight, with his head up, and his eyes focused straight ahead.

The next step for the player is to reach forward with both hands, keeping them no wider than his shoulders, and place both hands on the ground. By initially placing both hands on the ground the player will learn to keep his shoulders even and his back straight. Most beginning offensive linemen, when asked to get into a three-point stance, have a tendency to place the hand that is on the ground more into the center of the body, causing their shoulders to be tilted to one side or the other. In a four-point stance, this tendency is eliminated and the player should have no problem keeping his shoulders square. In the case of the offensive center, this is the time to place the ball into either the right or left hand in preparation for snapping.

Once the coach is satisfied that the player understands the proper hand placement, he can allow the lineman to remove one hand from the ground, allowing the hand and arm to rest on the inner thigh. This will leave the player in a proper three-point stance. The distance the player reaches forward will differ with the offense being run and the type of blocking being used, but, as a beginning point, the hand on the ground

should be slightly in front of the shoulder pads. The player should have a small amount of weight on his down hand, but not enough so that if it were removed he would fall forward on his face.

When the player is in a three-point stance, he naturally will want to move the foot on the side of the down hand back a few inches. It is best if this is a toe-to-instep relationship with the other foot, although some linemen feel more comfortable with a toe-to-heel alignment. Both coach and player must realize that the greater the stagger of the feet in the stance, the greater the difficulty the player will have in moving in all directions. Also, a player who has a greater stagger in his feet often will narrow the distance between his feet and diminish his balance.

Here are the basic rules to remember about the lineman's stance:

First, the stance must be comfortable. This allows the player to focus on the target he is assigned to block and to move as the ball is snapped. The more times a player practices getting in and out of his stance, the sooner the player will feel relaxed and comfortable in it.

Second, a player's stance must put him in the best possible position to execute the block that has been assigned to

him on the play being run.

Third, the player's stance must be balanced and allow for quickness of movement. Fast, short, choppy steps enable the offensive lineman to generate power into the block.

Fourth, offensive linemen should try to assume basically the same stance on every play so that the defensive player cannot tell prior to the snap of the ball whether the offensive lineman is blocking straight ahead, pulling to the left or right, or setting up in pass protection.

WINNING POINTS
- Feet shoulder-width apart.
- Shoulders even; back straight.
- One hand on ground, bearing small amount of weight, slightly in front of shoulder pad; other hand and arm resting on inside of thigh.
- Foot on side of down hand set back, toes even with instep or heel of front foot.
- Assume same stance on every play, run or pass.

Center Snap

On every down, guards and tackles must know the play, the snap count, and which defensive player they are responsible for blocking. The center has all these responsibilities, plus he has the added job of getting the ball to the quarterback.

Teaching an offensive lineman to be a center is not difficult. It does, however, require a great deal of practice in order for the center-quarterback exchange to be successful every play.

One of the easiest ways to introduce a young player to the center position is to have him get into a basic four-point stance. In this stance, the player's weight should be distributed evenly on the balls of both feet, his feet need to be parallel and spread about the width of his shoulders, and his back should be straight with his head up. The center's hands should be placed on the ground slightly ahead and inside of the outside points of his shoulders.

The coach should make certain that the player's shoulders are level and that the player's weight is distributed evenly on the balls of both feet and the fingers of both hands. Once the stance is correct, the coach should have the player charge straight ahead a few times, angle charge to his right and left a few plays, and set back as if he were pass protecting for the quarterback.

The next step is to have the offensive lineman, in his four-point stance, lift

When learning how to snap the ball, the center first assumes a four-point stance. Then, a football is placed, laces to the side, under one of his hands.

one of his hands off the ground. The coach then can place the ball on the exact spot where the player's hand had been. The player replaces his hand, only now he will be grasping the ball, rather than touching his hand to the ground. Eventually, with practice, the center will begin to feel comfortable with the ball as a normal part of his stance, an exten-

sion of his arm and hand.

It is important that when the coach places the ball on the ground, he does so with the laces pointing to the side away from the snapping hand, at the exact spot where the center's hand previously had been resting. As the center becomes more comfortable and proficient, the ball can be moved more into the center of his body in a position directly in front of his nose. With the ball in this location, the center can execute the snap with one or both hands on the ball. In either case, only one hand actually will grip and snap the ball. The other hand will merely rest comfortably on top of the ball to balance the center, or his non-snapping arm may rest on the inside of his thigh. These adjustments can come later; in the beginning it is easier to have success from a four-point stance.

As the center grasps the ball, his hand should be on the forward half of the ball, with the first knuckle of his thumb placed over the laces. The palm of the snapping hand would then rest on the outside of the ball and the four fingers of the center's hand should be spread, encircling the underneath portion of the football. The center should feel that he has complete control of the ball.

The next step is to remove the ball again in order to show the center the manner in which the ball should be exchanged with the quarterback. If the quarterback is not available, the coach or another center can play the quarterback calling signals and reaching under the center's buttocks so that the back of the top hand exerts slight upward pressure. Without any forward movement, the center should then reach back between his legs and shake hands with the top hand of the quarterback. This is the manner that the center should bring the ball up to the quarterback when he actually is making the exchange of the ball.

When the center has a feel for the proper path needed to bring his snapping hand up to shake hands with the top hand of the quarterback, the ball can be replaced under the center's snapping hand.

Using the ball, this simple drill can be repeated with the center actually placing the ball in the hands of the quarterback. Initially, because the emphasis must be on the actual exchange of the ball, neither the quarterback nor the center should move. The center should concentrate completely on making certain that he has brought the ball up correctly and that it is placed securely in the hands of the quarterback.

To get the feel for snapping the ball, the center reaches between his legs and shakes hands with the quarterback. He then repeats the same motion with a ball.

Once the snap and exchange are occurring without hesitation or a fumble between the center and the quarterback, movement should be added to the drill. Both the center and the quarterback will quickly feel the difference in the exchange when they actually are moving on a play.

In practicing this, the center should either drive straight ahead, to his right or left, or set up in pass protection. For all the running plays, where the center is moving forward, the movement of the quarterback should be down the line of scrimmage to his right or left, executing a reverse pivot to the right or left, or pulling away from the line of scrimmage to his right or left. When the center is executing a pass protection set, the quarterback should take a five-step drop and set up to pass.

The first few snaps incorporating movement can be done without the ball, thus enabling the center and quarterback to get a feel of actually moving off the line of scrimmage together in the same direction or, more difficult, of the center going in one direction and quarterback moving in the opposite direction or moving away from the line of scrimmage.

As quickly as possible, the ball should be reintroduced as part of the

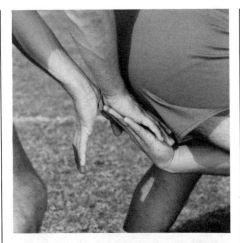

The center shakes hands with the quarterback's top hand. When the center actually snaps the ball, the laces hit the palm of the passer's top hand.

drill. There may be a tendency for beginning centers to shift their concentration to moving into their block and they may forget that the first—and most important—job that they have to do is to place the ball securely in the quarterback's hands.

Once the center is secure in his snapping motion, the actual quarterback (and not a coach or another lineman) always should be involved in the drill. The more these two players can work together and the greater the number of snaps that they practice as one unit, the less chance there will be in a game situation for the snap to be lost.

Run Blocking

The blocking techniques used by a lineman on running and passing plays naturally will be different, but there are some factors common to both.

Whether a run or pass is called, one of the most important traits for a blocker is aggressiveness. There is no better place to teach aggressiveness to a young offensive lineman than in run blocking. Coaches speak of great run blockers "blowing the defender off the ball," actually driving the defender back toward his own goal line. This is what run blocking is all about. The basic idea in run blocking is not only to place the

It is critical for a run blocker to quickly "get off the ball," or, in other words, fire out of his stance immediately upon the snap of the ball. A key to achieving this explosiveness is for the blocker to anticipate the snap count.

blocker between the defender and the offensive player with the ball, but also to forcefully move the defender away from his original location.

Run blocking should be attempted before pass blocking so that this attitude of physical and aggressive play can develop, an attitude that will carry over when pass blocking is learned.

It is important for offensive linemen to understand that there are different types of blocks that they will need to master in order to frustrate and defeat a defensive opponent. But prior to actually blocking an individual, it is important for offensive linemen to learn to "get off the ball," or, in other words, move with great quickness on the snap count.

Defensive linemen learn to react to the movement of the ball and the movement of the offensive player. An offensive player must learn to move on a sound and to anticipate the reaction of the defensive player. Not moving the in-

stant the ball is snapped almost always will result in an offensive lineman losing the battle to the defense. The snap count must be anticipated by the offensive player so that he can use his tremendous offensive advantage to its fullest potential.

DRILL:
Getting off the Ball

The coach stands behind the offensive linemen. They should be told the snap count and then asked to take their stances.

Once the coach sees that every offensive lineman is in his stance and is settled, he moves up behind the center, and simulates the quarterback calling out the cadence. From this position, the coach should accept the ball when it is snapped by the center as he moves forward.

Once the snap count is called out by the coach, the offensive linemen should instantly move forward out of their stances for five yards as quickly as they can. When coming out of his stance, each lineman should take quick, short, choppy steps, keeping his feet close to the ground. Both arms need to be pumping to give the player added forward thrust. His shoulders should stay low and square, and his back should be straight. He needs to keep his neck bowed and his head up. Each lineman should have his eyes focused straight ahead, looking at an imaginary target.

At first, it may be necessary for the coach to position himself five yards in front of the offensive linemen and have each player go one at a time. By doing this, the coach can be absolutely certain that the players are moving quickly on the snap count with proper steps and body position.

Drive Blocking

Of all the blocks that must be made by an offensive lineman, none is more basic than the drive block. The drive block is the block that the lineman uses when he is attempting to block a defender who is lined up on the line of scrimmage directly in front of him.

In a drive block, the job of the offensive lineman is to move the defender back toward the defender's own goal line, and, at the same time, keep the necessary relative position between the defender and the offensive player with the ball.

Because there is so little room between the defender and offensive lineman on this type of block, all errors must be eliminated and every advantage that the offensive lineman has must be used. The ability to execute a good drive block starts with a good, comfortable stance, an anticipation of the snap count, a very quick start at the instant the ball is snapped, and a complete focus on the target to be blocked.

The first step in teaching the drive block is to have the offensive linemen work against a blocking sled. Because the sled will not change its alignment or attack the offensive players, they can focus on the sled pads and concentrate on good blocking technique.

DRILL:

Drive Blocking vs Sled

The coach should line up one offensive lineman in front of each of the five interior pads on the sled. Then the coach should give the players the snap count so that they can move as one unit into the sled. On the command "Set!" by the coach, each offensive lineman should get into a comfortable three-point stance with his down hand one foot away from the sled pad that he is going to block. The offensive center should have a ball under his down hand.

Once the five players are completely set, the coach begins to call out the cadence used by the offense until he reaches the designated snap count.

The five players should be anticipating the snap count. The instant they hear the snap count, they should explode into the sled and continue to drive it back until the coach blows a whistle. It is important when coaching the offensive line to always begin each drill with a cadence and snap count, and, when it does not interfere with other drills elsewhere on the practice field, end the drill by blowing the whistle. This then becomes a conditioned reflex for starting and stopping a play, which the offensive linemen can automatically carry over into actual

Linemen should hit a blocking sled with a forward and upward motion, driving their legs with short, choppy steps and keeping their feet well apart.

alize that the block starts from the ground and goes up through his body into the pad on the sled. In order to generate the most power, the offensive lineman must have both feet on the ground at the moment of impact with the initial power generating up from his feet, through his calves, and into the big muscle groups of his upper legs and hips.

At the point of contact, the blocker should strike the center of the blocking pad with the heels of the palms of both hands. The blocker should keep his elbows close into his body as he hits with his hands. The hands only strike the pad —but the legs cause the explosion.

Each offensive lineman should think about the block as coming in a forward and upward motion. As contact is made with the sled, the blocker must keep his legs driving in short, choppy steps, making certain that he does not narrow his base but keeps his feet even with or slightly wider than his shoulders. The ideal drive block by an offensive lineman would have him physically get underneath the defensive player's chest and shoulders and drive him up and back. This forward and upward motion is what each blocker should strive for when blocking on the sled.

Finally, the offensive lineman must finish the block on the sled. This last effort

game situations.

When the offensive lineman hears the snap count, he should take a straight, short step toward the pad with his back foot. His shoulders should stay low and his back should remain straight. With his neck bowed and head up, the blocker

should focus his eyes on the center of the pad. While the target area is the center of the pad, it is important for the blocker to think of driving through the pad by actually aiming for a spot two or three feet behind the pad.

It is vital for the offensive lineman to re-is what separates the poor and average offensive lineman from the good, even great one. Great offensive linemen take enormous pride in the manner in which they finish any block and especially the drive block. In the beginning, it is up to the coach teaching the young players to demand that they finish every block.

Once the explosion has occurred and the hands have struck the pad and the legs are driving, it becomes essential for the offensive lineman to complete the block by thrusting the hips in a forward and upward motion. At the same time, using the back, shoulder, and upper arm muscle groups, the blocker must physically extend his arms in a forward and upward motion, actually lifting the sled up off the ground. The player then must keep driving and lifting, in one smooth motion, always keeping forward momentum, until he hears the whistle or the coach's command to stop.

Many linemen will come off the ball quickly and will hit the sled with explosion, but then will stop, hesitate, have to restart, and never finish the block. Those blockers may be able to stalemate the defensive player—to stop his penetration to the offensive side of the line of scrimmage—but they will not be able to drive the defender off the line to create big running lanes for the ball carrier to

The mark of a top lineman is the way he drives up and through to finish a block.

charge through. Wide running lanes only are created by offensive linemen who know the importance of, and continually practice, finishing the block.

If individual coaching is necessary, have the players block the sled one at a time. That way the coach can focus all his attention on the offensive lineman executing the block. The coach constantly should emphasize a quick start, explosion off the ground from both feet with a good wide base, a forceful striking of both hands into the pad, powerful hip thrust, continued leg drive, extension and pressing up with the upper body and arms, and a physical finish.

In all these drills, it is important for the center to snap the ball as he executes his movement into the sled. The coach or the backup center should take the snap, thus guaranteeing that the ball does not roll free on the ground and create potential for injury.

NOTE: *If you do not have a sled on which to work, you can run the same type of drill by using tall, hand-held individual dummies.*

Once the coach feels his offensive linemen have a good grasp of proper drive-blocking technique on the sled, it is time to advance the drill to the act of blocking a live defender.

For teaching and learning purposes, it is better to run the drills with offensive linemen serving as both blockers and the defenders. This can serve two important purposes: First, the coach can take as much time as is needed to work with and correct an individual offensive lineman without wasting the practice time of the defensive players. Second, it serves as a method of teaching the offensive lineman some of the skills used by the man he will be responsible for blocking during a game. He will gain some knowledge why a defender may line up in a certain position, and what the defender may do from that position.

When the offensive linemen have practiced the drive block against one another, the defense can be introduced

into the drill. It is important to remember that the introduction of the defense into the drill usually will cause greater competition. Many times the actual learning is decreased and the drill becomes more combative in nature. Because of this, early instruction in any skill or technique should take place in the more relaxed atmosphere of offensive players working against offensive players. Once the players get game experience, they may have less tendency to react aggressively during practice.

DRILL:

One-On-One Drive Blocking
When first setting up the blocking drill, the coach should position himself behind and to the side of the offensive line-

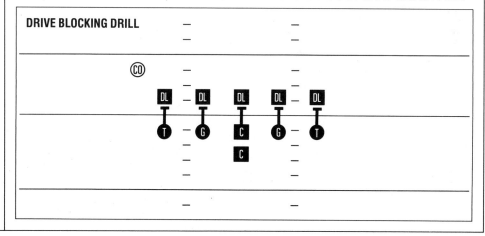

DRIVE BLOCKING DRILL

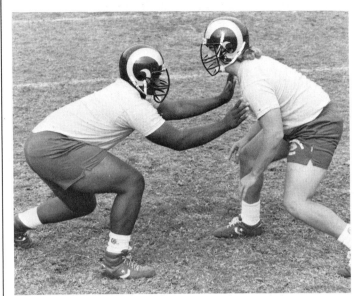 

In drive blocking, the offensive lineman fires out at the snap count, attempting to hit the defender, get up under his shoulder pads, thrust forward and upward, and drive the defensive man off the line of scrimmage.

man who is playing on defense. From this position, the coach can use hand signals to tell the offensive blocker when the ball will be snapped, without also telling the defender. The defender should line up directly in front of the blocker and get into a four-point stance. He should react to the blocker's movement and try not to be moved off the line of scrimmage.

It also is important for the coach to indicate to the blocker to which side the ball will be run, thus allowing the blocker

to also think about gaining relative position on the defensive man.

If possible, a center should snap the ball on every play, even though he is not blocking; the next center should take the snap as well as call out the cadence. The coach can call the cadence from the defensive side of the ball if he feels that it would be better for the drill.

As the offensive blocker takes his stance, he should begin to anticipate the snap count, focus his eyes on the jersey

numbers of the defender, and prepare to explode out of his stance.

The offensive blocker should use the same technique that he has practiced on the sled. The difference will now be that he is driving to get under the defender's shoulder pads, if possible, and that the defender is going to be moving at him, reacting and not staying stationary.

Because of the forward movement of the defender, the offensive lineman will find that he will make contact much quicker than he did on the sled. It will become imperative that he take short, quick steps, sliding his feet and maintaining a wide base. He must have both feet firmly planted on the ground when contact is made in order to have maximum power and explosion.

It also is important that the blocker keep his shoulders down and square, his head up, and his back straight. He should not raise upright, which would give the defender the advantage of getting under the offensive man's pads.

As contact is made, the offensive blocker must explode with his legs in a forward and upward motion, striking the defender in the numbers with the palms of both hands, and attempting to drive up and through him.

Then the offensive blocker must try to finish the block. He must thrust his hips forward, extend and press up and back with his upper body and arms, and continue to drive the defender back off the line of scrimmage.

At the same time, the offensive man should try to achieve relative position by ever so slightly positioning his body between the defender and the designated side of the ball. This movement, to one side or the other, never should cause the offensive blocker to stop driving the defender off the line of scrimmage.

NOTE: *A variation of the drive block, the "cut block," entails the lineman driving out, usually at a linebacker, and trying to cut the feet out from under the defender. But due to safety factors, a majority of high school and youth football leagues do not allow this type of block aimed at, or below, the knee.*

Hook Blocking

A hook block differs from the drive block in that the defensive player is lined up to the outside of the offensive blocker rather than directly in front of him. It will be almost impossible for the blocker to drive the defender off the line of scrimmage if the defender lines up in this outside position, although this still should be the blocker's goal.

Now the blocker must concentrate on stopping the defender's penetration and moving him laterally down, rather than backward away from, the line of scrimmage.

DRILL:

Hook Blocking

The offensive man who is on defense should align himself on one shoulder or the other of the offensive blocker. Later, when the offensive men have some skill in executing the hook block, the defenders can widen their set, moving off the blocker's shoulder and into the gap to the right or left of the blocker. When working on the hook block, the defensive player should charge straight ahead, across the line of scrimmage, when he

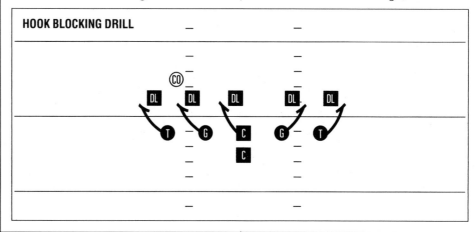

HOOK BLOCKING DRILL

sees the ball snapped or the offensive player move.

As the ball is snapped, the offensive blocker must insure that the defender does not get penetration across the line of scrimmage by taking a short two- to three-inch lateral step with the foot on the side of the block.

This drop step will open the offensive lineman's hips slightly, allowing him to step quickly across his body with the opposite foot. It is important that the blocker drive this foot forcibly into the ground because it will become the power foot for the hook block.

During this initial movement, it is essential that the blocker keep his shoulders low and square. If he raises up, there is an excellent possibility that the defender will get under the block and be in position to drive the blocker back into his own backfield.

As the power foot makes contact with the ground, the offensive blocker must thrust his far arm under the defender, driving up and through the defensive player's body. Using short, choppy steps, the blocker must drive his body in front of the defender's charge, stopping the possibility of any defensive penetration.

When many young offensive linemen learn the hook block, they have a ten-dency to narrow their base on their second step by actually trying to step too far. They find that their power foot never really has time to make contact with the ground before the defender reacts to them, knocking them off balance. If the offensive blocker is having this type of trouble, the defensive man can be moved off the line a few feet, thus giving the blocker more opportunity to set himself. As the blocker's skill level increases, the defender can be moved closer and closer to the line of scrimmage.

The coach must emphasize to the offensive lineman that on a hook block he must stay up, and not go to the ground. The blockers must continue to drive their legs, working up and through the defender, keeping physical contact with the defender until the whistle blows, and, if possible, moving the defensive man back.

Angle Blocking

While drive and hook blocks are used against defensive players who are lined up directly in front of or to the side of the offensive blocker, the angle block is used versus a defender who is lined up to the right or left of the blocker.

When executing an angle block, the offensive lineman is concerned not only with stopping the defender's penetration, but also with attacking the side of the defender's body exposed in his straight-ahead charge.

In the drill below, it is important for the man on defense to attack the offen-

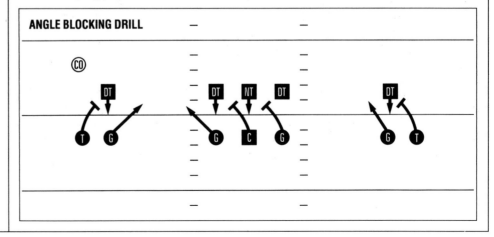

ANGLE BLOCKING DRILL

On an angle block, the offensive lineman takes a short angle step toward the man he is to block. He then power-steps across his body, explodes into the defender, and jams the palm of his far hand into the defender's side.

sive player directly in front of him before trying to react to the angle blocker coming from the side. By doing this, the offensive angle blocker will get experience executing the block under game conditions.

DRILL:

Angle Blocking

For this drill we have set up three separate groups of players. The coach will move from one group to another, having only one offensive player angle-block at a time.

The offensive player who is lined up in front of the defender to be blocked should move quickly on the snap count to the side opposite the angle block.

It is important for the angle-blocking offensive lineman to understand that the defender will not be focused on him, but will instead be moving toward the offensive player directly in front of him on the line of scrimmage.

As in previous drills, the coach should give the offensive men the snap count, call out the cadence, and observe the block, making certain that it is executed correctly.

On the snap, the offensive blocker

should take a short, two-inch, angle step down the line of scrimmage with the foot closest to the man he is attempting to block. This step serves two purposes. One, it allows the blocker to get his head in front of the defender, stopping penetration; and two, it allows him to open his hips, making it possible for him to attack the defender with a low, square, blocking surface.

The blocker must then bring his far foot quickly across his body, making certain that the step does not narrow his base. Because this second step serves to set the power foot of the angle block, the blocker must be sure to drive it aggressively into the ground.

As the power foot hits the ground and the blocker explodes into the defender, he should jam the palm of the far hand into the side of the defensive player with as much force as possible. Unlike the drive block, where the blocker can strike the defender with both hands, an angle block only allows for contact with one hand. This one hand should generate as much force and explosion as possible and should not be used merely to balance the blocker as contact is made.

Finally, the offensive lineman must finish off the block. Maintaining a wide base, he must continue to drive his legs, thrusting his hips forward and lifting up

and through the defender. The offensive blocker's goal on an angle block is not to drive the defensive player off the line, rather he should attempt to drive him laterally down the line of scrimmage until he hears the whistle or the command to stop.

During the entire block, the offensive lineman must concentrate on staying low, always trying to get under the shoulder pads of the defender. The blocker needs to take short, choppy steps, keeping his shoulders square and his back straight. As with all blocks, the offensive lineman must have his head up, neck bowed, and his eyes focused on the target.

Usually an offensive tackle or guard will execute an angle block going toward

the ball, although against certain defenses both players may find that they are required to execute this block when moving to the outside. The offensive center, because of his location, will use an angle block to both his right and left.

The Running Drive Block

In the previous sections we have dealt with methods of blocking a defender who is lined up on the line of scrimmage, either directly in front of, or to the side of, the blocker, or lined up on the line of scrimmage to the blocker's left or right.

The technique changes when blocking a defender who has positioned himself off the line of scrimmage, or a defender who is lined up in a position on

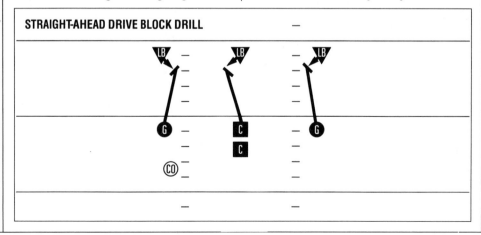

STRAIGHT-AHEAD DRIVE BLOCK DRILL

the line of scrimmage, but more than one man away from the blocker.

In executing both of these blocks, it is necessary for the offensive lineman actually to run a distance before physically making contact with the defensive man.

For the offensive lineman, the running drive block is used when firing straight ahead to block a linebacker who is lined up three or four yards off the line of scrimmage, or when the blocker is asked to pull laterally and trap a defender who is lined up on the line of scrimmage. Usually both offensive guards and the center have the most opportunities during a game to block straight ahead on a linebacker who is lined up off the line of scrimmage. Very few defenses align themselves in such a manner that the offensive tackle is called upon to make this type of block.

Because the initial movement of each of the blocks is different, it is best to set up two separate drills for the running drive block.

DRILL:

Running Drive Block I

One main difference between a regular drive block and a running drive block is that the defender has a greater opportunity to move to his right or left, reacting to the offensive blocker's path. Because of

A running drive block often is used against a linebacker, making quickness off the ball essential. The blocker must stay low and focused on his target.

this fact, the coach must not only tell the blocker the snap count, but also must make certain that the blocker understands where the ball will be going.

In the drill, the offensive lineman who is playing as the linebacker should react to the path of the blocker, moving forward to his right or left and attacking with his shoulders, arms, and hands.

The offensive blocker must make cer-

tain that he gets off on the snap count, and takes a good forward step with his back foot. Quickness off the ball is essential when blocking a linebacker.

The blocker should come off the ball in a low charge, making certain that he does not raise up into the air, and adjust his path so that he can achieve relative position to the defender and the side of the ball. As the blocker nears the linebacker he must shorten his steps and widen his base. If he makes contact with his feet too close together, it will be very easy for the defender to knock him to the ground. At the point of contact, the offensive lineman should flex his knees, lower his hips, and explode starting from the ground and up through the big muscle groups of the lower body. Using the palms of both hands to strike into the numbers of the linebacker's jersey, the blocker should punch up and through the defender.

Because the defender will be changing his position as the blocker approaches, it is vital for the offensive lineman to focus on the defender, keeping his head up and his eyes locked on the target area. The offensive lineman should finish the running drive block in the same way that he finishes the standard drive block, by trying to knock the defender back toward his own goal line.

The running or "pulling" drive block (also called "trap block") is predominantly used by offensive guards and tackles. However, now even centers are being asked to execute this block. Basically, in a trap play a defensive lineman is influenced across the line of scrimmage, then is blocked from the side by an offensive lineman pulling (leaving his position) and running down the line.

Because most players learn technique much faster when contact is eliminated, the coach should have the pulling linemen first go through their movements and steps, running over the spot where they will execute the block, without having any defenders in the drill. If necessary, a chalk path can be outlined on the ground for the blocker to follow. As the offensive linemen become more and more proficient at pulling, the coach can introduce the defensive players one at a time to the drill.

DRILL:

Running Drive Block II (Trap Block)

In this drill, the players on defense should charge straight ahead and then react to the trap block as they see it coming from one side or the other.

Prior to the snap, the pulling offensive lineman must make certain that he does not lean in the direction of his pull and

PULLING TRAP BLOCK DRILL (GUARDS) —

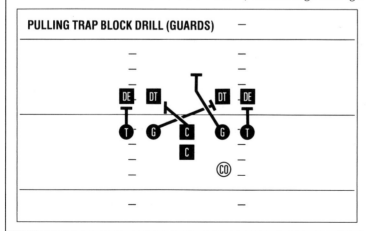

PULLING TRAP BLOCK DRILL (TACKLES) —

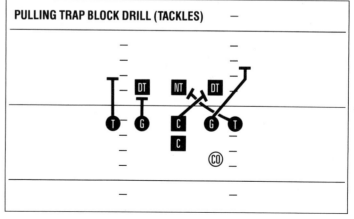

When pulling, the lineman swings his upper body around in the direction of his pull by pushing up and back out of his stance, jerking his arm to the side of the pull, and pushing off with the foot opposite the direction of the pull.

alert the defense as to which direction he is going to move.

When an offensive lineman is pulling and getting in position to execute a trap block, he must by necessity change the direction of his charge from straight ahead to either the right or left. Because of this, the blocker should use his first step with the foot in the direction of his pull to set his path. This should not be a long step, but it is vital that he cover some ground in the direction of the pull.

The offensive lineman then must swing his upper body around so that he is pointing in the direction of his pull. To accomplish this, the blocker should do three things. First, as he comes out of his stance, he should push off and back with the hand on the ground. Second, he must jerk the forearm around, with the arm to the side of the pull; many players describe this as swinging the arm around as if to hit someone standing behind them. Finally, he should push off the foot opposite the direction of his pull.

Once the blocker has redirected his charge, he must immediately pick up his target and focus on the blocking area. The path of the blocker should take him toward the defensive side of the line of scrimmage, allowing him to achieve an "inside-out" angle on the defender he is attempting to block.

If the block is a short trap—blocking a defender only two men away—the blocker must understand that the contact will come very quickly. It is essential, then,

As the blocker pulls down the line, he quickly must focus on his target.

that he maintain a wide base and anticipate the defender moving into his block.

Once the offensive lineman has started his pull, redirected his body and charge, focused on the target, and moved toward the defender, he is in position to execute a running drive block. Instead of executing the block straight ahead as on a linebacker, the blocker will attack the defender from the side.

At the point of contact with the defender, the basics of the block are the same as on other blocks. Explosion should be generated from both feet on the ground in a wide base, the charge should be low and hard, the palm of the hand should aggressively and forcibly attack the side of the defender, and the blocker must finish the block by hitting up and through

the defender, driving the defender out of the hole and toward the sideline, until the whistle blows or the coach calls the play to a stop.

DRILL:

Pulling Block vs. Linebacker

In this drill, the offensive guards and tackles pull long and then turn upfield and block on a linebacker.

The offensive men playing as the linebackers should focus on the man in front of them and, as they see the play develop, move forward, attacking the blocker who is moving toward them.

If the offensive player who is lined up in front of the linebacker is blocking beside the pulling lineman, it may become necessary for the pulling blocker's first

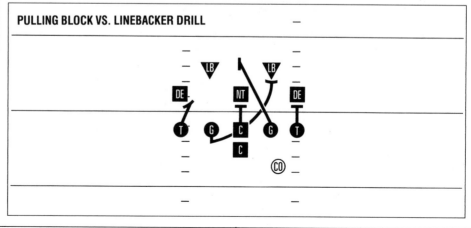

PULLING BLOCK VS. LINEBACKER DRILL

An offensive lineman pulling to block a linebacker may have to drop-step slightly to allow his teammate clearance to move to his block. The pulling lineman then locates his target and brings his shoulders into low blocking position.

step to be a short, two- to three-inch drop step. At the same time, the pulling lineman should slightly raise his lead shoulder higher than he normally would on a trap block. This technique will allow his teammate to move to his block and, at the same time, gives the blocker a greater clearance when pulling and driving up toward the linebacker. By the second and third step, the pulling lineman should bring his shoulders down into a low blocking position.

With the exception of plays where it becomes necessary to use the drop step, the offensive lineman should use the same pulling technique as in the previous drill. Because of the proximity of the linebacker, great emphasis must be placed on immediately finding and focusing on the target. Failure to instantly locate the linebacker often is the biggest reason for missing this block.

It is essential that the pulling lineman understand where the ball is going in the drill so he can get proper relative position on the defender. At the point of the actual block, the blocker should employ the technique of the running drive block.

Only one offensive lineman pulled

173

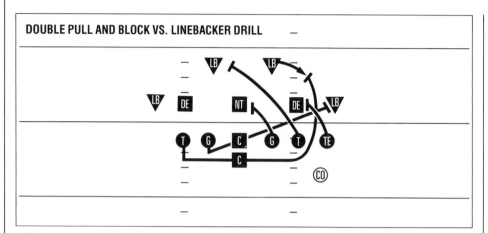

DOUBLE PULL AND BLOCK VS. LINEBACKER DRILL

each time in the previous drills, but in the next drill, both the guard and tackle from the same side of the ball will pull.

DRILL:

Two Pulling Linemen

The pulling guard will trap the linebacker at the end of the line of scrimmage and the tackle will pull up through the hole and block the linebacker who is pursuing from the inside.

Both linebackers should focus on the man in front of them and then move into position to take on a pulling lineman.

The guard's technique is the same as the one he used on a long trap play. The tackle also uses a long-pull technique and then turns upfield, locating, focusing on, and blocking the linebacker who is

moving from the inside.

Both offensive players must be reminded to move to the defensive side of the ball as soon as possible, to concentrate on having a wide base on contact, and to run through the defender, always completely finishing the block.

Combination Blocks

During the course of a game, two offensive linemen often will combine to block one defender (double team) or to block in unison on two defensive players (combo block).

Double-Team Blocking

The double-team block is the most forceful block that can be used by the offense. The size, strength, explosion, and

momentum of two men is pitted against only one defender. A double-team block is a combination drive and angle block. The offensive lineman directly in front of the defender will execute a drive block, while the blocker from the side will execute an angle block. It is a block designed to drive the defensive player laterally out of the hole and back toward his goal line. When executed properly, the double-team block will not only bury the defender or neutralize the key man of the defensive line, but also will cut off the pursuit by the other members of the defensive team, forcing them to go around the double-team block at a much deeper pursuit angle.

Double-team blocks are used by center-guard, guard-tackle, and tackle-tight end combinations. The technique used by each tandem is the same, but it is important for the coach to make certain that he has allotted enough time for each pair to get adequate practice time working together.

There are two different drills used in teaching the double-team block to young offensive linemen. The first uses the guards and center, the second uses the guards and tackles. If the tight end is available and is expected to be involved in double-team blocking, it will be necessary to set up a third drill using him and the tackle working together.

In Drill I, the double-team block is executed by the tackles and guards on both sides of the line. The center may snap the ball and then block away from the double-team block.

In Drill II, the guards and center execute the double-team block on the nose tackle. On the left, the left guard and center will work together, while on the right, the right guard and center will execute the block. The guard not involved with the double-team block should pull behind the block and run up the field.

NOTE: *The description of double-team blocking below, holds for either drill and for any combination of player positions. The important thing for the blockers to remember is that they are working as a team; they must work together and not against one another.*

DRILL:
Double-Team Blocking I (Guards and Tackles)

DRILL:
Double-Team Blocking II (Guards and Center)

The blockers first must align hip-to-hip in their block and generate all their force into and through the defender. Because the threat of penetration by the defense

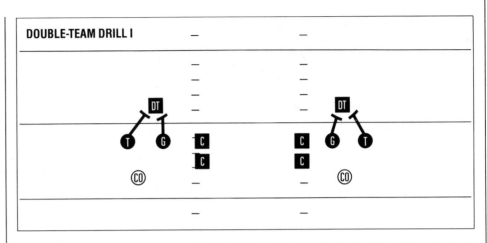

DOUBLE-TEAM DRILL I

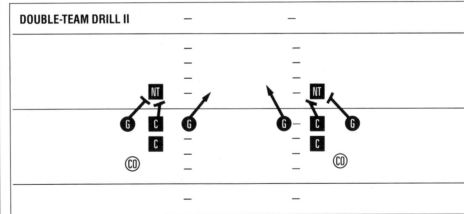

DOUBLE-TEAM DRILL II

is eliminated with this block, the angle blocker may take his first step toward his blocking companion and then drive hip-to-hip with his partner straight up the field. The drive blocker should take a first step directly at the defender and then try to "hip up" with the angle blocker, insuring that their momentum is being directed in the same path through the defensive player.

For a double-team block to be effective, both offensive linemen must attack the defender with a low, hard charge. They then get into position, hip-to-hip, drive the defender off the line of scrimmage, and finish the block together.

Both blockers must attack the defender with a low, hard charge, exploding into him and striking with the palm of the near hand into his body. At this point the blockers must drive the defender off the line of scrimmage, making sure that they stay hip-to-hip and drive up and through the defender.

If the blockers do not maintain the hip-to-hip relationship, the defensive man often will be able to create a wedge with his body and split the blockers apart.

Once the defender is being moved backwards, the two blockers should try to turn slightly and drive him away from the side of the angle blocker. It should be emphasized to young offensive players that it is more important to drive the defender off the line of scrimmage than it is to turn him out of the hole.

Both blockers must concentrate on finishing off the block together, coming up and through the defender, driving him onto his back if possible, and staying with him until the whistle blows or the coach calls "stop" to the drill.

Offensive linemen must be made to realize that there is no reason for a double-team block to fail, and that not only should the defender be blocked, but also he should be moved back and off the line to create a running lane for the ball carrier.

The reaction of the defensive player in the drills is important when working on the double-team block. In the beginning, the defender must attack the offensive lineman directly in front of him with both hands and then try to lean into the angle block as he feels it coming. As the offensive players become more proficient at the double-team block, the defensive man then can start dropping to the ground and creating a pile, making it harder and harder for the offensive blockers to move him from his original position.

Combo Blocking

In combo blocking two linemen start blocking on one defensive man. Then, based upon the defensive team's reaction, one of the blockers comes off the block and begins blocking another defender. Most combo blocks are used to block a defensive lineman on the line of scrimmage and a linebacker who is lined up off the line of scrimmage. (The uncovered lineman's phase of a combo block is referred to by the defense as a ''scoop'' block.)

As with the double-team block, we will set up two drills so that the guard-

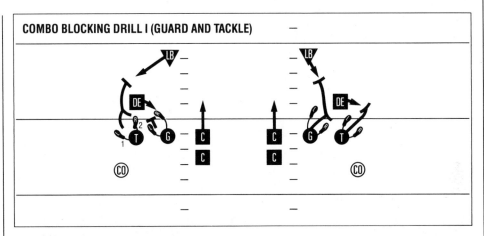

COMBO BLOCKING DRILL I (GUARD AND TACKLE)

In a combo block , two offensive linemen begin blocking one defender, then one blocker slides off and hits another defender, usually a linebacker.

take a short lateral step with their outside foot. On his second step, the tackle should strike the defensive end with the palm of his inside hand.

If the defensive end stunts to the inside, the tackle should let him go and continue upfield, turn toward the ball, and prepare to make contact with the linebacker who is coming from the inside. The offensive guard will also hit the defensive end and, with his second step, strike the body of the defender with the palm of his outside hand and arm. As the guard feels the defensive end coming to the inside, he should continue to move to the outside of the defensive end, making

If the end stunts to the inside (top), *the tackle lets him go and hits the linebacker. If the linebacker blitzes inside, the guard takes him* (bottom).

tackle and the center-guard combination both receive practice time.

DRILL:

Combo Block I (Guard and Tackle)

In this drill, the guard and tackle are responsible for blocking the defensive end and linebacker to their side. After making the snap, the center fires out straight ahead.

Both the tackle and the guard should

contact with his inside hand on the defender, and attempt to get a relative position on him as he drives him off the line of scrimmage.

While moving toward the defensive end, the guard must make certain that the linebacker is not blitzing to the inside. Should the guard see the linebacker on an inside blitz, he must immediately stop his movement to the outside and redirect his charge into the blitzing linebacker, meeting him square, stopping his penetration, and driving him off the line of scrimmage. The offensive tackle would then be responsible for the block on the defensive end.

Should the defensive end work to the outside, the offensive tackle will stay with him, blocking him for the duration of the play. As opposed to a play where the inside linebacker blitzes, if the linebacker is merely moving laterally, the guard can initially make contact with the defensive end and help the tackle move the defensive end off the line.

Once the guard feels the defensive end giving ground, or if he sees that the linebacker is about to move past him to the outside, he must leave the defensive end and execute a running drive block on the linebacker. Helping the tackle— when the defensive end works to the outside—should be of secondary impor-

The center (left) *in this combo block, must move away from his snapping hand. This means that he must hit the nose tackle with his free hand.*

tance to attacking and blocking the inside linebacker.

DRILL:

Combo Block II (Guard and Center)

When working a combo block with the guard, the center's technique should be the same as that of the tackle. The hardest part of this combo block occurs as the center moves away from his snapping hand. When this happens, it is necessary for him initially to strike the nose tackle with his free hand, even though it may not be the hand on the side of the combo-blocking guard.

There may be a time during a game, for example, against an even front, when it is necessary for the guard and center

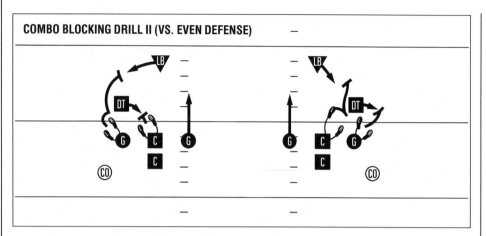

COMBO BLOCKING DRILL II (VS. EVEN DEFENSE)

to swap reads, assignments, and techniques as they execute the combo block. In this situation the guard will have a defensive tackle on the line in front of him and the center will be covered by a linebacker who is off the line of scrimmage. The coach will need to modify the drill if he knows that his offensive players will face this type of defense in an upcoming game.

In this drill situation it is the center who must check the linebacker for the inside blitz as he moves toward the defensive tackle on the side of the combo block.

Combo blocking is effective versus a stunting defense. By using a combo block, the offense can be sure to make fairly good contact with the defensive players no matter what type of stunt they might run. It is also the type of blocking which lends itself to an explosive option-style of running back, as holes often are developed all along the line of scrimmage and not merely at the designated area of attack.

The big disadvantage to combo blocking is that the offensive linemen do not have the all-out, completely-focused attack on one defender that they do with a drive block. Often coaches will find that the combo block is not executed with the same intensity and physical aggressiveness as other running blocks. However, when used with other types of running blocks, a good, sound, well-taught combo blocking scheme can be a very successful and efficient weapon.

Short-Yardage/Goal-Line Blocking

One special type of run blocking is used

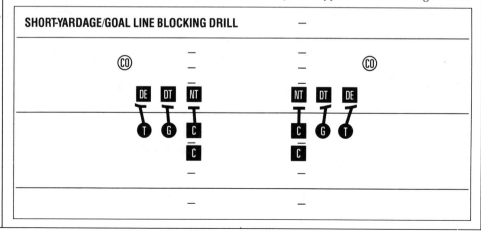

SHORT-YARDAGE/GOAL LINE BLOCKING DRILL

At the goal line or in short-yardage situations, linemen do not need lateral mobility because they only will be driving straight ahead. The four-point stance, with weight forward, contributes to an all-out charge.

for extreme short-yardage and goal-line plays. On these plays, the offense is not fooling anyone. Both the offensive and defensive players know that the offensive linemen are going to be blocking straight ahead and trying to move the defenders back a few inches or feet.

Often when blocking on these plays, offensive linemen completely adjust their stances. There's no need to be in a stance that allows for pulling to the right or left; the linemen only will be charging straight ahead. So many blockers revert to a four-point stance, reaching out with both hands four to six inches in front of their shoulder pads. In this position, the linemen put as much weight on their hands as possible.

The blocker should have his feet slightly wider than his hips. His hips should be up and his shoulders extended forward and lower than the level of his hips. His body must be aligned to allow him to explode straight ahead.

Once the lineman is set in a good stance the next most important thing for him to do is to concentrate on getting off on the snap count. Knowing the exact instant the play is to begin is a tremendous advantage for the offensive blockers, and utilizing this advantage to its fullest is even more important on short-yardage and goal-line plays.

DRILL:

Short-Yardage/Goal-Line Blocking

The defensive players assume a stance similar to that of the offensive blockers. Each defender's weight should be forward, shoulders low, hips up, and feet slightly wider than the width of the hips. As the defensive players see the ball snapped and the offensive men move, they should explode forward, driving their legs and trying to penetrate the offensive side of the line of scrimmage.

When first practicing this technique, only one offensive lineman at a time should block. As the efficiency and skill of the blockers increase, the drill can be run three-on-three.

The blocker must get off on the ball, exploding forward from the ground with the big muscle groups of the legs, hips, and lower back. He must keep his shoulders low and drive the defender back off the line of scrimmage with quick, short steps. It is important for the offensive lineman to focus on the defender, and expect him to come off the line in a low, hard charge. The offensive lineman should use his hands and arms only to finally push the defender. The initial con-

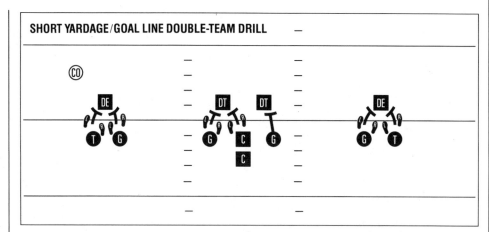

SHORT YARDAGE/GOAL LINE DOUBLE-TEAM DRILL

tact and force of the block must be made with the shoulder pads.

Each blocker must have the resolve and dedication to move the defensive man off the line of scrimmage in a short-yardage situation. This is neither the place nor the time to think of finesse blocking or trying to step laterally to get relative position on the defender. Short-yardage blocking is a "gut check" for the entire offensive team, especially the offensive line, and answers the question of who is the most physical, who has the most determination—the offense or the defense.

For each offensive lineman, blocking on goal-line and short-yardage running plays becomes a personal battle. Each

play is unique, determining if the blocker will push the defender straight back or the defensive player will penetrate the line of scrimmage and stop the play.

Before leaving short-yardage and goal-line blocking, be sure to work on double-team blocking. This usually consists of two-man blocks on one or more defensive linemen who are aligned on either side of the point of attack.

DRILL:

Short-Yardage/Goal-Line Combo Blocking

Both blockers must come off low and hard, charging hip-to-hip with short, powerful steps; exploding into the defender in unison with their shoulder pads together; and driving him back off the line of scrimmage.

Pass Protection

Protecting the quarterback as he attempts to pass is one of the most important jobs of any offensive lineman. While pass blocking, the offensive lineman is not asked to drive a defender off the line of scrimmage or to turn him away from the ball carrier. Instead, the blocker is asked to place his body in a relative position between the defender and quarterback.

Rather than firing out, the blocker is now asked to set up—but not retreat—on the offensive side of the line of scrimmage. Rather than initiating contact, he allows the defender to start his charge and reacts to his movement. Even though he is not firing out, the blocker must be aggressive at the moment of contact and strike the defender in a physical manner.

In pass protection, as in any type of offensive line blocking, pride becomes a major element in overall success. Great blockers hate to be beaten and refuse to quit until the whistle blows ending the play.

Prior to teaching the actual pass-protection techniques, the coach should spend some time with the offensive line discussing the mental aspects connected with pass blocking.

First, every offensive lineman must understand that pass protection is not passive. It must be physical and aggressive once contact begins.

Second, the offensive lineman must anticipate the charge of the defensive player. He must be aware of what the defensive man can do to rush the passer

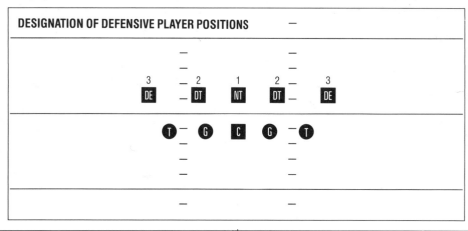

DESIGNATION OF DEFENSIVE PLAYER POSITIONS

If a quarterback is given enough time by his offensive blockers, he almost always will find an open receiver.

based upon his alignment prior to the snap of the ball. Before the snap, the blocker should determine if the defender is directly in front of him (a "one" position), on his outside shoulder (a "two" position), or lined up wide to the outside (a "three" position).

Finally, the blocker must remember that his job is to keep the defensive man from getting to the quarterback. Each offensive lineman must determine his set-up position; he must not allow the defensive man to dictate it. The blocker must realize that the target for the pass rusher is the quarterback and that he must maintain a relative position with his body between the quarterback and the rusher. The blocker must stop the defender's momentum toward the quarterback and cause him to restart his pass rush as many times as possible, thus giving the quarterback adequate time to throw the ball.

DRILL:

Setting Up for Pass Blocking

The first technique offensive linemen need to learn is how to quickly get out of the stance and set up as smoothly as possible.

In this drill we will not use any men on defense. Our only concern is to get the offensive player out of his three-point stance and into a body position to pass-protect. In the beginning, it is important for the coach to have only one player set up at a time. As the offensive linemen become more and more skilled in setting up, the coach can have the entire line set at one time.

In addition to telling the offensive lineman the snap count prior to each play, the coach also should tell the blocker where the defender is lined up, in a one, two, or three position.

The offensive lineman should line up in a balanced stance. The more weight he has on his down hand and the farther out in front of the shoulder pads the hand is, the harder it will be for him to set up. There should be just enough weight on the down hand that the offensive blocker can push off the ground with the fingers of the down hand, thus allowing him to get into a two-point stance for pass protection. There should not be a big stagger in the feet; a heel-toe or heel-instep relationship between the two feet is best.

Starting with the imaginary defensive player in a one position, the offensive player must push up and back with the down hand on the snap count. As his shoulders come up, he should take a slight step toward the center with his inside foot. This power step to the inside is necessary so he can be in position to stop the defensive player's inside charge.

The set-up technique is the same for a defender in the two position, except that now the first step of the offensive blocker—the power step—is taken with the outside rather than the inside foot.

At the same time he takes his power step, the blocker must lower his hips by flexing his knees (not by bending at the waist). He must keep his back straight and his head up, with his eyes focused straight ahead. The elbows of both arms should be in close to his body and bent so that the hands are four to five inches in front of his jersey. Both hands should be close together, thumbs almost touching, fingers up, palms facing toward the defense and even with the center of the offensive lineman's chest.

In the initial set-up with the defensive man aligned in a one or two location, it is very important that the offensive blocker always stay square to the line of scrimmage and not turn his body to the right or left.

When first teaching pass protection to the center, the coach must tell the center if he will set to his right or left with a defender in the one location.

The footwork for an offensive lineman in pass protection must change if he sees that the defender has lined up in a

The entire offensive line pass protects as a unit, each man setting up to best maintain relative position.

The pass blocking lineman must determine his set-up position and not allow the rush path of the defensive man to dictate it. The blocker power-steps back with his inside foot and waits for the rusher; he does not lunge.

three location. With the defender in this wide alignment, the blocker must kick his outside foot back with a 45-degree angle step and slide his inside foot to the outside so that his body remains in a squared, balanced position in the path of the pass rusher toward the quarter-back.

DRILL:

Pass Blocking I

Once the offensive line has mastered the technique for setting up on pass protection, it is time to introduce a defensive pass rusher to the drill. As with the run-blocking drills, use offensive linemen to play on both offense and defense.

Initially the men on defense should try only to run by the offensive blocker to the target area, which can be a dummy, a towel, or a chalk mark seven yards directly behind the offensive center. As the offensive linemen feel more comfortable in their footwork, the pass rushers can be given the flexibility of rushing to one side and then coming back to the other side of the offensive blocker.

The coach only will have one blocker and one defensive man work on each snap. In the beginning, when trying to build the blockers' confidence and foot-work, the coach should instruct the defenders to rush only to the outside from a one location.

On the snap, the blocker must power-step with his inside foot and assume a

PASS BLOCKING DRILL I

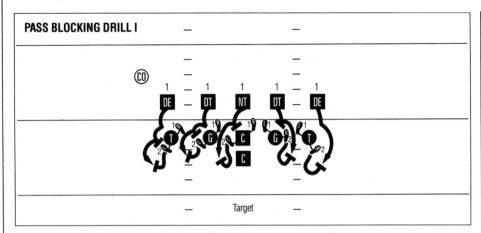

Target

pass-protection position, keeping his shoulders parallel with the line of scrimmage. As the defensive man starts his pass rush, the blocker must gather himself, lower his hips, straighten his back, position his hands and arms, raise his head, focus on the numbers of the defensive man, and prepare to strike the defensive player.

The force for stopping the momentum of the defender must start at the ground, come up through the big muscle groups of the blocker's legs and be transferred out through the palms of the offensive lineman's hands.

It is important that the offensive blocker not bend at the waist and lunge forward toward the defensive pass rusher. In this extended position he quickly will lose his balance and find that he will be unable to stay between the pass rusher and the target area.

The offensive lineman should deliver as hard a blow as possible with his hands. Once the palms have made contact with the defensive man, the blocker must press out with his arms and maintain separation from the pass rusher.

When the defensive man's momentum has been stopped, the blocker must reset his hands and arms and shuffle his feet so that he keeps his body between the pass rusher and the target area. By shuffling his feet, taking short, quick steps and keeping his feet close to the ground, the blocker can maintain a good, wide base. He cannot take long steps or cross his feet while he is pass-

protecting. He always must stay in relative position, maintaining his stance between the pass rusher and the target area and not going out to meet the defensive man, should the defender rush wide to the outside of the target area.

When the blocker sees that the defensive man once again starts his charge toward the target, he should gather himself and prepare to strike again, stopping the defensive man's momentum and causing him to restart his drive to the target area.

The blocker should continue this action until the whistle blows or the coach calls a stop to the drill. Without a quarterback in the drill, the coach can allow the men to make contact three or four times before stopping the drill and going to the next two players.

Remember, in this drill we are looking for a quick setup on the snap, a good hard blow by the blocker, balanced body position, quick-shuffling foot movement, and a well-maintained relative position by the offensive blocker on the defensive man.

DRILL:
Pass Blocking II
After the offensive linemen have demonstrated the ability to pass protect against an outside rusher who is starting in a one

PASS BLOCKING DRILL III

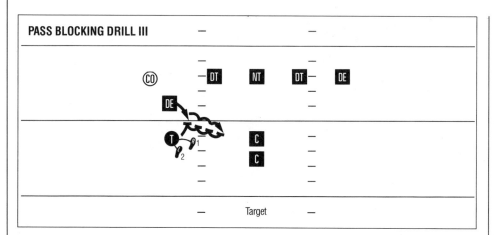

Target

location, the coach should align the defensive man on the shoulder of the offensive blocker in a two position.

At the start, the defensive man should rush in the same manner as in the previous drill. The big difference in blocking technique for the offensive lineman is that, with the defender rushing from this position, the blocker may be able to make contact only with his outside hand as he delivers the blow. All offensive linemen will have a tendency to attack the defender and turn to the outside to face the pass rusher. The coach must emphasize to the blocker that he must continue to shuffle back off the line, stay in relative position, and make certain that the defender must come through him to reach the target area.

DRILL:

Pass Blocking III

Next, the defensive man should take an inside charge from a one location. Because the defensive man is charging toward the inside, it is best to have the other players back and away from the drill area. This alignment will decrease the possibility of injury.

When the defensive player rushes to the inside, the blocker must stop his momentum to the target at all cost. He must strike the pass rusher at the line of scrimmage. Because the pass rusher is now moving directly at the target area and not wide to the outside, it is important for the blocker to maintain constant contact and not try to disengage from

the defensive man as he did when the defender rushed wide, away from the target area. The blocker must now drive the pass rusher down the line of scrimmage and keep him from penetrating the target area.

When a rusher takes an inside charge, the blocker maintains constant contact.

As the blocker drops back into pass protection, he must turn slightly toward a wide rusher, but not move to the outside away from the ball.

DRILL:

Pass Blocking IV

Finally, we will cover the technique needed to block a pass rusher who attacks the target area from a wide, or three, location. Remember that in this type of defensive location the blocker sets up by kicking back with his outside foot at a 45-

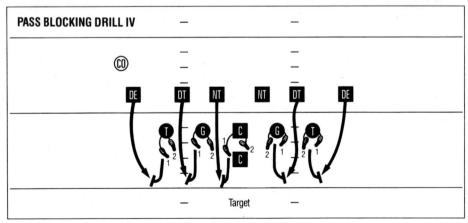

PASS BLOCKING DRILL IV

degree angle. This should be reviewed prior to starting the drill.

As with the other drills, we will have two men work at a time. The key to pass protecting against a wide rush is that the offensive man must, on the snap of the ball, turn slightly toward the defensive pass rusher.

As the blocker moves off the line of scrimmage, he must drop in a straight line, staying perpendicular to his original alignment and fighting the tendency to move to the outside, away from the ball and into the defender.

Another tendency is to give ground too quickly. When the blocker retreats off the line of scrimmage, he gives the defensive man an opportunity to rush straight to the target area by coming to the inside. The blocker must constantly maintain a position directly between the pass rusher and the target area.

As he moves off the line of scrimmage, the lineman must slide his feet, never crossing over, and shuffle back in quick, short steps. It is important that the feet stay low to the ground so the blocker is always in position to gather himself and strike the pass rusher as he attacks the target area.

When the defender moves toward the target area, the blocker must gather himself and prepare to strike with his outside arm. If the defender continues to rush upfield, the blocker should maintain contact, riding him up the field and past the

Offensive linemen must be careful not to give ground too quickly. He must maintain his position between the rusher and the passer, shuffling his feet in quick, short steps, and riding the rusher past the quarterback.

**PASS BLOCKING DRILL IV
(RIDING RUSHER PAST TARGET)**

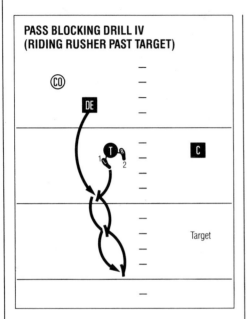

target area.

The blocker also must be prepared for the defender to rush over him or to the inside. If the defender attacks straight into the blocker, the pass protector should gather himself and strike out, stopping the defensive man's momentum. He must then extend his arms and, if possible, disengage from the defensive player's body. It is important for the blocker to realize that the defender generates more force and momentum rushing from the three position than he does from a one or a two location. Because of this,

the blocker must be sure he is in good hitting position, physically striking out at the defender. He must not get caught merely absorbing the rush of the defensive player.

Two-Point Stance

One adjustment a coach can make for his offensive linemen in sure passing situations is to allow them to start in an upright, two-point stance. This allows

In sure passing situations, some teams have their offensive linemen assume a two-point stance, which affords better body position for pass protection.

them to better focus on the rush of the defensive man, and to be in better body position to pass protect.

When taking a two-point stance the offensive lineman should flex his knees and place his outside foot slightly behind his inside foot. The blocker should place his hands on the inside of his thighs, keeping his elbows flexed so that he can push off on the snap. He should

---

WINNING POINTS
- Maintain relative position between defender and quarterback.
- Know location of defender and anticipate his charge.
- Get out of stance and set up smoothly and quickly.
- Lower hips by flexing knees; back straight; head up; elbows close to body; hands in front of jersey, thumbs almost touching, with fingers toward defender.
- Stop defender's momentum and make him restart his rush.
- Do not bend at waist or lunge toward rusher.
- Deliver hard, physical blow with palms of hands.
- Stay with defender, shuffling feet and making contact, until play ends.

---

keep his back straight, his head up, and his eyes focused on the man he is to block.

Picking-Up Stunts

Only after the offensive linemen have shown an ability to pass protect in one-on-one situations, should they work on stunt pick-up blocking.

During the course of a game it is necessary for two or more offensive linemen to work together to block defensive men who may be crossing, or stunting, with one another. These defensive maneuvers may be blocked by one of two methods: staying man-to-man or using zone blocking. In man-to-man (also called "man") pass blocking, the offen-

---

PICKING UP STUNTS I —

---

sive lineman stays with and blocks his assigned man, wherever he goes. In zone pass blocking, the offensive lineman retreats and blocks any defender who comes into his assigned area of responsibility.

Man-to-man blocking often seems the easiest to teach. The offensive lineman whose defender goes behind or second on the stunt will give ground and pick up the pass rusher when he appears from behind the stunt.

DRILL:
Picking Up Stunts

The offensive line is divided into three groups. Each group will work individually with the defensive men executing a stunt (one defender rushing behind the other) as they pass rush. The coach should designate which defensive man will go first in the stunt before the players take their stances.

Both the offensive guard and tackle should power-step with their inside foot protecting against a single inside pass rush. When the blocker sees that his man is not charging straight ahead but is looping around behind the adjacent defensive man, he must give ground. If his man is going away from the target area, the blocker merely can give enough ground to allow him to wait for the defensive player to reappear, once again attacking the target.

When the opposite occurs and the defender is stunting toward the ball, the blocker must not only give ground but also must slide behind his teammate, moving toward the ball and getting in a position to stop the defender's charge.

In the third drill, the center should work with one guard and then the other when learning stunt pick-up technique.

If you do not anticipate a great deal of stunting by the defense, stay with man-to-man pick-up for all stunts. Each offen-

PICKING UP STUNTS II

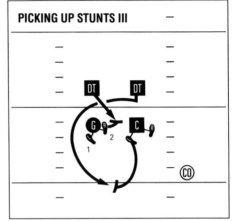

PICKING UP STUNTS III

In "zone" pass protection (left), the offensive lineman protects a certain area and blocks any rusher who approaches. In "man" pass protection (right), the lineman stays with, and blocks, his assigned man.

sive lineman knows which man is his before the ball is snapped. No matter the stunt, the lineman knows that it remains his responsibility to block that man until the play is over. Indecision is a great hindrance: with man-to-man blocking there is no indecision.

DRILL:

Uncovered Linemen

Against certain types of defensive fronts, one or more of the offensive linemen may find themselves uncovered (without a man in front of them on the line of scrimmage).

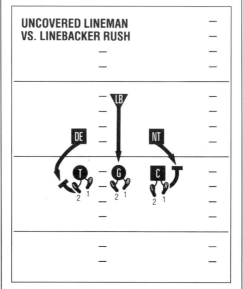

UNCOVERED LINEMAN VS. LINEBACKER RUSH	

An "uncovered" lineman has no one directly over him at the start of a play. The lineman's first responsibility then is the linebacker in front of him.

If the linebacker does not rush the uncovered lineman's area, the lineman retreats from the line of scrimmage, looks where helps is needed, and goes there.

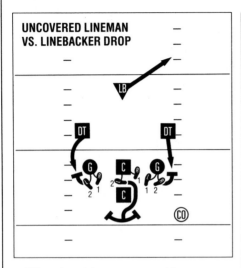

UNCOVERED LINEMAN VS. LINEBACKER DROP

When teaching uncovered linemen pass-protection technique, use the three-group approach (LT, LG, C; LG, C, RG; C, RG, RT). The coach, prior to the snap of the ball, should indicate to the person playing linebacker if he wishes him to rush or to drop off into coverage.

At the snap, the uncovered lineman's first responsibility is to block the linebacker positioned in front of him if the linebacker comes with a straight-ahead rush or stunts with one of the defensive linemen. If the linebacker does not rush, the offensive blocker should always back away from the line of scrimmage so that he can see where help is needed and move there.

DEFENSE

DEFENSIVE LINE

5

Defensive Line

- Stance   **203**
- Getting Off the Ball   **206**
- Defeating Run Blocking   **207**
- Understanding Blocking Progression   **217**
- Rushing the Passer   **220**
- Defensive Line Stunts   **231**
- Tackling   **239**
- Defensive Line Pursuit   **241**

Defensive linemen—players who have been described as the warriors in the pit—are the front line of the defensive team and are the first to feel the attack by the offense. Defensive linemen's reactions must be immediate because they are lined up only inches away from the offensive players who try to block them. They do not have the luxury of taking time to watch the play as it develops.

These two factors—the nearness of the blockers and the quickness of the attack—cause defensive linemen the most problems. These same two factors require that defensive linemen be trained to react automatically as a play develops. Their preparation must include many hours of repetitive quick-movement drills that simulate the type of blocking they actually will face in a game.

The modern defensive lineman must have the strength to defeat the blocker in front of him, the intelligence to analyze the play run by the offense, the speed to rush the passer and pursue quick offensive backs, and the mental and physical toughness to take a pounding play after play.

Great defensive linemen possess all the traits above, plus one more: They are fiercely competitive. Any player who desires to excel as a defensive lineman must develop his competitive instincts.

A defensive lineman must be a fighter, someone who accepts the challenge of one-on-one combat. He must take pride in physically defeating the man who is lined up in front of him. He must understand that by winning these individual battles he is making a great contribution to the defensive team's success.

A good defensive lineman must be totally unselfish, willing to sacrifice his own glory to allow one of his teammates to make the play. The lineman also needs to be self-motivated. Defensive linemen seldom receive the same recognition as linebackers or defensive backs. Great defensive linemen understand the importance of their role in the

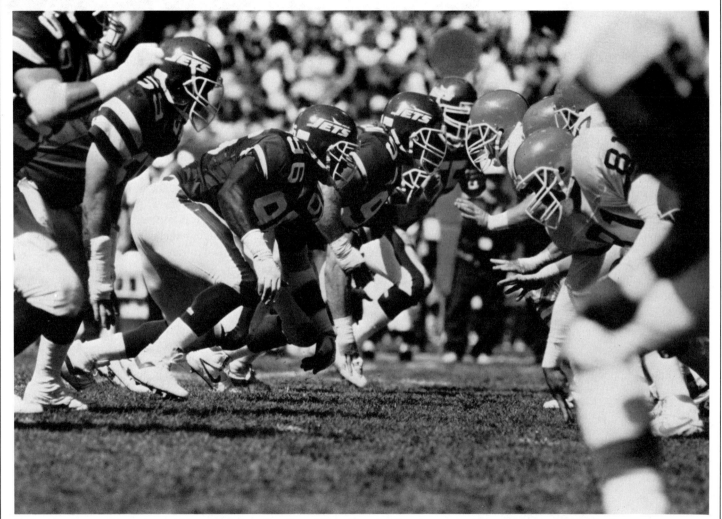

Defensive linemen must react immediately to the play of the offensive line because of the nearness of the blockers.

The closer a defensive lineman lines up to the offensive center, the more parallel his feet should be. This foot placement allows him better lateral mobility. The feet are staggered more away from center and in passing situations.

defense and play with pride and dedication.

Stance

The foot placement used by a defensive lineman varies according to where he lines up and according to the down and distance of the play being run. The closer a defensive lineman is to the offensive center, the more his feet should be parallel, allowing him to move with ease to his right or his left. A defensive lineman who is lined up in front of an offensive tackle may have a slight stagger in his foot placement.

Stance also varies with the situation. As the yardage needed by the offense for a first down becomes greater, increasing the probability of a pass, the more a defensive lineman should stagger his stance. This staggered stance allows for a quicker forward charge, which is essential in rushing the passer. A more squared stance affords the defensive lineman greater lateral mobility, necessary in stopping the running game.

Run Stance for Nose Tackle and Defensive Tackles

When an interior defensive lineman plays in front of either the center or guard, a good, square, level stance is essential. The player should stand upright,

To get into a proper defensive lineman's stance, stand with feet parallel, knees flexed, and bend forward, resting forearms on knees. Reach out with both arms, hands on ground. Then raise one hand, open, palm forward.

with his feet parallel, no wider than his shoulders. Next, the player should bend his knees until both his forearms rest comfortably on the insides of his thighs. The defensive lineman should have his back straight and his head up with his eyes focused directly ahead.

Once the player is in this position, he should reach forward with his arms, keeping both hands on the ground. Ultimately, the defensive lineman will place only one hand on the ground, but, by using both hands at the start, the player will get a feel for proper hand placement and learn to have his shoulders level. After the player is accustomed to placing his hands properly, he then may lift one of the hands from the ground, placing his forearm slightly above his thigh, with his hand open and facing forward. The distance a player reaches forward will vary with his body build, but he never should reach so far forward that his hips no longer are aligned directly above his feet.

In this position, the player's heels are off the ground with three-quarters of his weight resting on the balls of his feet. His legs are flexed enough so that his hips are slightly lower than his shoulders. The player's head is up, with his eyes focusing straight ahead. Initially, the player may not feel comfortable, but, after he gets in and out of his stance a few times, he will become much more relaxed in this position.

When a player is learning to get into a proper stance, it is important that he not move his feet backwards after he places his hands on the ground. Young defensive linemen often kick their feet back after they have gotten into their stance, causing their feet to be too far behind their hips.

Young players also have a tendency to have their shoulders uneven, one higher than the other, and to have their heads down with eyes focusing on the ground rather than straight ahead. Faults in stance should be corrected before beginning any drills.

Run Stance for Defensive Ends

The same progression as above is used when teaching proper stance to a defensive end. The only difference is the position of the end's feet when he is standing upright. Instead of having his feet parallel, a defensive end should have his inside foot back so the toe of the inside foot is even with the heel of the outside foot. This slight stagger allows the defensive end to move more easily to either his right or left. All the other important coaching points are the same. The feet are set no wider than the hips; the back should be straight; the shoulders square. The defensive end's inside hand should be placed on the ground directly beneath the front of his shoulder and in front of his inside foot. His other arm is held above his outside hip with his palm up and even with his helmet. His head is up and his eyes are focused ahead.

A defensive end's feet are set in a slight stagger, his inside foot back, toe even with the heel of the outside foot, and his inside hand is down.

Getting Off the Ball

Defensive linemen must learn to react to the movement of the center's hand as he brings the ball up to the quarterback. Because their start is so critical, all their drills begin when the ball is moved.

What follows are drills for three different techniques for getting off the ball —straight-ahead charge, lateral step, and slant step. They help teach the foot movements executed by the defensive linemen in most defenses. One or all of these get-off drills should be part of a defensive lineman's daily practice routine.

DRILL:

Getting Off the Ball

The coach kneels down with one hand on a ball that is placed on the ground directly in front of him. The drill is designed to teach the defensive linemen to move forward the instant the coach moves the ball.

All four defensive linemen get down into their stances, each making certain he can see the ball out of the corner of his eye. As the coach moves the ball, the four linemen should charge straight ahead, sprinting for five yards.

Once the coach sees the players reacting properly to the movement of the ball, he starts the drill by calling out, "Hit, hit, hit!," simulating a quarterback's cadence. This training is added to the drill so the defensive linemen will become accustomed to hearing an offensive cadence, while still understanding they cannot move until the center snaps the ball.

DRILL:

Lateral Step

This drill is designed to teach the defensive linemen to take a quick lateral step to the right or left before charging up the field. This is the type of movement a defensive lineman executes when he is responsible for the gap to his right or left. Once the players are in their stances, the coach calls right or left, indicating the direction they should step. As the ball moves, they take a short lateral step in

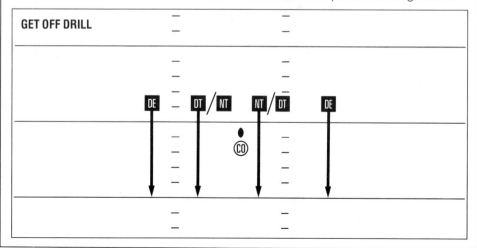

GET OFF DRILL

A quick lateral step positions the lineman for his gap responsibility.

the direction called and then charge straight up the field for five yards.

When first introducing this type of defensive line movement, the players should go one at a time so the coach may be certain they are stepping correctly.

DRILL:
Slant Step
This drill is similar to the previous one ex-

cept that now each defensive lineman steps with the foot opposite the direction called. His foot comes across his body toward the offensive side of the line of scrimmage, and he moves his arm on the same side in a ripping motion across his chest. The drill starts with the movement of the ball. The defensive linemen, after slant-stepping right or left, charge hard up the field for five yards.

A slant step comes across the lineman's body toward the offensive line.

The slant-step technique initially should be worked on one player at a time. After all the defensive linemen have mastered the technique, the entire line can do the drill simultaneously.

Defeating Run Blocking

A defensive lineman's success in playing against the running game starts with his understanding of who is blocking him, the different types of blocks he will be facing, and the techniques he needs to defeat each type of block. A good defensive lineman knows that he first must defeat the blocker before he can look for the ball carrier.

If he rises and looks for the ball carrier before defeating the blocker who is attacking him, he will be easily blocked away from the play.

It is good to start learning how to defeat a blocker by working against a blocking sled. The sled does not move or attack the defensive player, which allows the defensive lineman to focus on the pad in front of him and to learn to strike a blow in the proper manner.

Prior to starting the drill, the coach must emphasize to each of the defensive linemen that the only advantage they have over the offense is their ability to use their hands when fighting off blockers. This is countered by the offensive

A defensive lineman cannot stay upright and let a blocker get under him.

players' knowing where the play is to be run and when it will begin.

DRILL:

Defeating a Blocker (vs. Four- or Six-Man Sled)

In setting up this drill, one defensive player lines up directly in front of each of the pads on the sled. The player's helmet should be six inches away from the pad

in front of him. Going to one player at a time, the coach places the ball next to the man doing the drill and, when the player is in his stance, moves the ball to start the drill.

As the ball moves, the defensive lineman takes a short step forward, hitting the sled pad with his helmet and shoulder pads. At the same instant, the player hits the pad with the palms of both hands in a forceful, upward motion. When delivering this blow, the elbows should be directly behind the hands and slightly flexed.

After the initial contact is made, the defensive lineman extends his arms fully, separating his head and shoulder from the sled. It is important that the defensive lineman keep his knees flexed, has his feet under his hips, and drives in short choppy steps until the coach says, "Stop," and the drill ends.

Once each player has mastered the technique, the drill may be run with all four linemen firing into the sled at the same time. For this type of four-man drill, the coach positions himself in the center of the sled, making certain each of the defensive linemen actually can see the ball when it moves.

In the following drills, the sled is replaced by an actual blocker. For teach-

ing purposes, it is better, in the beginning, to run these drills with defensive players serving both as the offensive blocker and the defensive lineman. This serves two important purposes. First, the coach can take as much time as he needs with the defensive players without taking away from the practice time of offensive linemen. More important, it teaches the defensive linemen how to execute the various blocks they will face in a game.

By knowing how to execute the blocks, the defensive linemen recognize the blocks more quickly, making it easier for them to know how to defeat any offensive blocking scheme. All great defensive linemen have a solid understanding of offensive blocking techniques and principles.

Later, when the defensive players are proficient at defeating each of the offensive blocks, offensive linemen can be rotated into the drill, and the defensive linemen can be put to a true test. Be aware, however, that the introduction of offensive linemen causes greater competition; many times actual learning is decreased—another reason why the majority of the early instruction should take place in the more-relaxed atmosphere of defensive players working against defensive players.

DRILL:

Defeating Drive Blocking

Defeating the drive block is the first technique a defensive lineman needs to learn. This is the basic block used by an offensive lineman to defeat a defensive player who is lined up directly in front of him. The man playing on offense drives his head and shoulders into the numbers on the defensive man's jersey and attempts to move him straight back.

The coach tells the men on offense when the play will begin: first "hit," second "hit," or third "hit." The center moves the ball at the proper time, and the drill begins. When first learning to play against a drive block, only one pair of players should work at a time.

The man on defense needs to be told if his primary, or "gap," responsibility is to the right or left of the blocker. After meeting the blocker square with his shoulder pads, the defensive man slides his head to the side of his primary responsibility. As soon as the defensive lineman feels his shoulder pads making contact, he strikes out and up with the palms of both hands, delivering a blow to the blocker's chest area to stop his momentum. The defender then straightens his arms and fights to separate from the blocker. All the time he is doing this, the defensive

lineman must keep his feet under his hips and continuously take quick, short steps, driving the blocker backwards.

During all defensive drills of this type, special emphasis should be given to reminding the defensive player to keep his back as straight as possible, his body low by bending his knees and not his waist, and his head up. Serious injuries can happen to defensive players who neglect to keep these points in mind.

DRILL:

Defeating Hook Blocking

The hook block is used by the offensive player when he is trying to keep the defensive player from moving to his right or left. The blocker steps laterally, cutting

off the defensive player's forward movement. He then drives at the defensive player's hip.

The first thing the defensive lineman observes is the blocker moving laterally and not directly at him. He quickly sees he is not going to be able to meet pad on pad, and he delivers a blow with his hands, extending his arms and keeping the blocker from reaching his hips. He then tries to drive the blocker back across the line of scrimmage, keeping his head up so that he is in a position to locate the ball carrier.

Defensive linemen will see this type of block both to their inside and outside, so it is important to practice defeating the block to both sides.

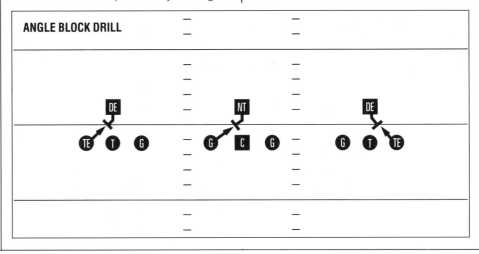

ANGLE BLOCK DRILL

DRILL:

Defeating Angle Blocking

For this drill, we set up three separate groups of players who work one at a time. Instead of reading the block of only the offensive player directly in front of him, the defensive lineman now must watch the man in front of him as well as the offensive blocker to his right and his left. This ability of a defensive lineman to see all three players is called "reading the triangle."

We are working only on defeating the angle block in this drill, so just the offensive lineman to the right or the left of the defensive player actually blocks. The player who is blocking steps with the foot closest to the defensive player and attempts to block him as quickly as possible and drive the defensive player off the line of scrimmage.

Because the first movement by the defensive lineman is straight ahead, he has very little time to react to an angle block. He is not able to meet the blocker squarely as he does when facing a drive block. The instant that the defensive lineman sees the man in front of him is not going to block him, he must determine where the block is coming from and step in that direction with the foot nearest the blocker.

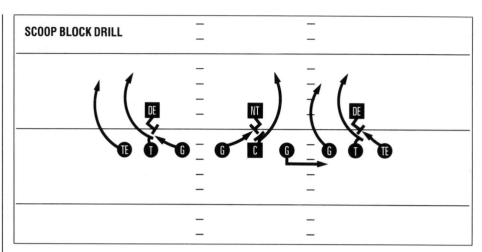

SCOOP BLOCK DRILL

When encountering an angle block, the defensive lineman must keep his knees bent, meeting the blocker with his near shoulder pad and then quickly striking a blow with his forearm on the side of the blocker. When the defensive lineman feels he has stopped the momentum of the blocker, he delivers a blow with the palm of his far hand and attempts to knock the blocker off balance.

The defensive lineman must not allow himself to be driven off the line of scrimmage and out of the hole. If he feels he cannot stop the momentum of the offensive blocker and is going to be driven out of the hole, the defensive lineman should drop to his hands and knees, creating as big a pile as possible with his and the

blockers' bodies.

When the defensive linemen regularly can defeat the angle block, the coach can call on the offensive player directly in front of the defender to drive block. This additional blocker forces the defensive linemen to step straight ahead, instead of waiting to see from which side the angle block is coming, and then stepping to defeat the angle blocker.

DRILL:

Defeating Scoop Blocking

To learn to defeat the scoop block, use the same drill set-up on the practice field as for the angle block. Again the man assigned to block the defensive lineman is coming from either the right or left.

The scoop block differs from the angle block in that the offensive blocker is not trying to drive the defensive lineman out of the hole. Instead the offensive lineman merely is trying to keep the defensive player from pursuing down the line. The first step of the offensive blocker is lateral and not directly at the defensive player; he then quickly moves his body into the defensive player. The man in front of the defensive player makes a movement like a hook block and then passes by the defender, allowing the scoop blocker to make contact. The fake hook-block action causes this to be a difficult block for the defensive man to recognize.

The defensive player first puts his hands on the man in front of him, reacting as to a hook block. As he feels the first blocker move away, the defender must charge up the field, redirecting his hands into the chest area of the oncoming scoop blocker. It is important for the defensive lineman to get his head and body in front of the scoop blocker, remaining in a position to pursue the ball carrier. One key for the defensive man to look for when trying to determine if he is actually facing a hook block or a fake is the height of the blocker's shoulder pads. On a true hook block, the shoulder pads of the blocker are much lower than when it is being faked to set up a scoop block.

DRILL:

Defeating Double-Team Blocks

In all the previous blocks that the defensive linemen had to defeat, they were being blocked by only one man. In a double-team block, two men block on one defensive lineman. The weight and strength of two offensive men make it difficult to defeat this block. The defensive player must struggle not to be pushed back; a double-team block is only successful if it drives him off the line of scrimmage.

This drill again uses the three-group set-up. The defensive lineman must read the triangle to see which players are executing the double-team block. For the defensive end, the double team usually

The defensive lineman reacts to the initial hook blocker, then charges into the scoop blocker, hitting him in the chest area with his hands.

DOUBLE-TEAM DRILL

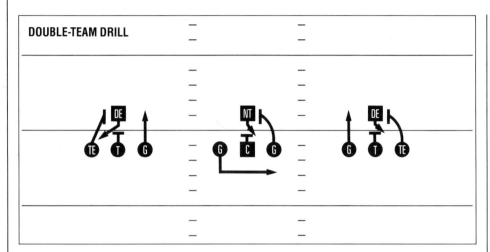

includes a drive block by the offensive tackle and angle blocking from the tight end. The nose tackle does not have it as easy because the double-team block may come from the center and either offensive guard.

For the offense, the double-team block is a combination of two blocks—a drive block by the man directly in front of the defensive player and an angle block by the man coming from the side. The drive blocker usually tries to stand the defensive player up, allowing the angle blocker to have a clear shot into the defender's side.

When the defensive lineman sees he is about to be double-teamed, he usually has both hands on the man in front of him, and the best he can do is to lean with all his body weight into the angle blocker. If he feels he is being driven back, the defensive lineman should drop his shoulder and knee to the side of the angle block, turn his body sideways in the gap between the two blockers, place his back to the angle blocker, and go to the ground. This action is the same for all defensive linemen.

DRILL:

Defeating Delayed Double-Team Blocks

One other type of double-team block, used against a nose tackle, is the delayed double-team block. In this block, the center begins a drive block just as in the regular double team. But instead of a guard serving as an angle blocker, either an offensive back or a tight end in motion becomes the delayed angle blocker.

In this drill, one of the tight ends or the fullback may serve as the delayed double-team blocker. The reaction and technique used by the nose tackle to defeat the block are the same as he used in defeating the regular double-team block. The big difference for the nose tackle is the slowness with which the block develops. He must be alert to this type of

Against double-team blocks, turn sideways into the gap between the blockers.

block and not concentrate all his energy and attention on defeating the center.

DRILL:

Defeating Trap Blocks

A trap block is different from any other type of run block a defensive lineman faces. In a trap block, the blocker isn't one of the players who form the reading triangle for the defensive player. The block also takes longer to develop due to the distance the blocker must travel to make his block.

The defensive lineman's first clue he is about to be trapped is that none of the offensive players in his reading triangle attempt to block him. This should be an automatic alert to look for a trap blocker.

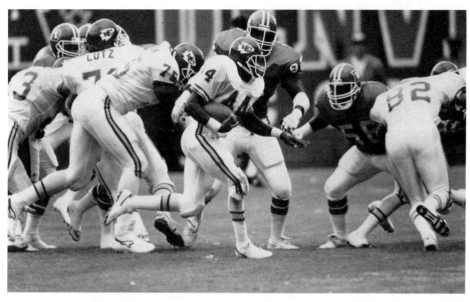

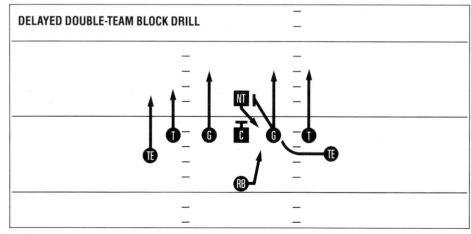

DELAYED DOUBLE-TEAM BLOCK DRILL

Defensive linemen must be alert to trap blockers (such as 75, above), who come from the other side of the ball.

For defensive ends, the trap block comes from the inside, from the direction of the ball.

The defensive tackles, who are lined up in front of the offensive guards, are trapped by a lineman from the opposite side of the ball. For the nose tackle, it is a much different story. Because of his central position, he can be trapped from either direction, with the blocker coming

TRAP BLOCK DRILL

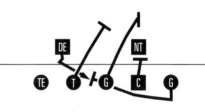
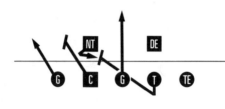

from the outside in toward the ball.

A trap block requires new techniques for the defensive players who are serving as the offensive men in the drill. The trapping lineman must step with the foot in the direction he wishes to go, swinging his foot and leg back, giving himself enough room to be able to run behind the offensive player who is adjacent to him. He must stay low as he runs, attempting to move across to the defensive side of the line of scrimmage as soon as possible. The trapper tries to get an inside-out angle on the defensive lineman he is to block. As he nears the target defensive lineman, the trap blocker shortens his stride and bends at his knees, keeping his back straight, head up, and eyes open. He then explodes into the defensive player.

A defensive end normally sees a trap play develop when the tackle and guard in his reading triangle both block in toward the ball. The defensive end's first reaction is to step out to the tight end, prepared to defeat an angle block.

The instant he senses the tight end is not trying to angle-block him, the defensive end must attack the line of scrimmage, slanting hard in toward the center. As he makes the move to the inside, the defensive end looks past the center, locating the offensive player attempting to trap him.

Once he has determined which offensive player is the trap blocker, the defen-

sive end gathers himself, turning square into the blocker. The instant the blocker reaches him, the defensive end brings his outside shoulder and forearm hard across the helmet and shoulder pads of the offensive man. This technique redirects the blocker's body back into the hole to which the ball-carrier is heading.

At the moment of contact, it is important for the defensive end to have a good bend at his knees, a straight back, and his shoulder pads at the same height as those of the offensive blocker.

One reaction the defensive end must avoid, if no one in his reading triangle blocks him, is charging straight across the line of scrimmage. The farther he moves into the offensive backfield, the easier it is for the offensive blocker to trap him.

A defensive tackle reacts to a trap the same way as the defensive end, except he is dealing with the guard and center in his reading triangle, and the offensive tackle instead of the tight end.

The clue for the nose tackle that he is about to be trapped is that no one in his reading triangle is blocking him. Usually he sees one guard firing straight ahead and the center and other guard moving in the other direction. Because the trap normally comes from the side away from the center's movement, the nose tackle

As soon as he determines who is going to block him, the defensive lineman turns square to the blocker and hits him with his outside shoulder and forearm.

first should look in that direction. When he determines which of the offensive blockers is trying to trap him, he uses the same technique to defeat the block as the defensive end. The man trapping a nose tackle generally is an offensive tackle, but it also may be a tight end; the nose tackle should be given the opportunity to work against both blockers.

DRILL:

Defeating Lead Blocks

The lead block differs from all other blocks in that the man executing the block is not an offensive lineman or a tight end. In a lead block, the man doing the blocking is one of the running backs. While most running backs don't have the size of a defensive lineman, they usually are much quicker and often have the leg strength to explode at the point of contact.

Running backs who are functioning as lead blockers present an additional problem for a defensive lineman. Normally, when a defensive lineman scans the backfield, he looks for the running back carrying the ball and fails to focus on the running back who is blocking. Defensive linemen must realize that they first must locate and defeat the man assigned to block them before they search for the ball carrier.

The technique used by many running backs when blocking a bigger defensive lineman is to come in low, driving their shoulder pads into the waist of the defensive player. If not played properly by the defensive man, the lead block often slides down the defender's leg to his knee.

The technique used by a defensive lineman to defeat the lead block is similar to that used in defeating a trap block, except the defender must not be quite as aggressive and must make certain he

Defensive linemen cannot allow themselves to focus solely on the running back carrying the ball. They first must locate and defeat any lead blocker.

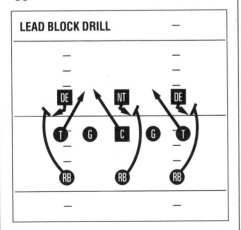

LEAD BLOCK DRILL

has his legs well behind his shoulders. Should the defensive player see his shoulder pads are above those of the lead blocker, he must extend both arms, striking the blocker's shoulder pads with the palms of both hands and pushing the offensive back to the ground.

Once the blocker is defeated and his momentum has been stopped, the defensive lineman must regain his balance, locate the ball carrier, and prepare to make the tackle. The better a ball carrier is, the closer he runs to the lead blocker. Consequently, there may be little time for the defensive lineman to react after taking on the lead blocker.

Understanding Blocking Progression

Once a defensive lineman understands how to defeat the various blocks he will face, he is ready to look at the entire offensive scheme. When a defensive lineman gets into his stance on the line of scrimmage prior to the start of every play, he quickly should review in his mind the order in which offensive players can attack him. Knowing this order allows the defensive lineman to go from one potential blocker to another in a logical and systematical manner, to look for certain types of blocks only when they can occur, and to determine the blocker and the type of block he is using. This is a mental rather than a physical exercise and is best practiced initially with no movement by the offense.

To introduce progression to a defensive lineman, have him stand up and point out the order of the offensive blocking progression relative to his position. When standing, it is easier for him to see and point out the players who are not in his immediate blocking triangle.

Once the player knows the correct progression, the player should assume his stance and call out the blocking progression from his playing perspective.

The next step is for the defensive lineman mentally and verbally to associate the various types of blocks that may come from each offensive player in the blocking progression. This is an excellent mental warm-up to use when the players first come on the field.

Later, blocking progression can be incorporated into the regular practice session in drill form, with the men on offense executing the proper blocks against the defensive players. This type of drill serves as the final examination for the defensive lineman versus the running game.

As with the teaching of most football techniques, it is best to start the drill at half-speed, allowing the defensive lineman time to focus on each blocker and become comfortable with the natural blocking progression without worrying about contact. When properly run at full speed, it demonstrates the defensive lineman's knowledge of blocking progression, his understanding of the different types of blocks used by each offensive blocker, and his grasp of the techniques he must use to defeat each type of block.

One final note: The defensive players who are portraying the offense in practice must understand they are learning how an offensive player attacks a defensive lineman and the different types of blocks that will be used in this attack. All players in the drill must work very hard, whether they are on offense or defense, helping each other to become better and more skilled.

Drills such as those that follow can be used not only to teach, but also to develop individual and team pride—vital ingredients in building a successful and winning program at any level.

DEFENSIVE END BLOCKING PROGRESSION

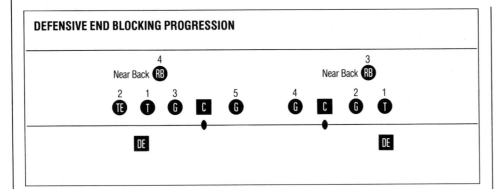

DEFENSIVE TACKLE BLOCKING PROGRESSION

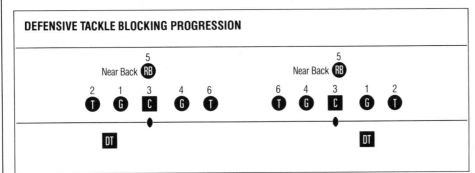

BLOCKING TRIANGLES

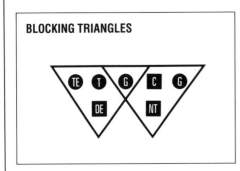

NOSE TACKLE BLOCKING PROGRESSION

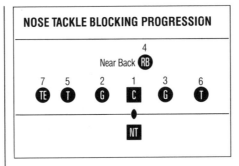

Defensive End Blocking Progression

1. Tackle   4. Near back
2. Tight end   5. Off guard
3. Near guard

Expected Block Types, By Position

1. Tackle—drive, hook, or double-team
2. Tight end—angle, scoop, or double-team
3. Near guard—angle, scoop, or double-team
4. Near back—lead
5. Off guard—trap

Defensive Tackle Blocking Progression

1. Near guard   4. Off guard
2. Near tackle   5. Near back
3. Center   6. Off tackle.

Expected Block Types, By Position

1. Near guard—drive, hook, or double-team
2. Near tackle—angle, scoop, or double-team
3. Center—angle, scoop, or double-team
4. Off guard—quick trap
5. Near back—lead
6. Off tackle—slow trap

Nose Tackle Blocking Progression

1. Center
2. Strongside guard
3. Weakside guard
4. Near back
5. Strongside tackle
6. Weakside tackle
7. Tight end

Expected Blocks, By Position

1. Center—drive, hook, or double-team
2. Strongside guard—angle, scoop, or double-team
3. Weakside guard—angle, scoop, or double-team
4. Near back—lead or delayed double-team
5. Strongside tackle—trap
6. Weakside tackle—trap
7. Tight end—trap or delayed double-team

NOTE: *Because the nose tackle is positioned in the middle of the offensive formation, he has a greater chance of blockers attacking him from his right or his left. Hence, it may take the nose tackle a longer time to understand and be able to recognize the blocking progression.*

DRILL:

Defensive End vs. Trap Block by Off Guard

To run this drill in practice, the coach stands behind the defensive end and, using hand signals, indicates which of the offensive players is to be the blocker and what type of block he is to use.

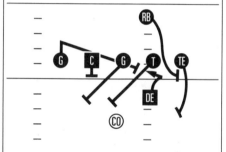

DEFENSIVE END VS. TRAP BLOCK BY OFF GUARD —

DRILL:

Defensive Tackle vs. Scoop Block by Center

The coach should indicate by the use of hand signals which of the offensive men is to block the defensive tackle and the type of block he is to use. The defensive tackle should be able to demonstrate his knowledge of block progression and his ability to use the proper technique in defeating the offensive blocker.

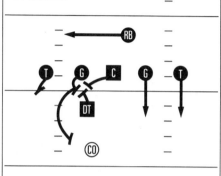

DEFENSIVE TACKLE VS. SCOOP BLOCK BY CENTER —

DRILL:

Nose Tackle vs Delayed Double-Team Block with Center and Near Back

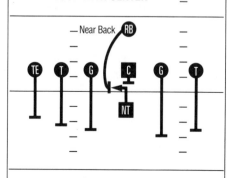

NOSE TACKLE VS. DELAYED DOUBLE-TEAM BLOCK WITH CENTER —

With the use of hand signals, the coach indicates the type of block he desires and the offensive player or players who are to execute the block. Once the nose tackle properly reacts to all the different types of blocks presented by the offense, the drill can be quickened to better simulate game conditions.

Rushing the Passer

For a defensive lineman, rushing the passer usually is the high point of playing the game. Against the running game, the offensive play selection dictates the style and type of reaction a defensive lineman must make. The defensive lineman's response to certain types of blocks or blocking schemes is predetermined. This all changes when the offense elects to pass the ball. Then, it is the defensive lineman who has the options, and it is the offensive player who must do the reacting.

Rushing the passer is a learned skill, one that can be assimilated in a systematic fashion. It also is a skill that allows for individuality, with the defensive lineman able to work on and adapt the pass-rush techniques best suited for his body structure and physical ability.

Before going onto the practice field, defensive linemen need to know some basic principles of rushing the passer.

For pass rushing, the stance is adjusted by decreasing the width of the feet, adding foot stagger, raising the hips, and putting more weight forward.

These are areas of mental rather than physical concentration. Once learned, they will increase the effectiveness of the pass rush greatly.

The defensive lineman first must understand the importance of "getting off the ball" if he is to have success. He should pay close attention to the down and distance for the offense, realizing that the longer the distance the offense needs to go, the greater the possibility there is for a pass. As the probability of a

Fighting through a wall of blockers and sacking the quarterback is one of the greatest thrills for a defensive lineman.

pass increases, the defensive lineman adjusts his stance. He decreases the width of his feet, adds a greater stagger in his stance, and places his front foot directly under his hip, closer to the line of scrimmage. His hips should be raised to a position slightly higher than his shoulder pads, and he should put more weight on the hand that is on the ground. When anticipating a pass by the offense, the defensive lineman should have his head up with his eyes focused on the ball, his body weight well forward. This style of stance allows him to move across the line of scrimmage the instant he sees the center snap the ball.

A defensive lineman's basic job against a pass play is to pressure the quarterback. He may not always be able to tackle the quarterback before he throws the ball, but he may be in position to force the quarterback to hurry his throw or to obstruct the pass. If a defensive lineman rushing directly at a quarterback sees the quarterback is about to throw, he should be prepared to stand tall, raise his arms into the air, and obstruct the quarterback's vision and passing lane. By thinking—and acting—in this manner, if the pass is thrown in his direction, the defensive lineman often will be in position to cause an incompletion, tipping the ball into the air or

Rushing defensive linemen must be ready to raise their arms to obstruct a pass.

knocking it to the ground.

The entire defensive team, and the defensive line in particular, must realize that an incomplete pass is the same as a running play that gains nothing. Often it is the hurrying of the pass or the tipping of the ball in flight that causes the pass to be incomplete or intercepted. Although the sacking of the opposing quarterback is an exciting and an important play for a defensive lineman, these two other types of play may be equally important to the outcome of a game.

Just as a defensive lineman understands the different types of blocks he may face on running plays, he also must have an insight into the different ways the offense blocks on the various types of pass plays: drop-back, sprint-out, play-action, dash, roll-out, and screen. These pass plays used by the offense should be introduced and explained in the classroom and then practiced, one at a time, on the field.

Regardless of the type of offensive pass play being executed, a defensive lineman first must defeat the offensive player assigned to block him. Defeating this player must be his number-one priority after he has determined that a pass play is coming. Once the blocker is defeated, the defensive lineman is in position to obstruct the pass or pressure the

quarterback. A young defensive lineman, in particular, usually looks for the quarterback immediately, never realizing that the quarterback probably is not in a position to throw the ball so quickly. It is during these first few moments of each pass play that a defensive lineman must concentrate on defeating the offensive blocker and not on the man with the ball.

Above all, the defensive lineman must develop an intensity and purpose in his pass rush. He must understand that he has to keep his feet moving and not be stopped, steadily boring in, collapsing the pocket, exerting more and more pressure on the quarterback. No matter how tempting it seems, this is not the time to push and shove the blockers around. The defensive lineman's goal always is to shed the blocker and get to the quarterback as quickly as possible.

There are seven basic individual pass-rush techniques that can be learned by a defensive lineman. No one defensive lineman will be able to become proficient at all of them. What each player needs to do, after he has been introduced to and practiced all seven techniques, is select the one or two that are best suited to him.

A defensive lineman who is short in stature will waste valuable practice time

trying to master an "arm over" pass-rush technique, and a defensive lineman who lacks upper-body strength may become frustrated if he is asked to "bull" rush time and time again. It is up to the player and the coach to find the correct rush techniques for each player. The defensive lineman should constantly practice these individually selected and specific pass-rush techniques until he becomes a master at executing each of them.

In all the following drills, defensive players are used for both the offense and defense. A defensive lineman's ability to rush the passer is greatly increased if he understands the techniques used against him by the offensive player. The best way to learn offensive techniques is to be forced to play the position in practice. Many times the starting defensive linemen are not asked to take their turn on offense. But instead of helping them by allowing them to rest, the coach actually is hurting their development by taking away a valuable learning experience.

Before a defensive lineman can learn individual pass-rush techniques, he must understand where he is trying to go with his pass rush. He needs a feel for where the target, i.e., the quarterback, will be located. The sprint drill is designed to give the defensive lineman a definite point at which to direct his rush.

It also serves to emphasize, above all else, that a defensive lineman must keep his feet moving toward the target.

DRILL:
Sprint, Touch, and Go

In this drill, the offensive players line up with their arms resting on their thighs. They don't move or block. As the center moves the ball, one defensive lineman at a time charges across the line of scrimmage, touches the offensive player in front of him with his near hand, and sprints toward the target (something such as a towel placed on the ground). He should be instructed to run through

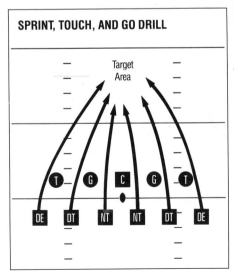

SPRINT, TOUCH, AND GO DRILL

Target Area

the target area. The depth of the target from the line of scrimmage can be changed each day to give the defensive linemen a feel for a five-, seven-, and nine-yard drop by the quarterback.

In the following drills, the offensive players are "live" and execute a pass-protection block against the rushing defensive linemen. The blocker attempts to stay between the pass rusher and the target area for as long as possible.

The drills feature only one defensive lineman rushing against one offensive blocker and begin with the command "Hit!" by the coach. The drills end when the coach says "Stop!" or blows the whistle. Blowing the whistle is the best way to end any drill because it conditions the defensive players to respond to a sound that stops play during an actual game. However, a whistle cannot always be used to end a drill, because it is distracting to other players who are practicing different techniques on nearby areas of the field.

DRILL:
Shoulder-Club and Slip

This pass rush technique starts with a fast outside charge by the defensive lineman. The first step is with the inside foot. If at all possible, the defensive line-

man should try to reach the offensive blocker by the time he takes his second step with his outside foot.

The defensive lineman then brings his outside hand hard under the outside shoulder pad of the offensive blocker. He pushes the blocker's pad up and in with his hand.

As the defensive lineman feels his hand make contact, he steps with his inside foot, drops his inside shoulder, and drives it under the outside armpit of the blocker.

Once he is in this position, the defensive lineman straightens his back, bows his neck and head back, and pushes up with the big muscle groups of his legs.

Next, it is important for him to force his hips forward and attempt to run by the offensive blocker. Most young players forget to force their hips forward, often completely stopping their foot movement, and merely lean on the offensive blocker and never reach the target area.

This is an excellent pass-rush technique for a defensive lineman who is average or short in stature but who has good speed off the ball.

DRILL:
Wrist-Club and Over-Arm

Again the rusher will use a quick outside charge, stepping first with the inside foot

In the shoulder-club and slip move, the defensive lineman brings his outside hand hard under the blocker's shoulder pad, then drops his inside shoulder and brings it up under the blocker's outside armpit and pushes by.

and then trying to reach the offensive blocker by his second step with his outside foot.

For this technique, the defensive lineman takes the outside arm and, with the forearm at a 45-degree angle, strikes a blow to the outside wrist of the blocker, driving the blocker's outside hand and arm across his chest.

As this contact is made, the defensive lineman takes his inside arm and reaches over the outside shoulder pad of the blocker. Once his arm is over the shoulder pad, the defensive lineman tries to drive the point of his elbow hard into the back of the blocker. This action serves to propel the defensive lineman past the blocker.

When contact has been made with the elbow, the defensive lineman once again forces his hips forward, accelerating past the offensive man toward the target.

A defensive lineman must have speed and adequate height in order to use this pass-rush technique effectively.

DRILL:

Rip-and-Run

Both of the previous pass-rush techniques involve outside charges. With the

In the wrist-club and over-arm move, the defensive lineman strikes the blocker's outside wrist with his outside forearm, then reaches his inside arm over the blocker's outside shoulder pad and drives back with his elbow.

rip-and-run technique, the rush goes to the inside of the offensive blocker. It also differs from the previous rushes in that the defensive lineman uses only one arm instead of two when executing the technique.

On the snap of the ball, the defensive lineman steps quickly with his outside foot across the front of the blocker. As he takes his second step, he lowers his outside shoulder, driving it under the inside armpit of the blocker. With his outside arm bent at the elbow in a 45-degree angle, the defensive lineman rips up and back, lifting the inside shoulder of the blocker as much as possible.

It is important for the defensive lineman once again to force his hips forward, driving with his feet and accelerating toward the target.

This is an excellent change-of-pace pass rush for the outside pass rusher who has speed and upper body strength.

DRILL:
Bull Rush
This pass-rush technique is most effective against offensive linemen who have a fast drop off the line of scrimmage. For most defensive linemen, it is difficult to reach the blocker by his first or second step. What the defender faces is an offensive player who is giving ground

The rip-and-run technique is an inside rush move. The defensive lineman steps quickly with his outside foot across the front of the blocker, rips up and back under the blocker's inside arm with his outside arm, and charges past.

quickly. Because this offensive part of the drill can be a problem to teach and simulate, it is best to have the offensive guards line up one yard off the line of scrimmage and the offensive tackles line up two yards off the line prior to the snap of the ball.

At the snap of the ball, the blocker starts retreating, ready to absorb the rush of the defensive lineman.

It is important for the defensive line-man to explode off the line with a low, hard charge, keeping arms bent, elbows near his sides, and hands open with the fingers up. As he nears the blocker, the defensive lineman drives the heels of his hands forward and up, punching them into the armpits of the blocker. When contact is made, the pass rusher extends his arms, keeping his feet moving with short, powerful steps. Keeping his back straight and the top of his helmet under the chin of the blocker, the defensive lineman drives the blocker straight into the quarterback. If necessary, the defensive player must be prepared to scramble directly over the blocker as he works toward the target area.

This is an excellent pass-rush technique for any defensive lineman to use against a soft, deep-setting offensive blocker. It is especially good for a big, strong defensive player who may not

Use the bull rush against blockers with a fast drop. The defender charges into the blocker, hitting him with the heels of his hands, and drives him backward.

have great speed off the ball.

DRILL:
Bull-and-Jerk

The bull-and-jerk technique starts off similar to the bull technique. The variation comes at the point of contact and involves both the offensive and defensive players.

When contact is about to occur, instead of continuing to give ground, the offensive blocker plants both feet and fires or lunges out at the pass rusher.

The defensive pass rusher must anticipate this adjustment by the blocker. When he sees it taking place, the defensive lineman should be prepared to change his technique. Instead of punch-

ing out with his hands, he now grabs the front of the blocker's jersey, and, using the blocker's own momentum, jerks him either to his right or left.

It is important to step across the blocker with the foot on the side of the jerk, thus allowing the pass rusher's hips to pass the blocker and giving the defensive lineman a free rush to the target area.

Big, strong defensive linemen who plan to use a bull-rush technique must be prepared to incorporate the jerk technique as part of their individual pass-rush package.

DRILL:
Bull-and-Slip

This is another variation of the basic bull-rush technique that should be used against a fast-setting offensive lineman, who, at the instant of contact, does not plant his feet and fire out but instead chops his stride, gathers himself, and does not permit the defensive player to push him back into the target area.

It starts at the snap of the ball with the same low, hard charge off the line of scrimmage. As the pass rusher feels the blocker getting stronger and stronger (but not overextending), he pushes up on the blocker's shoulder pads with one hand, steps across the blocker's body with the opposite foot, lowers his hips by bending his knees, and drives his free arm and shoulder pad under the blocker's raised armpit.

Once he is in this position, the pass rusher straightens his legs, lifting the blocker up. Keeping his back straight, the defensive lineman then keeps his feet moving, pushing his hips forward and up, allowing him to accelerate past the offensive blocker toward the target.

DRILL:

Shoulder-Club-and-Spin

This is the most difficult pass-rush tech- nique for young or beginning defensive linemen to master. It should be taught only after the preceding six pass rush techniques have been learned and per- fected.

In order to have success with this technique, the defensive lineman must

In the bull-and-jerk maneuver, the defensive lineman begins with a bull rush. But if the offensive blocker lunges at him, the defensive lineman grabs the front of the blocker's jersey and jerks him to the left or right.

The bull-and-slip is another variation of the bull rush. The defensive lineman charges, pushing up on one side of the blocker's shoulder pads. He steps across the blocker's body and drives his free arm under the blocker's raised armpit.

convince the offensive blocker that he is going to rush hard to his outside. The pass rusher starts exactly as he would if he were going to use a shoulder-club and slip pass rush against the offensive blocker.

The offensive blocker will be moving quickly away from the line of scrimmage, fighting to keep the pass rusher from getting to his outside. When the defensive lineman sees the blocker's momentum moving him away from the line of

scrimmage, he reaches out with his outside arm and starts the club move. Instead of slipping with the inside hand and arm, the pass rusher drives his inside forearm and hand into the rib cage of the blocker. This action should further propel the blocker away from the line of scrimmage.

As the inside arm and hand make contact, the defensive lineman leans into the blocker and spins to the inside. It is important that the defensive player spin toward the target area and not back toward the line of scrimmage. Frequently, a young player tries to spin before he has hit out with his arm and hand, allowing the blocker to stop his movement easily and drive him to the outside, away from the target area. Once the pass rusher feels he is free to the inside, he fights for separation and accelerates toward the target area.

This is an excellent technique for a quick outside rusher who wants to take advantage of an offensive player who retreats from the line of scrimmage too quickly.

One tendency all young defensive linemen have when first learning to rush the passer is to turn into the offensive blocker. This is why we start with the sprint-rush technique drill, showing defenders the proper path to the target area. Defensive linemen should have only a straight-on pass-rush path, rushing jersey number to jersey number when using one of the bull techniques. On all of the other rushes, it is important

for the defensive lineman to set and maintain the rush lane, exposing only one hip to the blocker.

Remember, a great pass rush comes from a player who has decided what technique he is going to use, has practiced and perfected the technique best suited for him, and has an intense desire to get to the target area.

Because pass rushing is an individual skill, it often is advisable, once all the techniques have been introduced by the coach, for the player to tell the coach what technique he is going to attempt. This is especially true when the pass-rush drill is run against actual offensive players.

Defensive Line Stunts

One of the most effective methods of rushing the passer is for the defense to run a pass-rush *stunt*, a rush technique that involves two or more defensive linemen looping or crossing, or a defensive lineman rushing in conjunction with a linebacker. This type of pass rush is an effective variation because it not only creates doubt in the offensive blockers' minds, it serves as an effective way to attack different types of pass protection.

Each stunt is designed with one player designated as the first rusher; the second player on the stunt attacks the line

of scrimmage before stunting behind the initial penetrator. However, the rush order (who goes first and who goes second) on a stunt can be switched if a "change" call is made, generally in the huddle.

When teaching pass-rush stunts it is best first to work on the stunts involving only the defensive linemen. All the principles taught to the defensive linemen carry over to combination defensive line and linebacker stunts.

There are two basic principles that should be explained to the defensive linemen before they begin to practice the stunts on the field. The first principle is that all stunts must be run on the offensive side of the line of scrimmage. The second is that the man who is second in the stunt (the defensive player who is coming behind the initial defensive lineman's charge) must never execute the stunt if his area is under attack by the offense.

NOTE: *In the NFL, and in the drills and diagrams that follow, stunts have names to make them easier to learn and remember. These names may vary by team, but the stunts are the same.*

DRILL:
Two-Man Stunt (End First)
In this stunt, the defensive end (DE) is

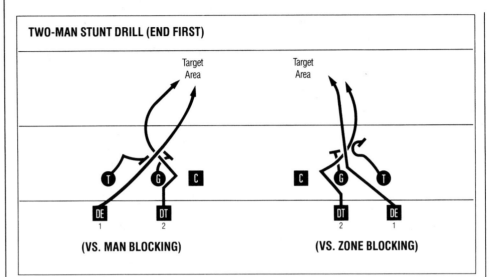

TWO-MAN STUNT DRILL (END FIRST)

Target Area

(VS. MAN BLOCKING)

Target Area

(VS. ZONE BLOCKING)

the first penetrator and the defensive tackle (DT) the second.

At the snap of the ball, the defensive end steps across the face of the offensive tackle with his outside foot. As he steps, it is vitally important that he stay low, using a rip technique with his outside arm on the offensive tackle. His primary role is to get penetration into the gap between the offensive guard and tackle, aiming for the outside hip of the guard. While he is penetrating the gap, the defensive end determines if the offensive tackle is staying with him (i.e., driving him in toward the center, thus indicating "man" pass protection) or is try-

ing to push him into the guard ("zone" pass protection).

If the defensive end determines it is "man" pass protection, he should try to execute a rip-and-run pass rush technique on the tackle. As the defensive end passes the guard, he tries to hit the guard in the buttocks with his inside hand and arm, knocking him temporarily off balance.

Should the defensive end feel the offensive tackle is trying to push him to the inside toward the guard ("zone"), he should use his inside forearm to club the near hip of the guard and instantly redirect his charge straight up the field to the

target area.

The defensive tackle takes a quick step directly at the guard with his outside foot, then takes a second step with his inside foot toward the gap between the guard and center, causing the guard to think that he is rushing to the inside.

As the defensive tackle takes his second step, he reaches out with his inside hand, touching the blocker on the inside shoulder pad. When the defensive tackle touches the guard, he pushes off of his inside foot, stepping to the outside and coming around behind the charge of the defensive end. The defensive tackle stays close to the rush of the end and doesn't run in a wide arc, which would take him completely away from the target area.

Prior to the snap of the ball it is impossible for the defensive linemen to know which of them will get free and be able to pressure the target area. Because of this, the defensive ends and tackles rush with the same intensity and desire. With this type of rush, the end and tackle often both come free and are in position to attack the target area.

When the defensive tackle, the second man in the stunt, sees that the offense is working a running play in his area, he reacts to the blocking scheme being used, plays the run, and doesn't carry out his stunt. Many defenses get burned for long runs on passing situations because they allow the second man to run his stunt without first determining if a run or pass play is being used.

This same type of stunt may be run with a defensive end and the nose tackle if you are using a 3-4 defensive alignment.

DRILL:

Two-Man Stunt (Tackle First)

All the principles of the previous stunt hold for the tackle-first stunt. The difference is that the defensive tackle now is the first penetrator.

At the snap of the ball, the defensive tackle steps across the face of the guard with his inside foot, using his inside arm to execute an outside rip-and-run pass rush. His second step takes him up the field, into the gap between the guard and tackle. His charge is toward the inside hip of the offensive tackle.

Like the end, the tackle must determine if it is "man" or "zone" pass protection. If the guard is staying with him, the defensive tackle continues his penetration into the gap. At the same time, the defender delivers a blow to the inside hip

of the offensive tackle with his outside forearm.

Should the defensive tackle feel the guard is trying to push him into the offensive tackle, the defensive tackle uses his outside forearm as a club into the side of the offensive tackle, fights for separation from the tackle, and redirects his charge straight up the field toward the target area.

The defensive end steps directly up the field with his inside foot and determines if it is a pass or run. When his area is under attack on a running play by the offense, the defensive end reacts to the run block and doesn't go through with the stunt.

If the defensive end sees it is a pass play, he should step toward the outside shoulder of the offensive tackle, reaching out and touching him with his outside hand on the tackle's outside shoulder. The instant he has made this move, the defensive end pushes off his outside foot, charging hard to the inside and coming around behind the charge of the defensive tackle. Again, it is essential for the defensive end to stay as close as possible to the defensive tackle's charge and not run in a wide arc.

This style of stunt also may be executed between a nose tackle and a defensive end.

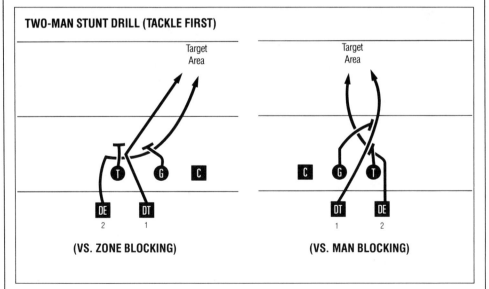

TWO-MAN STUNT DRILL (TACKLE FIRST)

Target Area

Target Area

(VS. ZONE BLOCKING)

(VS. MAN BLOCKING)

DRILL:

Defensive Tackles Stunt

This stunt is best used against teams that pull the center off the line of scrimmage and commit him to block either to his right or left. When the center leaves the middle of the line, there is a big area for the two defensive tackles to run the stunt.

In the stunt, the right defensive tackle is the first penetrator, executing a rip-and-run pass-rush technique on the guard who is in front of him. With the center leaving, the first tackle usually can be sure that the offensive team is trying to "man" pass protect. Because of

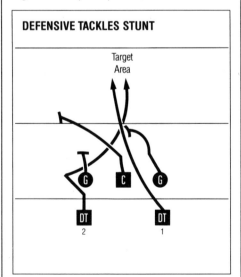

DEFENSIVE TACKLES STUNT

Target
Area

G C G

DT DT
2   1

When the center pulls, the defensive tackles have room inside to run a stunt. The right tackle is the first man in and must get good penetration.

this, it is vital for the first man to get good penetration, fighting up the field to the target area and not concerning himself with hitting the guard on the other side of the center.

The left defensive tackle steps with his inside foot directly at the left guard and determines if he is facing a pass or run. He doesn't carry out the stunt if his area is under attack on a running play.

If it is a pass play, the left defensive tackle steps into the gap between the guard and tackle with his outside foot, giving the guard the feeling that he is going to rush to the outside or run a stunt with the defensive end on his side. As soon as the tackle takes this step, he reaches out and touches the outside shoulder pad of the guard with his outside hand. He then pushes off his outside foot and charges to the inside, coming around as close as he can behind the right defensive tackle, and charging toward the target area.

DRILL:

Three-Man Defensive Line Stunt

This stunt requires a coordinated rush by three defensive linemen. The principles and techniques used in the two-man stunts also apply in the three-man stunt. The defensive end and the defensive tackle are first penetrators. They both execute an inside rip-and-run pass rush.

The nose tackle first steps directly at the offensive center, with his foot on the side of the stunt. He then steps into the guard-center gap away from the stunt with his other foot. After touching the center, the nose tackle comes around behind the charge of both the defensive end and tackle. The nose tackle must anticipate good penetration by both his teammates, staying as tight as he can to their paths and not looping around them in a big arc.

DRILL:

Defensive End and Outside Linebacker Stunt

When running this stunt, the defensive

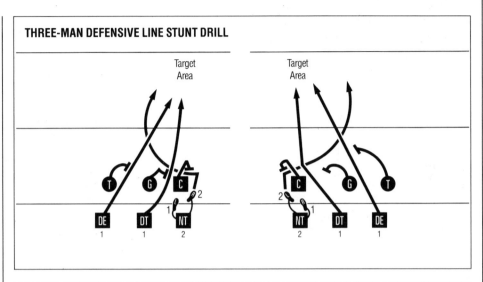

THREE-MAN DEFENSIVE LINE STUNT DRILL

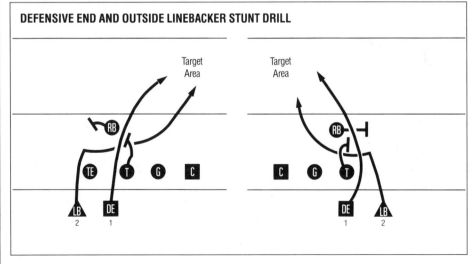

DEFENSIVE END AND OUTSIDE LINEBACKER STUNT DRILL

end is the first penetrator, using a hard outside rush on the offensive tackle who is lined up in front of him.

The outside linebacker is the second man on the stunt, coming behind the defensive end with a rush to the inside. The outside linebacker charges straight up the field, staying outside the rushing defensive end for at least three steps and making certain that he runs the stunt on the offensive side of the line of scrimmage. This is important regardless which offensive player is assigned to block the linebacker—the tight end, near guard, or near back.

Should it be a wide offensive run to the side of the stunting linebacker, he doesn't go through with the stunt. Instead, he plays the run with proper run-block defeating technique. If the offense runs the ball away from his side or up the middle of the formation, the outside linebacker executes the stunt because it puts him in a better position to make the tackle.

DRILL:

Defensive End and Inside Linebacker Stunt

The defensive end again is the first penetrator and uses the same techniques he learned on the previous pass-rush stunt.

The inside linebacker is the second man on the stunt. It is important for him to

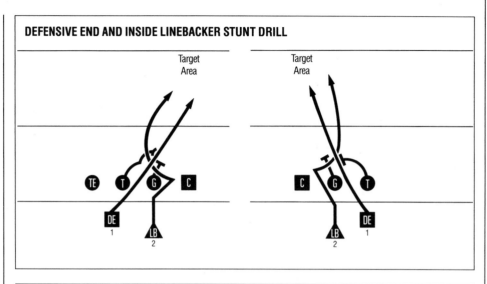

DEFENSIVE END AND INSIDE LINEBACKER STUNT DRILL

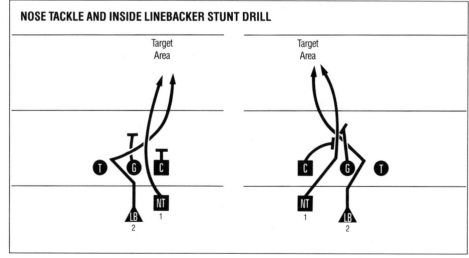

NOSE TACKLE AND INSIDE LINEBACKER STUNT DRILL

attack straight at the offensive guard. As the inside linebacker nears the guard on the offensive side of the line of scrimmage, he touches the guard with his inside hand and fakes into the inside guard-center gap. Pushing off his inside foot, the inside linebacker then comes to the outside behind the defensive end, keeping as tight an arc as possible to his rush.

As with all pass-rush stunts, if the inside linebacker sees that his area is being attacked by an offensive run play, he doesn't execute the stunt.

DRILL:

Nose Tackle and Inside Linebacker Twist

The nose tackle is the first penetrator on this stunt. He charges to the side of the stunting inside linebacker. The nose tackle uses the same techniques and reads that he used on earlier pass-rush stunts.

The inside linebacker is the second man on the stunt, as he was on the previous pass-rush stunt. The difference on this stunt is that, as he nears the guard, he reaches out and touches him with his outside hand, while faking a move to the outside. Pushing off his outside foot, the inside linebacker then charges back toward the center, coming behind the rush of the nose tackle.

The play of the inside linebacker in

NOSE TACKLE AND TWO INSIDE LINEBACKERS STUNT DRILL

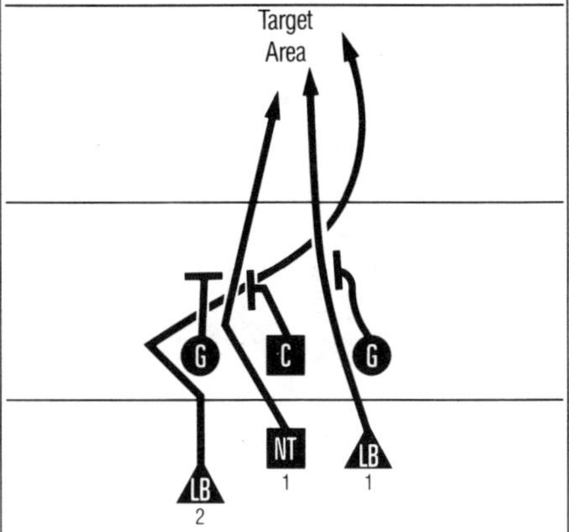

case of a running play remains the same.

A "twist change" call tells the inside linebacker that he is going to be the first penetrator on the stunt ("twist" referring to the stunt and "change" referring to the rush order of the players). If this call is made, the inside linebacker lines up on the line of scrimmage so he quickly can get penetration into the guard-center gap when the ball is snapped.

DRILL:

Nose Tackle and Two Inside Linebackers Stunt

This is another variation of a three-man coordinated pass-rush stunt. Instead of

---

involving three defensive linemen, this stunt utilizes the nose tackle and both inside linebackers (in a 3-4 alignment).

Both the nose tackle and the inside linebacker away from the direction of the call are the first penetrators on the stunt. They both charge into the gap to their left, using a rip-and-run pass-rush technique against the offensive lineman in front of them. Remember, any time the inside linebacker is a first penetrator, he must line up on the line of scrimmage prior to the snap of the ball.

The inside linebacker to the side of the call runs the stunt, using the same techniques he uses on a twist pass-rush stunt. The things he must remember are that he must now allow two men to penetrate up the field and that he must come behind both the nose tackle and the other inside linebacker as he executes his pass-rush stunt.

Other Stunt Combinations

There are any number of pass-rush stunt variations and combinations that involve defensive linemen and linebackers. These variations and combinations utilize both linebackers and the defensive end on one side of the ball; both outside linebackers and the two defensive ends; or a defensive end, nose tackle, outside linebacker on one side, and an inside linebacker on the other side. All of these combination stunts are merely two-man stunts that are simultaneously, using techniques previously learned.

Regardless of the variation of pass-rush stunt used or who is running the stunt, the two basic stunting rules are the same: (1) All pass-rush stunts are run on the offensive side of the line of scrimmage, and (2) the second man on

WINNING POINTS
- Adopt pass rush techniques best suited to body type and physical ability.
- Adjust stance by decreasing width of feet; adding greater stagger in feet; placing front foot directly under hip; raising hips slightly higher than shoulder pads; and putting more weight on hand on ground.
- Get off ball quickly; be prepared to raise hands in air.
- Defeat blocker first, then pressure quarterback.
- All stunts are run on offensive side of line of scrimmage.
- Second man does not execute stunt if his area is attacked by offense.

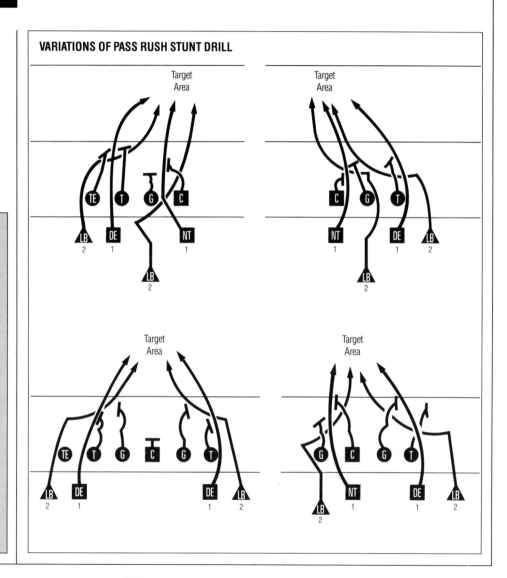

VARIATIONS OF PASS RUSH STUNT DRILL

any pass-rush stunt must not go through with the stunt if his area is attacked by an offensive running play.

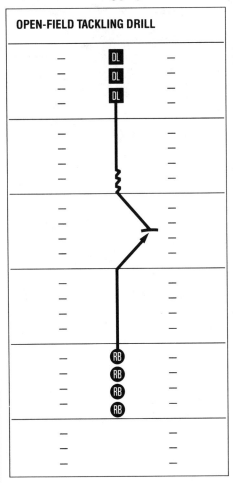

OPEN-FIELD TACKLING DRILL

Tackling

Defensive linemen seldom have the opportunity to make picture-perfect tackles similar to those made by linebackers and defensive backs. More often than not, when working in the pit with blockers attacking quickly from all directions, a defensive lineman will be hard-pressed to wrap up a ball carrier by himself. But it still is important for defensive linemen to know proper position for making a tackle.

Tackling should be taught slowly—at half speed—until the players are using the correct technique and have overcome their natural fear of contact. Body position and technique are much more important than the force of the hit.

The two most important elements of tackling for all defensive linemen are: bending at the knees, not the waist; and keeping the head up and never looking down at the ground. If a defensive lineman remembers and practices these elements, he should become a solid tackler with a decreased chance of suffering serious injury. One other element—desire—cannot be taught, but is instrumental in tackling success.

DRILL:

Open-Field Tackling

The defensive linemen are divided equally into two groups, 15 yards apart, facing one another. The members of one group serve as the ball carriers and the other group members are the tacklers.

On the command "Hit!," one ball carrier and one tackler run straight ahead five yards. The ball carrier then cuts, without faking, at a 45-degree angle to his right or left and runs in that direction.

As the tackler nears the end of his five yards, he shortens his stride and momentarily hesitates until he is absolutely certain of the direction of the cut by the ball carrier. Once the tackler determines the direction of the cut by the ball carrier, he breaks in that direction and prepares to make the tackle. It is important for the tackler to shorten his stride as he comes closer to the ball carrier, gathering himself so he can explode up and through the man with the ball.

At the moment of contact, the tackler pushes off his foot nearest the ball carrier, keeping his back straight, his head up, and his eyes open. He should place his head in front of the ball carrier's chest striking the ball carrier with his shoulder pad. The tackler pounds the insides of his elbows and forearms into the chest and back of the man with the ball. The instant his arms make contact, they will have a tendency to bounce off, and the tackler will feel his hands making contact

In the furious action of the pit, defensive linemen rarely get a chance to make a textbook-style open-field tackle.

with the ball carrier. When this occurs, the tackler grabs the ball carrier's jersey with both hands, thus preventing him from advancing up the field. It is important for the ball carrier to keep running and not stop when he sees that contact is about to occur.

The tackler should not drive the ball carrier to the ground but should explode into the ball carrier, grab his jersey, and stop his forward movement.

It is important to remember to have both players run at half speed when first teaching open-field tackling. As confidence builds and tackling techniques improve, the speed of the drill can be increased. Regardless of the speed of the drill, proper technique and not the force of the hit are what should be emphasized.

After the tackle has been made, the two men change places, go to the end of the proper line, and wait their turn. The drill continues until each defensive lineman has had an opportunity to make a tackle to his left and right.

DRILL:

Shed and Tackle

In this drill, there is an offensive blocker for the defensive lineman to shed before he tackles the ball carrier. This drill simulates game conditions for the defensive lineman. A majority of the tackles made

by defensive linemen are made in this manner.

The offensive blocker fires out into the defensive lineman, but doesn't try to drive him off the line. Remember, this is a drill to teach how to tackle and not how to shed a block.

Initially, the defensive lineman is given responsibility to make the tackle only on one side of the blocker (the side of his *gap responsibility*), and the ball carrier cuts and runs to that side.

On the command "Hit!," the blocker charges into the defensive lineman. The defensive lineman meets the charge of the blocker with his shoulder pads and helmet, always keeping his head to the side of his gap responsibility. As the de-

SHED AND TACKLE DRILL

fensive lineman's shoulder pads make contact, he strikes a blow with both hands into the upper chest area of the blocker, pushing the blocker away from the defensive lineman's gap responsibility. As the defensive lineman sheds the blocker, he gets his head up and locates the ball carrier.

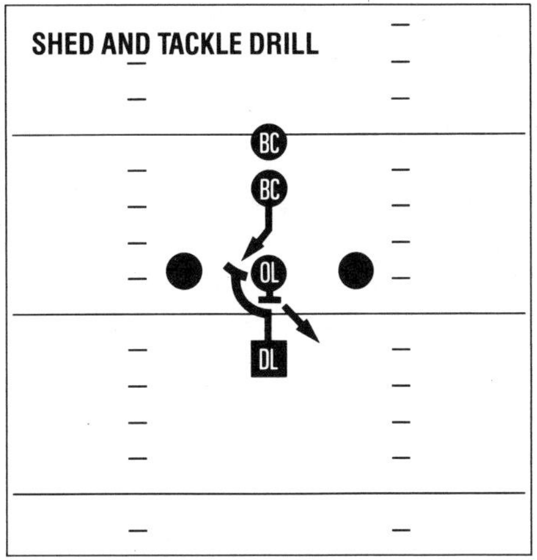

The ball carrier runs directly at the blocker, then cuts to the side of the defensive lineman's gap responsibility. It is important for the ball carrier to cut near the hip of the offensive blocker, to keep running, and not to stop when he sees the tackle is about to be made.

At the point of contact with the ball carrier, the defensive lineman explodes up and through the ball carrier, keeping his back straight and using the big muscles in his legs to stop the ball carrier's momentum. The defensive lineman wraps both arms around the ball carrier and attempts to drive him back a few steps. In this drill, it is not necessary for the tackler to drive the ball carrier to the ground.

Each defensive lineman should have an opportunity to make a tackle going to his right and left. During this drill, players should rotate from the roles of ball carrier, blocker, and defensive player.

Defensive Line Pursuit

Defensive success often can be traced to

the desire and discipline that the defensive line demonstrates as it pursues a play. Wanting to pursue and make the tackle is important, but without a knowledge of where to go on each type of play, most defensive linemen will get in on few tackles—especially on offensive plays that don't directly attack the defensive lineman's area. The following drills outline and teach the proper pursuit paths for defensive linemen to take on various types of offensive plays they can expect to encounter during the course of a game or season.

DRILL:

Running Lateral Pursuit

In this drill, each defensive lineman moves laterally, down the line of scrimmage, always keeping the ball carrier in his vision. When the ball carrier turns and drives toward the line of scrimmage, the lineman makes the tackle.

At the command "Hit!," the ball carrier turns and starts to run toward the sideline. The defensive lineman shuffles down the line of scrimmage, keeping his hips facing up the field, and not turning his body to the sideline. The defensive lineman stays a step behind the ball carrier. At first, this drill should be run at half speed.

At some point before reaching the

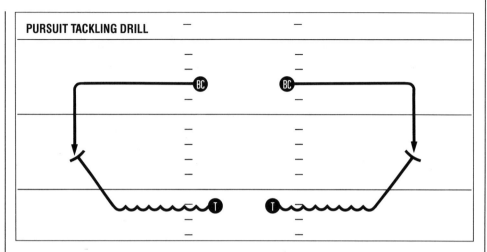

PURSUIT TACKLING DRILL

sideline, the ball carrier turns and attempts to run straight up the field. When the defensive lineman sees the ball carrier make his cut, he shortens his stride, bends his knees, and makes a tackle, using the techniques taught in the open-field tackling drill.

As with the other tackling drills, all defensive linemen should have an opportunity to make a tackle moving in both directions. The ball carrier and the tackler should change positions after the tackle has been made.

When the players become more proficient in running the drill, it is fun to allow the ball carrier to fake, cut, and try to make the defensive lineman miss the tackle.

DRILL:

Wide Pursuit

The object of this drill is to teach the defensive linemen where to pursue on wide running plays to the right and the left. The only defensive lineman who is blocked is the defensive end on the side to which the ball carrier is running. The drill is designed to be run by a five-man line, which allows all defensive linemen to practice at the same time even if the team alternates between a 3-4 and a 4-3 set.

As the ball carrier starts running wide toward the sideline, the offensive tackle on the side of the run tries to hook block the defensive end who is lined up to his outside.

At the snap of the ball, each of the five defensive linemen steps forward, hitting the shoulder pads of the offensive man in front of him with both hands, and then locates the ball carrier and determines the direction of his run.

The defensive end on the side of the run reacts to the hook block, making certain that he holds his position and does not start to widen until the ball carrier has crossed his nose. Once he sees the ball carrier moving to his outside, the end pursues down the line of scrimmage, staying one or two steps behind the ball carrier.

After the two defensive tackles and the nose tackle make contact with the offensive players in front of them, they determine the direction of the run and start moving down the line of scrimmage in the direction of the ball carrier. Once they move down the line to the next offensive player, they take a pursuit angle toward the numbers on the field. The defensive tackle on the side of the run goes five yards deep, the nose tackle 10 yards deep, and the defensive tackle on the side away from the run 15 yards deep.

The defensive end on the side away from the direction of the run charges across the line of scrimmage. He goes upfield until he is even with the running

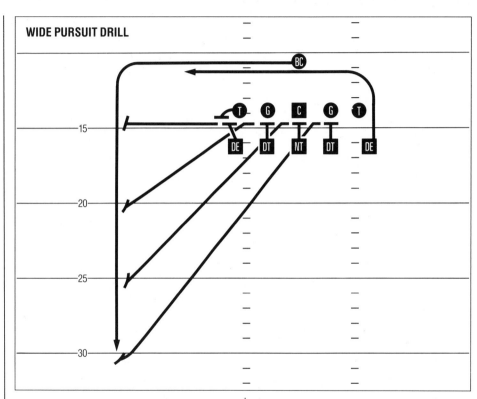

WIDE PURSUIT DRILL

back who is moving away from him. Once he reaches this depth, he then starts to chase the ball carrier, tracing his path. In chasing the ball carrier, the defensive end insures that the offense does not attempt to run a reverse.

The man with the ball runs wide, toward the sideline, until he reaches the numbers, then turns straight up the field, running in that direction for a full 20 yards. Each defensive lineman should touch the ball carrier as he runs up the field. Because this is a drill designed to teach proper pursuit, the ball carrier should not be tackled.

It is important that each defensive lineman have an opportunity to pursue to both his right and his left.

This is a good drill to run at the end of practice, instead of running wind sprints, because it also aids conditioning.

DRILL:

Screen Pass Pursuit

All the defensive linemen should realize that a screen pass is nothing more than a running play that originates on one side of the field or the other, instead of in the backfield.

Once the screen pass is thrown by the quarterback to the running back on either his right or left, all defensive linemen stop their pass rush, turn away from the quarterback, and begin running down the field in their proper pursuit paths, as they would on a wide running play.

The defensive end on the side of the screen aims for a point seven yards outside his original alignment on the line of scrimmage. The defensive tackle aims for a point three yards downfield and at the numbers. The nose tackle's path is midway between the numbers and the hashmarks. The defensive tackle away from the side of the screen takes a path to the outside of the hashmarks. Finally, the defensive end away from the screen sprints to the center of the field.

The pursuit paths and the relationships of one defensive lineman to another, which we have started in our screen pursuit drill, are easily adapted for passes that are thrown downfield to either the right or left of the ball. The difference obviously is the defensive lineman's depth of pursuit. On a deeper pass, the defensive linemen go all the way downfield to the ball.

It is very important to emphasize to all the defensive linemen the importance of stopping their pass rush, turning, finding their proper pursuit path, and pursuing the pass down the field. The tendency of most young defensive linemen is to slow down and become a spectator once the ball leaves the quarterback's hand.

DRILL:

Downfield Pass Pursuit

Because offensive linemen do not block in this drill, it is necessary for the quarterback to line up six yards off the line of scrimmage, drop back to nine yards,

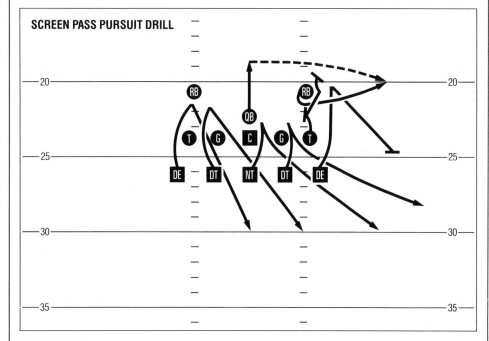

SCREEN PASS PURSUIT DRILL

and then throw the ball downfield to either his right or left. The quarterback doesn't throw the ball until the defensive linemen have had an opportunity to rush up the field.

When the receiver catches the ball, he waits for the defensive linemen to pursue downfield and then runs laterally across the field, allowing each of the defensive linemen to touch him.

As are all pursuit drills, this is an excellent combination drill for teaching proper pursuit and working on the conditioning of the defensive linemen.

DRILL:

Draw-Play Pursuit

A draw play is an offensive play that starts out looking like a drop-back pass, then becomes a run after the defensive team has reacted to the potential pass. The offensive linemen drop back as they do on a pass play and attempt to block the rushing defensive players away from the ball. The quarterback starts his pass drop. As he comes even with the two halfbacks, who have set up to pass block, he hands the ball to one of them. The back with the ball then runs up the field.

The most important technique for defensive linemen to learn is that once they see that the play is a draw, they must turn

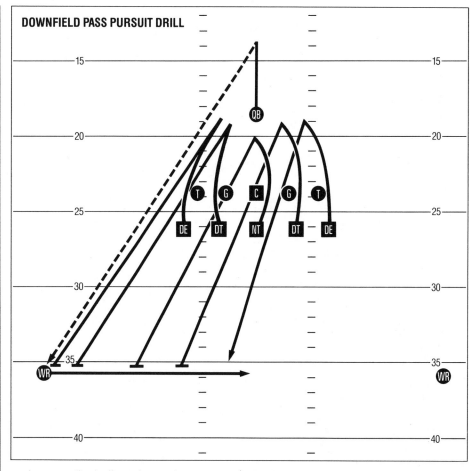

DOWNFIELD PASS PURSUIT DRILL

and pursue the ball carrier on the same path they were using to rush the passer.

If the defensive end was rushing to the outside, he stops and retreats back to

the line of scrimmage, staying outside the offensive tackle. If his rush had taken him inside the offensive tackle, the defensive end then comes back on the same path.

The nose tackle usually has committed his pass rush to the right or left of the center. The nose tackle stays on that side when he sees the draw develop, then retreats back to the line of scrimmage.

If the defensive linemen react to the draw play in this manner, it becomes much easier for the rest of the defensive team to know how and where to react in order to stop the play.

WINNING POINTS

- In tackling, bend at knees, not at waist; keep head up, eyes open; never use helmet as initial point of contact or weapon.
- Shorten stride approaching ball carrier; explode up and through man with ball; stop ball carrier from advancing.
- Always maintain proper pursuit paths.
- On screen passes, stop pass rush and pursue—don't become a spectator.
- On draw plays, stop pass rush, turn, and retrace rush route.

LINEBACKERS

Linebackers

- Stance **249**
- Defeating Blockers **252**
- Linebacker Blocking Progression **260**
- Tackling **261**
- Linebacker Pursuit **264**
- Zone Pass Defense **266**
- Man-to-Man Pass Defense **277**
- Intercepting the Ball **282**
- Blitzing **285**
- Stunts **290**

As offenses have expanded the use of both the forward pass and formations that utilize the entire field, the need for quick, agile players at the linebacker position has increased. Today's linebackers must be able to step up, take on blockers directly in front of them; move from side to side; make tackles from sideline to sideline; rush the quarterback on pass plays; and play pass defense by dropping into deep zones or covering swift offensive backs man-to-man. The modern linebacker combines the strength of a big defensive lineman and the nimbleness of a defensive back with the hitting and intensity already associated with the position.

One of the most important traits of a great linebacker is leadership. It is not necessary to be a shouter or a sideline screamer to lead. Great linebackers lead more by example than words. To develop this necessary leadership quality, a linebacker must become a dedicated student of the game. He must comprehend as much of the total plan of the de-

fense as possible. In addition to understanding the skills needed to play his position, he also should be familiar with the responsibilities of the other defensive players on the team. He must take it upon himself to set the tempo of practice, working hard from the moment he walks onto the field until the last play of practice.

Good, hard, clean, aggressive tackling is a skill possessed by every good linebacker. Nothing can fire up a defensive team quicker than a linebacker's hard tackle that stops a ball carrier in his tracks.

Stance

Foot and body positions vary slightly for inside linebackers and outside linebackers. Comfort and balance are constants regardless of which position a linebacker is playing.

Inside Linebackers

An inside linebacker's stance starts with the feet parallel to the line of scrim-

Inside linebackers stand square to the line of scrimmage with feet spread no wider than their shoulders. The elbows are held in, hands held chest-high with palms out.

An outside linebacker over a tight end needs a staggered stance, inside foot up.

mage, no wider than the player's shoulders. Remember, the wider apart the feet, the harder it becomes for the player to move to the right and left. Prior to the start of the play, the player should roll up on the balls of his feet so that he is not caught flat-footed when action be-

gins. There should be a slight bend in the knees, the back should be straight, with the shoulders slightly in front of the player's feet. Elbows should be at the player's sides. His hands should be in front of his chest, number high, with his wrists cocked and fingers extended and

separated, with the palms facing the offensive man directly in front of him. The inside linebacker's head needs to be up to give good vision, with his neck bowed.

Outside Linebacker Playing Over Tight End
An outside linebacker playing over a

The outside linebacker keeps his shoulders even with the tight end's.

An uncovered outside linebacker can relax more in his stance; he stands more upright, with his inside foot forward and his arms hanging down.

tight end must adjust his stance to be able to react quickly and compensate for the nearness of the offensive player. Instead of his feet being parallel, it is now important that he have the front of his outside foot even with the instep of his inside foot. The space between his feet should be no more than the width of his shoulders. This proper foot alignment decreases the possibility of his being hook-blocked on wide running plays. It is necessary for the outside linebacker to have a greater bend in his knees, squatting down until his shoulders are even with the shoulders of the tight end while keeping his back straight. The proximity of the blocker makes it even more important that the player keep his arms and hands in proper position—elbows against his sides, hands in front of his chest number-high,

251

wrists cocked, fingers extended and separated, with his palms facing directly at the tight end in front of him. The outside linebacker's head should be up, with the neck firmly bowed and set, eyes locked on the man in front of him.

Uncovered Outside Linebacker

Relaxation is the key in the stance of any outside linebacker who does not have a potential offensive blocker lining up directly in front of him. His stance can be more upright, with the inside foot forward, and the front of the outside foot in position behind the heel of the front foot. There is little need for much width in the foot placement. In this upright stance, only a slight knee bend is needed. The back still is straight, and the head up, giving the player a full view of the offensive formation. Without the threat of an immediate blocker, the player may allow his arms to hang loosely at his sides, knowing he will have ample time to get his hands up when he determines which of the offensive players is assigned to block him.

Defeating Blockers

Most successful blocks against linebackers result not from the superb skills of offensive players, but from linebackers looking for the ball carrier instead of fo-

The first thing a linebacker must do to defeat a straight-ahead block is stop the blocker's momentum by pushing out with his arms to separate from the blocker.

cusing their eyes on the men coming to block them. A good linebacker not only understands who can block him, but he also has a feel for the different types of blocks that each offensive man will use in any situation.

Defeating Drive Blocking

In order to play any of the linebacker po-

sitions, a player must be able to stop a blocker who attacks him straight-on. Offensively, this is called a "drive block," a block that an inside linebacker commonly faces from the offensive lineman positioned directly in front of him. An outside linebacker sees the same type of block from a tight end. In this maneuver, the offensive man tries to drive his head and shoulders into the numbers of the linebacker's jersey, attempting to drive him off the line of scrimmage. The linebacker must meet the blocker shoulder pad to shoulder pad, punching out with the heels of both hands, separating himself from the blocker.

Once the offensive man's momentum has been stopped, the linebacker is in a position to shed the blocker to one side or the other; he then can concentrate on locating the ball carrier and making the tackle.

The important thing to remember in frustrating this type of block is that the linebacker never should take a side until he has defeated the block. He must stay square, or it will be easy for the offensive man to turn him, thus providing a running lane for the ball carrier.

DRILL:

Moving and Striking (vs. Four- or Seven-Man Sled)

When practicing this drill, all the players line up to the right of the sled. At the coach's command of "Hit!," the players move down the sled, shuffling their feet and stopping at each pad to step forward with their inside foot and strike a blow with the palms of their hands against the pad. After striking the blow, they retreat a couple of steps, shuffle to

the next pad, and strike again. This action continues until each of the players has gone the length of the sled. Then the entire procedure is repeated in the opposite direction. Because there is no

Once the linebacker stops the blocker, he can shed him to the side.

running back to tackle and there is no fear of the pads hitting back, this drill is a good way to introduce moving, focusing the eyes, and striking a blow. Remember, players should not bend at the waist; instead they should bend their knees and flex to get to the proper height to strike the sled.

DRILL:

Facing One-on-One Blocking

In this drill, the sled is replaced with live blockers. For teaching purposes, it is better to use linebackers as the defensive and offensive linemen and tight ends. The role of the player on offense is to drive the defensive player straight backward off the line. The coach must tell the defensive player where his primary responsibility is—on the right or the left side of the blocker. After meeting the blocker squarely with his shoulder pads, the defensive man should slide his head to the side of his primary responsibility. As soon as the defensive player feels his shoulder pads meeting the blocker's, he should strike out with the palms of his hands, trying to deliver a blow to the area near the blocker's numbers, thus stopping the blocker's momentum. It is important that the defensive man have a straight back, lowering his body by bending at the knee and not the waist.

Bending at the waist when making contact with another player is the leading cause of back problems for a player at any position. The coach should end the action by blowing a whistle, conditioning the men to stop on the same sound that stops play in a game.

DRILL:

Defeating Drive Blocking (vs. Live Offense)

There are two new elements for linebackers to handle in this drill. First, the blockers actually will be offensive players. Second, the linebacker has the opportunity to tackle a man with the ball after he defeats the blocker. When running this drill it is important to have towels lying on the ground, limiting the area where the ball carrier can run.

The quarterback starts the play by using his normal cadence, handing the ball to a running back, who is either charging straight ahead or moving quickly to his right or left. The skills that the linebacker has learned in the previous drills now must be transferred into instant action on the field. Focusing initially only on the blocker, the linebacker must meet the blocker pad on pad and then strike out with the palms of his hands. He must stop the blocker's forward movement. After the blocker is in control, the linebacker must locate the ball carrier, shed the

blocker, re-flex his knees, and prepare to make the tackle. Should the linebacker try to hit the blocker with his hands first, he will find that his shoulders will naturally go up and back, and the offensive player will have an easy time driving him off the line. A whistle blown by either an offensive or defensive coach should end the play, just as in a game.

Defeating the Cut Block

The cut block is a variation of the drive block. It differs in that the blocker aims at the linebacker's feet and ankles instead of driving at the linebacker's numbers. If the defensive player has not focused his eyes on the blocker and is looking for the ball carrier, this can be an effective offensive tool. One minute the linebacker will be standing up; the next second he will find himself sprawled on the ground.

DRILL:

Escape From Cut Blocks (vs. Bags)

This drill is similar to the drive-blocking drill used on the blocking sled, except that a line of bags lying on the ground takes the place of the pads on the sled. Starting on the right side of the bags, each linebacker moves down the line, extending his arms, pushing the bags into the ground, and kicking his feet

back in the same motion. As his feet hit, the linebacker must push up with his arms in order to regain his balance and shuffle down the line to the next bag. When using this technique, it is again important that the player keep his back straight and not merely bend at the waist.

DRILL:

Facing One-on-One Cut Blocking

This is set up in exactly the same way as the one-on-one drive-blocking drill. The only difference is that the offensive player tries to knock the linebacker off his feet with a cut block instead of driving him off the line. The linebacker's reaction to this type of block also must be different. He no longer can meet the blocker pad to pad. Now he must extend his arms, forcing the blocker into the turf. As his hands strike the blocker's pads and push down, he must kick both feet backwards, eliminating any chance of the blocker knocking him off his feet. There always is a chance for injury in this drill. Consequently, it is advisable to start the drill with the players going only half speed. As the players become better at defeating this type of block, the speed of the drill may be increased.

Defeating the Angle Block

Inside linebackers are much more likely

When facing a cut block, low to his legs, the linebacker must extend his arms and force the blocker to the ground as he kicks both feet backwards.

to see an angle block used against them than are outside linebackers. The angle block normally will be used by an offensive tackle when he is blocking down on an inside linebacker to his inside. But it also may be used by the offensive tackle when he is blocking an outside linebacker who is lined up on the tight end, to his outside.

DRILL:

Defeating Angle Blocking
Because of lack of time to see the blocker coming, the inside linebacker normally will not be able to take on an angle block squarely. Consequently, the tech-

nique used to defeat this blocking is different from that used in playing the drive block. The instant the linebacker determines that the offensive player directly in front of him is not going to block him, he must look to the next-closest offensive player. If he sees the player coming to block him, he quickly must step directly at him with his nearest foot, keeping his knees bent, meeting the blocker with his near shoulder, then striking a blow with his forearm. When the linebacker feels

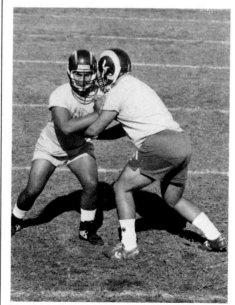

The linebacker steps directly at an angle-blocker, hitting him with his forearm.

255

he has stopped the momentum of the offensive blocker, he should deliver a blow with the palm of his far hand, attempting to knock the blocker off balance. It is vital that the linebacker not be driven out of the hole.

At times, the outside linebacker playing over the tight end may face a similar block from the offensive tackle. Naturally, the block will come from the inside rather than the outside. The drill requires two defensive men to play the offensive blockers.

The defensive player has an advantage because he knows that he will be working against an angle block. After running the drill a few times, the coach can call for either a drive or an angle block, guaranteeing concentration.

Defeating the Hook Block

A hook block is used most commonly by tight ends when they are trying to block the outside linebacker to their side on wide running plays. It is similar to a cut block, but, instead of firing straight out at the linebacker's feet, the tight end now will step to the outside and then drive for the outside foot of the linebacker. The offensive tackle also may use this type of block on an outside linebacker if he comes behind the tight end.

DRILL:

Defeating Hook Blocking

The hook block should be easy for an outside linebacker to defeat if he remembers two important points stressed earlier. First, he must take a stance with his outside leg slightly behind his inside leg. Second, he must focus all his attention on the tight end.

At the snap, the linebacker will realize that the tight end's shoulders are moving laterally and not coming straight at him. He instantly knows that he will not be able to meet the block pad on pad. Consequently, he immediately should extend his arms, striking his palms into the blocker. At the same time, he should be stepping out and back with his outside foot, keeping slightly outside the blocker. As in playing the cut block, when the linebacker senses the tight end is starting to drive at his outside foot, he must push down with both hands, kicking back with both of his feet. The instant he is free of the blocker, the linebacker must regain his balance, and be ready to locate the ball carrier and make the tackle.

Defeating the Trap Block

A trap block is used by the offense against inside and outside linebackers. It differs from other blocks because con-

tact does not occur the instant the play begins, and the blocker usually comes from the opposite side of the ball, or at least two players away. A trap block's success depends on the linebacker's inability to locate the man blocking him and the possibility that the linebacker will charge straight across the line of scrimmage.

DRILL:

Outside Linebacker Trap

In a trap situation, the outside linebacker must quickly determine that neither the tight end directly in front of him nor the offensive tackle to his inside is going to block him. He then immediately looks farther in toward the ball, seeking the offensive guard who probably is attempt-

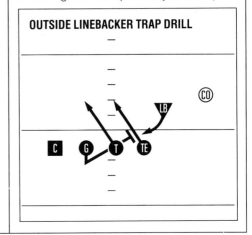

OUTSIDE LINEBACKER TRAP DRILL

ing to trap him. Because the guard has an opportunity to run a short distance and build momentum, the linebacker cannot afford to wait to take on the blocker. As the trapping lineman begins to throw his block, the linebacker should bring his outside shoulder and forearm hard across the blocker's helmet and shoulder pads, redirecting the blocker's body into the hole in which the ball carrier eventually will try to run. As with taking on a drive block, it is important that the linebacker keep his knees bent, his back straight, and his shoulders at the same height as the blocker's shoulders.

DRILL:

Inside Linebacker Trap

An inside linebacker has a difficult job in

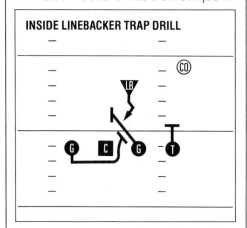

INSIDE LINEBACKER TRAP DRILL

As soon as an outside linebacker locates the trap blocker, he attacks him, throwing his outside shoulder and forearm across the blocker's helmet and pads.

playing the different types of blocks because he not only must look at the man in front of him, but he also must be aware of blockers coming at him from both the inside and the outside. Playing as an inside linebacker has been compared to spinning in a revolving door, with someone trying to hit you every now and then.

The instant the linebacker sees the lineman in front of him block toward the ball, he must shift his attention to the tackle on his outside, making certain that he is not coming on an angle block. If neither of these men is blocking him, the linebacker must attack the line of scrimmage, slanting toward the center. As the linebacker moves forward, he must look past the center to the linemen on the other side of the ball. As soon as he determines which of these offensive men is the trap blocker, the linebacker must set, gathering himself to defeat the blocker.

As the blocker reaches him, the linebacker should bring his outside shoulder and forearm hard across the helmet and shoulder pads of the offensive man, redirecting the blocker's body into the hole in which the ball eventually will be run. At the moment of contact, the linebacker must have a good bend in his knees, his back must be straight, and he should attempt to keep his shoulders at the same height as the blocker's shoulders.

Defeating the Lead Block

The lead block differs from other blocks because the man executing it will be a running back, not an offensive lineman or a tight end. While most running backs will not have the size of offensive line blockers, they usually will be much quicker and often will have better explosion at the point of contact. Running backs who are blocking present an additional problem because, when the linebacker looks into the backfield, he naturally seeks out the man carrying the ball; he may miss the man who is leading the rusher through the hole.

DRILL:

Outside Linebacker vs. Lead Block

The technique used by the outside linebacker to defeat the lead block is much the same as that used against a trap block. The main difference is that the linebacker cannot be quite as aggressive because the running back may throw a cut block rather than attempting to drive the linebacker out of the hole. If the back comes in high, the linebacker can use the outside shoulder and forearm technique; but, if there is any doubt, the linebacker must play the blocker with his hands. If the blocker attempts to cut the linebacker, driving at his feet, the linebacker must extend his arms, push-

ing the blocker to the ground, while kicking his feet back. The important thing to remember is that the linebacker must keep his eyes focused on the blocker until he has defeated his block.

DRILL:

Inside Linebacker vs. Lead Block

It is important that an inside linebacker see where the offensive backs are lined up prior to the start of every play. This is necessary for a number of reasons, but the primary one is that it gives the linebacker advance knowledge of the possible direction of a lead block. As with the outside linebacker, the inside linebacker must locate the running back who will be attempting to block him, once he deter-

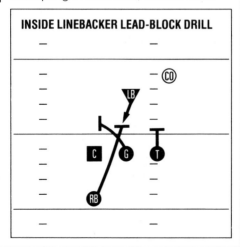

OUTSIDE LINEBACKER LEAD-BLOCK DRILL

INSIDE LINEBACKER LEAD-BLOCK DRILL

Outside and inside linebackers can use the shoulder and forearm technique if a lead blocker comes in high, but must be alert for a potential cut block. An unblocked inside linebacker must attack the line of scrimmage aggressively.

mines that he is not going to be blocked by an offensive lineman. The linebacker immediately must attack the line of scrimmage, heading directly at the blocker, gathering momentum as contact is made. If the linebacker doesn't attack the line of scrimmage, he may defeat the lead blocker, but he will have opened up a running lane in depth rather than width for the ball carrier. If the blocker is coming in high, the linebacker can use the far shoulder and forearm technique that he practiced against the trap block. Realizing that it is possible for the running back to use a cut block, the linebacker must be prepared—should he see the back driving toward his feet—to extend his arms, striking the blocker's pads with his palms and pushing the blocker to the ground. While doing this, the linebacker must kick his feet back, eliminating the possibility of being knocked off balance or down. Once the blocker is defeated, and his momentum is stopped, the linebacker must regain his balance, then prepare to locate the ball carrier and make the tackle. Good ball carriers will run as close to their lead blockers as possible so there probably will be little time to react off the block.

> **WINNING POINTS**
> - Identify offensive blockers before looking for ball carrier.
> - Stop blocker's momentum; defeat block first, then commit to a side and shed blocker.
> - Bend at knees, not waist, and keep back straight when making contact.

Linebacker Blocking Progression

All linebackers must understand which offensive players can block them and

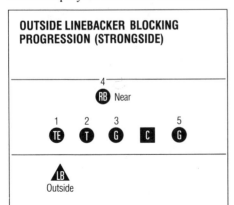

OUTSIDE LINEBACKER BLOCKING PROGRESSION (STRONGSIDE)

OUTSIDE LINEBACKER BLOCKING PROGRESSION (WEAKSIDE)

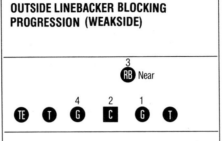

INSIDE LINEBACKER BLOCKING PROGRESSION

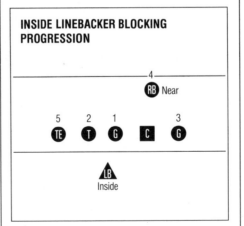

the order in which they will do so. This is a mental, rather than physical, exercise and is best introduced with no movement by the offense. A good time to work on it is when the players first

come on the field before they have had the opportunity to warm up.

A progression drill later can be incorporated into the regular practice, with the men on offense actually executing the proper blocks against the inside and outside linebackers. When running the progression drill, the coach should stand behind the defensive player and indicate who is to block by hand signals

> **Outside Linebacker Blocking Progression**
>
> The blocking progression that an outside linebacker must understand and the order that his eyes must follow are as follows:
> 1. Tight end   4. Near back
> 2. Near tackle   5. Far guard
> 3. Near guard
>
> Once the linebacker knows the progression, the next step is to associate the various types of blocks with each offensive player who might use them:
> 1. Tight end—drive or hook block
> 2. Near tackle—angle or hook block
> 3. Near guard—trap block
> 4. Near back—lead block (drive or cut technique)
> 5. Far guard—trap block.

Inside Linebacker Blocking Progression

The blocking progression for inside linebackers is:

1. Guard in front of him
2. Tackle to outside
3. Far guard
4. Near back
5. Tight end

The possible blocks from opposing offensive players include:

1. Onside guard—drive or cut block
2. Onside tackle—angle block
3. Offside guard—trap block
4. Near back—lead block drive or cut technique
5. Tight end—possible late angle block

to the men on offense. This drill serves as a final exam on the running game for linebackers, demonstrating the player's knowledge of blocking progression, of the different blocks that he will face, and of the techniques that he must use to defeat each of the blocks.

In all of these drills, the emphasis is on teaching the defensive players how to play the game. But it also is important that the coach stresses to the defensive players who are simulating the offensive blockers that they are learning what the

offense can do and how they will do it. In order for the linebackers to get better, they continually must help each other, working as hard in offensive roles as they do on defense. Developing group pride is just as important as instilling pride in individual players.

Tackling

The art of good tackling has been described as 70 percent desire and 30 percent technique. This may be true, but if a player—especially a young player—does not learn correct tackling techniques, he may increase his natural fear of contact, thus automatically decreasing his desire. Proper tackling skills, like the techniques used in defeating blocks, must be taught slowly, with the initial emphasis on proper body position and not on the force of the hit.

The two most important elements of body position must continually be emphasized when teaching tackling. They are that the defensive player must bend at his knees and not his waist, and that he always must keep his head up, never looking down at the ground, which can expose his neck to injury. It also is crucial for a linebacker to realize that he may not always make what could be called a picture-perfect tackle. Sometimes in a game situation all a lineback-

er can do is grab the ball carrier any way that he can. He may have a chance only to catch the ball carrier's jersey or to grab a leg. The player's desire often will determine if he gets shaken off or if he brings the ball carrier down.

DRILL:

Open-Field Tackling

The linebackers are divided into two groups, 15 yards apart, facing one another. One group will serve as the runners; the other group will be the tacklers. The linebackers who are being tackled should be carrying a ball. On the command of "Hit!," both the ball carrier and the tackler sprint five yards toward one another. After covering the first five yards, the tackler hesitates, running in place, keeping his eyes focused on the ball carrier's numbers until he determines which way the ball carrier is going to cut. After running straight ahead for five yards, the ball carrier will cut, without faking, at a 45-degree angle to his right or left. Once the linebacker sees the ball carrier cut, he will break in that direction and prepare for the tackle.

It is important that the tackler shorten his stride the closer he gets to the ball carrier, bending his knees more, gathering himself so that he can explode up and through the ball carrier. At the mo-

Linebackers must be among the surest tacklers on the team, able to take on ball carriers individually or as a unit.

ment of contact, the tackler should push off his inside foot, keeping his back straight and his head up. He should place his head in front of the ball carrier and pound the insides of his forearms and elbows into the runner's chest and back. The instant his elbows make contact, they will bounce off, and the linebacker will feel his hands hitting the ball carrier. When this happens, the tackler should grab the ball carrier's jersey, stopping any further advance. In this drill, it is not necessary for the linebacker to drive the ball carrier to the ground as he would in a regular game, though it is important that the man with the ball attempt to keep running and not stop when he sees he is about to be hit.

After the tackle, the ball carrier should go to the end of the line of the men preparing to tackle, while the tackler goes to the end of the ball carrier line. When first using this drill, it is good to have both players run at half-speed. As the tackling techniques become better, the speed of the players can be increased. Also, towels or markers should be placed on the ground to indicate sideline boundaries and limit the live area of the drill.

DRILL:
Sideline Tackling
Sideline tackling differs from other tack-

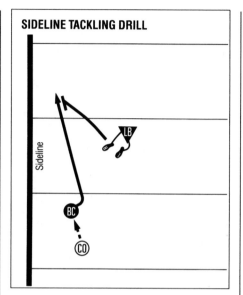

SIDELINE TACKLING DRILL

ling in that the ball carrier and the tackler usually are in the open with no other offensive or defensive players close at hand. The job of the linebacker is to make absolutely certain that the ball carrier does not get by him. If the tackler must allow the man to gain a few extra yards, so be it, but he must get his hands on the ball carrier or force him to run out of bounds.

In this drill, the ball carrier and the tackler are only five yards apart. The man who is to serve as the ball carrier lines up one yard from the sideline, facing the coach with his back to the defensive

player. The tackler lines up four yards inside the sideline with his feet straddling the yard line and his body at an angle facing the ball carrier. The coach tosses a ball to the ball carrier to start the drill. He spins around and faces up the field as soon as he catches the ball. At the same time, the tackler takes two or three steps forward and stops, running in place, still maintaining his angle toward the sideline. Now the ball carrier is free to go anywhere he desires, faking any number of times he wishes. The tackler must wait in position until the ball carrier starts to cross his nose, coming to the inside or trying to run up the sideline. At that instant, the defensive man must step, with his foot in the direction that the ball is going, then move on a path that will bring him in position to make the tackle after the ball carrier has run two or three more yards. If the linebacker does not open up (step) to start his movement, but crosses over with his feet, he never will make the hit.

DRILL:
Gang-Tackling
When working on gang (group) tackling, several essential points must be emphasized. All defensive players stop when the whistle blows. There is no excuse for getting a penalty for a late hit and giving

the offense extra, unearned yardage. Control is essential. The first man to the ball carrier has the job of controlling the player. The second and third men have important jobs as they converge on the ball carrier from either side. If the tackler advances on the ball carrier on the side he is holding the ball, the tackler must concentrate on knocking it loose. Should he approach from the side that is away from the ball or from behind, he should concentrate on tackling the ball carrier's legs.

In teaching this skill, all three players should converge on a six-foot stand-up dummy, one from straight ahead, and one from either side. The linebacker who is attacking from straight ahead is the primary tackler and should wrap his arms around the upper part of the dummy. Prior to the start of each turn in the drill, the coach will designate which side of the dummy has the ball. The linebacker on this side will hit with a hard forearm about halfway up the dummy while the tackler from the other side will execute his tackle on the bottom of the dummy. The players should rotate so that they find themselves executing each of the techniques. The intensity of the hit is not nearly as important as making the linebackers think of gang tackling as a single technique with purpose and not merely jumping on the ball carrier. The action of the drill ends with the coach blowing the whistle. Sometimes it should be blown before the players ever reach the dummy, making certain they stop.

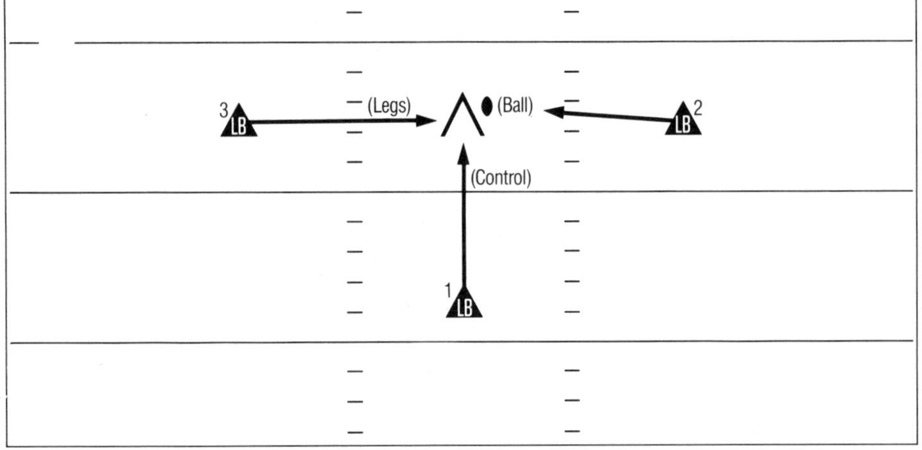

Linebacker Pursuit

Most long runs by the offense are the result of defensive players taking an improper pursuit angle. Linebackers, with their mobility and positioning on most running plays, should clearly see the pursuit paths that they must take. A major mistake in pursuit is over-running the ball, getting between the ball carrier and the sideline, thus allowing the ball carrier to cut back and have a large portion of the field in which to run. The proper line of pursuit for each linebacker will vary with his relationship to where each specific play is being run. The farther the linebacker is away from the play, the deeper his pursuit path ultimately should become.

DRILL:

Strongside Pursuit/Weakside Pursuit

When running a pursuit drill, two of the linebackers should play on offense, one as quarterback and the other as a running back. Towels should be placed on the ground to simulate the placement of the offensive tight end and linemen. The position of the man running the ball

GANG-TACKLING DRILL

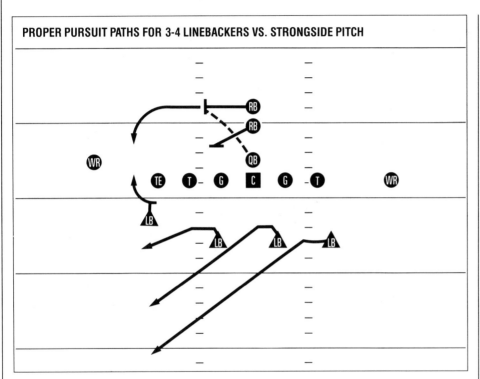

PROPER PURSUIT PATHS FOR 3-4 LINEBACKERS VS. STRONGSIDE PITCH

The same type of drill can be run to the weakside, away from the tight end, with

should occasionally be changed from a set behind one tackle or the other to directly behind the quarterback.

Once the runner is given the ball, he should have the option to rush wide or to cut back in any of the areas between the towels. As long as the running back is on the offensive side of the line of scrimmage, the linebackers should shuffle in the direction that he is running, always

careful not to get in front of the ball carrier.

When the runner makes his cut, the linebacker nearest the ball carrier should attack him while the other linebackers should start getting depth in case the tackle is not made. None of the linebackers, no matter their distance from the ball, should think that the play is over until the whistle has blown.

The linebackers must pursue a ball carrier as a unit, staying in their pursuit lanes. The farther each is from the ball carrier, the faster he must go; the closer the linebacker is to the ball carrier, the more controlled his movements must be.

the same pursuit rules enforced. Remember, this is not a tackling drill; it is to make certain that the linebackers are moving as one unit in response to a ball carrier's movement. Always keep in mind that the farther the linebacker is from the ball carrier, the faster he must move; the closer he is, the more controlled his movement must become.

Zone Pass Defense

All linebackers must demonstrate six basics in order to be effective in playing good zone pass defense: (1) play recognition (is it a run or a pass?); (2) a knowledge of their individual zone responsibility; (3) an understanding of the proper techniques that the linebacker should use in getting to his zone; (4) an ability to recognize offensive pass patterns; (5) the capacity to know when to focus on the quarterback; and (6) the talent to react properly to the ball once it is thrown. A deficiency in any of these

can render the linebacker ineffective and can contribute to a poor performance by the defense. Linebackers also must realize that the number of underneath zones will vary from four, five, or six, depending on the type of zone coverage that has been called in the defensive huddle.

NOTE: *On teams that use only three linebackers, the middle linebacker will take the place of the inside linebacker in the drills that follow.*

Linebackers must be able to recognize pass plays and patterns, drop into coverage, and react when the ball is thrown.

As soon as linebackers have learned the various deep and underneath zones of the field, they can begin practicing dropping into coverage as a unit. It is critical that each linebacker knows where to go in a particular defense.

DRILL:

Learning the Zones of the Field

In this drill, the linebackers learn zone location and what the different zone names refer to in relation to the field. There will be no offensive team to complicate the drill, and the coach will not throw a ball. Instead, he will point to one linebacker at a time and call out the zone to which he wants him to go. On command, the linebacker will run to that zone as quickly as he can. Because this is a mental drill, little if any time should be spent on teaching the technique that the linebacker will use in moving to his assigned zone.

Once the players individually become comfortable with the designated zones, the coach then should tell each of them where he wants them to go and have them drop as a four-man unit. Later, as the players learn their designated areas on a particular zone defense, the coach will merely have to call out the defense, and the linebackers should drop to their respective areas on the field.

THE SEVEN UNDERNEATH ZONES

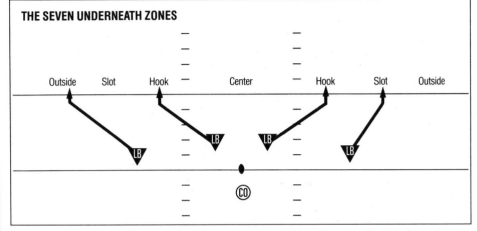

Outside — Slot — Hook — Center — Hook — Slot — Outside

DRILL:

Zone Drop Technique

Once the players know where the different zones are on the field, they must learn the proper techniques to use when going to their assigned zones. The farther a linebacker must go, the shallower an angle he should take and the faster he should sprint to get to the area. Great distances cannot be covered on the football field by casually jogging. Linebackers must realize that they have to reach their designated area while the quarterback is dropping back.

Linebackers cannot afford to leisurely drop into pass coverage—they must sprint into their assigned zones while the quarterback still is in the process of dropping back. The farther a linebacker has to run, the faster he should go.

Once a linebacker has sprinted to the necessary depth, he can swing his body around and begin to backpedal. The linebacker immediately focuses on the quarterback, and stops retreating as soon as the quarterback sets to throw.

Once a linebacker has reached his necessary area, he then can swing his body around and start to backpedal to get depth. The minute a linebacker begins his backpedal, he should focus on the quarterback. When he sees the quarterback preparing to throw, the linebacker should stop getting depth, move his feet in place, bring his shoulders slightly in front of his feet, and prepare to move to his right or left, depending on where the pass is thrown. In this drill, we are working only on linebacker drop technique; the coach should raise the ball when he wants the players to stop getting depth.

DRILL:

Pass Pattern Recognition I (Back to Either Side Running "Wide" Pattern)

This drill is run without throwing the ball. It teaches the linebackers to watch where the running backs are going in order to know what patterns the wide receivers are running and to adjust their drops accordingly.

If the back to the linebacker's side runs a "wide" pattern, the wide receiver will be running a hook pattern to the inside. The linebacker with the outside zone knows that he must stay as wide as the back. The next linebacker to his inside then must widen his drop, anticipating the wide receiver coming to the inside.

DRILL:

Pass Pattern Recognition II (Backs to Either Side Running "Stop" Pattern)

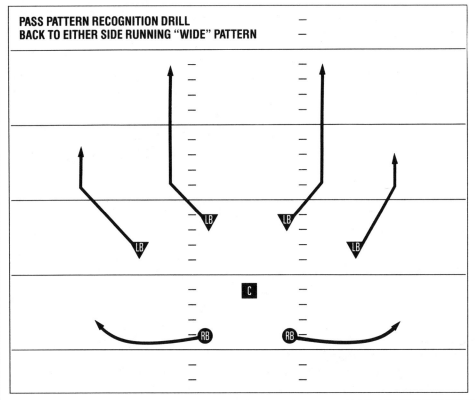

**PASS PATTERN RECOGNITION DRILL
BACK TO EITHER SIDE RUNNING "WIDE" PATTERN**

Linebackers key on the running backs to learn the wide receiver routes.

When the back to a linebacker's side runs a "stop" pattern, both linebackers on that side should be alerted that the outside receiver is running an "out" pattern. The linebacker in the outside zone now understands that he must get wider in order to be in position to break up the pass.

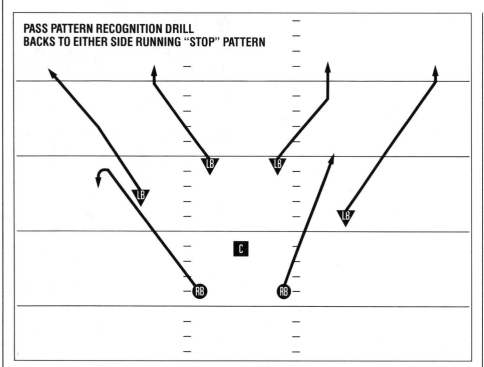

PASS PATTERN RECOGNITION DRILL
BACKS TO EITHER SIDE RUNNING "STOP" PATTERN

DRILL:

Pass Pattern Recognition III
(Back to Weakside Running "Angle" Pattern)
(Back to Strongside Running "Angle" Pattern)

When the linebackers see an offensive back to their side run an "angle" pattern, they should realize that the wide receiver will be trying to run a deep "in" pattern.

The outside linebacker no longer needs to get width and should try to slide in with the wide receiver. The inside linebacker must realize that he must get as much depth as possible if he is to stop the pass.

DRILL:

Pass Pattern Recognition IV
(Both Backs Away from Tight End, First Back "Wide")

(Both Backs Away from Tight End, First Back "Stop")

Each of the linebackers must read the movement of both running backs when the side of the offensive formation with the three receivers changes. The outside linebacker away from this movement

A linebacker must know what plays can be run from specific offensive sets.

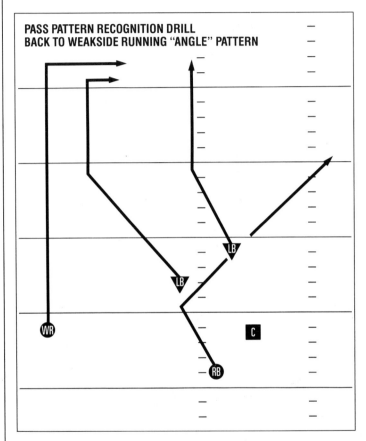

PASS PATTERN RECOGNITION DRILL
BACK TO WEAKSIDE RUNNING "ANGLE" PATTERN

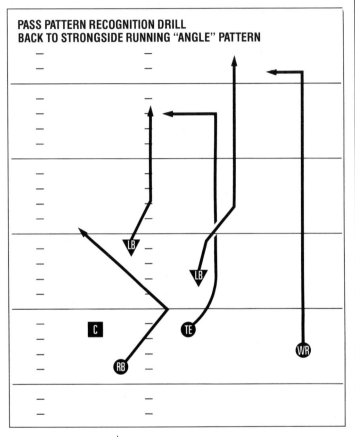

PASS PATTERN RECOGNITION DRILL
BACK TO STRONGSIDE RUNNING "ANGLE" PATTERN

knows that there is only one receiver out wide, so he can stop thinking about width and drop back on a straighter line. The inside linebacker on the same side now must come back more to the center, directly in front of the quarterback. The

two linebackers on the side of the backs' movement now must read the first back's pattern for a key to the wide receiver's pattern. If the back goes wide, they should expect a hook pattern by the wide receiver.

Should the first back run a "stop," they should look for an "out" pattern, and all the linebackers should adjust their drops for the anticipated pattern. The outside linebacker should widen his drop to be in position to stop the "out" pass.

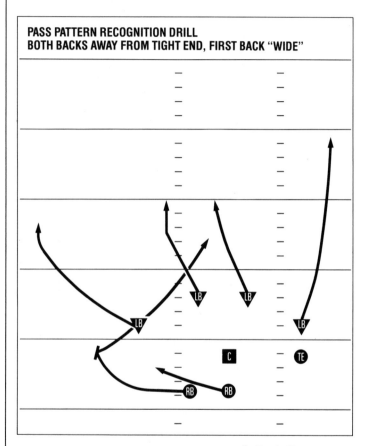

**PASS PATTERN RECOGNITION DRILL
BOTH BACKS AWAY FROM TIGHT END, FIRST BACK "WIDE"**

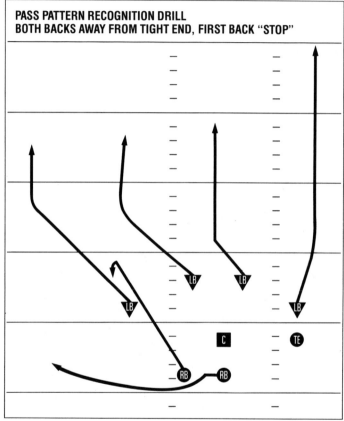

**PASS PATTERN RECOGNITION DRILL
BOTH BACKS AWAY FROM TIGHT END, FIRST BACK "STOP"**

DRILL:

**Pass Pattern Recognition V
(Both Backs Away From Tight End, First
Back "Angle"
(Both Backs Away from Tight End, First**

Back "Deep")

When the first back runs an "angle," the linebackers automatically must think of an "in" route run by the receiver on the outside. The inside linebacker on the side of the two backs must keep his

depth and not succumb to the natural temptation of following the crossing back.

If the first back runs deep up the field, this is an indication that the outside receiver also is running a deep route. The outside linebacker should be alerted to

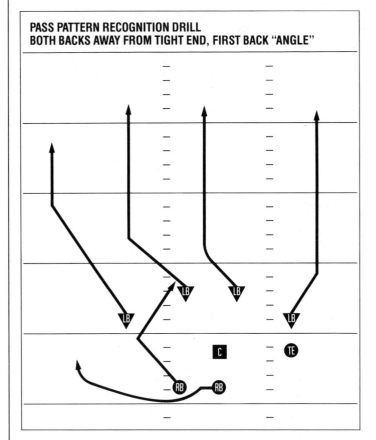

PASS PATTERN RECOGNITION DRILL
BOTH BACKS AWAY FROM TIGHT END, FIRST BACK "ANGLE"

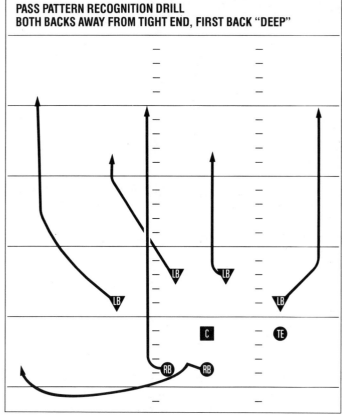

PASS PATTERN RECOGNITION DRILL
BOTH BACKS AWAY FROM TIGHT END, FIRST BACK "DEEP"

get more depth, expecting the back to try to get behind him near the sideline.

Watching the Quarterback

If linebackers concentrate on the quarterback, they can react when the ball is thrown and either intercept the pass or at least deflect it, causing an incompletion. As far as the defense is concerned, an incomplete pass has the same result as a running play that is stopped for no gain.

DRILL:

Quarterback Focus
(Three Steps Throwing to Right)

The objective of this drill is to force the linebackers to focus their attention on the

The linebackers must learn to watch the quarterback at all times as they drop into pass coverage. As soon as the quarterback stops his drop, the linebackers should be ready to react to the quarterback as he steps to throw.

quarterback and to move to the correct side of the field as he steps to throw. The drill is run with four linebackers, plus a defensive player acting as the quarterback. The coach calls the defense, determines that all the linebackers know where they are going, and then tells the quarterback to start his drop, either a three-step (used for short passes), a seven-step (used for medium pass patterns), or a nine-step (used for deep passing). As the linebackers begin to drop to their zones, they should watch the quarterback his first three steps to make certain that he is not throwing a short pass.

DRILL:

Quarterback Focus
(Seven Steps Throwing in Center)

After determining that it is not a short pass, the linebackers should get their necessary width and, as they start their backpedal, they should once again focus their attention on the quarterback. When he stops getting depth, the linebackers know that they also must stop getting depth and prepare to react either to the right or left. Before passing the ball, the quarterback will step to his right or left, or straight ahead. The linebackers then should break, as a unit, in the direction of the quarterback's step.

DRILL:

Ball Reaction

In this drill, two receivers align themselves in a stationary position, six yards on either side of the linebacker and 13 yards from the line of scrimmage. The quarterback does not drop back, but

Linebackers quickly should turn and break in the direction of a pass.

lines up at seven yards. The linebacker takes his position between the two receivers, but only 12 yards deep, and starts running in place while focusing his attention on the quarterback. When the quarterback sees the linebacker is concentrating on him, he will step directly at one of the receivers and throw the ball to him. The instant the quarterback steps to throw, the linebacker should roll over the foot in the direction of the pass and attempt to deflect the ball.

When linebackers become more proficient at reacting to the pass, the distance between the two receivers can be widened. The drill should be set up in different positions on the field, giving the linebackers a chance to see the ball coming from different angles.

Man-to-Man Pass Defense

Linebackers who are playing man-to-man pass defense generally will be asked to cover running backs coming out of the backfield. There usually will be two types of coverage in which they will be involved—when they are asked to cover the back in conjunction with another linebacker, and, more difficult, when they must cover the back without any help. Linebackers need to learn techniques for both types of coverage. They must realize that they cannot prop-

Linebackers working man-to-man must stay on one side or the other of a back.

erly cover a back, alone or with help, if they allow him to get "square" with them. They must stay on one side or the other of the back running the pattern. Also, a linebacker must recognize the pattern the back is running, keeping a cushion, and breaking into coverage once the linebacker has recognized the pattern. Unlike zone pass defense, the

In man-to-man coverage, it is essential for linebackers to be able to backpedal effectively. The secret is to run by stepping backwards, not pushing backwards, while keeping the feet under, and no wider than, the hips at all times.

linebacker must focus on the man he is covering, only looking for the ball when he is breaking with the running back and is close enough to touch him.

If the running backs do not release, each linebacker in coverage should drop to a depth of five yards, stay on the outside shoulder of his running back, and be alert for a screen or delay pass to the man he is covering.

DRILL:
Backpedaling
The ability to backpedal is essential for a linebacker if he is to succeed when playing man-to-man pass defense. The player learns in this drill how to run backwards correctly. Linebackers should start the drill, each in his normal stance but with a slight stagger, five yards away and facing the coach. At the coach's

Linebackers must be able to leave their backpedals and change direction or angle without crossing their legs or losing the back-pedal rhythm. This is done by swinging the leg opposite the direction he wants to go.

command of "Hit!," they should push off their front foot, stepping backwards with their back foot. Their feet should remain under, and no wider than, their hips. Their shoulders should remain slightly in front of their hips. The arms should swing in a normal running motion, with the em-

phasis on stepping backwards rather than pushing backwards with their feet. They should continue this running action for at least 10 yards. Linebackers who push, rather than run, backwards soon will find themselves losing their balance and falling backwards. Speed is not

nearly as important as technique when first running this drill.

DRILL:
Angle Backpedal
Once a linebacker has a feeling for running backwards in a straight line, he

must learn to change direction or angle without crossing his legs or being forced out of his normal backpedal. A good receiving running back will try to force a linebacker to leave his backpedal and turn the linebacker to one side or the other as quickly as he can.

This drill starts like the previous backpedal drill, with the linebacker five yards away and facing the coach. At the command "Hit!," the linebacker starts straight back. After he has covered five yards, the coach will point in one direction or the other. The linebacker then must change the angle of his backpedal and move in the designated direction. The coach will allow the player to backpedal that way for five yards. Then he will signal him to go straight back for another five yards, before pointing for the linebacker to angle back into the center of the drill. In total, the linebacker will run 20 yards, so it is not necessary for him to practice the entire drill at full speed, especially at the beginning. To stay in a backpedal the entire drill, the linebacker must change directions by swinging his leg opposite the direction in which he is attempting to go.

DRILL:

Calling Out Patterns

One of the linebackers serves as a run-

When calling out patterns, inside linebackers should try to stay on the running back's inside shoulder; outside linebackers stay on the outside shoulder.

ning back. He must run the pass pattern called for by the coach as well as he can. This not only gives the man on defense a proper picture to see, but it also teaches the patterns to the man who is running the offensive play. The linebacker must focus his complete attention on the running back, recognizing when he actually is breaking on a route. The line-

backer should point in the direction the back is breaking and call out the pattern. The only physical action for the linebacker will be to start his backpedal when the back releases from the backfield, and then continue backpedaling, staying either inside or outside and pointing when the back makes his break.

This is not a coverage drill, except that

CALLING OUT PATTERNS DRILL

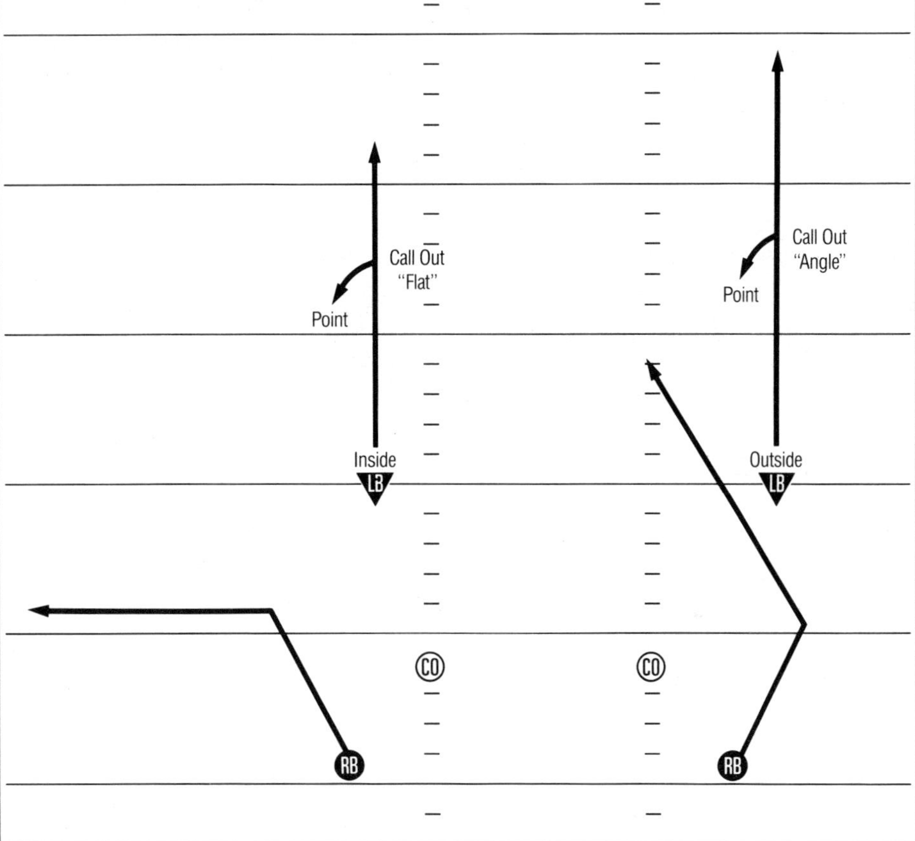

Call Out
"Flat"

Point

Inside
LB

Call Out
"Angle"

Point

Outside
LB

CO

CO

RB

RB

out the pass route run by the back, the coach can see who really is concentrating and who knows the patterns he will face in a game.

DRILL:
Roll-Over

Once the linebacker has learned how to backpedal straight back and at an angle, and once he has demonstrated that he knows how to focus on the back and recognize the patterns that he will face, he must learn the proper method of leaving his backpedal, changing his momentum, and running to cover a pattern. The key element in this drill is the linebacker's ability to roll over the foot in the direction that he needs to go rather than planting and stepping in that direction.

The coach will start the player moving backwards. After he has backpedaled at least 10 yards, the coach will point in the direction that he wants the player to run, either to his right or left or indicating a deeper angle to his right or left. When the linebacker sees where the coach is pointing, he immediately must roll over the foot in that direction and begin running straight ahead at full speed.

DRILL:
Live Coverage

This drill is a final examination for the

the inside linebackers should fight to stay on the inside shoulder of the back, and outside linebackers should attempt to remain on the outside shoulder of the back as he releases up the field. Both linebackers should try to stay at least three yards farther upfield than the back. With the linebackers pointing and calling

281

linebackers in man-to-man coverage. It includes actual offensive players running the pass routes. At the start of the drill, the outside and inside linebackers on one side will have two-on-one coverage on the back as he runs his pattern. Both linebackers will use their backpedal technique, keeping their three-yard cushion, but, instead of trying to play on the back's shoulder, they will stay two yards either inside or outside of him. If the running back runs a route toward the sideline, the outside linebacker will cover him. If the pass route is back toward the center of the field, the coverage responsibility belongs to the inside linebacker. The drill is run with the quarterback passing to one side and then the other. After the linebackers have had a few turns of running two-on-one coverage, the coach should ask them to try to cover by themselves, designating which linebacker has the coverage before the play begins.

With the introduction of offensive players who know how to run the routes and get open, and a quarterback who has the skill to pass the ball, it is almost certain that the competitive nature of the linebackers will surface and the techniques on which they have worked so hard quickly will disappear. Proper technique must be re-emphasized.

A linebacker intercepting a high pass must hold his hands with thumbs together, extending his arms so he can see the ball and his hands as he makes the catch.

Intercepting the Ball

Big plays such as interceptions do not just happen; they must be planned, practiced, and talked about by everyone on defense. Interceptions of any type usually start with a player executing the defense properly, understanding what the offense probably will do, and knowing the correct technique for catching a ball. Many potential interceptions are dropped, and an important play is lost to the defense, not because of desire, but because the player is not concentrating on how to catch the ball. Catching the ball is a skill linebackers must practice, just like backpedaling, tackling, or taking on a trapping guard.

DRILL:

Interceptions

When the coach raises the ball to a passing position, the linebacker who is first in line moves up to the yard stripe and begins running in place, prepared to break to his right or left or to come straight ahead. The coach then steps in the direction in which he desires the linebacker to move and throws the ball. As the linebacker sees the coach step, it is important that he not only move in that direction, but that he also break on an angle that brings him forward. As the ball approaches the linebacker, he must keep his eyes glued to the ball, bringing his hands into a position so that he can see his fingers and the ball at the same time. It is vital that the linebacker look at the ball all the way into his hands.

Should the pass be chest high or lower, the linebacker must cup his hands so that his little fingers are together. If the pass comes at his shoulders or above,

In a tip drill, the first linebacker runs forward and tips the ball into the air.

The second linebacker in the tip drill comes up to make the interception, making sure he keeps his eyes on the ball and cocks his wrists.

the linebacker then must cock his wrists back and form a cup with his thumbs touching, rather than his little fingers. Most high passes are not easily intercepted. Instead they are knocked to the ground because the interceptor does not cock his wrists back properly, and, when the ball makes contact, it is deflected toward the turf.

DRILL:

Tipped Balls

As the coach raises the ball in preparation to throw, the nearest linebacker runs straight at the coach and the first man in the line behind also runs in the same direction. The coach will throw the pass high to the first linebacker, who then tips the ball high into the air. The second linebacker must adjust his path and move into position to catch it, making certain that he catches the ball at its highest point whenever possible.

While it is true that during a game, most balls will be tipped by linebackers to defensive backs, sometimes one of the defensive linemen will reach up and deflect a pass, and the linebacker must be prepared to make the catch. This is a good drill to run at the end of practice with no one allowed to go in until every one of the linebackers has made an interception.

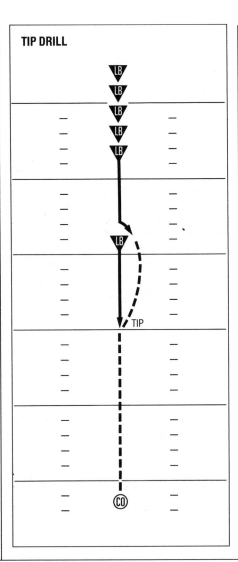

TIP DRILL

DRILL:

Team Interceptions

This is a team drill that emphasizes the importance of everyone working together when an interception is made. Each player needs to understand that the minute a defensive player catches the ball the entire team switches from defense to offense. Defenders also must realize that the two members of the offensive team who will know that an interception has been made are the quarterback and the intended receiver. These two must be blocked on every interception.

After calling out the defense he wants the team to play, the coach will start the drill by backing up toward the goal line. He may go straight back, or drop to his right or left. The rush men must count to three, and then they can start to pursue the coach, making certain that they allow him to throw the ball. The remaining men on the defense drop into their respective zones. As the pass is thrown, all members of the defense, including the rush men, break towards the ball, with the closest man calling out, "I've got it! I've got it!" When the interception is made, the man making the catch should break for the nearest sideline, sprinting toward the end zone. The next closest man to the ball must simulate blocking the in-

WINNING POINTS

- The farther a linebacker must go to reach his zone, the faster he must run and the shallower an angle he must take.
- Watch running backs to determine wide receiver patterns; adjust drops accordingly.
- Watch quarterback's first three steps to determine if he is throwing short pass; stop getting depth when the quarterback steps to throw; break in direction of pass.
- In man-to-man pass defense, never allow receiver to get "square;" keep a cushion and focus on assigned receiver, never looking for the ball until receiver breaks and is close enough to touch.
- Backpedal by running, not pushing; change direction while backpedaling by swinging leg opposite desired direction; leave backpedal by rolling over foot in desired direction.
- To intercept pass number-high or below, keep little fingers together; for pass at shoulders or above, have tips of thumbs touching and wrists cocked back; "look" ball into hands.
- Stay alert for tipped balls.
- Block intended receiver and quarterback on all interception plays.

tended receiver, while the rest of the team should turn toward the end zone, running hard to place themselves in a position to block. One of the rush men on the side of the return should seek out the quarterback.

Blitzing

A team may decide to blitz a linebacker either to stop running plays or to put added pressure on the quarterback. If a team elects to send only one linebacker, it still has the option of playing some sort of zone defense. But when the decision is made to blitz two or more linebackers, the defense is forced into man-to-man pass defense, with no possible help for any of the coverage men. Linebackers must understand the enormous pressure the coverage men are under in this type of blitz situation, and they must realize that speed is essential in getting to the man with the ball. Great blitzing linebackers take extreme pride in rushing and sacking the quarterback. Like everything else in football, blitzing the

quarterback is a learned skill.

DRILL:

Outside Linebacker Blitz

The first thing the blitzing linebacker must do, as the quarterback starts his drop, is determine which man—the

The blitzing outside linebacker uses a rip maneuver with his inside arm.

When linebackers are added to the defensive pass rush, the effect on opposing quarterbacks can be devastating.

guard or running back—is assigned to block him. Once he has determined who the blocker is, the linebacker must focus all of his attention on defeating him. Should he see the guard pulling out to block him high, the linebacker should lower his inside shoulder, ripping his inside arm forward and up, and lean in to take the guard's hit. If the running back is setting up to block, the rushing linebacker should try to get square on him. As he gets within two steps of making contact, the linebacker either should step inside or outside the blocker, knowing that his final move will be quickly in the opposite direction. Grabbing and pulling the blocker behind the shoulder pads with the near hand, the linebacker should reach over the blocker's helmet, driving the back of his upper arm into the blocker's shoulder blades, and propelling himself by the blocker.

Should the blitzing linebacker find that the running back is the type of blocker who fires out, he must be prepared to use both hands to avoid the block. As the back fires out, the linebacker should move to one side, grabbing the blocker by the back of the shoulder pads with both hands, and use the blocker's momentum to help accelerate himself.

If the running back is going to try to cut, or block at the feet of, the linebacker, the latter then must use the same tech-

As the back sets to block, the linebacker pulls his pads and reaches over.

nique that he used when defeating the cut block on a running play. As the blocker drives towards the linebacker's feet, the linebacker must extend both his arms, striking the blocker's shoulder pads with the palms of both hands.

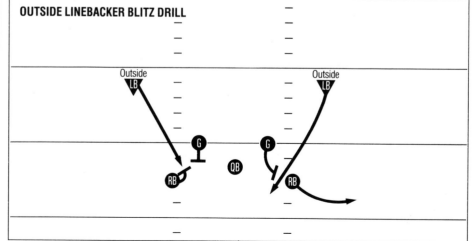

OUTSIDE LINEBACKER BLITZ DRILL

A blitzing inside linebacker uses the wrist-club and arm-over technique. He hits the blocker with his near hand, then reaches over and drives past using his elbow.

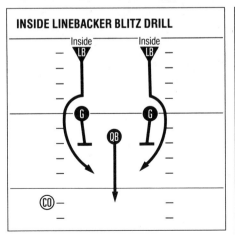

INSIDE LINEBACKER BLITZ DRILL

Pushing the blocker into the turf, on one side or the other, the linebacker then must move his feet quickly in the opposite direction, push up with his arms to regain his balance, and rush the quarterback. If the blocking back falls to the turf early, the linebacker may find that all he has to do is leap over the blocker's body.

DRILL:
Inside Linebacker Blitz

When an inside linebacker blitzes over a guard, he has a much more difficult job than an outside linebacker blitzing over a running back. The guard is bigger and usually will be a much better blocker. As in the outside rush, if the inside linebacker can start directly at the guard and stay squared up on him, the linebacker has the advantage and element of surprise because he can go either left or right. The guard must try to guess the ultimate direction of the linebacker's rush.

The inside linebacker can start with

When blitzing against a tall guard, the linebacker uses an under-arm technique. Instead of reaching over the guard's shoulder, the linebacker jams his far shoulder under the arm of the blocker and lifts, then charges by.

the same over-arm technique that was taught to the outside linebackers, faking in one direction, grabbing or hitting with the near hand, reaching over with the far arm, and finally pulling and pushing himself past the blocker.

Because of the height of the offensive guard, it often may be difficult for the linebacker to reach over. Thus, it is important that inside linebackers also learn to use an under-arm rush technique. The difference in this rush is that when the

linebacker starts his final move, instead of attempting to reach over the guard's back, he now drives with his far shoulder and rams it under the arm of the blocker. The far arm should be driven hard across the blocker's chest with the forearm and hand landing on the back of the blocker's shoulders. As the blitzing back makes contact with this arm, he must lift up, allowing himself enough room to move by the blocker.

One final technique that may be used

by a blitzing inside linebacker is a bull rush. This is effective only if the linebacker sees that the guard has his weight back on his heels, leaning backwards, and is not in a position effectively to take on the rushing linebacker. The linebacker should bend his knees, making certain his back is straight, and run directly over the blocking guard while trying to keep his shoulder pads under the blocker's shoulder pads. When contact is made with the shoulder pads, the blitzing line-

A bull rush is an effective technique against a fast-retreating blocker who has his weight back on his heels. The blitzing linebacker gets his palms against the blocker's chest, then tries to run over him or knock him backwards.

backer should punch out with the palms of both hands into the blocker's chest and attempt to knock him over backwards.

Stunts

In a game, all linebackers will be called upon to run stunts with other linebackers and defensive linemen. There are many kinds of stunts, but there are some principles common to all of them. First, the defense should try to run as much of the stunt as possible on the offensive side of the line of scrimmage. The first men in the stunt must drive hard and

fast through their designated gaps, fighting for penetration. The second (or last) man coming behind or around on the stunt must charge straight ahead and not loop at the start of the stunt, making certain that the ball is not being run in his direction before he begins his rush.

Here are some examples of linebacker/defensive linemen stunts. When you practice these stunts against your own defensive people, the men on offense should offer minimum resistance and allow the stunt to be run at full speed. There will be ample opportunity to run the drill with full contact when it is prac-

ticed against the offense.

DRILL:

Outside and Inside Linebackers/ Defensive End Stunts

When running this stunt the defensive end and the outside linebacker both slant hard to the inside, fighting to get on the offensive side of the line of scrimmage. At the same time, the inside linebacker charges directly at the guard for two steps, making certain that the ball is not being run straight at him. After two steps, he then pushes off his inside foot, scraping around behind the penetrating

OUTSIDE AND INSIDE LINEBACKERS/ DEFENSIVE END STUNT

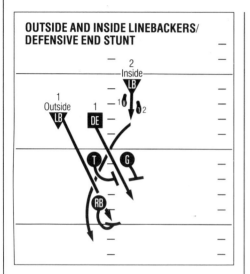

OUTSIDE AND INSIDE LINEBACKERS/ DEFENSIVE END STUNT

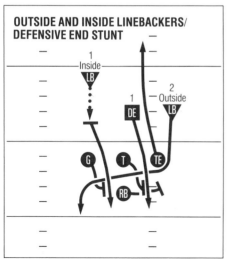

Linebackers stunt in combination with other linebackers and defensive linemen.

INSIDE LINEBACKERS/NOSE TACKLE STUNT

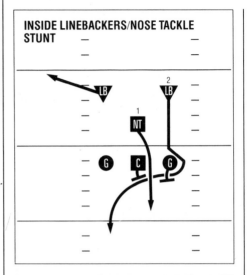

INSIDE LINEBACKERS/DEFENSIVE END STUNT

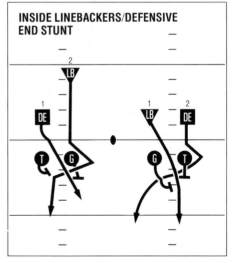

end and outside linebacker. It is important that he come as close to their charge as possible. In running these stunts, inside and outside, if an inside linebacker is designated to go first, he must cheat up to the line of scrimmage prior to the snap of the ball.

WINNING POINTS
- When blitzing, determine who blocker is and defeat him, then blitz with speed and intensity.
- Run stunts on offensive side of line of scrimmage; last man on stunt must make sure ball is not being run in his direction before beginning his rush.

DEFENSIVE BACKS

Defensive Backs

- Stance — **297**
- Start — **299**
- The Backpedal — **300**
- Man-to-Man Technique — **302**
- Pattern Reaction Keys — **307**
- Bump-and-Run Technique — **310**
- Zone Pass Defense — **313**
- Ball Stripping — **319**
- Interceptions — **323**
- Tackling — **328**
- Run Force — **332**
- Blitzing — **335**

A defensive back's life is filled with pressure—one mistake can result in a game-breaking score for the opponent. A missed tackle by a defensive lineman can be covered up by a linebacker or defensive back, and a pass coverage blown by a linebacker often will be picked up by an alert defensive back. But the defensive back is on his own. As the last line of defense, the defensive back is expected to compensate for the mistakes of others, constantly aware that there is no one on the field to cover for him.

The prerequisites for a great defensive back include better-than-normal speed, perfect body control, the toughness needed to stop the run, good hands, and confidence—plus an overall attitude that dares the offense to come his way.

But one of the most important traits of any good defensive back is his intense desire to compete. Poor defensive backs enter a game *fearing* that the ball will be thrown their way. Great defensive backs hope that *every* pass will be thrown to the man they are covering. They long to test and re-test their abilities. The better the offense they will face, the more emotional they are in preparing for the game.

In order to develop this necessary attitude, a good defensive back must be a dedicated student of the game. He must continually practice and develop the physical skills he needs to accomplish his job. He also must understand all the coverages he will use, and he must study the tendencies of the team he will face. He must be familiar not only with the movement and style of the man he expects to cover most often, but also with the other receivers he might occasionally face in the game.

While sure, aggressive tackling is important, a good defensive back must understand that he can't miss any tackle, sometimes sacrificing a hard hit for a game-saving shoving out of bounds.

He also must take the knowledge that an incomplete pass—a pass deflected or knocked down—is the same as a running play stopped for no gain, and

Along with speed and toughness, a top defensive back needs an attitude that dares the quarterback to throw his way.

A cornerback should stand with his feet shoulder-width apart. He puts his outside foot forward, in line with his chin and turned so the outside edge is facing the line of scrimmage. His arms hang down loosely at his sides.

balance it with the knowledge that making an interception often can be the spark that ignites his team. In other words, he must know when to lay back and when to take a risk.

Stance

An improper stance often can be the reason a defensive back is beaten on a pass pattern. Consequently, the correct stance must be taught, practiced, and reinforced each day. When first teaching or learning a proper defensive-back stance, it is important to be strict and specific in the positioning of each part of the body. The closer the defensive back is to the man he is to cover, the more disciplined he must be when taking his stance.

Cornerbacks

When getting into a proper stance, a cornerback should start by standing upright, feet spread shoulder-width apart. He then should lean forward at the waist while stepping with his outside foot, bringing it forward and in, until it is lined up directly under his chin. In the beginning it is advisable to turn the front foot so that the outer edge of the foot is facing the line of scrimmage. He then should bend his knees slightly, feeling most of his body weight on the front foot. His arms should hang down in a relaxed manner, and his head should be up, tilted slightly to the inside, looking at the ball. The young player may feel awkward and uncomfortable, but, as he gets into his stance over and over, he soon will relax.

Strong Safety

Because the strong safety often will be lined up one or two yards outside of the tight end, whom he will cover, it often is advisable for him to take a stance similar to a cornerback's. But the safety also can be more upright so that he can see into the offensive backfield.

The strong safety (above, left) is more upright than the cornerback. The free safety (right) stands almost upright with his feet parallel to the line.

Starting in an upright stance with his feet the width of his shoulders, the strong safety should lean forward while stepping forward with his outside foot. The placement of his front foot can be more forward and need not be directly under his chin. However, it still is important that the safety's weight be on the ball of his front foot. He should bend at his waist, bringing his shoulders to a position in front of his hips. He also should have a slight bend in his knees.

His arms should hang down from his shoulders in a relaxed fashion, and his head should be up and tilted toward the ball so he easily can have the tight end and the quarterback in his field of vision.

Most strong safeties will find this stance comfortable right from the start. If not, they must practice getting into the proper stance over and over again until it becomes second nature.

Free Safety

Most of the time, the free safety will be lined up deeper than the other defensive backs, and, more often than not, he will not have coverage responsibility for a specific receiver. Because of these two factors, the free safety can assume a much more upright stance, with his feet parallel to the line of scrimmage, spread no wider than the width of his shoulders.

He should have a slight bend in his knees, and his head and shoulders should be slightly ahead of his hips. His arms should hang down from his shoulders in a relaxed manner, and he should feel as comfortable as possible in his stance. In this position, the free safety should have his head up and his eyes focused directly on the quarterback.

If the offensive formation, or the coverage that is to be used, calls for the free safety to cover a specific receiver, then it is important that he adjust his stance to the one used by the strong safety. Coaches often will make the mistake of asking the free safety for tight coverage, while never allotting practice time and instruction for the adjustment of the player's stance.

With his weight forward, the defensive back can push off into his start.

Start

Most defensive backs are beaten in the first two steps of a play rather than at some other time in their coverage. Realizing this, it is imperative that a defensive back get a proper start on every play. A defensive back cannot have a good start unless he first has lined up in a correct stance. By having his weight on his front foot prior to the start of the play, a defensive back is now in position to push off the front foot, while simultaneously taking a short step backward with his back foot. This explosive push and step motion is similar to the initial movement that a shot-putter uses in his explosive move across the ring.

The defensive back's shoulders should slowly and naturally come up, always staying slightly in front of the player's hips. The most common mistake for a young defensive back is to try to start by leaning back with his shoulders, causing him to step up with the back foot rather than taking a step backwards. This mistake results in the defensive back having poor balance and occasionally even falling backwards. It also forces him to take two steps, while never moving from his original alignment, as the offensive player sprints two steps closer to him.

When teaching this technique, the

Backpedaling is a technique for running backwards. The defensive back must visualize lifting his feet, stepping, and pulling his body in the direction he wants to go. He stays bent at the waist, shoulders in front of his hips.

coach should line up the players five yards away from him, check their stances, then, on the command "Hit," have each of them push off the front foot and take a step backwards with the rear foot.

The Backpedal

The ability to run backwards, or back-pedal, is a technique essential for a player to learn if he wants to play defensive back. All kids naturally learn the art of running forward at an early age, but the ability to run backwards is one that must be practiced, then perfected.

Unfortunately, many players and coaches fail to realize the importance of this basic technique for defensive backs and will stop practicing backpedal drills once the season has begun. Backpedal drills must be incorporated into the individual drills that are executed every practice day by the defensive backs.

Certain elements in running backwards are necessary for the player to understand if he is to be proficient as a defensive back. Most important, the defensive back must understand that backpedaling truly means running backwards, and not pushing backwards and shuffling his feet to move his body. The defensive back must picture in his mind what he must do, actually lifting his feet and stepping backwards, pulling his body in the direction that he wishes to go.

DRILL:

Backpedaling

The focus of this drill is on teaching and practicing the proper technique for a defensive back to use in his backpedal. The drill is run with the defensive backs lining up, one at a time, five yards away from the coach. After the coach sees that the player is in the proper stance, he will give the command "Hit!" The player then will push off his front foot, stepping back with his other foot and running backwards a full 15 yards.

During the backwards run, the player must keep his feet under, and no wider than, his hips. His waist should be bent so that his shoulders remain slightly in front of his hips, with his head up, looking directly at the coach. The player's arms should swing naturally in a normal running motion.

In this drill, speed is not important; what we are developing is proper backpedal technique.

DRILL:

Angled Backpedal

Once a defensive back has mastered

A defensive back must change direction without crossing his legs.

the technique of running backwards in a straight line, he then must learn to change direction, or angle, without crossing his legs or being forced out of his normal backward-running motion. When running any type of pass pattern, a good receiver quickly will attempt to get the defensive back to leave his backpedal, forcing him to turn his body to one side or the other.

The practice starts the same as the normal backpedal drill, with the defensive back lined up five yards away from, and facing, the coach. At the command "Hit!" the defensive back starts straight back. After he has run for five yards, the coach will point in one direction or the other. The player then must change the angle of his backpedal, moving in the direction designated by the coach. The coach allows the player to continue in this new direction for five yards, then signals the player to go straight back for another five yards, and finally directs the player to angle for the final five yards back to the center of the drill. In order for the player to remain in his backpedal for the entire 20 yards, it is necessary for him to swing his leg around opposite from the direction he desires to go instead of crossing over with his legs. Again, remember, we are working on technique and not speed in this drill.

Man-to-Man Technique

The techniques we have covered—stance, start, backpedal, and angle backpedal—all are necessary for a defensive back to master if he is to have success in playing either man-to-man (one-on-one coverage) or zone (assigned area of responsibility) pass defense. These are techniques that can and should be practiced without a receiver in the drill.

Now we are ready to introduce a receiver into the action to teach defensive backs the additional skills they will need to play man-to-man pass defense.

The first skill a defensive back must learn is that he cannot allow the man he

A defensive back cannot allow the man he is covering to get square on him.

is covering to get *square* (directly in front) on him. Based on the coverage called, the defensive back always must shade the receiver on one side or the other.

The next important skill is to know and recognize the different patterns that a receiver may be trying to run. The defensive back also must understand the importance of keeping a *cushion* (not allowing the receiver to get too close to him) during the play, and he must know how and when to leave his backpedal to cover the pattern run by the receiver.

Finally, the defensive back must realize, when playing man-to-man pass defense, that he must focus on the man he is assigned to cover and that he can look for the ball only when he is breaking with the receiver and is close enough to reach out and touch him.

DRILL:

Pattern Depth Recognition
At the start of each play, a defensive back must understand that he does not have to think about all the different patterns that an offensive receiver may run at him. Instead, he can break the patterns down by the depth at which they are run, concentrating on recognizing only those patterns that are run in a certain area.

In man-to-man coverage, the defender must focus totally on the receiver, never looking for the ball until the receiver breaks.

The faster a defensive back can recognize a pattern being run, the faster he can defense it. When running pattern recognition drills, the defensive back keeps his cushion and points out the direction of the receiver's route.

There are three distinct depths in which pass patterns are run by the wide receivers or the tight end: short (up to five yards), medium (6 to 12 yards), and deep (more than 12 yards).

In this drill, the defensive back lines up seven yards away from the receiver (played by one of the other defensive backs). At the coach's command of "Hit!" the receiver comes off the line, running straight up the field. The defensive back starts his backpedal and calls out the different areas as the receiver runs through them; "short, short, short" for the first five yards, "medium, medium, medium" for yards 6 through 12, and "deep, deep, deep" for the remainder of the run. This is *not* a coverage drill, but the defensive back should try to keep at least three yards between himself and the receiver during the entire play, and he should attempt to stay on one shoulder or the other of the receiver.

DRILL:

Short Pattern Recognition

This drill teaches defensive backs the different patterns a wide receiver or tight end may run in the short area (up to five yards). We want each defensive back, whether a safety or cornerback, not only to recognize the pattern, but also to call out the pattern verbally the instant he recognizes it.

In order to do this, the defensive back first must have been taught the names of each pattern he will see. When conducting the drill, one of the defensive backs will serve as the tight end or wide receiver and will run the pattern called for by the coach. This not only gives the defensive back a proper pattern to see but also teaches the man playing offense the patterns.

The defensive back lines up seven yards from the line of scrimmage. At the start of the play, he begins his backpedal, moving straight back. The instant he knows the pattern, he should point in the direction that the receiver is going and call out the proper name of the pattern.

By forcing the defensive back to point and call out the name of the pattern, it becomes an easy matter for the coach to tell which defensive players actually are concentrating and recognizing the patterns run.

SHORT PATTERN RECOGNITION DRILL

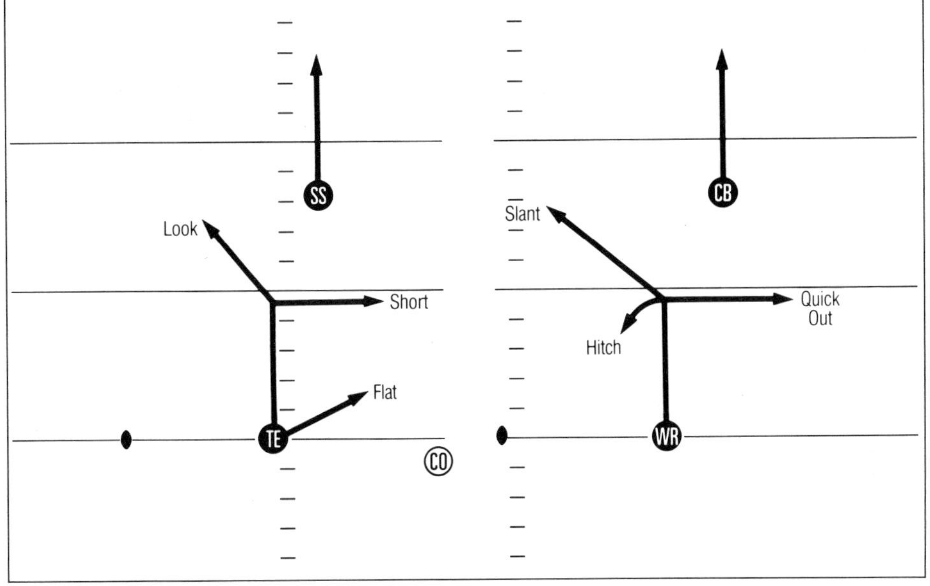

DRILL:

Medium Pattern Recognition

This drill is set up in the same way as the short-area drill, except now the defensive back must call out the patterns to be run in the medium area (6 to 12 yards). Once again, the player running the pattern, which is called by the coach, will be another defensive back. Remember, these are not coverage drills; they are recognition drills. But the defensive back still should keep his cushion and stay on the proper shoulder when doing the drill. It is not necessary for the receiver to run at full speed right away. As the players' recognition of each pattern improves, the speed of the drill may be increased.

The defensive back must understand that he is looking only for the patterns that are run in the medium area. The instant the defensive player recognizes the pattern, he should point in the direction the receiver is running and call out the proper name of the pattern.

DRILL:

Deep Pattern Recognition

As soon as the defensive backs have mastered the ability to recognize and call out short and medium patterns, move on to deep-pattern recognition (more than 12 yards). Because we do not want the defensive player to be forced out of his backpedal in this drill, it is crucial in the beginning that the receiver not run at full speed. As in the previous drills, the defensive man in coverage should point out and call out the pass pattern the instant he recognizes it. It is possible that the defensive player will call out two patterns ("post"—"post-corner, corner"

—"up, up-comeback"—"comeback"). By doing this, the defensive player learns that one pattern is run after the start of another pattern, and he sees exactly what the difference is in the running of the two patterns. Remember to change the location of the ball as the drills are run, and to have the free safeties as well as the strong safeties cover

the tight ends to learn their patterns.

DRILL:
Roll-Over

Once a defensive back has learned to start properly, to backpedal both straight and at an angle, and once he has demonstrated that he can focus on a receiver and recognize the pattern being run, he

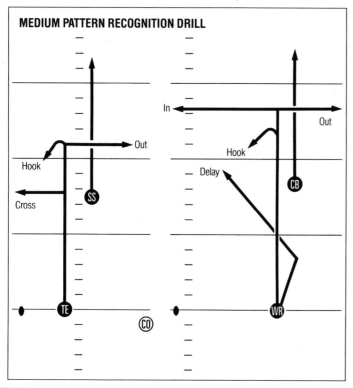

MEDIUM PATTERN RECOGNITION DRILL

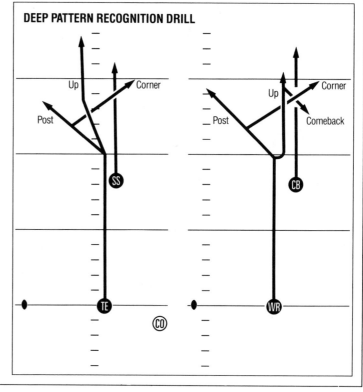

DEEP PATTERN RECOGNITION DRILL

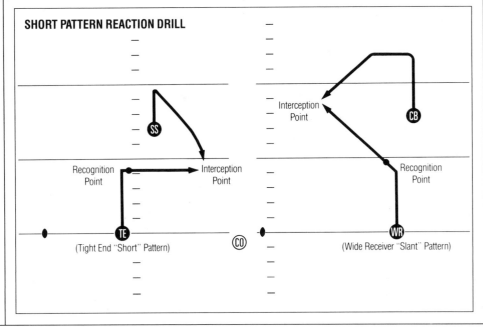

To leave a backpedal, roll over the foot in the direction you need to go.

must learn the proper method of leaving his backpedal, changing his momentum, and running to cover the pattern.

The focus of the drill is to teach the defensive back to roll over the foot in the direction that he needs to go, rather than planting a foot, stopping his momentum, and stepping in that direction. Starting

five yards apart, the coach will give the command "Hit!" and the player will start moving straight back in his backpedal. After the player has covered 10 yards, the coach will point in the direction that he desires the player to run. The coach either will point straight out to his right or left, indicate a deeper angle to the left or right, or have the player come directly back to him. When the defensive back sees the direction that the coach is pointing, he immediately must lean in the direction he desires to go, roll over the foot

in that direction, and begin running straight ahead at full speed. In the usual practice sequence, this drill immediately follows the angle backpedal drill.

Pattern-Reaction Keys

There are three points about pattern reaction that need constant emphasis:

(1) The defensive player should concentrate on the distance the receiver is running (short, medium, deep) and on the patterns that can be run in each specific area;

SHORT PATTERN REACTION DRILL

Interception Point

SS

Recognition Point — Interception Point

TE — CO

(Tight End "Short" Pattern)

Interception Point

CB

Recognition Point

WR

(Wide Receiver "Slant" Pattern)

The instant the defensive back recognizes the receiver's pattern, called the "recognition point," he leaves his backpedal and runs to the "interception point" 6 to 10 yards away, depending on the depth of the pattern.

(2) The defensive player must understand that the instant he recognizes the pattern, called the *recognition point*, he leaves his backpedal, rolling over the proper foot;

(3) The defender must concentrate on the fact that the receiver will not catch the ball at the recognition point, but rather about 6 yards from the recognition point for inside patterns coming toward the ball and about 10 yards from the recognition point for patterns going away from the ball.

The point where the ball actually will be caught is called the *interception point*, and it is here that the defensive back must run if he is to break up or intercept the pass. When conducting the following pattern-recognition drills, the receiver first will run short patterns, next medium patterns, and finally deep patterns. To give the defensive players a true idea of where to go, it is advisable to put out cones or chalk marks at the interception points. But as the drill is repeated, the cones should be removed, forcing the defender to judge the distance on his own.

DRILL:
Short-Area Pattern Reaction
In running this drill, make sure each player has an opportunity to see all the patterns that are thrown in the short area, to see how the interception point changes with the direction of the pattern (toward or away from the ball), and to calculate the length of time the pass must be in the air. The defensive players must stay in the habit of calling out each pattern as they recognize it, and then breaking toward the interception point. It also

should be pointed out to the defensive backs that at the start of each play, they will be looking at the quarterback (determining run or pass), and they often will see the quarterback take two steps, rise up, and prepare to throw the short patterns. This movement by the quarterback should alert the defensive player to focus quickly on the receiver and be prepared to break in the direction of the pattern being run.

DRILL:
Medium-Area Pattern Reaction
As the distance a receiver is running from the line of scrimmage lengthens, the more time he has to get square with the defensive back. Because of this, the defensive back must concentrate on staying on one shoulder or the other of the receiver, physically taking away one direction and staying prepared to break in the other.

When running this drill, be sure that each of the players works against all the medium patterns and make certain he continues to call out the patterns as he reacts to them. Each defensive back should have a feeling, at the end of the drill, for the different locations of the interception points. In the case of the "hook" pattern, he actually will be coming directly at the back of the receiver.

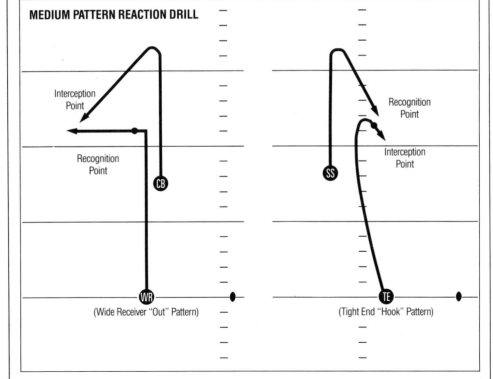

MEDIUM PATTERN REACTION DRILL

Interception Point

Recognition Point

CB

Recognition Point

Interception Point

SS

WR

(Wide Receiver "Out" Pattern)

TE

(Tight End "Hook" Pattern)

DRILL:

Deep-Area Pattern Reaction

Because of the length of the deep pat-terns run by the tight end and wide re-ceivers, the interception point is farther away from the recognition point, and the time the defensive back has to react is greater. Even on the "post" pattern, the receiver will run at least 10 yards before he catches the pass.

By understanding this, the defensive back can adjust his path so he can go di-rectly to the interception point and not have to chase the receiver up the field. This understanding is especially true when covering a double-move pattern, such as a "corner" or a "comeback" pass. In all probability, the defensive back will have left his backpedal and be running toward the "post" or the "up" pat-tern when he recognizes the actual pat-tern being run by the receiver. In the case of a "corner" pattern, the defensive back must know that he has time to turn his back to the receiver, wheel around while keeping his momentum, locate the receiver, and still break up the pass.

NOTE: *In the drill diagram the ball has been moved to the right of the receivers as a reminder to run the drill on both sides.*

Bump-and-Run Technique

Bump-and-run man-to-man coverage is different from regular man-to-man cov-erage in that the defensive player, usual-ly a cornerback, lines up at the line of scrimmage in front of the receiver whom he is to cover for the length of the play. In order to use this technique, the defen-

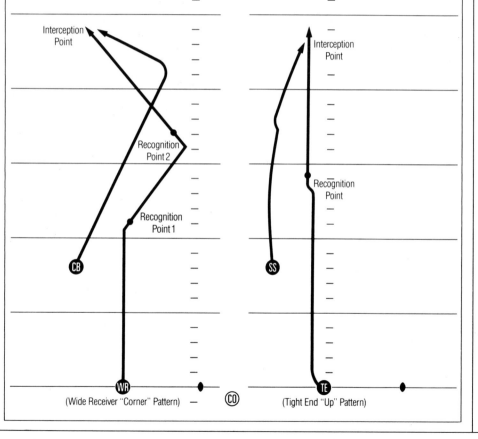

DEEP PATTERN REACTION DRILL

Interception Point

Recognition Point 2

Recognition Point 1

CB

(Wide Receiver "Corner" Pattern)

CO

Interception Point

Recognition Point

SS

TE

(Tight End "Up" Pattern)

sive player must be of equal or better speed than the man he is to defend. Bump-and-run coverage is ideal to use in any man-to-man coverage situation in which the defensive player will not have any help. Bump-and-run coverage also cuts down on the effectiveness of a slower wide receiver who may make good moves as he runs his routes. This type of coverage is similar to man-to-man coverage in basketball.

Bump-and-run style of coverage is challenging and rewarding for competitive defensive backs. It is up to them to make certain that the receiver lined up in front of them does not catch the ball during the entire length of the play. Learning to master this type of coverage is essential for cornerbacks because often it is the only type they will be able to use when playing goal-line defense.

Bump-and-Run Stance and Hit

The defensive player should start in a stance in which he aligns himself either inside or outside the man he is covering. If there will be no help, the defensive back assumes a stance on the inside of the receiver. Should there be inside help on the coverage, the defensive back may assume an outside alignment. The idea for the defender is to place his body in a position so that the offensive

player can release off the line only in one direction. Facing the receiver at a 45-degree angle, the defensive back should be in a solid stance, with his feet spread the width of his shoulders. He should have a good bend in his knees— almost a quarter-squat position. His back should be straight, his head up, and his eyes focused on the man in front of him. The defensive back's elbows should be close to his waist and flexed, the palms of both hands should be held at chest level, and his fingers spread and open.

DRILL:

Bump-and-Run (Inside Stance)

In this drill, the outside foot of the defensive back should be in front of the nose of the wide receiver. The defensive player should set up at a 45-degree angle to the offensive man. Again, as in many other drills, both positions are played by defensive players. Starting at one side, on the command "Hit!" from the coach, the wide receiver charges straight up the field. The defensive player jams the palm of his outside hand into the sternum area of the offensive player. The idea is not to injure the offensive player but merely to stop his momentum and interrupt his timing.

When first teaching this drill, players

should go at half speed. As skill levels develop, the speed of the release by the offensive player can be increased.

DRILL:

Bump-and-Run (Inside-Outside Release)

When the wide receiver releases off the line in this drill, he attempts to run to the inside or outside of the defensive player instead of charging straight up the field. At the start, it is important for the receiver to go directly inside or outside. After the drill has been run a number of times, the receiver may first fake one direction and then go the other way. Never lose sight of the fact that we are instructing the defense to play bump-and-run and not working on the receiver's release off the line.

As the receiver releases, the defensive man must step in the direction in which the receiver is going and start running with him. If he has an opportunity to bump him he may do so, but he never should step up to make the hit. The bump should be attempted only if the receiver makes a move directly into the defensive man.

The first step by the defensive player should occur when the receiver starts to pass the defensive player's nose. When the receiver releases to the inside, the defensive back should step back with

The defensive back playing man-to-man bump-and-run positions himself so that the receiver can release off the line of scrimmage in only one direction.

DRILL:

Mirror Running

The next step in teaching bump-and-run coverage actually is running with the receiver up the field. This is not a pattern-recognition drill. The offensive player will release to the outside and then run straight for 10 to 15 yards.

As the receiver releases off the line to the outside, the defensive player should step with his outside foot and start running with the receiver up the field. In this drill, we want the defensive player to maintain a position where his belt buckle is slightly ahead of the inside hip of the receiver. He should be a foot away from the receiver to the inside, so that the receiver cannot lean into him and push off. As the defender runs up the field, his hands should be up so that he can hit the receiver should he try to run to the inside. He should attempt to stay even with the receiver as he races upfield. During the entire drill, the defensive back never should take his eyes off the receiver.

DRILL:

Bump-and-Run (Pattern-Reaction)

When incorporating pattern reaction with bump-and-run coverage, it is not necessary for the receiver to run the entire pattern at the start. The receiver need only

his inside foot, hitting the receiver with the palm of his inside hand, and attempt to push the receiver down the line of scrimmage toward the coach.

With an outside release, no contact will occur. Instead, the defender steps first with his outside foot and runs up the field

with the receiver.

Lunging at the receiver and stepping with the improper foot are the two biggest mistakes made in this drill. The defensive player must be certain of the receiver's direction before he makes any movement.

PATTERN REACTION DRILL (BUMP-AND-RUN)

Bump ... CB ... CB

WR ("In" Route) ... CO ... WR ("Out" Route)

"comeback." The defender should keep as close as possible to the receiver when he runs these new routes.

> **WINNING POINTS**
> - Do not let receiver get "square;" always shade receiver on one side or the other.
> - Always keep cushion on receiver.
> - Concentrate on distance/depth receiver is running to gain keys to potential patterns.
> - In man-to-man coverage, look for ball only when receiver breaks and he is close enough to touch.
> - When leaving backpedal, roll over foot in direction desired.
> - In bump-and-run coverage, assume stance and body position to allow receiver to release off line in only one direction.
> - Never step up to bump receiver or lunge at receiver on inside release; let him come to you; do not bump on outside release.
> - When running with receiver, keep hands up and eyes on receiver; stay between receiver and goal line as pattern is run.

run up the field six or seven yards and then either run an "out" pattern or try to get to the inside. As the ability of the defensive player progresses, the patterns can be run at their normal depth by the receiver.

Should the receiver attempt to come to the inside, the defensive back must jam him with the heels of both hands, stop his momentum, and then be prepared to roll inside as the receiver runs to the center of the field. If he can, the defensive back should force the receiver back toward the line of scrimmage, keeping his body between the receiver and the defender's goal line. In this position, the defender

can see through the receiver to the quarterback.

When the receiver runs to the outside, no collision will occur. The defender then must round off his run, keeping between the receiver and his own goal line, and drive for the interception point while still focusing on the numbers of the receiver. By doing this, the defender will be prepared to change his path should the receiver suddenly turn up the field.

After the defensive backs react correctly to the inside and outside routes, the coach may instruct the receiver to run different patterns such as the "out-and-up," "post," "corner," "up," and

Zone Pass Defense

Once a defensive back has mastered the

skills and techniques needed to play man-to-man defense successfully, he is ready to take the physical skills he has learned and adapt them to playing zone defense.

There are two basic differences between the two types of defenses. The first is that in man-to-man, the responsibility of the defensive player is to run with a particular receiver wherever he might go. In zone defenses, the defensive player is assigned to cover an area (or zone) on the playing field, with the responsibility of breaking up any pass thrown to any receiver in his zone. The defensive backs rotate either right or left into their zones. Two players may be assigned to share the responsibility for the deep area of the field (*two-deep zone*), or three players may go deep (*three-deep zone*). The remaining defensive back, or backs, cover the zones closer to the line of scrimmage (*underneath zones*).

The second difference is that in man-to-man coverage the defensive player focuses his eyes and attention on a particular receiver for the duration of a play. In zone defense the defender's focus is on the quarterback, not on a receiver.

When the defensive back understands these two differences between man-to-man and zone pass coverage, he is pre-pared to learn the five basic elements needed to play good zone defense. These elements are: (1) play recognition (is the offense running or passing the ball?); (2) understanding the type of zone being played and responsibility within a particular zone; (3) the techniques to use when moving to a zone; (4) recognition of offensive pass patterns as they develop; and (5) proper reaction once the ball has left the quarterback's hand.

A weakness by a defensive back in any one of these areas will cause his play to be ineffective and may result in a breakdown of the entire defense.

Great zone defense requires smart, hard-hitting, disciplined players. Zone defense can be played only by defensive players who are willing to study on and off the field, who take pride in the team's performance, and who never gamble or leave their zone because they *think* something may take place.

Before introducing zone defense on the field, the defensive players should be taught the different types of zone coverage a team is going to use throughout the year. For example, they should know they will use a three-deep zone (with either four or five underneath zones) and/or a two-deep zone (with either five or six underneath zones).

DRILL:

Learning the Zones

In this exercise, the defensive backs learn the locations of the different zones on the field, and to what the names of each refer. We will not use offensive players, and no ball will be thrown.

The coach calls upon one player at a time, naming the particular zone to which he is to move. On the command "Hit!," the defensive back moves to the designated zone. This is strictly a mental drill. In the beginning, little, if any, time should be spent in teaching the proper technique to be used by the defensive player.

Once all of the players become comfortable moving individually to the designated zones, the coach should tell each of them where he desires them to go and have them move to their zones as a coordinated four-man unit. Later, as the players learn their designated areas, based on a call of a particular zone defense, the coach will specify a particular defense, and the players should correctly drop to their zones.

When first teaching the various zones to the defensive backs, it is advisable either to mark the practice field with chalk or to place cones, thus giving the players a point of reference. After the drill has

THE ZONES OF THE FIELD

Deep Half   Deep Half

Deep Outside   Deep Middle   Deep Outside

Outside   Slot   Hook   Center   Hook   Slot   Outside

FS   SS

CB   CB

CO

take an outside underneath zone. Which one takes this responsibility is determined by a call from the safety on that side. If the call is "Sky," the safety has the outside underneath zone, but if the call is "Cloud," the cornerback assumes the responsibility. In either case, the three remaining defensive backs share the coverage of the deep zones. The coach should allow the calls to be made prior to starting the drill.

DRILL:
Zone Left With "Sky" Call

On the command "Hit!," both cornerbacks drop straight back into one of the deep outside zones. Because they are lined up to the outside prior to the start of the drill, they do not have to worry about getting any wider; they can use the backpedal technique they practiced in man-to-man coverage.

The safety away from the call must turn toward the center of the field and sprint until he is in the middle of his zone, when he also can get into his backpedal. The safety on the side of the call should turn and run to the outside, aiming for a spot six yards from the sideline and 12 yards deep. When he reaches this point, he should go into his backpedal.

All four players should be looking directly at the coach as they backpedal.

been run a few times, the artificial boundaries should be removed, forcing the players to locate their proper zones based upon the usual game-day markings they will find on the field.

DRILL:
Three-Deep Zone Drop Technique

The four defensive backs line up across the field, eight yards from the position of the coach. Prior to the start of the drill, the coach calls out the direction in which he desires the zone to *rotate* by saying, "Zone right" or "Zone left." His choice always should be in relation to the direction in which the players are facing.

Either the cornerback or the safety to the side of the direction of the call will

In zone pass defense, the defensive backs focus their attention on the quarterback rather than a specific receiver.

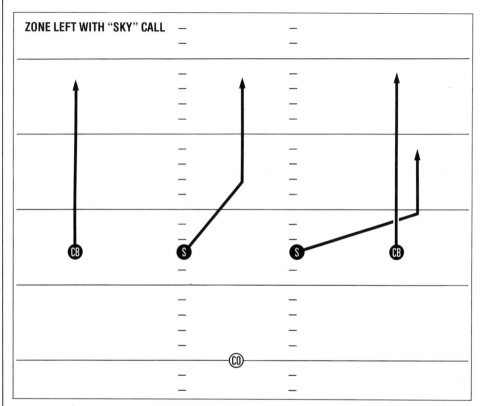

ZONE LEFT WITH "SKY" CALL

tioning drill. It teaches the players how to go to their zones, focusing on the man with the ball, and then breaking the instant they see the ball being thrown. A ball is not used because time is spent later coaching the players on how to properly intercept the ball.

DRILL:

Zone Right With "Cloud" Call

In this drill, the cornerback on the side of the call will be in the outside underneath zone on his side. Because he has no need to worry about getting wider, he can step forward, set into an outside bump-and-run position, simulate bumping the receiver who would be releasing off the line of scrimmage, and then start his backpedal.

Both safeties must turn to their right and sprint at 45-degree angles into their zones. Once they have reached the proper width, they both can return to their backpedal and focus on the coach. The cornerback away from the call should backpedal and focus on the coach.

Once all the players have reached their correct depths, the coach simulates throwing the ball, and the players break in that direction, then sprint as a group back to the line of scrimmage.

It is important in this type of drill that

The coach then simulates throwing a pass either to the right, left, or middle. All four players should immediately stop their backpedal, change their momentum by rolling over, move toward the area where the pass would have been thrown, and then sprint as a group back to the original line of scrimmage.

Ideally, the coach should allow the three deep players to reach a depth of 18 to 20 yards before he starts his throwing motion. As soon as the players on the field cross the line of scrimmage, the next group should be lining up across the field, waiting for the coach's call.

This drill is not designed to be a condi-

the coach make certain that all players have an opportunity to move to the different zones.

DRILL:

Two-Deep Zone Drop Technique

The four defensive backs line up across the field in the same manner as for the three-deep drill. The big difference in the drops of the players when using a two-deep zone is that a "cloud" call is given on both sides, instructing both cornerbacks to cover the outside underneath zones. The two safeties, then, must divide the field so each is in the center of his half.

After both safeties have called out "cloud" to the cornerbacks, the coach gives the command "Hit!" and the drill begins. The movement of both cornerbacks should be the same. They should take two steps toward the line of scrimmage and to the outside, where a receiver would be releasing up the field. They then should set into an outside bump-and-run position, simulate hitting the receiver, then backpedal as quickly as they can into their proper zones, while directing their eyes to the quarterback/coach.

At the same time, the two safeties also should move as one. Both should open to their outside and sprint to get their

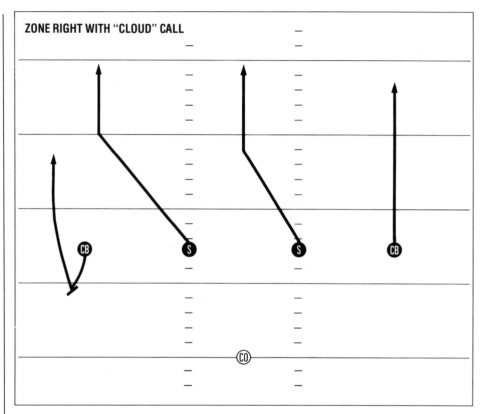

ZONE RIGHT WITH "CLOUD" CALL

needed width and depth. Both safeties must think "deep" if a two-deep zone is to have success. Once the safeties are in the center of their zones, the should swing into their individual backpedals and focus on the quarterback/coach.

When the four players have reached their zones, the coach makes a throwing motion. The players move in that direction and then sprint as a group to the original line of scrimmage.

In both the two-deep and three-deep technique drills, we first are making certain that the correct call is made before the drill begins. Next, we want to make

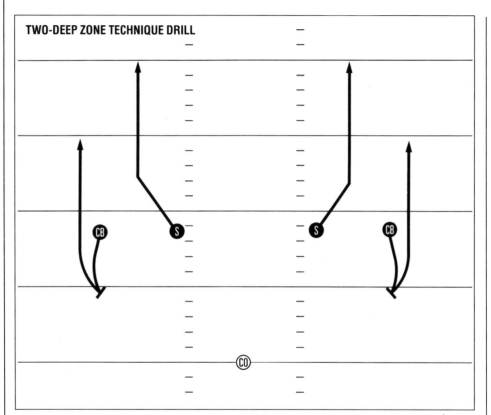

TWO-DEEP ZONE TECHNIQUE DRILL

the entire four-man group should be required to repeat the drill. It is the coach's responsibility to the players to make certain that everyone does the drill correctly and with maximum effort.

> **WINNING POINTS**
> - In zone coverage, watch quarterback until ball is thrown, then react to ball.
> - Rotate correctly into assigned zone; quickly reach proper depth and begin backpedal.

Ball Stripping

Many times the defensive back is not in position to deflect the pass away from a receiver. But he may be in position to strip the ball from the receiver's hands. The ability to strip the ball from a receiver is as much mental as it is physical. The defensive back must be thinking about stripping the ball before he ever reaches the receiver. He must understand the physical mechanics that go into catching a pass, and he must be alert enough not to make contact with the receiver until the instant that the receiver first touches the ball.

Many coaches talk about this skill, yet in practice they don't conduct drills that teach defensive backs the actual skills necessary to get the job done. If a coach

certain that each of the four players goes to the correct zone, and that he moves there with proper technique. Then we want to see all the defensive backs get into their backpedal, concentrating and focusing on the coach who serves as the quarterback. Finally, as the throwing motion occurs, we want to see all four players immediately change from their backpedal and run in the direction where the ball would have gone, sprinting as a group back across the line of scrimmage.

Because defense is played as a team, if one of the players does not perform correctly in any one of the techniques,

There are five locations where a receiver will have his hands to catch a pass. The first three are: directly in front of him (left); high above his pads to the right (middle); or above his pads left (right).

wants his players proficient at something, he must show them what he wants.

Remember: An incomplete pass is the same as a running play stopped for no gain.

DRILL:

Ball Stripping

This is not a full contact drill; the players run at three-quarter speed. It is designed to teach defensive backs how to properly strip a ball away from a receiver, which arm should be attacked, and the technique that should be used to cause an incompletion.

Next, the players should be shown that the receiver's arm on the same side as the pass is the one they must attack. If the defensive back sees the pass coming to the left of the receiver, he should take his left arm and reach over, pulling down and back on the left arm of the receiver. If the pass is to the right, he uses his right arm to attack the right arm of the receiver.

This "reach-and-pull" technique first should be taught with the players standing still, the receiver merely reaching to simulate one of the five receiving positions, and the defender, who is standing directly behind him, pulling down and back on the correct arm. Once the coach is satisfied that the players understand which arm to attack, and the proper method of doing it, they can proceed to the actual drill.

At the start of the drill, both the receiver and the defensive back face one sideline or the other. The defender stands 10 yards away from the receiver. At the command "Hit!" the receiver starts running directly toward the sideline, and the defensive back angles toward the receiver on the sideline, aiming at a point six or seven yards ahead of the receiver, running on a path so that he will reach the receiver as the ball arrives.

After the receiver has run a few yards,

The final two locations to expect a receiver's hands are: behind him; or low to the left or right. Knowing these locations aids in stripping the ball.

Prior to running the drill, the coach should demonstrate to the players the five different locations where a receiver may have his hands when he catches a pass: with the ball in front of him, his hands below or above his shoulder pads; behind him with his hands below or above the shoulder pads; and with the back of the receiver directly in front of the defensive player.

The receiver's arm on the side of the pass is the one defenders must attack in attempting to strip the ball. The defensive back reaches over with his own arm on that side and pulls down and back on the receiver's arm as he touches the ball.

the coach passes the ball to him. At the moment the receiver's hands touch the ball, the defensive back, having seen through the receiver to the location of the pass, makes contact, reaching over and pulling the correct arm, causing the ball to fall to the ground. His other arm should be making contact with the back of the receiver, his elbow hitting the small of the receiver's back, and his hand then grabbing the jersey of the receiver in case the ball does not fall free and he has to make a tackle.

The coach must make certain that he throws the ball in positions in front of and behind the receiver so that the defensive back learns to recognize which arm he must attack while the ball is in the air.

When working on stripping a pass to a receiver who is stopped and has his back to the defensive player, the drill is set up the same way, except that the receiver doesn't move; he begins the drill facing the coach waiting to receive the ball. The coach tosses the ball either to the right or the left of the receiver. As the pass is thrown, the defensive back sprints toward the receiver, attacking the arm on the side of the pass, pulling it away from the ball and causing the incompletion.

To repeat: Stripping the ball is as much mental as it is physical. While there is little movement or hard contact in the drill, each time a defensive back executes the drill properly he gets a mental picture of what he can do during a game to cause a receiver to drop a pass.

Interceptions

For a defensive back, there is no greater thrill than intercepting an opponent's pass, then avoiding the offensive players who are trying to tackle him, and returning the ball for a touchdown. An interception by a defensive back can cause a shift in the momentum of the game, giving a tremendous boost to the intercept-

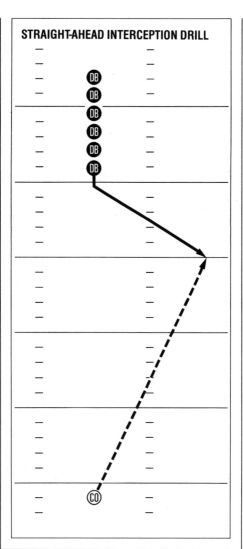

STRAIGHT-AHEAD INTERCEPTION DRILL

ing team.

Defensive backs who make great interceptions do so not because of blind luck but because of hard work, hours of studying the opponent so that they mentally can see the pass before it ever is thrown, and correctly playing the defense called. More often than not, when a player returns to the sideline after making an interception, the first words he says are, "I knew he was going to throw the pass in my direction." Interceptions, like any great plays in a football game, are the result of careful planning, dedication to detail, and an intense desire by the player to make a significant contribution to his team's chances for victory.

DRILL:

Straight-Ahead Interceptions

The defensive backs line up 20 yards away from, and facing, the coach. When the coach raises the ball to a throwing position, the defensive back who is first in line steps in the direction that the coach is going to throw the pass. As the coach takes his step and throws, the defensive back rolls over his foot in that direction, and starts running that way while coming at a forward angle toward the ball.

The defensive back must keep his eyes focused on the ball as it approach-

Interceptions are not lucky occurrences; they result from studying the opponent and correctly playing the defense called.

es him, bringing his hands into a position so he can see his fingers and watch the ball all the way into his hands. He must not look downfield or think about running the interception back for a touchdown.

If the defensive back sees that the pass is going to be caught at his chest or lower, he must cup his hands, palms up, with his little fingers touching, ready to receive the ball.

If the pass is at shoulder level or above, the defensive back then must cup his hands, cock his wrists so that his palms are slightly up, but now have his thumbs, rather than his little fingers, touching. Many high passes that should be intercepted are not caught because the defensive back has not cocked his wrists, and his palms are not up but actually are facing the ground. Instead of catching the ball, the defensive back deflects it to the ground; a big play is lost for his team.

On any high pass, emphasis also must be placed on the defensive back leaping to catch the ball at its highest possible point rather than waiting for it to come down.

DRILL:

Angle Interceptions

Most defensive backs never are directly in front of the quarterback during a

Correct hand position for intercepting a pass is the same as for offensive receivers —little fingers together for low passes, thumbs touching for high passes.

game. In this interception drill they actually see the ball coming at the same angles as they will in game situations.

This drill is run the same as the previous one except that the players spread across the field so they are in positions similar to those they will be in during an actual game. When initially running the drill, the coach should designate only one player to try to make the intercep-

tion. After the players become accustomed to the drill, the coach may activate two adjacent players to see which of them actually gets to the ball.

Often players will make an interception with ease during practice when there is no possible chance for a collision, but they will shy away if there is a possibility of contact. Contact is likely to occur in a game, so it is important to run this type of

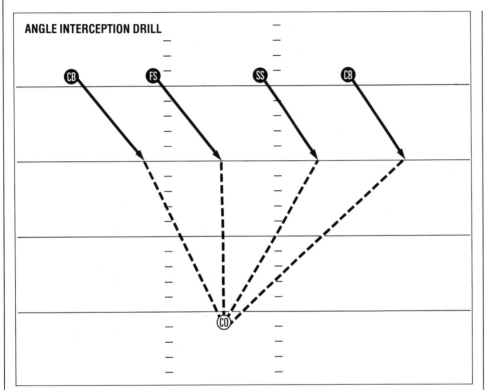

ANGLE INTERCEPTION DRILL

To intercept an over-the-head pass, reach up with little fingers together.

drill to allow the defensive backs an opportunity to become accustomed to making an interception with people around them. If one player in the two-man drill sees that he is going to make the interception easily, he should start yelling, "I have it, I have it," so that his teammate does not run into him, causing him to drop the ball.

All the important techniques that were emphasized and taught concerning the proper way to catch the ball should continue to be reinforced during this drill.

DRILL:
Over-the-Head Interceptions
Occasionally during a game, a defensive back has an opportunity to make a diffi-

cult interception—when he has to catch a ball coming directly over his head as he is running toward his own goal line. To prepare for this situation, it is important for the defensive backs to practice this type of catch and to learn the proper

OVER-THE-HEAD INTERCEPTION DRILL

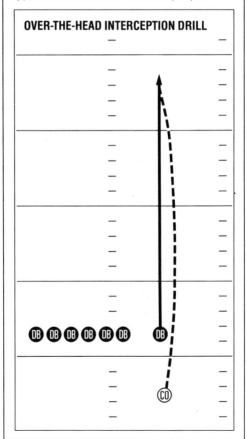

technique to use in making the interception.

One at a time, the defensive backs line up five yards directly in front of the coach, facing down the field. When the coach yells "Hit!," each player begins running down the field away from the coach. After the defensive back has run five yards, the coach lobs the ball over the player's head. As the player runs, he should lean his head back as far as possible and attempt to see the ball as it starts its downward path. When he locates the ball, the defensive back should raise both arms upward, his hands forming a cup, little fingers together, palms up, and wrists cocked.

When making this type of catch, the defensive back must bring his hands high enough so he can see the ball and his hands at the same time as the interception is made. Without running this type of drill, most players will keep their hands at chest level, will never see their hands near the ball, and will lose an opportunity to make an interception because they are unable to watch the ball all the way into their hands.

DRILL:

Tipped Passes

Many times during the course of a game, defensive backs will have the opportuni-

A tipped pass usually will be deflected high into the air and slowed.

ty to catch a pass that has been touched, tipped, or somehow deflected by either another defensive player or by an offensive receiver. These balls will not come on a level path but usually will be

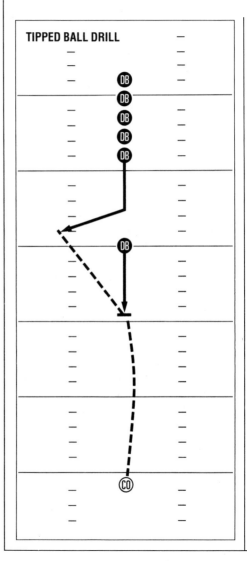

TIPPED BALL DRILL

knocked high into the air, thus diminishing the original velocity of the pass. Often players will have to make diving catches when making this type of interception, catching the ball just before it hits the ground.

To set up the drill to simulate tipped balls, have the players line up, single-file, facing the coach. When the coach raises the ball, the first defensive back starts toward the coach with the second man in line following directly behind him. The coach then throws a high, easy pass to the front man, who tips the ball into the air rather than catching it. The trailing defensive back then must adjust his path and do everything he can to intercept. If the ball is tipped high into the air and the defensive back easily can run under it, he should not forget to jump up to make the interception, always trying to catch the ball at the highest possible point.

Tackling

Missing a tackle is one of the worst sins a defensive back can commit. The other defensive players may miss a tackle and know there always will be someone else between the ball carrier and the goal line who can prevent the touchdown. Defensive backs don't have that luxury.

Because defensive backs are the last line of defense, missed tackles in the secondary usually result in long gains or touchdowns. There is no lonelier feeling on the football field than the one felt by a defensive back when he is out in the open field, alone with a ball carrier, with no help in sight, and all the fans and his coaches and teammates watching to see if he will make the tackle or if he will allow the ball carrier to score.

While correct tackling style and technique should be emphasized and taught, it also is important that the defensive back understand he must grab the ball carrier any way he can. Even if it is not a picture-perfect tackle, he must hold on to the ball carrier and wait for help to arrive from his fellow defensive players.

WINNING POINTS
- To intercept pass at numbers or below, hold hands with little fingers together.
- To intercept pass at numbers or above, hold hands with thumbs together; cock wrists back.
- To intercept pass over shoulder or head, reach for ball with little fingers held together; look ball into hands.
- Call for interceptions to avoid collision with teammates.

Defensive backs must have correct body position for tackling: knees bent with no forward lean at the waist; back as straight as possible; head up; and eyes open.

More often than not, a defensive back is asked to tackle an offensive player who is much larger than he is. Tackling someone larger takes guts, but is not difficult to attempt if the player is taught safe and proper techniques from the beginning. These skills must be taught slowly, with the initial emphasis on proper body position and not on the force of the hit. Little or no learning can take place when the player is afraid of being injured.

When teaching correct body position for tackling, constant emphasis must be placed on the tackler bending his knees and not leaning forward at the waist, thus keeping his back as straight as possible. He always must keep his head up, never looking down at the ground and exposing his neck to injury. Tackle with the shoulder pad and not the helmet.

Knowledge of proper tackling technique is one of the greatest assets in helping a player overcome his natural fear of injury. It will give the player the desire and determination to take on ball carriers in the open field.

DRILL:

Open-Field Tackling

It is best to start with straight-ahead tackling when first working with defensive backs, even though most tackles they will make will not be of this type. What we are teaching is proper tackling technique, not trying to simulate game conditions.

For this drill, the defensive backs are divided into two groups. One group does the tackling, while the members of the other group serve as the ball carriers.

On the command "Hit!," both the ball carrier and the tackler move straight ahead for five yards. As the tackler nears the end of the five yards, he should shorten his stride and hesitate momentarily, keeping his eyes focused on the

OPEN-FIELD TACKLING DRILL

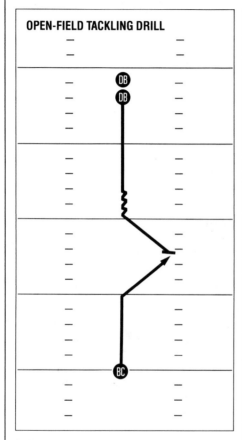

ball carrier's numbers until he is certain which way the ball carrier is going to cut.

The ball carrier, after running straight ahead for five yards, cuts, without faking, at a 45-degree angle to his right or left and runs in that direction.

The tackler, once he sees the direction of the ball carrier's cut, also breaks in that direction and prepares to make the tackle. The tackler must shorten his stride as he gets closer to the man with the ball, gathering himself so he can explode up and through the ball carrier. The ball carrier must attempt to keep running on his course and not stop when he sees that the tackle is about to be made.

At the moment of contact, the tackler should push off his foot nearest the ball carrier, keeping his back straight, his head up, and his eyes open. He should place his head in front of the ball carrier's chest and pound the inside of his elbows into the ball carrier's chest and back. The instant the defender's elbows make contact they will bounce off, and the tackler will feel his hands coming in contact with the ball carrier. When this happens, the tackler should grab the ball carrier's jersey, stopping any further advance up the field. In this drill, it is not necessary for the tackler to drive the man to the ground, but we do want him to explode into the ball carrier, grab his jersey, and stop his forward movement.

After being tackled, the ball carrier should go to the end of the line of the players preparing to tackle, and the tackler should go to the end of the line of the ball carriers.

When learning the basics of tackling, it is important that both players in the drill run at only half speed. As techniques become better, fear will be reduced and the confidence of the players will improve. The speed of the drill then can be increased. The drill continues until each player has had an opportunity to make a tackle on the ball carrier going both to the right and left.

DRILL:
Angled Open-Field Tackling
This drill starts with the ball carrier and the tackler eight yards apart. On the command "Hit!," the ball carrier will run straight up the field for five yards, then cut at a 90-degree angle, running straight for the sideline.

At the same time the defensive back is backpedaling five yards, and, when he sees the ball carrier make his cut, he rolls over his foot and drives to a point 10 yards in front of the ball carrier to make his tackle. As he reaches the ball carrier, he uses all the same techniques and assumes the same correct body positions that were described in the preceding drill.

This drill is used to simulate the type of tackle that most defensive backs will be called upon to make during the course of a game following a reception by an offensive receiver. The tackler must make

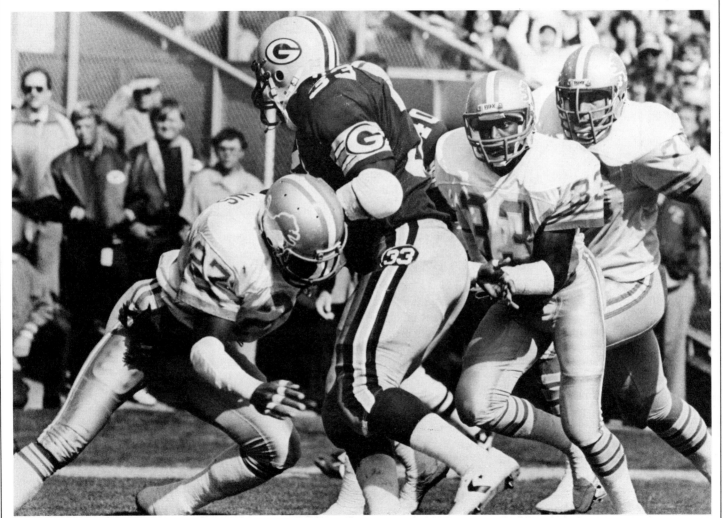

Defensive backs are a team's last line of defense, often the only men between a fleet ball carrier and the end zone.

ANGLE OPEN-FIELD TACKLING DRILL

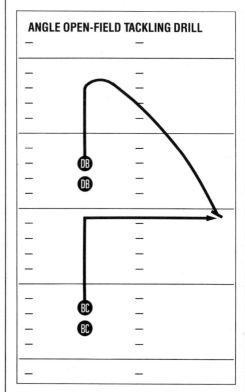

certain that he does not allow the ball carrier to be in position to turn up the field. Each player should have the opportunity to make a tackle to his right and his left before the drill ends.

DRILL:
Close Sideline Tackling
This is one of the most important tackling drills for defensive backs. It often is up to them to make certain that a ball carrier does not have the opportunity to run free up the sideline for a touchdown. It may be necessary to allow the ball carrier to gain a few yards, but he must not be allowed to break away.

In setting up this drill, the ball carrier and the tackler line up five yards apart. The defensive back who is to serve as the ball carrier lines up one yard from the sideline, facing the coach, with his back to the tackler. The tackler lines up four yards from the sideline, straddling the yard line, with his body angled, facing the back of the ball carrier.

The coach starts the drill by tossing the ball to the ball carrier. The instant he catches it, the ball carrier spins around and faces up the field. At the same time the tackler takes two steps forward, stops, and runs in place, while still maintaining his angle toward the sideline.

At this point, the ball carrier is free to go in any direction he desires, faking any number of times, before making his final dash for the open field. The tackler must wait in position, not committing one way or the other until the ball carrier starts running to the inside or trying to run straight up the field. When the runner crosses his nose, the tackler must open up with the foot in the direction the ball carrier is going, and move on a path that will put him in position to make the tackle after the ball carrier has run two or three more yards. If the tackler crosses his feet instead of opening up, usually he will miss the tackle and merely chase the ball carrier. In this drill, the defensive back should remember that he must grab the ball carrier and that he is trying to buy time that will allow his teammates to come to his aid.

CLOSE SIDELINE TACKLING DRILL

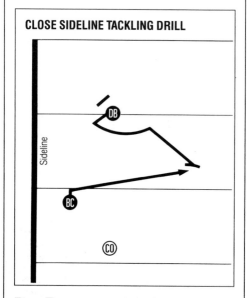

Run Force

Defending against the pass is the primary responsibility of defensive backs. But

Close sideline tackling is one of the most important skills for a defensive back. The tackler must time his move to the ball carrier so that he is in position to make the tackle two to three yards after the runner turns upfield.

they also are called upon to help stop the running game. A defensive back who can play only pass defense and can't play the run is a serious handicap to his team. The need for this type of action by a defensive back usually arises when the offensive team attempts a wide run-ning play.

One of the defensive backs, who is lined up on the side of the run, must quickly come up and turn the ball carri-er back to the center of the field. This type of maneuver is called *run force*, and it is one of the hardest jobs a defen-sive back has. The difficulty is caused by the size of the blockers, usually offen-sive linemen, who are in front of the ball carrier.

Once the defensive back determines that the play is a run to his side, he must charge across the line of scrimmage, quickly attacking the blocker before the ball carrier has the opportunity to get outside the linebackers and defensive linemen and start upfield.

DRILL:

Run Force

The coach calls out which one of the defensive backs he wants to force the run by calling "sky" for the safety and "cloud" for the cornerback. As in previous drills, the offensive positions should be played by defensive backs.

The defensive back who has the responsibility to force the run should focus on the tight end. If the tight end blocks the defensive player directly in front of him, the force man charges the line of scrimmage, aiming for a point two yards across the line and three yards outside the tight end.

The defensive back must charge to this point, for, if he does not cross the line of scrimmage, the back easily can turn up the field; if he comes up any wider, the ball carrier has a running lane between the force man and the next defensive player to the inside.

The quarterback begins the drill by saying "Hit!" He turns and pitches the ball to the halfback. The tight end blocks the defensive player in front of him, showing the defensive back that it is a

running play.

The fullback is the lead blocker and should run in front of the ball carrier. In order to avoid injury, the fullback should carry a lightweight blocking shield in his right arm. Instead of actually blocking the defensive back, he should hit him with the shield.

The defensive back who is the force

man will charge to his point and attack the fullback with his inside shoulder and forearm. He should deliver as hard a blow as possible with his forearm to the shield the fullback is carrying. It is important for the defensive back to stay on his feet and to keep his outside arm free. Should the ball carrier attempt to run around him to the outside, he must be in

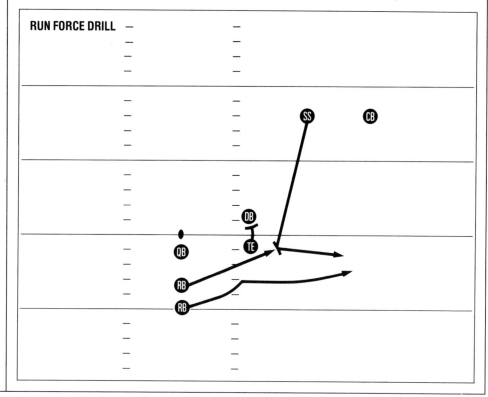

RUN FORCE DRILL

handing him the ball. This allows the force men to see the different locations and paths from which a blocker may attack. It also shows the defensive back the different paths the running back may take when trying to run to the outside.

After the defensive backs have become accustomed to running the drill, the coach may call a pass for the offense and have the tight end release up the field instead of blocking. Should the force man still come charging up when the tight end releases, there is a good possibility the defensive back is looking into the backfield and not concentrating on the tight end.

Blitzing

In some defenses, the cornerbacks and safeties occasionally are used to rush the passer. When defensive backs are called upon to blitz, they always must keep four points in mind:
1. Get off on the snap of the ball.
2. Come through the proper pre-designated rush lane.
3. Know and understand which offensive players can block you and be in position to avoid those blockers on your way to the quarterback.
4. Be prepared to obstruct the pass if the quarterback throws in your direction. Anytime a defensive back comes on a

The defensive back who has run force responsibility charges across the line of scrimmage and attacks the lead blocker with his inside shoulder and forearm.

position so he can turn and make the tackle or force the ball carrier out of bounds.

It must be remembered this is not a tackling drill. We are teaching the defensive back where to force and how to take on the lead blocker. After the ball carrier has run to his right a number of times,

the drill should be reversed so that the defensive backs on the other side of the field have an opportunity to practice their force.

The next time the drill is run, the lead blocker should line up as a guard on the side of the run; the halfback should be in a split position, with the quarterback

blitz, he must realize that the other defensive backs are forced into single coverage. So it is imperative that the blitzer get to the quarterback as quickly as possible.

WINNING POINTS
- When tackling, bend at knees, not waist; keep back straight; head up; eyes focused on ball carrier's numbers. Remember to make contact with shoulder pad and not helmet.
- Shorten stride and do not cross legs before contact on tackle; explode up and through ball carrier; do not let ball carrier turn upfield; never use helmet as contact point.
- Defensive back with run force responsibility keys on tight end.
- To force run, charge two yards across line of scrimmage, three yards outside tight end; take on lead blockers with inside arm and shoulder; keep outside arm free.

THE KICKING GAME

8

The Kicking Game

- Punting   **341**
- Directional Punting   **354**
- Punting In Wind and Rain   **355**
- Punting From the End Zone   **358**
- Placekicking   **359**
- Soccer-Style Kicking   **361**
- Straight-Ahead Kicking   **368**
- Snapping for Kicks   **373**
- The Holder   **376**
- Soccer-Style Kickoffs   **379**
- Straight-Ahead Kickoffs   **382**
- Returning Kicks   **385**

Of all the positions on a football team, punter and placekicker may be the least understood and least appreciated by fans and even some coaches. Yet these two positions are extremely important to any team's success. These players often fall into two groups: starters at some other position who work on kicking only part-time, or kicking specialists who don't play any other position.

The more advanced a football program, the more specialized the two kicking positions. The importance of a dependable punter and placekicker cannot be emphasized enough. The outcome of many games depends on how well these two players execute.

The importance of skillful punting is best seen when a superior punting team slowly wins a battle of field position over its opponent. For a good punting team, each kick has the potential to gain 10 or more yards of field position. In the course of a game, if everything else is equal, a superior punting team should start an offensive series at least once or twice on the opponent's side of the 50-yard line.

Good punting is both an offensive and defensive weapon for a football team. For the offense, it can result in starting each series closer to the opponent's end zone, while for the defense it can mean starting each series on the opponent's side of the field. Both ultimately can be factors in the outcome of a game.

With a good placekicker (who will be referred to as "kicker"), the situation is different. The result of having a superior kicker is the actual scoring of points, either on points after touchdown (PAT) or field goals. A kicker who has the leg strength and accuracy to kick field goals from a great distance tremendously enhances his team's ability to win games.

Knowing an opponent has a great kicker puts added pressure on the opponent's defense, and often forces it to gamble more on stopping the offense farther from its goal line, thus keeping the kicker out of the game.

A superior placekicker with the leg strength to kick field goals and extra points accurately is an asset to any team.

Having a superior kicker for kickoffs also can result in a field position advantage, but this advantage is most often gained by better punting. While kickoffs are important, the primary focus of the kicker must be kicking field goals and PATs.

Punters and kickers don't have to be overly big, well-muscled, or strong. These two positions can accommodate the much smaller player who would have little or no success at any other position. Size does not determine a kicker's ability to perform.

However, mental toughness is absolutely vital. Both punters and kickers must have great confidence in their ability. They must be able to shut out the pressure that comes with each kick, and to focus completely on kicking the ball properly.

Unlike players at other positions, punters and kickers are under pressure to perform correctly on every opportunity. A receiver may drop a pass but come back to catch 10 more; a linebacker may miss one tackle but still make numerous others; a quarterback may throw an errant pass but knows he will have many other chances for completions. For the punter and kicker, though, there may only be a few opportunities to perform in each game. There may not be another chance later on in the game to redeem oneself following a bad kick. So the pressure exists on each and every kick.

Also, the punter and kicker must always be ready on the sideline. They never know when their moment will come, but they must be mentally prepared to do the job when the coach calls on them.

Punting

Anyone who has the responsibility for coaching and developing a young punter must understand that good punting is built on good form. Each separate technique is essential if a punter is to enjoy success. The elements of punting are best taught separately. Then, under a coach's guidance, the parts all are brought together into one smooth, even motion. A punter must have a good understanding of each segment of the punting motion before even attempting to kick a ball.

Should the punter be experiencing difficulty with his kicks, it is vital for the coach to analyze each segment of the punter's motion and determine which segment is being done incorrectly. Yelling or screaming at a boy who is having trouble with his punting will only cause him to lose his concentration and lose confidence in his ability.

Punting is such an individualized and pressure part of football that coaches must correct and encourage rather than constantly berate a boy who is not having success.

Punting Stance

Prior to ever taking a snap from center or actually punting the ball, the punter, like all players, needs to learn proper stance. When first getting into his stance to receive the snap from center, the punter must assume a position that feels relaxed; it is vital that his body not be rigid.

When practicing punting, it often is best for the punter to stand on the sideline, facing across the field with his feet straddling a yard line. The punter's feet should be set no wider than the width of his shoulders, though many punters have them closer together. Standing up straight, with his feet the proper width and straddling the line, the punter should then take a small step forward with his kicking foot, bringing the heel of his kicking foot even with the instep of the foot that has not moved. He should shift his weight to the balls of his feet and slightly bend his legs at the knees. The punter's shoulders and upper body should be leaning forward, slightly in front of his hips. His head should be up with eyes focused straight ahead. He must feel that, if necessary,

A punter needs to take a relaxed, comfortable stance to receive the ball. His weight should be balanced so he can move in any direction to catch an errant snap.

he can step quickly straight ahead or to his right or left, jump high into the air, or bend to the ground.

The coach should line up 10 yards away and directly in front of the punter. From this position he can make certain that the punter's shoulders are pointing straight across the field and that his foot placement is not too wide or too narrow. In the beginning it is also important for the coach to view the punter from the side, checking on the position of his front foot, making certain that there is not too great a bend at his knees or waist, and seeing that he is balanced on the balls of his feet.

Once the punter is in a comfortable stance, the coach, by use of hand signals, should have the punter move quickly to the right, left, and straight ahead, jump up, and bend to the ground. When the punter moves right or left, it is important that his first step be with the foot on the side which he needs to move. If the punter has his feet too wide, or if he has his weight back on his heels, he will not be able to move swiftly. For now, forget about the ball; the punter has the luxury of learning to concentrate on moving correctly and not about catching the ball and kicking it.

Punting Steps

It is especially important for a young punter to realize that punting is based on balance and correct body position. Quick jerky steps, unnecessary body movement, and ungainly attempts at power decrease the punter's efficiency and do not add to the distance of a kick. A proper stance and correct steps are the fundamentals needed to become a good kicker.

Different punters will use either two or three steps when kicking the ball. Be-

When practicing punting, it is best to stand with feet straddling a yard line.

cause two-step punting lessens the chances of having a punt blocked, it is preferred.

The same approach that was used to introduce the proper stance to the punter should be used to teach the proper

steps. The initial position of the punter and the coach should be the same and, as before, no ball is used.

Punting steps should not be exaggerated. Instead, the steps should be taken in a normal walking motion. The entire distance covered by the two steps will never be more than three to three-and-a-half yards. Remember, balance and proper body position are the most important factors in the stepping motion of the punter. Elongated steps will cause the punter to lose his balance and will not add to his punt.

Because balance is so important to successful punting, the punter should place his hands on his hips when working on his steps. With his hands in this position, he will not be able to use them to keep his balance and both the punter

and the coach will quickly see if he has stepped correctly.

The punter's first step is with his forward foot. This should be a small forward step moving slightly away from the yard line the punter is straddling. The punter's forward foot should come down so that he lands on the ball of the foot, with the toe angled slightly away from the yard line. Angling the toe allows the punter to open his hips for the actual punting motion.

The second step should be a normal walking stride. The punter's leg should come across the yard line with his back foot landing just across the line on the same side as the first foot. The toe of the foot should be at the same angle as the toe of the other foot. If his foot ends up aiming straight downfield, the punter

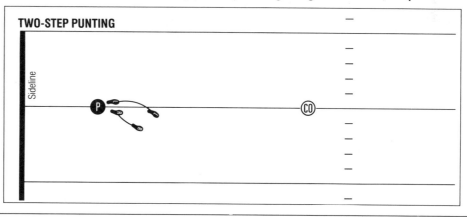

TWO-STEP PUNTING

In two-step punting, the punter's first step (above, left) *is with his forward (kicking) foot. The second step* (middle) *should be a normal walking stride—not an exaggerated stride—or the final kicking motion* (right) *will be awkward.*

will be unable to have a smooth punting motion.

As with the first step, it is vital that the punter land on the ball of his foot. If the punter lands on the heel of his foot, all of his momentum will be directed into the ground and not forward to help his punting motion.

During the entire two-step process, the punter's body should remain in the same position as it did in the stance. The punter should keep his hips over his feet, he should be bending forward at the waist, and his shoulders must remain in front of his hips. The punter's head should be up with his eyes focused straight ahead.

When first learning the proper steps,

the punter should move at a very slow speed. The speed and tempo should be increased only after the punter feels comfortable and the coach determines that the steps are correct. After taking the second step, the punter can swing his kicking leg forward in a relaxed fashion, keeping his ankle locked and the toe of his kicking foot pointed downward.

The beginning punter should slowly go through the steps again and again until this part of his kicking motion becomes automatic. At this point in the punter's development, the coach must make certain that the punter is moving correctly and his steps are the same on each practice kick. Don't be in a hurry to move to other segments of punting until the proper stance and steps are mastered.

Position of Arms and Hands

Once the stance and steps are second nature, the punter can move his hands off his hips and place them in a position to receive the snap. As before, no ball will be used.

From the stance position, the punter should remove his left hand from his hip and extend it forward with the palm facing upward. The elbow should be bent and the arm relaxed. The left hand will

The punter forms a target with both hands (left), *then extends his arms, little fingers touching, to receive the snap.*

serve as the target for the center. The hand should be aligned in the center of the punter's body, even with the bottom of the numbers on the punter's jersey.

After the left hand has been properly placed, the right hand should be removed from the hip and extended forward. Unlike the left hand, the right hand should be held higher, even with the middle of the jersey numbers. The palm of the right hand will face down toward the ground. The right hand should be higher and slightly to the right of the left hand. This forms the roof of the target for the center. The right hand will not stay in this position when the ball is snapped, but it is important for the punter always to form the target first when preparing to punt. If he doesn't establish this target area, the punter risks a snap that is erratic and off target.

After the punter has established the target area for the center, he should move the right arm and hand down so

As the punter takes his second step, he drops his left arm and swings it back.

that it is even with the left hand. In this position the right hand is turned palm upward and the little fingers of both hands should nearly touch. It must be emphasized that the punter have his arms extended so that he is able to see the ball and his hands at the same time when receiving the snap. The center knows the punter is ready to receive the ball when he sees the right hand move from the roof position to the receiving position.

After the punter can correctly place his hands while he is in his stance, it is time to work on arm and hand movement during the two-step punting action.

As the punter takes his first step, the hands should remain together in position to receive the snap. As the second step is executed, the left hand should fall away and swing back above and outside of the left hip. By removing his left hand in this manner the punter can keep his balance during the kick and drop the ball properly.

When the left hand is moving away from the ball, the punter should fully extend his right hand forward and to his right until it is even with the outside of his right thigh. From this position the punter will be able to properly drop the ball to his foot.

The most important objective for the

The football's back tip should be held between the right thumb and forefinger.

punter at this time is the incorporation of body balance, body position, and the additional movement of the hands and arms. Before the ball ever is introduced, the punter must go through each of these procedures—stance, step, hand position, and action—over and over again in the same order until they become automatic.

The left hand lightly rests on the lower front inside of the football.

The ball always is held with laces up. As the left arm is swung back, the right arm and hand are extended forward and slightly to the right.

Handling and Dropping the Ball

The punter finally is ready to begin using a football to learn how to properly cradle the ball in his hands, how to remove the left hand and extend the right hand and arm, and finally how to drop the ball.

While straddling the yard line and holding the football, the punter should first make certain that the laces of the ball are facing upward. The back tip of the football should be nestled into the palm of the right hand in the curve that is formed by the "V" between the thumb and forefinger. The seam with the laces should be up and placed midway between thumb and forefinger. The thumb and first two fingers of the right hand should be located on the top panels of the ball and the ring and little fingers should be on the bottom outside panel of the ball.

When the ball is correctly placed in the right hand, its point should be turned inward toward the center of the punter's body. The left hand should rest on the front inside of the ball. The fin-

The ball is held level and dropped from slightly above the punter's waist.

gers of both hands should lightly grasp the ball with a minimum of pressure. The punter should hold the ball with the same light pressure that he would need to lightly grasp a round sponge. Most of the control is with the right hand.

Standing still, the punter should pull his left hand away from the ball, allowing it to swing back to a position above and to the outside of his left hip. As the left hand swings back, the right hand should be extended forward and slightly to the right. Moving the left hand and arm should cause the upper torso to twist slightly, which will force the right shoulder forward and make it easier for the punter to extend his right hand and arm properly.

The right wrist should be locked and the arm fully extended in this position. The ball should be held as level as possible and should be at a height that places it between the bottom of the jersey numbers and the punter's waist. The front of the ball should be pointed in exactly the same direction as the punter's hips at this time.

When his arm is fully extended and is positioned to the outside of his right thigh, the punter should pull his right hand away from the ball and allow the ball to drop to the ground in a level manner. If the ball is dropped properly, it should bounce directly back to the punter's right leg after striking the ground.

Both the coach and the punter must be aware of the bounce of the ball after it hits the ground. By focusing his eyes and concentrating totally on the drop of the ball, the punter will instantly know if his drop has been correct. If the ball bounces forward, away from the punter, it means the ball was dropped with the back of the ball lower than the front. When the ball bounces toward the kicker, but goes to the right or left, it is an indication that the ball was dropped with the front point striking the ground first.

Because we are teaching the drop without incorporating the steps used in punting, it is possible for the punter to practice the drop a number of times in a very short period. Once the punter understands that the ball should bounce directly back to his right leg when it is correctly dropped, he quickly can tell if his drop is correct and make any necessary adjustments.

Uneven pressure by any of the fingers or the thumb of the right hand, or pushing of the ball rather than pulling the hand away, will cause the ball to drop unevenly and will result in a poor kick.

Mock Catch and Drop

The next step is to combine all these techniques and put them together in a simulated kicking motion. We are not concerned about distance or height of the punt. In fact, the kicking leg should move in an easy and smooth motion. The essentials for the punter to concen-

In taking his first two steps, the punter must land on the ball of his stepping foot and not on the heel. Once he completes his second step, the punter drops the ball onto his right foot and swings his leg in a smooth kicking motion.

trate on are the movement from his stance, his steps (with proper hand and arm action), and watching the ball make contact with his kicking foot at the desired point.

Using the same alignment as previously, the punter assumes his stance holding the ball in both hands with the laces up. On the coach's command of "Go," the punter will start his motion by stepping forward with his right foot, making certain that his body stays in balance. At this point he should still have both hands on the ball. Again, it is important that the punter land on the ball of his right foot and not on his heel. If the coach sees that the punter is landing on the heel of his front foot he should immediately check the length of his step. If he's overstriding, the punter will not be able to land on the ball of his foot on the first step.

As the punter begins his second step with his left foot, his left hand should start to come away from the ball. At the same time the right hand and arm, with the ball, should extend and move to the outside of the punter's leg. Again a check must be made to determine that the punter is landing on the ball of his left foot and not on his heel. Should the punter be making contact with his heel on the second step, there are two points that must be checked. As with the first step, the first check must be the length of the step. If the length of the step is correct, then the coach must make certain that the punter is not leaning back with his shoulders and head.

Once he completes his second step, the punter is in position to drop the ball onto his right foot, easily swinging his right leg in a smooth kicking motion. Remember, we are not concerned about the distance or height of the punt. We are concerned with a good, level drop of the ball, the pointing of the punter's right toe and locking of his right ankle, and solid contact between the football and the punter's right foot.

Because this is the first time that the

The punter's body should be positioned in front of the snap. His hands and arms should be extended so that he can see them and the ball as he catches the snap.

young punter actually is kicking the ball, it is important for the coach to emphasize that the drill is not designed to kick the ball long or far.

The first few times that the punter practices this mock catch and drop, he will have a tendency to forget the important elements of punting previously taught. He often will move in a jerky motion, will overstride, will lean back with his head and shoulders, will keep the ball in the center of his body, or will not drop the ball level.

The role of the coach at this stage is to calm the punter and not let him try to kick too hard or become frustrated. The coach must observe and analyze each step in the punter's movement, and make certain that he is executing each

and every step of the punting motion correctly.

Catching the Snap
In the first punting practice, we emphasized the importance of a good stance, which allows the punter to move easily in any direction and thus stay in front of the ball as it is snapped from the center.

We are now at that stage in the punter's development where he learns how to catch the snap and then proceed with his normal kicking motion. To keep the punter focused on the catch, the ball will be dropped outside of his right leg instead of on his right foot. The ball will drop to the ground instead of being kicked downfield.

If a center is available, he should be

used to make the snap about 10 yards away from the punter. If a center is not available, a coach may line up ten yards in front of the punter and simulate a snap by throwing the football to the punter with an underhanded motion. The speed of the snap is not nearly as important as having the ball spiral and come as close as possible to the target area established by the punter's hands.

As the punter views the ball approaching, he should adjust his position so that his body is in front of the snap, making certain that his hands are extended far enough in front of him so that he can see the ball and his hands at the same time. It is important that the punter "look the ball" all the way into his hands and not jerk his head down at the last instant to locate his hands.

The little fingers of the punter's hands should be together and the palms of both hands should be facing upward. As the ball nears the punter's hands, he should start his first step with his right foot. He should spin the ball as he catches it to bring the laces up and adjust the ball into the groove of his right hand.

The punter then will continue with his second step and extend the ball out in his right hand in preparation for the drop. However, instead of dropping the

Drop the football to the outside of the kicking leg and watch its bounce.

ball onto his foot, the punter drops the ball to the outside of his kicking leg. The coach should observe the bounce of the ball to determine if the drop was executed correctly. Because he doesn't actually kick the ball, the punter will be able to

concentrate on the most important aspect of this drill—catching the snap. It can't be emphasized enough that there's no chance for a successful punt unless the punter correctly catches the snap from the center.

Catch, Step, Drop, and Punt

Now all the elements of the punting motion should be put together. We set up in the same manner as before, with a slight adjustment in the position of the center in relation to the punter—the center should place the ball to the left of the yard line prior to the snap. In addition, he should align his feet so that he is favoring the left side of the yard line, with the center of his body to the left of the line. In the beginning the center should be 13 yards in front of the punter. If the center has the strength to accurately snap the ball for a greater distance, this gap may be increased to 15 yards.

With this adjustment the punter should find that he has lined up the center of his body directly behind the middle of the right side of the center's body. This is how the punter should line up behind center in a game situation. Because we are teaching proper punting form, we have moved the center and will continue to allow the punter to have the yard line as a point of reference as he goes through his entire punting motion. Obviously, once we move out onto the field of play, it's up to the punter to align himself slightly to the right of the center.

The entire emphasis is on the punter. He must assume a proper stance, catch the ball properly, execute the proper steps, go through proper arm and hand action, drop the ball correctly, concentrate on locking the ankle and pointing the toe of his kicking foot, swing his kicking leg in a smooth and straight line, see the football making contact with the top of the ball of his kicking foot, and finally follow through with his kicking leg up toward his right shoulder. It is important for the coach to make certain that the punter's kicking leg is swinging straight downfield and is not coming across his chest.

NOTE: *Be sure the punter has adequately stretched and warmed up prior to this phase of practice. Flexibility exercises are essential for any punter.*

This is a form practice; we are not concerned with the distance, height, or hang time (the time the ball is in the air) of the punt. Do not allow the punter to try to power the ball. We are concerned with the smoothness of the punter's movement and that he correctly executes each step in his punting maneuver. If the snap is not in the target area, if

The punter's kicking leg follows through up toward his right shoulder.

the ball is to the right or left, or if it is very high or low, stop! Do not allow him to punt the ball. We want to practice punting form only with good accurate snaps at this stage. A bad snap will throw a young punter's steps and bal-

ance off and he will end up practicing poor punting form. Practicing poor technique in any phase of football only perfects the bad technique and does not make the player any better. Practicing incorrect punting technique in particular is disastrous and often will lead to diminished ability and confidence.

If the punter is executing each stage of his motion properly, the ball should leave his foot with a nice spiral and travel straight downfield. If the back of the punted ball comes down first, it usually is a result of an improper drop with the back of the ball striking the punter's foot first. Should the punt go end-over-end, the opposite is true (i.e., the punter has dropped the ball unevenly with the front of the ball first making contact with his foot).

Following a kick which does not result in a nice, straight spiral down the field, the coach should ask the punter what he did incorrectly on the kick. If the punter understands each step in the correct punting motion, he should be able to analyze, explain, and demonstrate his mistake for the coach. This indicates to the coach that the punter understands what has been taught and also that he is concentrating on every punt.

Both the coach and the punter must

The punter stands along a yard line, 13 yards away from the center, with arms and hands extended to receive the snap.

If the punting motion is smooth and each stage is executed properly, the ball should spiral straight downfield.

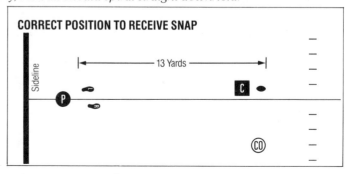

CORRECT POSITION TO RECEIVE SNAP

Sideline

|← 13 Yards →|

P   C

CO

realize that it is far more valuable to a punter's development to kick a few punts properly than to kick a large number with incorrect form. That is why it is essential that after each poor punt the practice be stopped, the poor kick analyzed, and corrections made before resuming.

If the punter is having no success, if each kick is worse than the one before, if the punter seems confused and frustrated, it is often advisable to abandon the complete drill and return to practicing each segment of punting form independently. Once the punter has reviewed and practiced each step, he is ready to attempt the complete drill again.

Directional Punting

Often during the course of a game, the punter will need to kick either to his right or left rather than straight down the field. Kicking to either side starts with a slight adjustment in the stance. This is especially true when the punter first starts trying to kick to his left. When working on directional punting, align the punter once again on the sideline directly over a yard line. Allow the punter to hold the ball in his hands to eliminate the worry of catching the snap.

When kicking to his left, the punter should point the toes of his left foot

WINNING POINTS
- Adopt a balanced stance that allows for movement in all directions—hips over feet, forward bend at waist, shoulders in front of hips, head up, eyes focused ahead.
- A two-step punting motion is preferred; do not exaggerate or elongate punting steps. Land on balls of feet, not heels.
- To receive snap, extend left hand, palm facing up, level with center of body; extend right hand, higher and slightly right of left hand, palm down. When ready to take snap, move right hand down, even with left hand, palm up, little fingers of both hands nearly touching. Look ball into hands.
- Kicking motion should be smooth, with level drop of ball, right toe pointed and right ankle locked. Ball should be kicked with top of ball of kicking foot. Follow through with kicking leg up toward right shoulder.

slightly to the left, rather than straight down the field. From this stance, the punter will not feel uncomfortable when he takes his first step with his kicking

foot toward the yard line rather than away from it as he normally would do. If the left foot is not slightly turned to the left, the punter will feel that he is stepping across his body with his first step and he will not have his hips and upper body in proper position to correctly kick the ball.

For a punt to the left, the punter's right foot should make contact with the ground directly on the yard line. The instep of the right foot should land squarely on the line with the toes of the right foot landing on the left side of the yard line. The second step also should go to the left, with the left foot staying on exactly the same line and pointing in exactly the same direction as the right foot. Remember that the punter's hips, upper body, and shoulders must always face squarely in the direction he needs to kick the ball.

When kicking to the right, the opposite slight adjustment in the punter's stance is required. Because the punter has a natural tendency to step to the right with his first foot, the left foot will need to be turned only slightly to the right. The first step, by the right foot, must establish the line in which the body is going to move so that the hips, upper torso, and shoulders end up pointing slightly to the right rather than

When punting to the left or right, the punter's hips and body must face that same direction. The first step must establish the direction of the punt.

straight down the field.

All the other segments of proper punting form remain the same.

Punting In Wind and Rain

Weather conditions affect all phases of football play. But adverse weather conditions really can wreak havoc on the kicking game. High winds can cause a punter to doubt his ability unless he knows how to cope with the elements.

Adjustments must be made in the normal punting motion as wind conditions change. First, the punter must determine wind direction. Is the wind blowing straight into his face, does it come from the side, or is it coming from behind his back? Each direction will necessitate a corresponding and separate adjustment in punting style.

When forced to kick into a wind which is blowing directly into his face, the punter must realize that the most important thing is to keep the trajectory of the ball low. Should the ball get up high, it will be caught in the wind and the distance of the kick greatly decreased.

In order to keep the kick low, the punter must adjust the height of the ball when he executes his drop. The ball should be dropped from a point just below the waist, with the ball making contact with the foot at a point just below the knee. When kicked from this height, the ball will have a lower trajectory, becoming more of a line-drive type of kick. The front point of the ball will have a tendency to turn over more quickly, thus not allowing the ball to be caught up in the wind. All other segments of the kicking motion remain the same. The low drop should be practiced even when there is no wind to concern the punter.

It is important for the punter to alert the other players on the punt team when he'll make this type of kick. They must know that the punt will not have as much hang time, which will result in a greater opportunity for a runback. Also, a low kick is easier to block.

The height of the drop is adjusted to compensate for a strong wind. When kicking into the wind, the drop is lower (left) *to keep the punt lower; when kicking with the wind, the drop is higher* (right) *to gain height and distance.*

When the wind is coming from behind the punter, it is important to determine if it is blowing from his left or right. With a wind coming from behind and to the right, the punter should make no adjustment in his steps, but he should raise the point from which he drops the ball to a position in the lower portion of his numbers. A ball dropped from this height will result in a higher punt, which will allow the ball to get up into the wind, thus increasing distance.

Should the wind be coming from behind and to the left, the punter should use the same form as he would when trying to make a directional kick to the left. Remember, when kicking to the left the punter must adjust his stance prior to receiving the snap. Just as when the wind is coming from behind and to the right, the ball must be dropped from a higher point.

Should the wind be blowing directly across the field, the punter must retain

Punting is a highly-specialized part of the game and the pressure on punters to perform consistently is intense.

his basic punting form and not change the height of the drop point. The proper adjustment in this case is to kick to the side of the field from which the wind is blowing, letting the ball fly into the wind and ride down the field. Do not make the mistake of kicking at too great an angle to the right or left and chance a short kick that goes out of bounds.

The ideal wind, if there is such a thing, is a slight wind coming at the punter from either the right or left. In these conditions, the punter should aim the ball into the wind and allow the ball to get good height and a good hang time.

The coach must remind the punter constantly during practice sessions that there are proper techniques to use when faced with adverse wind conditions. By knowing how to punt in all wind conditions, the punter will gain confidence and not be distracted when faced with the situation in a game.

Punting in Wet Weather

There are so many things for a punter to concentrate on when he is kicking, the addition of any type of wet weather only makes the punter's life that much more complicated. In addition to remembering all the techniques that must blend together smoothly to make a successful punt, the punter now must worry about the slipperiness of the ball and the field.

When kicking on a wet field, the punter must give special emphasis to three areas of his kicking motion. First, he must make certain that he catches and handles the snap properly. More than at any other time, punters should be alert for a bad snap in wet weather. No matter how good the long snapper may be, if the ball is really soaked and slippery, there is always the chance for the snap to miss the target. Even though the punter will want to stay in his normal rhythm, he may have to slow his start until he is certain that he has caught the ball and has placed it correctly in his hands.

The second thing the punter must concentrate on is landing on the balls of his feet and making absolutely certain that he keeps his feet directly under his hips. Should the punter land on the heel of either foot, he will slip and the punt will be ineffective. A long stride with either leg also may result in a slip.

Finally, the punter must make certain that he keeps his arms extended, not succumbing to the tendency to keep the ball in close to his body where he feels he has better control.

If there's a strong possibility that a game will be played in wet weather, it is important that the punter has an opportunity to kick with a wet ball. This easily can be accomplished by placing a ball in a bucket of water for a few minutes and then having the center snap the ball back to the punter. The punter will then quickly get a feel for catching and punting a wet ball.

Punting From the End Zone

Whenever a punter is forced to kick from his own end zone, he must assume that he will be facing a 10-man rush by the defensive team. There also is the possibility that he will not be able to line up a full 15 yards away from the center, which means that the rush team must cover a shorter distance before attempting to block the kick. In addition to these two major concerns, the punter also must realize that he needs to get as much distance on the punt as possible.

When the punter kicks from deep in his own end zone, he must first make certain that he lines up with both his feet in the field of play. As the snap comes, the punter must step forward, and even if the snap is to one side or the other, he must not step back on the end line or a safety will be called.

Because of the concern of having the kick blocked, it is important for the punter to quicken his steps and to make certain that he des not lengthen his stride.

To punt out of the end zone, use a low drop as on a kick into the wind.

Next, in order to get distance on the kick, the punter should use a lower drop, just as he would if he were kicking into a wind blowing directly into his face. This lower drop, from below the waist, will cause a lower, longer punt, driving the ball away from the punter's goal line.

The punter should remind the members of the punting team of two things before the team breaks the huddle. First, he must check that everyone is certain of his blocking assignment. Next, he must remind the coverage men that with this type of low, long-distance punt there will not be a great hang time. Consequently, there will be a good possibility of a return, so the coverage men must be downfield quickly possible.

Placekicking

The role of the placekicker in professional football has increased in importance. In today's game, leading kickers in each conference score more than 100 points each season and make a significant contribution to their teams' winning records.

A placekicker's (kicker's) job is much different from that of the punter. One difference is the actual number of opportunities each player has during a game. The kicker often will have only two or three attempts to demonstrate his ability, while the punter will usually have six or more chances during each game. And while the punter has control of the ball as he is kicking it, the placekicker must rely on another player to properly catch the ball and place it in a correct position for his kick.

The most dramatic difference between a punter and a placekicker, however, is that a kicker has the opportunity to put points on the scoreboard while a punter merely changes the possession and field position of the ball. Because of this, the pressure on a kicker is great. Punters often can afford the luxury of getting off one bad punt and not having it make a difference in the outcome of the game. But every time a placekicker runs out on the field for a field goal or extra point, his kick may be for the points that win or lose the game.

It is important for every coach to recognize and understand the enormous pressure on every placekicker. The pressure is especially difficult for the beginning placekicker to deal with; it is the coach's job to constantly support and encourage the young kicker. In many games, the placekicker may be asked to demonstrate his skill on the very last play, with the outcome of the game hanging on his ability. At these times, the coach must calm the kicker, telling him that he can do the job, and reminding him to stay within his motion and meet the ball correctly.

It always is amazing to hear a coach tell a kicker prior to an attempt at a game-winning kick, "You make sure you do *not* over-kick." The kicker runs on the field having been told what *not* to do, rather than being told what *to* do: "Kick it right between the uprights."

In all placekicking, the kicker does not look at his target; he keeps his head down and concentrates on hitting the ball solidly.

More often than not, the young place-kicker will do exactly what he has heard last from the coach, regardless if it is positive or negative instruction. Negative coaching will usually lead to negative reinforcement and, more often than not, will lead to the exact action which the coach does not desire.

Placekicking, more than any other position, has gone through a metamorphosis in style and technique. In the "old days," the placekicker would also play another position. Today, the placekicker plays no other position on the team and often has never played a regular position in any football program. In addition to being a true specialist, he's almost always a soccer-style kicker rather than a straight-ahead kicker. In the following pages, we will discuss the technique needed to kick with either style, but it should be emphasized that the soccer style is by far the most popular.

Soccer-Style Kicking

When being introduced to the art of placekicking, it is important to concentrate on three vital areas before ever kicking the ball. First, a kicker must learn how to align himself properly with the kicking tee. Next, he must learn the correct stance. And, finally, he learns the proper kicking motion.

Proper kicking alignment begins with the kicking foot directly behind the tee.

Placekicking is much like bowling or putting in golf. A bowler does not look at the pins but instead focuses on a spot located at the front of the lane. When putting, the golfer lines up the putt, then instead of looking at the hole, which may be a number of feet away, concentrates on the ball resting on the ground directly in front of him. In placekicking, the principle is exactly the same. The kicker knows where his target is and keeps his head down, concentrating on the ball.

NOTE: *All instructions are given for right-footed kickers. No tee is used on field goals and extra points in the NFL and NCAA play. If you use a tee, place it centrally over the spot where the holder will place the ball.*

DRILL:

Soccer-Style Kicking Alignment

When first working with the kicker on proper alignment, it is often better to use the sideline and yard line positioning that was used in learning the initial skills for punting. Without the goal post to look at, the kicker will focus more easily on his relationship to the tee.

The kicker should take the tee, place it on the ground, and make certain that it is facing directly down the yard line. He then should align his body so that it is in a direct line with the yard line and the tee. The kicker should place his left foot to the side of the tee. His right foot then is placed directly behind the tee. This alignment will remain constant every time he starts to kick.

To get into soccer-style placekicking position, the kicker takes three steps of normal length, starting with his right (kicking) foot, away from the tee and down a yard line. The kicker should end up with his right foot on the line.

After taking his three backward steps, the kicker takes two sideways steps left with each foot at a 90-degree angle away from the yard line. The kicker then turns and faces the tee, which should be pointed at the goal post.

From this position, the kicker should then take three steps of normal length, starting with his right foot and backing away from the tee. At this point the coach and the kicker should check the position of the kicker's feet, making certain that he has not wandered off to the left or the right as he has taken his steps away from the tee. The kicker should end up with his right foot on the yard line and his left foot to the side of the yard line. Should the kicker stand with his feet in any other position on the yard line, he often will end up in a final kicking motion with his plant foot either too close or too far away from the tee. That is why it is imperative to get the kicker's first three steps grooved and not have them change with every kick.

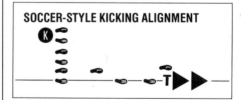

SOCCER-STYLE KICKING ALIGNMENT

After taking the three steps directly backward away from the tee, the kicker should take two side steps left with each foot at a 90-degree angle away from the yard line. Now, the kicker can turn, face the tee, and concentrate on a proper stance. This position always will remain constant. The thing that will change is the placement of the tee so that it is pointed directly at the center of the crossbar. If the ball is in the center of the field, there are no problems. But when the ball is on one hashmark or the other, the beginning kicker often will align with the field and forget to line up with the tee.

The problem the beginning kicker will experience when first moved off the yard line (where he is always kicking directly down the line), is that he will have a tendency to wander to the left or right on his first three steps. In early practices, the coach may use a string which has been previously measured to the kicker's step to help him with gauging distance from the tee and achieving the proper 90-degree alignment. With the tee pointing at an angle toward the target, the kicker always must check his body position after taking his three steps back from the tee, making certain that he still is in proper alignment, with his kicking foot lined up in a straight line through the tee to the target point (the center of the crossbar).

The kicker and the coach can move the position of the tee all over the field to practice the proper alignment from different angles. But when the kicker fails to practice kicking from all angles on the field, he does not learn correct alignment and usually is not prepared properly to kick in a game.

Soccer Stance

After taking his final two side steps, the kicker must turn his body so that his hips are facing toward the tee. As he turns, he should place his left foot, his plant foot, slightly ahead of the right foot, the kicking foot. The width of the feet should be slightly less than the width of his shoulders.

It is important for the kicker to have his weight on the balls of both feet and to have his knees bent slightly. He should bend at the waist so that his shoulders are in front of his hips. His arms should hang down in a relaxed fashion and his head should be down with his eyes focused on the kicking tee. In this position, the kicker's weight is shifted forward and he is prepared to move toward the tee without hesitation. Remember, for a kicker to become proficient, it is necessary for him to keep each segment of the kicking motion the same on every kick.

Steps and Kicking Motion

With the kicker in a proper stance, facing toward the tee, the proper steps and

The preferred motion for placekicking, like that for punting, includes only two steps. Facing the tee, the kicker begins his movement toward the ball by taking a smooth and relaxed first step with his right (kicking) foot.

The second step, with the left foot, is longer than the first step and should come down even with, and six inches to the left of, the tee. This step is called the "plant step;" it is critical in determining kicking direction.

The "plant foot" should come down pointed in the same direction as the tee.

body movement necessary to kick the ball can be learned. It generally is best to practice without a ball on the tee. A ball quickly can be added to the practice when the coach feels the player is ready to progress. Once the ball is added, though, there may be a tendency for the kicker to rush every movement.

In practice, the coach stands to the right of the tee, where the holder would be on an actual kick. From this position he can check the kicker's stance and observe him as he moves toward the tee.

The two-step kicking motion starts, after the coach's command of "Go," with a step toward the kicking tee with the right foot. This step should be smooth and relaxed. The second step, with the left foot, is somewhat longer and should come down even with, and six inches to the left of, the kicking tee. This second step is called the plant step, with the left foot often referred to as the plant foot.

It is the placement of the plant foot that often determines the direction of the kick. When the left foot is too close to the tee, the ball usually will be pushed or sliced to the right. If the plant foot is too far away from the tee, the ball will hook to the left. When the plant foot comes down ahead of the kicking tee, the result is a low, line-drive kick. It also is important for the plant foot to come down facing the same direction as the tee, rather than turned at an angle to the right or left.

Once the plant foot hits, the right leg (the kicking leg) begins its forward movement. The leg should come from a high arc, fully extended and with a slight bend at the knee. The position of the right foot is crucial to a successful kick.

Once the plant foot hits, the kicking leg comes forward from a high arc.

The toe should be pointed down and the ankle fully locked. As the kicking motion begins, the kicker must lead with his hips, using the full force of the lower body to generate power for the kick. The right knee will lead the motion for the kicking leg.

As the leg comes through its swing, the toe of the foot should pass just right

The toe should be pointed down and the ankle fully locked for kicking.

of the tee, and the top center of the left side of the kicking foot should sweep over the center of the tee. *The top inside part of the kicker's foot, and not the underside of the instep as many people believe, makes contact with the ball.* At this point the kicker's hips should be facing directly downfield to the target. The kicker's head should be down with his eyes focused on the tee.

After the kicking foot passes over the tee, the kicker's body must follow through directly toward the target. To check if the kicker is following through correctly, the coach should adjust his position to a point four yards in front of the tee, where he has a good view of the kicker. If the kicker falls away to the left of the tee, it often is a result of leaning backward and bringing the leg across his body instead of extending it. When the kicker ends his motion with his hips pointing to the right of the target, the coach should check that the kicker is not leaning forward too much and that his plant foot is pointing straight toward the target. The coach must remind the kicker that his body needs to stay balanced, that his shoulders must stay in front of his feet, and that his hips lead the way toward the target.

When the coach and the kicker feel that the kicking motion is smooth and balanced, it is time to introduce the ball to the practice. In the beginning, a center will not be used; the coach acts as the holder. Prior to kicking the ball, the kicker must be required to go through all the preliminaries on each kick. He should place the tee on the yard line—remember, we have not started kicking toward the goal post—take his proper steps, and assume his stance.

Once the kicker is in his stance, the coach should extend his left arm down the yard line and pick up the ball in his right hand, holding it away from his left. On the command "Go," the coach will bring the ball to his left and place it on the tee with the laces pointing straight down the yard line. When the kicker hears the command, he should start his movement toward the tee and smoothly kick the ball, *making contact one inch below the center of the ball.* When kicked correctly, the ball should travel straight down the yard line. Distance is not as important as accuracy.

Should the kicker start hooking the ball to the left or slicing it to the right of the yard line, the coach must remove the ball and calmly go over each phase of the kicking motion with the kicker until the kicker calms down and is ready to try again. The natural tendency of any young kicker is to power the ball and forget the techniques needed for a successful kick.

DRILL:
Game Kicking
Once the kicker is in a good kicking groove, he is ready to move out on the playing field. Introduce a center and holder to simulate actual game kicking.

When first starting this drill, the distance of the kicks should be kept as short as possible. Accuracy is the most important asset any kicker can have. It is much more important to be able to consistently kick with accuracy than it is to kick for great distance.

The kicker should place the tee on the ground seven yards away from the ball and the line of scrimmage, making certain that it is lined up directly with the center of the crossbar. The kicker should then take his steps and assume his stance. Once the kicker is in his stance,

the holder should look up and the kicker should say "Ready," indicating that he is prepared to kick. The holder then will extend his hands toward the center, showing the center that both he and the kicker are ready for the snap. It is important for the kicker to focus on the kicking tee and to see the ball being snapped with his peripheral vision. The kicker should start his kicking motion the moment he sees the ball snapped to the holder. If the kicker waits until the ball is placed on the tee, he will undoubtedly have it blocked during a game. These three men—the cen-

ter, the holder, and the kicker—must work as a team and should practice together as much as possible. Successful kicking depends on each of these players and they must have intense pride in their respective jobs.

Straight-Ahead Kicking

In the past 15 years, soccer-style kicking has become the most popular style in college and professional football. Most young players want to emulate the professional and collegiate kickers and are interested in learning the soccer style of kicking, but there is a good reason for a coach to know how to teach the other style.

Straight-ahead kicking has one major advantage: it is easier to line up the tee and the kicker with the target. This is especially beneficial for kicks at an angle. On wet fields, the straight-ahead kicker usually will have better balance and less chance of slipping. Because straight-ahead kicking is easier to teach, it is recommended for any player who is a backup kicker and who may be playing as a starter at another position.

However, there are two major drawbacks to straight-ahead kicking. One is that it requires a specially made, extremely costly square-toed shoe, which the kicker must put on and take off if he

The kicker starts his kicking motion the moment he sees the ball snapped to the holder. Any hesitation in the kicker's movement could lead to a blocked kick.

In the correct stance for straight-ahead placekicking, the kicker's weight is mostly on the left (non-kicking) foot; the right knee is flexed. The kicker is bent forward at the waist, his head is down, and his arms hang loosely.

is playing another position. The second drawback is that the range of the kicker is usually less than that of a soccer kicker. This is because the power of a straight-ahead kicker is dependent upon the strength of his leg and not upon the power generated by the movement of his lower body.

Stance for Straight-On Kickers

When working on straight-ahead kicking, again use the yard-line set-up for practice; goal posts won't be involved until later.

STRAIGHT-AHEAD KICKING ALIGNMENT

The kicker should place the tee facing directly down the yard line. Once the tee is in place, he should place the toe of his kicking foot directly behind the tee, and his left foot to the left and even with the tee. He should be facing straight down the yard line.

From this position, the kicker takes three natural steps backward, straight along the yard line. These steps are right foot, left foot, and right foot, then aligning the left foot with the right. The kicker should end up with his right foot on the

The kicker places the toe of his kicking foot directly behind the tee; his left foot is to the left of, and even with, the tee. He then takes three natural steps backward, beginning with his right (kicking) foot.

yard line and his left foot to the left of the yard line.

Once he has taken his three steps back, the kicker should move his right foot forward so that the instep of the right foot is even with the toe of the left foot. The kicker's feet should be six to eight inches apart, and the weight should be mostly on the left foot, thus allowing the kicking leg to be more relaxed. The kicker's right knee should be flexed and there should be a slight bend in the left knee.

It is important in straight-ahead kicking for the kicker to have his weight forward. Consequently, when the kicker gets in his stance, he must bend forward at the waist, move his shoulders in front of his feet, keep his head forward, and focus his eyes on the kicking tee. The kicker's arms should hang down and forward in a very relaxed fashion. The coach should make certain that the kicker's shoulders are even and that he is not leaning to one side or the other, as this can affect the final kick.

Steps for Straight-On Kicking

The straight-ahead kicker uses a two-step motion when kicking the ball. The first step, with the right foot, should be an easy, relaxed step which starts his body moving forward. The second step,

After the third backward step, taken with his right foot, the kicker aligns his left foot with his right, six inches apart. He then moves his right foot forward so that the instep of the right foot is even with the toe of the left foot.

with the left foot, must be more of an attacking step, with the left foot landing eight inches behind and to the left of the kicking tee. This spot for the plant foot is different from soccer-style kicking, where we want the plant foot to be even with the tee. During the entire kicking motion, the kicker must keep his shoulders and weight forward, constantly moving straight ahead toward the target.

As the plant foot hits, the kicker should bring his kicking leg forward in as big an arc as possible. For straight-ahead kicking, the ankle of the kicking foot must be locked so that the sole of the foot is even with the ground. The toes of the kicking foot may be relaxed. If the kicker locks his toes upward, he often will hit the ground with the heel of his kicking shoe prior to making contact with the ball. If the toes are locked down, as in soccer kicking, the toe of the kicking shoe will drag on the ground before the kick.

As the kicking foot moves over the tee, the kicker's body also should move straight ahead over the tee. His head and shoulders should remain forward and move straight down the yard line. The kicker's arms will have a tendency to widen during the kick and should be used to maintain proper balance. When kicking without the ball, the coach should not require the kicker to swing his leg with great velocity.

DRILL:
Straight-Ahead Kicking

Once the coach and kicker feel comfortable lining up the tee, taking proper steps away from the tee, assuming a good stance, and completing the kicking motion, the ball can be added in a drill situation. Again, instead of using the goal post, we will start the drill on the yard line.

The coach may serve as the holder. He must make the kicker go through all the preliminary motions prior to the kick. Once the kicker is in his stance, he should tell the coach, "Ready." The coach then will extend his left hand down the yard line and on the command "Go" he will bring the ball, which is in his right hand, to his left, place it on the tee, and spin it so that the laces are pointed down the yard line.

When the kicker hears the command "Go," he should start forward with his kicking motion. He must not overextend with his first step or he will find that his plant foot is much too close to the ball. Remember, at this stage we are not concerned with distance, but we are concerned that the ball be met squarely and that it travels in a straight line away from the tee.

Power for straight-ahead kicking comes from the power in the kicking leg, but the coach should not ask the beginning kicker to kick with all-out power. Not until the kicker can consistently kick the ball straight down the yard line should the goal post, the center, and holder be integrated into the practice. Then, start the drill with the ball in the center of the field, a short distance from the goal post. For example, begin with the ball on the 5-yard line and eventually move back to the 15-yard line. Kickers should not overkick when first learning the skill.

Once the kicker is in his stance, he should tell the holder, "Ready." The holder will extend his hands toward the center, alerting the center that they both are ready for the snap. The kicker should keep his eyes focused on the tee and start his kicking motion when, with his peripheral vision, he sees the ball snapped by the center.

When the kicker has perfected the kicking motion, he will feel his body actually coming off the ground as he follows through. The kicker must understand that the ball is not just propelled by the initial contact, but that in all kicking, the ball stays in contact with the kicking foot for a slightly longer time. Because of this, the kicker must always work on following

The straight-ahead kicker uses a two-step motion. The plant foot should land eight inches behind, and to the left of, the tee. As his kicking leg swings forward, the kicker's body should move straight over the tee.

through with determination.

The final stage of practice is to move from one hashmark to the other, selecting points in between and forcing the kicker to line up the tee toward the center of the crossbar. As mentioned earlier, a straight-ahead kicker usually will find it much easier to line up any angle kick.

Snapping for Kicks

The center has a great impact on the success of the kicking teams. His ability to snap the ball correctly to the punter and the holder is as important as the skills of the kickers.

When learning to snap, the player needs to work first on the proper grip. The player should grip the ball so that his right hand is just forward of center of the ball, fingers over the seam, and his little finger just covering the laces. The center should then lightly place his left hand, fingers pointing downfield, on the top left side of the ball.

DRILL:

Center Pass

It often is best to have the beginning players use a simple drill to develop snapping skills. The center kneels on his right knee, grasping the ball properly in both hands. He then takes the ball off the ground and holds it over his head. With the ball behind and over his head, arms fully extended, he should pass the ball forward to another center, who is also kneeling and facing him 10 yards away. It is important for the coach to emphasize that the center follow through after the pass and that the fingers of both hands end up reaching out toward his partner. The same motion is used when snapping the ball between the legs.

Center Stance

The center should approach the ball so that it is at arm's length in front of him. The center should take a stance with his feet slightly wider than his shoulders and the front of his right foot even with the instep of his left foot. The center may wish to have his feet even; that is fine if he feels more comfortable. The center then should bend his knees and reach

To practice for kick snaps, the center kneels and holds the ball over his head.

forward and out, grasping the ball in his right hand. At this point, a coach must check to make certain the center's shoulders are square and his back is level. If the center's hips are higher than his shoulders, the ball will tend to have a higher arc. When the hips are lower than the shoulders, there is a greater chance for a low snap.

The center passes the ball forward to another center 10 yards away.

Setting the Ball

After taking the proper stance, the center should concentrate on setting the ball properly. Prior to gripping the ball, the center should reach out and turn it so that the laces are to the right and slightly past the center of the ball, facing toward the ground. He then will take his stance and reach out with his right hand, gripping the ball at the laces as discussed above. From this position, he needs to slightly turn his hand so that it is more under the ball. After he has rotated the ball slightly in his right hand, he should place his left hand lightly on top of the ball with the fingers pointing forward. The center must remember that it is the right hand that passes the ball while the left hand is used to guide it.

Once the holder sets the target and signals that he is ready, the center passes the ball to him, extending his arms and reaching back as he releases the ball.

The center's shoulders should be square and his back level. In gripping the ball, he turns it so that the laces are slightly to the right and facing down.

Center Snap for Placekicks

When snapping for a placekick, the center should keep the ball level as he grasps it in his right hand. The distance of the snap is only seven yards and the height of the snap is the level of the holder's extended hands. After gripping the ball, the center should look back between his legs and focus in on the holder, who is kneeling seven yards away. Once the holder extends his arms, the center knows that he is ready to receive the snap. The holder's hands are the center's target. The center needs to pass the ball back to the holder, extending his arms fully and reaching out and back with his fingers toward the holder as he releases the ball. If his arms properly extend back, the center will feel his entire body moving toward the holder.

Because the kicker has enough to concentrate on, the coach should be certain that the holder and center practice together and have the snap perfected before asking the kicker to join the drill. The kicker must not be concerned with the snap or the hold, only with kicking the ball. In the end, these three men must function as one cohesive unit. As the center becomes better and gains more skill, he will be able to snap the ball so that it reaches the holder with the laces pointing toward the goal post, and the holder will not need to spin the ball.

Center Snap for Punts

Snapping for a punt is very similar to

snapping for placekicks. The difference is the distance of the snap, 15 yards, and the height, the numbers on the punter's jersey. To compensate for these two differences, the center must make some adjustments. The first is that as he grasps the ball, instead of keeping it flat, the center must lift the front point of the ball so that the ball is at an angle. The next adjustment is the velocity of the

pass, which is faster on punts.

The center uses the two outstretched hands of the punter for his target. Once the center sees the top and bottom of the target, he watches for the punter to extend both hands with the palms up. This alerts the center that the punter is ready to receive the snap. When making the snap, the center must follow through with both arms propelling the ball back to the punter. Again, it is important for the center to end the snap by reaching back toward the punter's jersey numbers with the fingers of both hands. Because the center uses more velocity on the long snap to the punter, his arm action will cause him to move backward.

For the center on the punt team, there is only one job to be concerned with and that is getting the ball back correctly to the punter. Blocking and covering the kick are of secondary importance.

The Holder

The final player involved in the kicking game is the holder for placekicks. Naturally, one of the first prerequisites of a holder is his ability to catch the snap. Coaches talk of holders having "good and sure hands," and often the holder is either a quarterback or a wide receiver. One big drawback of having the starting quarterback as a holder is that it is diffi-

Snapping for punts differs from snapping for placekicks in that the ball is held at more of an angle by the center; the follow-through is the same.

The holder on placekicks lines up seven yards from the center. He sets a target for the center, signals for the snap, and catches the ball, placing it down and holding it with his index finger. He spins the ball so the laces point forward.

cult to find adequate practice time for the kicker, holder, and center to work together. Coaches must realize the importance of these three players working together and should schedule as much time as necessary so that they learn to work as a team.

The holder should line himself up seven yards from the center so that his body is even with and to the right of the kicking tee. From this alignment, the holder then should kneel down, placing his left knee on the ground and his right knee up. He should then lean slightly forward and place his left hand on the center of the tee.

When first practicing without the kick-er, the holder should look up to where the kicker will be standing and ask if he is ready. Pretending to get a positive reply from the kicker, the holder will extend his right arm and hand, palm down and fingers pointing toward the center. The height of the right arm and hand should be even with the middle of the holder's jersey numbers. The extended right hand becomes the top of the target for the center. Once the kicker indicates that he is ready, the holder will remove his left hand from the tee, bringing it up to his right hand so that the thumbs of both hands are together.

The center will know that both the kicker and the holder are ready for the snap when he sees the holder extending both his arms and hands toward him.

When the ball is snapped, the holder must first make certain that he catches the ball. As he brings the ball down to the tee, the holder should try to turn the ball so that the laces are pointed directly at the center of the goal post. As the ball is placed on the tee, the holder should lightly hold the top of the ball with the index finger of either his right or left hand. If the holder sees that the laces of the ball are not facing forward, he should use his free hand to spin the ball and bring the laces to the front. The holder must avoid ever having the laces facing the kicker.

Because timing is so crucial on placekicks, the kicker, holder, and center must function smoothly as one unit.

Soccer-Style Kickoffs

Learning to kick off with consistency is one of the most difficult tasks facing any kicker. As with punting or placekicking, there always is room for slight adjustments in kickoff technique. A coach must be aware of a kicker who constantly is changing his alignment or steps prior to kickoff. This is usually a good indication that the kicker is not comfortable and does not believe in his kicking style. Experimentation can be allowed and practiced once the kicker gains experience, but it often is a coaching mistake not to force a young kicker to stick with and perfect one style.

For kickoffs, the ball is placed in the tee with a slight backward lean.

The soccer-style kicker positions himself for kickoffs by taking nine steps backward away from the tee and five side steps left. He then faces the tee.

Ball Placement

A two-inch tee should be used by all beginning kickers. The tee may be the conventional tee or the soccer style kickoff tee that was developed by Jan Stenerud, formerly an outstanding NFL soccer-style kicker. If you have access to the Stenerud type of tee, I would recommend it since it was especially designed to assist a soccer-style kicker.

Use a yard line, for orientation, just as in learning the other kicking skills. The tee should be placed so that it is facing straight down the yard line. The ball should then be placed on the tee with a very slight lean toward the kicker. It is important for the laces to face forward, aimed in the direction of the kick.

Positioning for Kickoffs

Once the ball is placed properly on the tee, the kicker should line up with his right foot directly behind the tee and his left foot to the left of the tee. He then takes one step with his right foot directly away from the ball. At this point, he should turn and take an additional eight steps away from the ball. He then turns back and faces the ball, making certain that he has not strayed to the right or left. The kicker's right foot should be on the yard line.

When the kicker determines that he is lined up straight with the tee, he should take five normal steps to his left, again forming a 90-degree angle, and turn and face the tee.

Stance

At this point the kicker should put his right foot five to six inches in front of his left foot. It is not necesary for the kicker to bend far forward, but he should have his knees flexed and have his shoulders slightly in front of his hips. The key thing is that the kicker feel relaxed in his stance and that he not tense up.

Kickoff Steps

The kicker should start his movement toward the ball by taking a relaxed step

The kicker begins his motion toward the ball with a relaxed step with his right (kicking) foot. He approaches in a relaxed manner for five more yards.

step forward with his right foot. He then should continue his approach in a relaxed manner for the next five yards. Each step should be slightly quicker, but we do not want the kicker to run these first five yards. For the last five yards as he approaches the tee, the kicker should quicken his steps and begin to attack the ball.

Kicking Motion

As the kicker nears the ball, he must place his plant foot two to four inches behind and six inches to the left of the tee. The foot should point straight downfield in the desired direction of the kick.

When the plant foot makes contact, it is important that the kicker keep his head down, his eyes focused on the tee and ball, and his shoulders in front of his hips. As in soccer-style placekicking, motion starts with the forward movement of the kicker's hips. The kicking leg should move with a high arc, the kicking toe needs to be pointed down, and the knee of the kicking leg should precede the foot.

At the point of contact, the inside part

In the last five yards of his approach, the kicker quickens his steps and begins to attack the ball. In soccer-style placekicking, motion starts with the forward movement of the kicker's hips. The shoulders stay in front of the hips.

of the instep of the kicker's foot will make contact one inch below the center of the ball. Remember, if the beginning kicker is having trouble with his steps and plant, it often is a good idea to remove the ball and allow the kicking foot to fly over the empty tee. Even with the ball, the coach should stress excellent form, steps, and consistency, rather than distance, when first teaching kickoff technique.

When finally kicking with full power, the kicker should feel himself lifted off the ground as he makes contact with the ball and he will land two to three feet in front of the tee.

The next step is to move onto the field and line up in the same manner as in a game, at the kicking team's 35-yard line. Beginning kickers should have their kicks clocked for hang time (the time the ball is in the air) and the distance of their kicks. A young kicker usually will have a hang time of about 3.2 seconds. As he improves, that should increase to 3.7 or 3.8 seconds. When determining the hang time of a kick the coach starts the watch the instant the kicker's foot hits the ball and stops it when the ball is caught or hits the ground.

If the kicker has a strong wind at his back, he will want to make contact a little lower on the ball, lifting the ball high-

The plant foot lands two to four inches behind, and six inches left of, the tee.

er into the air and allowing the wind to take it farther downfield. When kicking into a headwind–a wind blowing into the kicker's face–the kicker should attempt to hit the ball more in the center, driving it low into the wind. This type of kick is extremely difficult for kick returners to catch.

When kicking to the right or left, the kicker can use two methods. The first, and by far the easiest, is to set the tee and the ball on the left or right hashmark. This keeps the kicker's motion constant.

The second technique is for the kicker to turn his plant foot, pointing it in the direction he desires the ball to go. His hips will follow the plant foot and he will find his kicking foot moving in the desired direction.

Straight-Ahead Kickoffs

For a straight-ahead kickoff, the kicker should make certain he uses a conventional two-inch kicking tee and not attempt to use the Jan Stenerud-design soccer kicking tee.

The ball should be placed on the tee with a slight lean toward the kicker. The laces should be aligned facing directly downfield. Having the laces in this position allows for the best height and distance possible on the kick.

The straight-ahead placekicker lines up 10 yards away from, and in a direct line with, the ball for a kickoff. He assumes a stance with his feet five to six inches apart, his right (kicking) foot in front of his left.

Lining Up

It is easy for a straight-on kicker to line up properly. He should move back 10 yards from the ball. First practice kicking down a yard line; the coach measures off and marks 10 yards for the kicker so that he consistently is starting at this distance from the ball. Kicking down the yard line makes lining up and approaching the ball straight easier.

Once the kicker lines up at 10 yards, he should make certain that his body is positioned in a straight line with the ball and tee. The kicker should assume a stance with his feet five to six inches apart and his right foot in front of his left. In this stance, the kicker should have his knees slightly bent with a bit more weight on the ball of his front foot. He should bend forward at the waist so that his shoulders are slightly in front of his feet, keeping his head down, and his eyes focused on the tee. The arms should hang down in a relaxed fashion.

Movement to the Ball

The kicker should start his movement toward the ball with a slow step forward with his right foot. For the first five yards the approach should gain momentum with the steps gradually becoming quicker. The kicker should use the sec-

ond five yards to increase his momentum and to attack the ball. These last five yards will be covered with three steps: left, right, and left, then finally a kick with the right foot. The third step with the left foot becomes the plant step; it should come four to six inches to the left of, and eight inches behind, the tee.

Kicking the Ball

Most young kickers feel they have to lean back with their head and shoulders in order to get the ball well into the air. This is the exact opposite of what to do at the moment of contact with the ball. The kicker must keep his shoulders for-

WINNING POINTS

- In all placekicking, keep head down, eyes on ball.
- In soccer-style kicking stance, hips are facing tee (or placement point); weight on balls of both feet; knees bent slightly; bend at waist so shoulders are in front of hips.
- Plant step should come down even with, and six inches to left of, kicking tee.
- Lead with hips into kicking motion. Kicking leg moves in high arc, fully extended, with slight bend at knee, ankle locked with toes down. Contact ball an inch below center with top inside of kicking foot. Follow through with body directly toward target.
- In straight-ahead kicking, plant foot is eight inches behind, and to left of, tee.
- In kicking motion, keep shoulders and weight forward, ankle of kicking foot locked with sole of foot even with ground. Widen arms to maintain proper balance during kick and follow through smoothly with body moving over tee and lifting off ground.

The straight-ahead kicker begins his motion to the ball by taking a slow step forward with his right foot. He gradually gains momentum in the first five yards.

The last five yards to the ball should be covered in three steps—left, right, and left (plant step)—followed by the kicking of the ball and follow-through.

ward, his head down, and his eyes focused on the ball. The right foot must be locked at the ankle so that the foot resembles a hammer. The toes of the right foot should not be pointed up or down, but should be relaxed so that the foot is in a flat, even position. Contact should be one inch below the center of the ball so that the full, hard, flat surface of the front of the kicking shoe will strike the ball. Distance comes from the momentum gained from the approach and the power generated by the kicking leg. The follow through needs to be smooth and forceful so that the kicker finds himself lifted off the ground.

When kicking off to either the right or left, the kicker should first set the tee so that it points in the desired direction and then walk back in a straight line away from the tee. This will angle the kicker, through the tee, to the area of the field where he wants to kick the ball.

Returning Kicks

One of the most difficult and yet most important jobs on any football team is returning kicks. It is a job that requires a special, dedicated, and highly motivated player if each return is to have any chance of success.

Kick returners are a special breed of football player who must posess a fear-

The kick returner gains forward momentum as he makes the catch, then sprints to the area designated for the return.

lessness that is not required in any of the other positions on the team. On many returns, the kick returner will find himself being hit by numerous tacklers just as he makes the catch. A good kick returner must be able to block out the coverage people converging upon him and to totally concentrate on catching the ball. A return man never must forget that any successful kick return must start first with catching the kick.

The importance of a change of ball possession during the course of a football game cannot be emphasized enough to any football player and especially to young players. For any player who desires to return kicks, this emphasis is doubly important. Catching and securing the ball must be priorities for any kick returner on punts or kickoffs.

A long return of a kick is one of the most exciting plays of any football game and it often is a play that greatly adds to a team's opportunity to win the game. Each player who has the opportunity to return a kick must understand the importance and responsibility of the job. A great kick return may result in a touchdown or, at least, an enormous change in field position, putting the offense in a much better position to score.

Kick returners may be asked to field and run back both punts and kickoffs, but because of the different natures of each, most teams usually will employ different players to return either type of kick.

Kickoffs differ from punts in a number of ways. First of all, on a kickoff the return man knows that he is almost always guaranteed that he will have ample opportunity to make the catch without any of the coverage men being near him. His concentration must be on getting "in front of the ball" and judging the distance of the kick.

The second big difference is that on kickoffs the ball will be tumbling end-over-end as it flies through the air and not in a spiral as it generally does on a punt. The path of a kickoff usually will remain constant once it has left the kicker's foot and its distance can usually be determined by the height of the kick. A high kick usually will travel less distance that a kick of average height, but both will be determined by the kicker's leg strength.

Kickoff Returns

As a beginning rule of thumb for a kickoff return man, he should line up 10 yards farther downfield than he expects the kicker to kick the ball. In no instances should the return man ever line up in his own end zone. The farthest back he ever should go is the goal line, for example following a penalty that puts the kicker closer to the goal line.

As the ball leaves the kicker's foot, the returner must move so that he is in a direct line with the fight path of the ball. Once the return man has taken this position, he should quickly determine the distance of the kick and move to the point on the field where he can make the catch. His hands should be held palms up with the little fingers and outside edges of his hands touching. His elbows should be held close to his body.

It is much better for the return man to be moving slightly forward as he makes the catch than it is for him to be too far up the field and have to be moving back toward his own goal line.

By moving slightly forward as he makes the catch, the return man will be in a position to always see his hands and the ball at the time of the catch, allowing him to concentrate and see the ball all the way into his hands, thus helping to guarantee the catch. He also will have his momentum moving up the field toward his opponent's goal line as he makes the catch and secures the ball. A return man moving into his catch will find that it will be easier for his teammates to properly time their movement up the field into their blocks, as well as having the advantage of already gaining speed as the catch is made.

If the return man has misjudged the distance of the kick and has moved too far up the field prior to the catch, he must first stop and retreat toward his own goal line. If the return man has to make the catch over his shoulder or head, there always is the possibility that the ball will make contact with his shoulder pads and not his hands, resulting in a fumble. Obviously, in this situation, if the return man does make the catch, he will have to stop and re-direct his momentum back up the field, thus losing time and hurting the timing of the return.

Once a kick has been caught, the return man must sprint to the area of the field where his blockers are setting up the return. A kickoff return is not a play for the faint of heart. Instead, it requires a player who is willing to sprint up the field without hesitation, attacking the return area at full speed.

As he sprints up the field, the return man must stay alert for a slight crack or seam in the coverage lanes of the kicking team as they come down the field and are blocked by the return man's teammates. The player must know that this seam usually will open only for a brief moment, that the opening will

not be very large, and that it must be hit at full speed if he is to get through the opening before the coverage men have an opportunity to react to the blockers.

Kickoff return men who hesitate, stop, or continually try to change direction from the left to right seldom, if ever, have a successful return. As they change direction, they often cause their teammates to be placed in a position where they are trying to block a coverage man who suddenly turns, thus causing an illegal block and a penalty. More often than not, this type of soft or hesitant kickoff return man will cause his offense to start each of its drives deep in their own end of the field.

Once the return man sees that he is about to be tackled, it is important that he concentrate on securing the ball, making certain that he does not fumble it to the opposition.

For kickoffs which go into the end zone, the return man must know if the rules allow for a return. Even if they do, the return man should listen for his teammates to tell him if he should run the ball out or not. Usually, the best decision for any kickoff return man is not to try to return a kickoff which sails into the end zone. More often than not it is much better to take the touchback and allow the offense to begin its next series

on the 20-yard line.

If the kick is a squib type, low and on the ground, the return man must concentrate all of his attention on getting in front of the ball as it comes down the field. It is important that the player move up the field toward the ball and get set. He must expect the ball to bounce to either his right or left and move in front of it as he is making the catch. If at all possible, the return man should try to secure the ball and return it up the field. Only as a last resort should a return man fall on the ball and not try to bring it up the field. Many return men get into trouble and fumble this type of kickoff because they look up to check the coverage, take their eyes off the ball, and are not prepared when the ball bounces to one side or the other.

While every kickoff return man must hope for and think about taking each kickoff back for a touchdown, he must understand that this seldom will happen. Instead it is important for him to know that his primary job is to make the catch, and return the ball as far up the field as possible, allowing his offense to start with the best field position on the next offensive series.

All return men must understand that on a kickoff the ball is a free ball and if the kicking team can fall on the ball they will gain possession. It is very important for the return men to make absolutely certain that they take possession of every kickoff—even those long kicks that sail into the end zone and are not going to be returned.

WINNING POINTS
- Line up 10 yards deeper than anticipated depth of kick.
- At kick, move into direct line with flight path of ball.
- Move forward as catch is made, holding hands palms up, little fingers and outside edges of hands together, elbows close to body.
- Secure ball before being tackled.
- On squib kicks, get in front of bouncing ball.

Punt Returns

For a punt return man, the problems encountered are much different than those of a player who has the responsibility of running back kickoffs. One big difference is that the punt returner will not always be able to see the ball immediately as it leaves the kicker's foot. More often than not, his view of the kicker will be obscured by the members of the punt team and his teammates as they work to set up the return. For the punt returner,

the first sight of the ball usually will be after it is well in flight.

The first thing the punt returner needs to do is to gauge the flight path of the ball. As he makes this assessment, he should start moving in the direction of the punt and try to set up in a position in line with the ball's flight.

One of the hardest things a beginning punt returner has to learn is if he really has an opportunity to safely make the catch or not. All punt returners must never forget that, unlike a kickoff, the ball belongs to his team once it leaves the punter's foot. It is not necessary for him to make the catch in order for a change of possession to take place. If the punt returner feels that he cannot safely make the catch or if the ball is bouncing on the ground, the return man should move away from it and call out to his teammates also to move away. It is much better to allow a ball to roll an extra few yards, than it is to muff the catch and give the kicking team a chance to recover the muffed ball.

If the punt returner thinks the ball is catchable and has positioned himself in line with the flight of the ball, the next thing he must do is focus on the front point of the ball. Because the ball is usually moving in a spiral, the punt returner must try to see how the ball starts

its descent. If the front of the ball turns over and starts the descent, the return man knows that the ball will have a longer flight and will usually carry to his right side. When the return man sees the back of the ball starting to drop first, he knows that the kick usually will not be as long and will have a tendency to go to his left side.

The actual catching of a punt is very similar to the catching of a ball anywhere on the football field. Because the ball is dropping into the return man's hands, it is important for the return man to reach up for it. He should form the receiving area with his hands by placing his palms up, the outside edges of his hands close together with his little fingers touching. With his hands in this position, the return man should extend his hands up toward the ball so that he is able to see his hands and the ball as he makes the catch.

The three biggest reasons for a punt return man not to catch a punt are: (1) trying to catch a punt that is kicked too far from his original position; (2) taking his eyes off the ball and looking at the approaching coverage men; and (3) not catching the ball in his hands and allowing it to bounce off his chest. Any one of these errors can, and usually does, result in a muffed punt and the opportuni-

The most important thing for a punt returner is to make the catch; he then can focus on breaking a long return.

ty for the kicking team to recover the ball and retain possession downfield.

The punt returner needs to practice catching kicks time and again. Once the punt returner and the coach feel that the punts are being caught correctly, and with consistency, make the practice a drill by adding one or two coverage men.

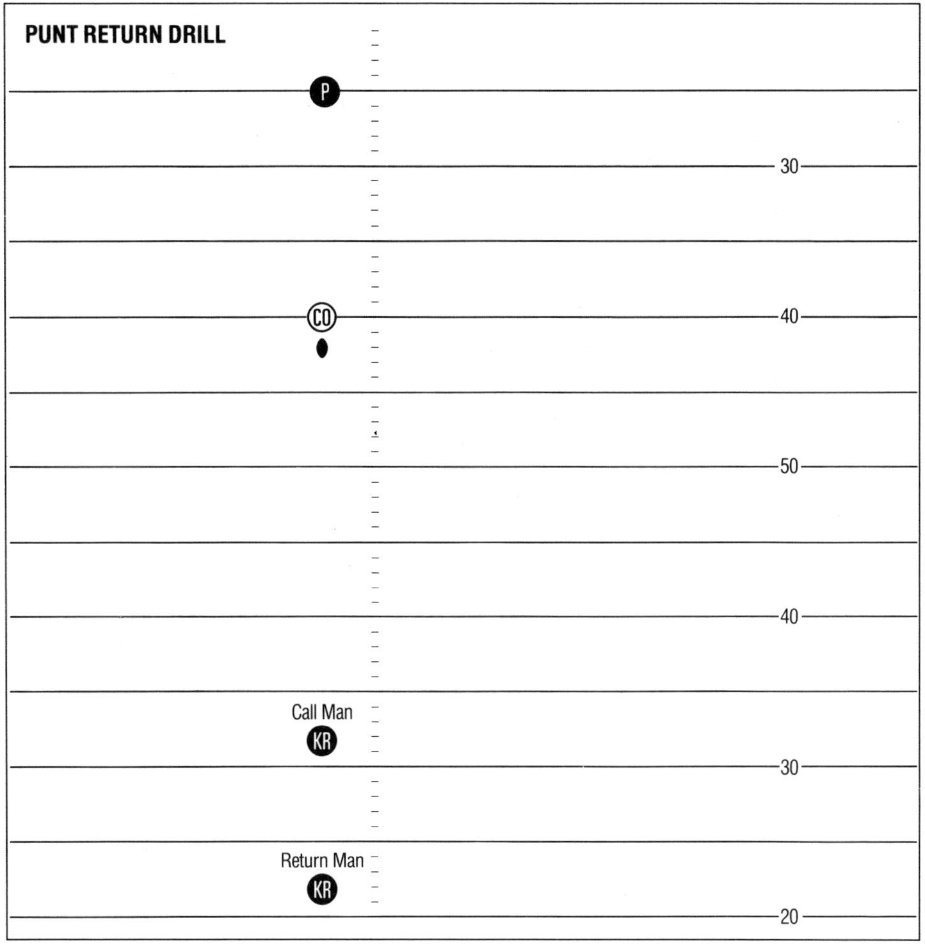

DRILL:

Punt Returns

In the beginning it is good to have two return men working together as a team. These two players can line up at the same depth on the field, or one man can line up ten yards in front of the other, serving as the call man plus fair-catching any short kick.

The man who is not going to make the actual catch should have the responsibility of telling the return man to return or fair-catch the punt. Once this call has been made by the call man and is received, it should be acknowledged by the punt returner with a call of "Got it. Got it." When the call man is certain that the call has been received, he then should attempt to block the first coverage man coming down the field.

The call man must never forget that his first responsibility is to serve as a second pair of eyes for the return man. While the return man focuses on the ball, the call man must focus on the coverage. When he calls for a fair-catch, the call man should keep his eyes on the return man and make certain that the punt returner is correctly signalling for a fair catch by vigorously waving a hand and arm over

PUNT RETURN DRILL

his head.

If the team is facing an exceptional punter, the call man may not be necessary. On a long kick, the return man will usually have time to move in front of the flight of the ball, steal a peek down the field to determine if he should fair-catch or return the punt, and still have time to re-focus back on the ball.

A punt returner must have a recklessness about him similar to that of a kick-off return man. He must know where the ball is to be returned (left, right, or middle), and, after making the catch and securing the ball, he must try to get to the return area as quickly as possible.

Often, if the ball is kicked completely away from the side of the return, the return man should be content to make the catch, returning the punt straight up the field and gaining as many yards as possible.

Sometimes, too, recklessness must give way to caution; the punt returner must know when to make a fair catch.

On any phase of a punt return it is important for the return man to keep the ball securely in his grasp. This is especially true when the punt returner sees that he is going to be tackled; he must make certain that he has a good grip on the ball.

WINNING POINTS
- Move in direction of punt and get in line with ball's flight path.
- Let ball go if catch cannot safely be made.
- Focus on front point of ball; make catch with hands extended, palms up, little fingers and outside edges of hands together. Look ball into hands.
- After catch, quickly get to return area.
- Call man makes call for return or fair catch, then blocks first coverage man downfield.

GLOSSARY

Glossary

Angle block—A block by an offensive player on a defender lined up to his inside or outside.

Audible—A change of plays made by the quarterback at the line of scrimmage.

Backfield—**1.** The area behind the line of scrimmage where the running backs set and the quarterback passes. **2.** The term for the quarterback and running backs. **3.** An alternate term for the defensive secondary, as in "defensive backfield."

Backpedal—Backward running to drop into pass coverage.

Blindside—To tackle a quarterback from behind or from the side opposite his passing direction as he sets up to pass.

Blitz—An all-out pass rush involving defensive backs or linebackers individually or in combination. Sometimes called a "dog."

Blocking progression—The order in which offensive blockers probably will attack a defensive player. Each defensive lineman and linebacker has his own blocking progression to learn.

Blocking triangle—The three offensive men directly opposite a defensive lineman (the one in front and the two to either side). The defensive lineman "reads his blocking triangle" to determine who can block him.

Bomb—A long pass.

Bootleg—A quarterback fake; he fakes a handoff, then hides the ball against his hip and runs around one of the ends.

Bump-and-run—A pass defense technique in which the defender bumps the receiver as he releases off the line then covers him man-to-man on his route.

Burst—The last phase of a pass pattern when the receiver makes his final cut prior to catching the ball.

Call man—The "up," or forward, man on a kick return play who has the responsibility to tell the kick returner whether to field the kick or to make a fair catch. The call man then blocks the first coverage man downfield.

Center—**1.** The middle man of the offensive line responsible for snapping the ball to the quarterback, punter, and placekick holder. **2.** The action of snapping the ball.

Cheat step—A very short step forward taken by a quarterback at the line of scrimmage, with the foot opposite his passing hand, to guarantee he does not pull away from center before he has received the snap.

Chuck—A quick shove or push of an opponent who is in front of a defender. The tactic is used primarily against pass receivers.

Clipping—An illegal block caused by throwing the body against the back of an opponent (who is not a running back) or hitting an opponent below the waist from behind. Clipping is not called within three yards of the line of scrimmage, where it is considered "close line play."

Cloud—The code term often used to indicate that a right or left cornerback (depending upon the direction of zone rotation) will take an outside underneath zone and has run force responsibility on a particular play.

Combination block—A block involving more than one player, usually referring to a double-team or combo block.

Combo block—A block by two offensive linemen versus two defensive players with final assignments determined on the move.

Cornerback—Two of the players of the defensive secondary, one set wide to each side of the formation, responsible for pass coverage and stopping running plays.

Coverage—Pass defense. Also used to designate the exact type of coverage used, as in "double coverage."

Crackback block—An illegal block thrown by any offensive player who has lined up more than two yards outside the offensive tackle, as he comes back toward the ball.

Crossbar—The horizontal bar of a goal post over which a field goal or extra point kick must go.

Crossover step—A start or change of direction maneuver, usually by a running back, in which the player first leans in the direction he wants to go then steps across his body with the opposite leg.

Cutback—A maneuver by a ball carrier reversing his direction against the flow of the play.

Cut block—A low block, illegal at many levels of the game, in which the blocker aims at the knees or ankles of his target.

Dash pass—A pass thrown outside the pocket in which the quarterback takes a five-step drop, then releases to either his left or right to throw.

Dead ball—When the ball no longer can be advanced, it is whistled dead by the officials. Penalties committed after the whistle are considered "dead ball fouls."

Deep Zone—Any one of the zones occupied by a defensive back to guard against a long pass.

Defense—1. The team *without* the ball. 2. The tactics of that team.

Defensive backs—The players in the defensive secondary; the cornerbacks and safeties.

Defensive ends—The two widest set of the defensive linemen, responsible for stopping the run and rushing the passer. The defensive ends usually set opposite the offensive tackles.

Delay pass—A pass to a running back who waits for a three-count, then goes over the middle to make the reception. Also called a "check pass."

Dime—A situational pass defense that features six defensive backs.

Dive—A quick-hitting running play on which the running back lines up almost directly behind the hole he is to run through, taking the handoff from the quarterback with no faking involved.

Double coverage—Two pass defenders covering one receiver.

Double-team block—A powerful block involving two offensive blockers hitting one defender and driving him off the line of scrimmage and out of a hole.

Down—1. A play from scrimmage; the offense gets four downs numbered in sequence, first to fourth, to gain 10 yards and make a new first down. 2. When a ball carrier is tackled, his knee touches the ground, or his forward progress is stopped, he is considered *down* and the play ends. 3. On a punt, the kicking team may touch the ball before it is whistled dead and *down* it at the spot it is touched, ending the play. On a kickoff, the receiving team may *down* the ball in the end zone for a touchback by indicating the kick will not be returned. The ball then is brought out to the 20. 4. A defensive lineman in a 3- or 4-point stance is called a "down lineman."

Draw play—A delayed running play that in the beginning is made to look like a pass to the defense.

Drive block—A basic, straight-ahead block used to drive a defender off the line of scrimmage.

Drop—1. The backward movement of

the quarterback after the snap as he retreats into the backfield to pass. Quarterbacks use either a three-step, five-step, or seven-step drop, depending on the depth of the pass to be thrown. **2.** The movement of a defensive player as he retreats into pass coverage. **3.** The punter's release of the ball onto his kicking foot.

Drop step—A step back from the line of scrimmage taken by a lineman to get into position to block or pull. Also called a "set step."

Eligible receiver—Any of five offensive players who can receive a pass—the two end-men and three backfield men (lined up a yard or more behind the line of scrimmage). An interior lineman can be eligible if he is the widest man on either side of the ball. The quarterback also can be eligible, but only if he does not take a snap from under center.

Encroachment—A penalty called when a player is in the neutral zone and makes contact with an opponent before the ball is snapped. (*See also: "offside"*)

End around—A variation of a reverse play in which a wide receiver or tight end becomes the ball carrier on a wide running play.

End line—The line at the back of the end zone.

End zone—The area, 10 yards deep,

bounded by the end line, goal line, and both sidelines, into which the offensive team must move the ball in its possession to score a touchdown.

Even defense—A defensive set with an equal number of defensive linemen aligned on both sides of the ball.

Extra point—The one-point play (NFL) allowed a team after scoring a touchdown. It may be attempted by run or pass, but almost always is attempted with a placekick. Also called the "point-after-touchdown" (PAT) or "conversion." Outside the NFL, a conversion that is scored by a run or pass is worth two points.

Fair catch—A unhindered catch by the receiver of a punt or kickoff. To signal a fair catch, the returner raises one arm high over his head. Once he makes this signal, the player cannot run with the ball nor can he be touched. Penalties are assessed if either occurs.

False start—A penalty called when an interior offensive lineman moves after assuming a set stance. A quarterback also may be called for a false start if his signal cadence or actions at the line of scrimmage are judged by the officials to be an obvious attempt to draw an opponent offside.

Far—A term referring to an opposing player lined up on the other side (right

or left) of the ball, such as the *far* running back, or a trap block by the *far* guard.

Field goal—A scoring kick worth three points that may be attempted from anywhere on the field. The kicked ball must go between the goal post's uprights and clear the crossbar.

Finish—The final phase of a lineman's block in which he drives up and through the man he is blocking.

Flat—The offensive backfield area near the sidelines.

Flanker—The wide receiver on the tight end's side of the field who usually lines up one or two yards off the line of scrimmage.

Flood—An offensive tactic that sends two or more receivers into one area to create confusion and a numerical mismatch in a zone defense.

Flow—The direction or motion of a play or offensive players, especially the running backs.

Forward pass—A ball thrown, usually with an overarm motion, in the direction of the offense's goal line.

Formation—The alignment of offensive or defensive players on a play.

Four-point stance—A weight-forward stance, with both hands on the ground, that affords a powerful straight-ahead charge; used by offensive linemen, tight ends, and sometimes defensive linemen, usually in short-yardage/goal line situations.

Four-three—A defensive formation featuring four linemen and three linebackers. Also called "forty-three."

Free kick—The kick that puts the ball into play following a safety. The ball usually is punted.

Front—A defensive front or front line, such as the four down linemen in a four-three defense.

Fumble—Loss of possession of the football by the ball carrier, handler, or passer. *(See also: "muff")*

Gadget play—A trick play.

Game plan—The strategy and list of plays chosen for each game.

Gang tackling—More than two defensive players tackling the ball carrier at the same time.

Gap—**1.** The space between two offensive linemen. **2.** A defense with a man aligned over every gap.

Gap responsibility—The side of an offensive lineman that a defensive lineman or linebacker is assigned; he must stop any running play attacking that area.

Glide—The second phase of a pass pattern, in which the receiver alters his path up the field to get into the best possible position to make the reception.

Goal line—The field stripe separating the end zone and the field of play that must be touched or crossed to score a touchdown. *(See also: "plane of the goal")*

Guards—The two offensive linemen on either side of the center. Guards often pull to lead the blocking on runs.

Half—A 30-minute period, divided into two 15-minute quarters. There are two halves, the first and second, in a game.

Halftime—The intermission between the first and second halves of a game. During halftime, the teams rest and discuss second-half strategy.

Handoff—Giving the ball to another player, most often from a quarterback to a running back.

Hang time—The amount of time a punt or kick stays in the air, measured from the moment the ball leaves the kicker's foot to the time it is caught or hits the ground. Good hang time allows the kick coverage team more time to get downfield and stop a runback.

Hashmarks—The short lines that are used for spotting the ball, running the length of the field and lined up with the uprights of both goal posts in pro football. In college and high school play, the hashmarks are set one-third of the way in from each sideline.

Holding—The penalty called for illegal grabbing or grasping of another player. Holding can be either an offensive or defensive penalty, though it most often is called on offensive linemen.

Hole—**1.** A space in the offensive line opened by offensive blockers for a ball carrier to run through. **2.** A numbered space in the offensive line.

Hook block—A block on which an offensive blocker steps laterally for position, then drives for the defender's hip to stop his movement.

Huddle—A brief gathering for play- and signal-calling by the offense and defense between plays.

I-formation—A backfield formation featuring two running backs in line directly behind the quarterback.

Incomplete pass—A forward pass that is not caught or intercepted.

Influence—Deception by the offensive line, denying keys to the defense and leading it away from the play.

Inside—**1.** The area between the two offensive tackles where running plays can be directed or pass rushers make their charge. **2.** The area of the line of scrimmage between a player and the offensive center. **3.** The direction of movement of a receiver toward the center of the field. **4.** The position of a pass defender between a receiver and the center of the field.

Intentional grounding—A penalty

called when the quarterback purposely throws the ball away to avoid being tackled for a loss.

Interception—A change of possession when a defensive player catches a pass intended for an offensive player.

Interception point—The point where a pass actually will be caught and can be intercepted.

Interference—A judgement penalty called when either an offensive or defensive player interferes with another player's opportunity to catch a pass.

Keeper—A play in which the quarterback keeps the ball and runs with it.

Key—**1.** An alignment or movement that can tell a defensive player where the ball is going and what blocks to expect. **2.** To specifically watch one player to gain clues to a play.

Lateral—A toss or pass backward from the direction of play.

Lead block—A block by a running back, preceding another running back into the line and hitting the first defender in his path.

Lead step—A start technique used by running backs to move directly toward the line of scrimmage. The running back's first step is with the foot on the side of the desired movement; he then pushes off with the other foot.

Linebacker—The all-purpose defenders who play between the defensive linemen and the defensive backs. Linebackers are designated "inside" and "outside" in 3-4 alignments, and "right," "left," and "middle" in 4-3 alignments.

Line call—Signals called at the line of scrimmage in some offenses, generally by the offensive center, to alert offensive linemen to their blocking assignments.

Man-to-man—A type of pass defense where linebackers and defensive backs are assigned a potential receiver to cover individually for an entire play.

Man-blocking—A pass-blocking scheme in which each offensive lineman is assigned a defender to block and stay with, wherever he goes. The opposite of "zone blocking."

Midfield stripe—The 50-yard line.

Mirror block—A type of block used primarily by wide receivers on running plays. The receiver runs his route, then waits for his coverage man to react to the running play. As soon as the defender commits to a side, the receiver hits and stays with him.

Mirror running—A technique used by pass defenders covering a receiver off the line of scrimmage in which the defender maintains an exact relationship with the receiver throughout a pass route.

Misdirection—Deception by the offense to lead the defense away from the flow of a play.

Motion—The action of a running back or receiver running parallel to, and behind, the line of scrimmage (never forward) before the snap. Only one man may be *in motion* before the snap.

Muff—The touching of the ball by a player in an *unsuccessful* attempt to gain possession of a free ball; no possession is implied.

Near—A term referring to an opposing player lined up on the same side (right or left) of the ball, such as "near running back."

Neutral zone—The area between the offensive and defensive lines as wide as the length of the ball.

Nickel defense—A defensive formation in which an extra (fifth) pass defender, the "nickel back," is brought into the game.

Nose tackle—The defensive tackle in a 3-4 alignment who lines up opposite the offensive center.

Odd defense—A defensive alignment that has a man set directly over the offensive center.

Offense—**1.** The team *with* the ball. **2.** The tactics of that team.

Offside—A penalty called when a player is across the line of scrimmage before the ball is snapped.

One position—The numbered position of a pass rusher when he is lined up directly in front of an offensive lineman.

Onside kick—A short kickoff that carries just the required 10 yards to allow the kicking team a chance to recover the free ball.

Option pass—**1.** A play in which the quarterback has the option of throwing on the run to any one of a number of receivers. **2.** A play in which the runner has the option to run or pass, and elects to pass.

Option play—A play in which the quarterback moves parallel to the line of scrimmage and has the option to hand off, pitch, or run.

Outside—**1.** The area between the tight end and the sideline on one side of the line of scrimmage and the the weakside tackle and the sideline on the other. **2.** The area of the line of scrimmage between a player and the sideline away from the offensive center. **3.** The direction of movement of a receiver toward the near sideline. **4.** The position of a pass defender between a receiver and the near sideline.

Overshift—A defensive formation in which all, or some, defensive linemen shift one position over toward the strong side.

Overtime—The extra 15-minute period added on to NFL regular season games to try to break ties. In NFL postseason games, as many overtime periods as needed are played. Also called "sudden death" or "sudden victory" overtime, because the first team to score in any manner immediately wins the game.

Passing tree—A map of the pass routes run by a receiver. Wide receivers, tight ends, and running backs each have their own passing trees.

Pass pattern—The route a receiver runs on his way out to catch a pass.

Pass protection—Keeping defensive players away from the passer until he releases the ball.

Pass rush—The charge by defensive linemen, linebackers, and sometimes safeties and cornerbacks to sack or pressure the quarterback as he attempts to pass.

Penalty—An infraction of the rules that can result in a loss of yardage and/or down. It also can result in nullification of a play.

Penalty marker—The yellow flag thrown by officials to indicate a penalty.

Penetration—Movement of the defensive linemen or linebackers across the line of scrimmage.

Pitch—An underhanded toss, usually in the backfield from the quarterback to a running back. Also called a "pitchout" or "toss." A "lateral" is similar, but generally refers to a sideways or backwards toss in the open field.

Placekick—The general term used to encompass kickoffs, field goals, and extra points, where the ball is kicked from a fixed point and is held by a holder or is set on a tee.

Plane of the goal—The imaginary plane extending upward from the goal line that must be broken by a player in possession of the ball in order to score a touchdown.

Plant foot—**1.** The foot opposite a placekicker's kicking foot that serves as a base for his kicking motion. **2.** The foot used by the quarterback to take his set step.

Play-action pass—A play in which the quarterback fakes a running play, then passes. The line blocks as if for a run.

Pocket—The area of protection around a passer formed by his blockers.

Possession—Grasp and control of the ball by an individual; control of the ball by a team.

Prevent defense—A defensive alignment, usually featuring deep zone coverage, designed to stop long passes.

Primary receiver—The designated first receiver the quarterback will look for as he drops back to pass.

Pull—When an offensive lineman

leaves his position and runs down the line of scrimmage to lead a play or execute a trap block.

Punt—A type of kick used primarily on fourth down that ordinarily results in a change of possession.

Pursuit—The predetermined movement of the defensive team to the action of a ball carrier.

Quarter—A 15-minute playing period; four quarters, first through fourth, make up a game.

Quarterback—The player who leads the offense. The quarterback calls plays and signals, hands off the ball and passes it, and sometimes runs with it.

Quarterback draw—A fake pass play in which the quarterback starts to drop back to pass, then runs the ball up the middle.

Quarterback sneak—A short-yardage or goal-line play in which the quarterback takes the snap and immediately runs or dives over center.

Quick count—An abbreviated signal count used by the offense to initiate a play faster and catch the defense off balance.

Quick hitter—A quick short-yardage inside running play.

Read—1. The quarterback's observation of the defensive alignment at the line of scrimmage. 2. The observation of keys, the action of the offense, or the action of a specific offensive player by the defense or an individual defensive player.

Recognition point—The instant or spot at which a defensive player identifies a pass pattern being run.

Relative position—The placement a pass blocker seeks to maintain between an oncoming pass rusher and the quarterback.

Release—1. The action of a receiver leaving the line of scrimmage. 2. The action of the passer letting go of the ball during his throwing motion.

Reverse—A trick running play in which the quarterback fakes in one direction, then hands off to a running back or receiver going by in the opposite direction. If the running back or receiver hands off to *another* ball carrier going by, the play is called a "double reverse." A reverse to a receiver often is called an "end around."

Rollout—1. A pass where the quarterback leaves the pocket, following both running backs to either his right or left to throw the ball. 2. The pass play of the same name. *(See also: "dash pass," "sprint pass," and "waggle pass")*

Rollover step—A change of direction technique used by linebackers and defensive backs in which the player rolls over the foot in the direction he wants to go.

Rotation—The movement of the defensive secondary into predetermined zone coverage.

Run force—The defensive responsibility of a safety or cornerback to turn a running play toward the middle of the field. Occasionally a linebacker has run force responsibility.

Running backs—The players who are the main ball carriers in the ground game, serving as lead blockers for each other, and who act as receivers coming out of the backfield. Running backs are designated "halfbacks," "fullbacks," and "tailbacks" in some offenses.

Running drive block—A drive-type block thrown on the run, most often used by pulling linemen on trap plays or against linebackers.

Rush lane—The predetermined path of a pass rusher toward the quarterback.

Sack—When the quarterback is tackled in the backfield while attempting to pass.

Safety—1. A two-point scoring play most often caused by the tackling of a ball carrier or passer in his own end zone or an offensive penalty in the end zone. 2. The position played by two players in the defensive backfield, usually designated the "strong" and "free" safeties. The strong safety generally lines up on the tight end's side of the formation and is responsible for covering the tight end. The free safety (also called the "weak" safety) usually is not assigned any particular player to cover, lines up to the side away from the tight end, and plays the deepest of the defensive backs.

Safety blitz—A surprise pass rush by one of the safeties, usually the free safety.

Scoop block—The second part of a combination block, from the perspective of the defender.

Scramble—When the quarterback runs evasively in the backfield to avoid being sacked.

Screen pass—A delayed pass play in which the quarterback drops back to pass and the offensive linemen allow the pass rushers to get by, then drift out to a designated area to form a screen, or wall, of blockers. The ball then is thrown to a running back or receiver behind this screen. There are delayed screen passes and speed screen passes.

Scrimmage (line of)—The imaginary line running from sideline to sideline through the ball before it is snapped; the line from which a play begins.

Seams—The areas between pass coverage zones.

Secondary—1. The area of the defensive backfield beyond the line of scrim-

mage. 2. The personnel of the defensive backfield: the two cornerbacks and two safeties.

Set—1. The offensive or defensive alignment. 2. The action of an offensive player getting into his stance and remaining motionless before the snap of the ball. 3. The stance of a player.

Set step—The final step of the quarterback's drop that stops his backward motion and helps bring his body under control to throw a pass.

Shift—The movement of the offense or defense, in unison, into a different formation prior to the snap of the ball.

Shotgun—An offensive formation in which the quarterback takes the snap from center five to seven yards behind the line of scrimmage.

Sidelines—The lines running the length of the field, from end line to end line, marking the outside boundaries of the field and end zones. The sideline itself is out of bounds.

Signals—The number and word codes called by the quarterback at the line of scrimmage. Signals also are called by the defense prior to a play, usually by a linebacker.

Situational substitution—Substituting players with specialized skills in specific situations.

Sky—The code term often used to indi-

cate that one of the safeties (depending upon the direction of zone rotation) will take an outside underneath zone and/or has run force responsibility on a particular play.

Snap—The action of the center passing the ball between his legs to the quarterback, punter, or placekick holder to begin a play. Also called the "exchange."

Snap count—The signal on which the ball will be snapped.

Sound (going on)—A quick variation of the snap count; the center snaps the ball at the first sound the quarterback makes.

Spearing—A dangerous penalty called when a defensive player dives head firs into a downed offensive player.

Special teams—The players who make up the units in all phases of the kicking game.

Spike—The action of a player slamming the ball to the ground after scoring.

Split—The distance a player is separated from another player.

Spot—The placement of the ball by the referee after a play or penalty.

Spot of enforcement—The spot from which a penalty or foul is marked off; it varies depending on the situation.

Spot pass—A pass pattern predicated on timing and coordination; the quarterback throws to a predetermined spot on the field before the receiver actually gets there.

Sprint—The third phase of a pass pattern, including the last four steps of the glide phase, in which the receiver tries to convince the defender that he is going to run by him just before making his final break.

Sprint pass—A pass play where the quarterback leaves the pocket following one running back, moving to either his right or left to throw the ball.

Square—To be directly in front of, and facing, another player. A defensive back never allows a receiver to get "square" with him.

Squib kick—An intentionally low kickoff that bounces along the field and is difficult to handle.

Stack—When a linebacker stands directly behind a defensive lineman.

Start—The action of any player as he begins to leave his stance.

Straight-arm—A technique used by a ball carrier, usually in the open field, to ward off a tackler by extending one arm into the face of the defender.

Strong side—The side of the offensive formation with the tight end.

Stunt—A planned rush involving two or more defensive linemen and/or linebackers, in which they loop around each other instead of charging straight.

Sudden death—*See "overtime."*

Sweep—A wide running play around the end, usually led by pulling linemen.

Tackle—**1.** To bring down a ball carrier. **2.** The offensive linemen positioned on the outside of the guards. **3.** The defensive linemen playing inside the defensive ends. In a three-man front, the defensive tackle is called a "nose tackle."

Tee—A specially designed stand used to hold a football upright on placekicks.

Three-four—A defensive formation that features three defensive linemen and four linebackers. Also called a "thirty-four."

Three-point stance—A stance used by offensive and defensive linemen and running backs in which one hand is touching the ground.

Three position—An outside set by a defensive player versus an offensive lineman that affords a wide pass rush.

Tight end—A receiver/blocker positioned outside the offensive tackle. The position of the tight end determines the strong side and weak side of the offensive formation; the tight end's side is the strong side.

Time out—A halt to game action called by either team or the referee. Each team is allowed three charged time outs per half.

Tipped ball—A deflected pass.

Touchback—When a ball is whistled dead on or behind a team's own goal line (e.g. on a kickoff that goes into the end zone). The ball is put in play on the receiving team's 20-yard line.

Touchdown—A six-point scoring play that occurs when one team crosses the other team's goal line with the ball in its possession.

Trap—A running play in which a defensive lineman initially is unblocked, then is influenced across the line of scrimmage and is blocked by a pulling guard, tackle, or tight end.

Trap block—A running drive block thrown by a pulling lineman or tight end against a defender who was intentionally left unblocked.

Twist change—A defensive call that changes the order of penetration on a stunt.

Two-minute offense—A time conserving, quick-play (usually passing) attack used primarilly in the last two minutes of a game or half. Also called a "two-minute drill" and a "hurry-up offense."

Two-minute warning—The notification given to both benches by the officials that two minutes remain in a game or half.

Two-point stance—An upright stance used by running backs in the I-formation; receivers to gain a quicker release; offensive linemen in certain passing situations; linebackers; and defensive backs.

Two position—Placement of a defender on the outside shoulder of an offensive lineman.

Unbalanced line—An offensive formation with a lineman shifted to overload one side of the line.

Uncovered lineman—An offensive lineman with no defender set directly in front of him.

Underneath zones—The seven pass coverage areas between the line of scrimmage and the deep zones.

Undershift—A defensive formation in which all or some defensive linemen shift one position toward the weak side of the formation.

Uprights—The two vertical poles of a goal post between which a field goal or extra point kick must pass.

Waggle pass—A pass play in which the quarterback leaves the pocket, first faking to the running backs going in one direction, then, with a lineman in front of him, moves in the opposite direction to throw the ball.

Weak side—The side of the offensive formation without the tight end.

Wide receiver—A pass receiver who is set outside the offensive tackle. A team may use from one to three wide receivers on any given play.

Zone defense—A type of coverage in the defensive secondary in which the cornerbacks and safeties are assigned specific areas to watch (as opposed to watching specific players in ''man-to-man'' coverage).

Zone blocking—A type of pass blocking in which offensive linemen are assigned a particular area to protect; they block anyone who comes into that area.

INDEX

Index

Angle blocking: by offensive linemen, 166-168; by tight end, 141

Angle blocking (defeating): by defensive linemen, 210; by linebackers, 254-256

Backpedal: by linebackers, 270, 278-280; by defensive backs, 300-301; angled backpedal, 279-280, 301; change of direction in, 281, 301, 306-307. *See also* roll-over step

Ball stripping, 319-323

Blitz: by defensive backs, 335-336; by linebackers, 285-290

Blocking: angle blocking, 141, 166-168; combination blocking, 174-180; combo blocking, 177-180; cut blocking, 165; double-team blocking, 75-76, 142-143, 174-177; drive blocking, 139, 160-165, 168-174; hook blocking, 139-141, 165-166; lead blocking, 69-76; man blocking, 193-195, 232-233; mirror blocking, 135-137; pass blocking, 76-81, 182-196; short-yardage/goal-line blocking,

143-145, 180-182; trap blocking, 168-174; vs. blocking sled, 160-163; zone blocking, 193-195, 232-233

Blocking progression: 217-220, 260-261; for defensive ends, 218-219; for defensive tackles, 218-220; for nose tackle, 219-220; for inside linebackers, 260-261; for outside linebackers, 260-261

Blocking triangle, 210, 211, 213, 217-218

Bootleg pass, 49

Bump-and-run, 310-313

Burst (phase of pass pattern), 114-115

Call man (on punt returns), 391

Center: quarterback-center exchange, 18-20, 155-158; snapping for kicks, 373-376; snapping for punts, 376; stance, 155-157. *See also* blocking

Change of direction: inside cut, 67-68; using crossover step, 66-67; using roll-over step, 281, 306-307; spin technique, 68-69

Cheat step (by quarterback), 21-22, 28

"Cloud" call, 315, 317-318

Combination block, 174-180

Combination block (defeating): by defensive linemen, 210-213

Combo blocking, 177-180

Cornerbacks: in man-to-man defense, 302-313; in zone defense, 313-319; run force responsibility of, 332-335; stance, 297-298

Crossover step, 58, 66-67

Cut block, 165

Cut block (defeating): by linebackers, 254

Dash pass, 48-49

Defensive backs 295-336. *See also* cornerbacks, safeties

Defensive ends: blocking progression for, 218-219; pass rushing, 220-233, 235-238; stance, 205, 220-222; stunts involving, 231-233, 235-238

Defensive tackles: blocking progression for, 217-219; stance, 203-205; in stunts, 231-233, 235-238. *See also* nose tackle

Delay pass, 94-95

Dive (handoff for), 24
Double-team blocking: with center and guard, 174-177; with guard and tackle, 174-177; with tight end and tackle, 142-143, 174-175
Double-team blocking (defeating): by defensive linemen, 211-213
Draw play, 96-97
Drive blocking: by offensive linemen, 160-165; by tight ends, 139; vs. blocking sled, 160-163. *See also* running drive block
Drive blocking (defeating): by defensive linemen, 208-209; by linebackers, 252-254
Drop: by quarterback into pocket, 28-31; by defensive backs into coverage, 299-302, 306-307; by linebackers into coverage, 266-282; of ball by punter, 347-359
Drop step, 172-173
Extra point. *See* placekicking
Fair catch, 391-392
Field goal. *See* placekicking
Finish (of block), 161-162, 165
Five-step drop (by quarterback), 29-30
Forward pass. *See* passing
Four-point stance: by offensive linemen, 154, 180-182; by tight end, 143-145; in short-yardage/goal-line situations, 143-145, 180-182

Free safety. *See* safeties
Gang tackling, 263-264
Gap responsibility, 206, 209
Glide (phase of pass pattern): by tight end, 113; by wide receiver, 111-113
Guards: pulling, 170-174; stance for, 153-155, 180-182, 192-193. *See also* blocking
Handoffs: faking, 25-26, 44-46; making, 24-25; quarterback footwork on, 20-24; quarterback responsibility, 20; running back responsibility, 60; running back forming pocket for, 60-61
Hang time, 352, 358, 382
Holder (on placekicks), 376-377
Hole numbering, 59-60
Hook blocking: by offensive linemen, 165-166; by tight end, 139-141
Hook blocking (defeating): by defensive linemen, 209; by linebackers, 256
Inside linebackers. *See* linebackers
Interceptions, 282-285, 323-328; angle, 325-326; hand position for, 283-284, 325-327; over-the-head, 326-327; straight-ahead, 323-325; tipped passes, 284, 327-328
Interception point, 308-310
Lead block (by running back), 69-76
Lead block (defeating): by defensive

linemen, 215-216; by linebackers, 258-260
Lead step start, 58-59
Linebackers: 249-292; blitzing, 285-290; blocking progression for, 260-261; in pass coverage, 266-285; in stunts, 290-292; pursuit paths for, 264-266; stances for, 249-252; tackling, 261-264
Man blocking: 193-195, 232-233. *See also* pass blocking
Man-to-man (pass defense): 277-282, 302-313; recognizing, 145-148. *See also* bump-and-run
Mirror blocking, 135-137
Mirror running, 312
Muff (of kick), 389, 391
Nose tackle: blocking progression for, 219; in stunts, 235, 237-238; stance, 203-205
Option pass, 63-64
Option pitch, 63-64
Outside linebackers. *See* linebackers
Pass blocking: by running backs, 76-81; man blocking, 193-195, 232-233; setting up for, 185-187; two-point stance for offensive linemen, 192-193; picking up stunts, 193-196; zone blocking, 193-195, 232-233
Pass coverage recognition, 145-148
Pass defense: ball stripping, 319-323; bump-and-run, 310-313; man-to-man,

277-282, 302-313; zone, 266-277, 313-319

Passing: by running back, 97-98; delay passes, 94-95; five-step drop, 29-30; follow-through, 32; from quarterback to running back, 36-44, 86-95; from quarterback to tight end, 40-42, 129-135; from quarterback to wide receivers, 34-40, 121-129; grip for, 27-28; play-action, 44-46; release, 32, 36; rollout passes, 46-49; screen passes, 91-94; set step in drop, 30, 31; seven-step drop, 30; three-step drop, 29; throwing motion for, 31-34

Passing tree: for running backs, 36, 90; for tight ends, 41, 130; for wide receivers, 34, 123

Pass pattern reaction, 275-277, 307-310

Pass pattern recognition: by defensive backs, 302-307; by linebackers, 270-275

Pass rushing: by defensive backs, 335-336; positions for, 183-185; defensive lineman techniques, 220-231; linebacker techniques, 285-290; stunts, 231-239, 290-292

Pitch play, 23, 62-64

Placekicking: center snap for, 373-376; directional kicking, 354-355; holder forming target for

snap, 377; holder placing ball for kicker, 377; holder receiving snap, 377; placement of ball on tee, 361, 368, 379-380, 382; soccer-style kicks, 361-368, 379-382; soccer-style kick alignment, 361-364; soccer-style kickoffs, 379-382; soccer-style kickoff alignment, 380; soccer-style plant step for kicks, 366; soccer-style plant step for kickoffs, 381; soccer-style stance, 361-364; soccer-style steps for kicks, 366; soccer-style steps for kickoffs, 380-381; straight-ahead kicks, 368-373; straight-ahead kick alignment, 370-371; straight-ahead kickoffs, 382-385; straight-ahead kickoff alignment, 383; straight-ahead plant step for kicks, 372; straight-ahead plant step for kickoffs, 383; straight-ahead stance, 371, 383; straight-ahead steps for kicks, 371-373; straight-ahead steps for kickoffs, 383-385; tees for, 361, 380

Plant foot. See placekicking

Play-action passing, 44-46

Pulling (by offensive linemen), 168-174

Punting: 341-359; directional, 354-355; drop of ball, 347-359;

follow-through for, 352; forming target for center snap, 345-346; from end zone, 358-359; in rain, 358; in wind, 355-358; stance, 341-342; steps for, 3342-345, 349-350; taking snap, 350-351

Pursuit: by defensive linemen, 241-246; by linebackers, 264-266

Quarterback: 15-50, 60-64; delay passes, 94-96; dropback passing, 28-31; forward passing, 26-50; handoffs, 20-26, 44-46, 60-64, 96-97; passing to running backs, 42-44, 91-96; passing to tight ends, 40-42; passing to wide receivers, 34-40; play-action passes, 44-46; screen passes, 91-94; stance, 16-18; taking center snap, 17-20

Recognition point, 308-310

Relative position, 165, 183-188

Release (by quarterback). See passing

Release (by receivers): tight end, 108-111; wide receivers, 107-108

Returns: interception, 284-285, 323; kickoff, 385-389; punt, 385-387, 389-392

Rollout passes, 46-49

Roll-over step, 281, 306-307

Rotation (of zone pass defense), 314-319

Run blocking: by offensive linemen,

159-183; by running backs, 69-76; by tight ends, 137-144; by wide receivers, 135-137

Run force, 332-355

Running backs: 20-26, 44, 48-49, 53-98; as ball carriers, 64-69; as lead blockers, 69-76; as passers, 97-98; as pass blockers, 76-80; as receivers, 81-97; in play-action passes, 44-46; passing tree for, 90; stances for, 54-58; starts, 58-60; taking handoffs, 60-64

Running drive block, 168-174. *See also* blocking

Safeties: in man-to-man defense, 302-313; in zone defense, 313-319; stance, free safety, 297-299; stance, strong safety, 297-299. *See also* pass defense

Scoop block (defeating), 210-211

Screen passes: 91-94; defensive line pursuit of, 244

Set step, 30, 31

"Sky" call, 315-317

Snap: to quarterback, 17-20; for placekicks, 373-376; for punts, 373-374, 376

Sprint (phase of pass pattern), 113-114

Sprint pass, 46-48

Start: by running backs, 58-59; for receivers, *see* release

Strong safety. *See* safeties

Stunts: 231-239, 290-292; picking up, 193-196

Tackle, offensive: stance, 153-155, 180-182, 192-193. *See also* blocking

Tackling: angled open-field, 330-332; gang, 263-264; open-field, 261-263, 328-330; sideline, 263, 332

Tee, kicking, 361, 368, 379-380, 382

Three-point stance: for defensive linemen, 203-205; for offensive linemen, 153-155; for tight ends, 106-107

Tight end: 103-105; blocking, 137-145; burst, 114-115; glide, 113; hand position on receptions, 115-121; passing tree, 130; pass patterns, 129-135; reading coverage, 145-148; release, 108-111; sprint, 113-114; stance, 106-107, 143-145. *See also* blocking

Tipped balls, 284, 327-328

Trap blocking, 168-174

Trap blocking (defeating): by defensive linemen, 213-215; by linebackers, 256-258

Twist change, 237

Two-point stance: by cornerbacks, 297-299; by linebackers, 249-252; by offensive linemen, 154, 192-193; by safeties, 297-299

Uncovered linemen, 195-196

Waggle pass, 49

Wide receiver: 101-103; blocking, 135-137; burst, 114-115; glide, 111-113; hand position for receptions, 115-121; passing tree, 123; pass patterns, 121-129; reading coverage, 145-148; release, 107-108; sprint, 113-114; stance, 105-106

Zone defense: defensive backs in, 313-319; linebackers in, 266-277; recognizing, 145-148

Zone blocking, 193-195, 232-233. *See also* blocking, pass blocking

Drills

Quarterback

Quarterback-Center Exchange	20
Shallow Handoff Footwork	21
Deep Angle Handoff Footwork	21
Far Back Handoff Footwork	22
Reverse Pivot Handoff Footwork	22
Reverse Pivot Pitch Footwork	23
Dive Handoff	24
Deep Handoff	24
Three-Step Drop	29
Five-Step Drop	29
Seven-Step Drop	30
Screen Drop	30
Passing Delivery	32
Hook Pass	35
In, Out, and Up Passes	35
Post, Corner, and Comeback Passes	37

Hitch, Slant, and Quick Out Passes 38
Tight End Passes 41
Play-Action Passes 45
Passing on the Move 46
Roll-Out, Dash, and Waggle Passes 48

Running Back
Crossover Start 58
Lead Step Starts 59
Dive Handoff 60
Reverse Pivot Handoff 61
Fake Toss/Inside Trap 61
Pitch Play 62
The Option Pitch 63
Cut and Crossover 66
Inside Cut 67
Spin Technique 68
Dummy Blocking 70
Blocking the End Man 70
Blocking Defensive Tackles 71
Lead Block on a Linebacker 74
Double-Team Block 75
Setting Up to Pass Block 77
Blocking an Inside Pass Rush 78
Blocking an Outside Pass Rush 80
Hand Position 82
Ball Reception I 84
Ball Reception II 84
Short Patterns 86
Medium Patterns 88
Deep Patterns 89
Slow Screen 91
Speed Screen 93

Delay Pass 94
Draw Play 96
Run Pass 98

Receivers
Wide Receiver Release 107
Tight End Release 108
Wide Receiver Glide 111
Tight End Glide 113
Wide Receiver/Tight End Burst 114
Hand Position I 116
Hand Position II 118
Hand Position III 119
Pass Depths 122
Short Patterns 123
Medium Patterns 126
Deep Patterns 126
Short Tight End Patterns 131
Medium Tight End Patterns 131
Deep Tight End Patterns 133
Mirror Blocking 135
Drive Block 139
Hook Block 139
Angle Block 141
Double-Team Block 142
Short-Yardage/Goal-Line Blocking 143
Pass Coverage Recognition 145

Offensive Line
Getting Off the Ball 159
Drive Blocking vs. Sled 160
One-On-One Drive Blocking 163
Hook Blocking 165

Angle Blocking 167
Running Drive Block I 169
Running Drive Block II (Trap Block) 170
Pulling Block vs. Linebacker 172
Two Pulling Linemen 174
Double Team Blocking I (Guards and Tackles) 175
Double Team Blocking II (Guards and Center) 175
Combo Block I (Guard and Tackle) 178
Combo Block II (Guard and Center) 179
Short-Yardage/Goal-Line Blocking 182
Short-Yardage/Goal-Line Combo Blocking 182
Setting Up For Pass Blocking 185
Pass Blocking I 187
Pass Blocking II 188
Pass Blocking III 189
Pass Blocking IV 190
Picking Up Stunts 193
Uncovered Linemen 195

Defensive Line
Getting off the Ball 206
Lateral Step 206
Slant Step 207
Defeating a Blocker (vs. Four- or Six-Man Sled) 208
Defeating Drive Blocking 209
Defeating Hook Blocking 209
Defeating Angle Blocking 210
Defeating Scoop Blocking 210
Defeating Double-Team Blocks 211

Index

Defeating Delayed Double-Team Blocks 212
Defeating Trap Blocks 213
Defeating Lead Blocks 215
Defensive End vs. Trap Block by Off Guard 219
Defensive Tackle vs. Scoop Block by Center 219
Nose Tackle vs. Delayed Double-Team Block with Center and Near Back 219
Sprint, Touch, and Go 224
Shoulder-Club and Slip 224
Wrist-Club and Over-Arm 224
Rip-and-Run 225
Bull Rush 226
Bull-and-Jerk 228
Bull-and-Slip 228
Shoulder-Club and Spin 229
Four-Man Stunt (End First) 231
Four-Man Stunt (Tackle First) 233
Defensive Tackles Stunt 234
Three-Man Defensive Line Stunt 235
Defensive End and Outside Linebacker Stunt 235
Defensive End and Inside Linebacker Stunt 236
Nose Tackle and Inside Linebacker Twist 237
Nose Tackle and Two Inside Linebackers Stunt 237
Open-Field Tackling 239
Shed and Tackle 241

Running Lateral Pursuit 242
Wide Pursuit 242
Screen Pass Pursuit 244
Downfield Pass Pursuit 244
Draw-Play Pursuit 245

Linebackers
Moving and Striking (vs. Four- or Seven-Man Sled) 253
Facing One-on-One Blocking 253
Defeating Drive Blocking (vs. Live Offense) 254
Escape From Cut Blocks (vs. Bags) 254
Facing One-on-One Cut Blocking 254
Defeating Angle Blocking 255
Defeating Hook Blocking 256
Outside Linebacker Trap 256
Inside Linebacker Trap 257
Outside Linebacker vs. Lead Block 258
Inside Linebacker vs. Lead Block 258
Open-Field Tackling 261
Sideline Tackling 263
Gang Tackling 263
Strongside Pursuit/Weakside Pursuit 264
Learning the Zones of the Field 268
Zone Drop Technique 269
Pass Pattern Recognition I 270
Pass Pattern Recognition II 271
Pass Pattern Recognition III 272
Pass Pattern Recognition IV 272
Pass Pattern Recognition V 274
Quarterback Focus (Three Steps Throwing to Right) 275

Quarterback Focus (Seven Steps Throwing in Center) 276
Ball Reaction 277
Backpedaling 278
Angle Backpedal 279
Calling Out Patterns 280
Roll-Over 281
Live Coverage 281
Interceptions 283
Tipped Balls 284
Team Interceptions 284
Outside Linebacker Blitz 285
Inside Linebacker Blitz 288
Outside and Inside Linebackers/Defensive End Stunts 290

Defensive Backs
Backpedaling 301
Angled Backpedal 301
Pattern Depth Recognition 302
Short Pattern Recognition 304
Medium Pattern Recognition 305
Deep Pattern Recogniton 305
Roll-Over 306
Short-Area Pattern Reaction 309
Medium-Area Pattern Reaction 309
Deep-Area Pattern Reaction 310
Bump-and-Run (Inside Stance) 311
Bump-and-Run (Inside-Outside Release) 311
Mirror Running 312
Bump-and-Run (Pattern Reaction) 312
Learning the Zones 314

Three-Deep Zone Drop Technique   315
Zone Left With "Sky" Call   315
Zone Right With "Cloud" Call   317
Two-Deep Zone Drop Technique   318
Ball Stripping   320
Straight-Ahead Interceptions   323
Angle Interceptions   325
Over-the-Head Interceptions   326
Tipped Passes   327
Open-Field Tackling   329
Angled Open-Field Tackling   330
Close Sideline Tackling   332
Run Force   334

The Kicking Game
Soccer-Style Kicking Alignment   361
Game Kicking   367
Straight-Ahead Kicking   372
Center Pass   374
Punt Returns   391

Notes